# Jane's

# BATTLES WITH THE
# LUFTWAFFE

# BATTLES WITH THE
# LUFTWAFFE

Theo Boiten and Martin Bowman

HarperCollins

**THIS BOOK IS DEDICATED TO THE MEMORY OF HAP GALFUNT.**

In the UK for information please contact:
HarperCollins*Publishers*
77-85 Fulham Palace Road
Hammersmith
London W6 8JB
Great Britain
www.**fire**and**water**.com

In the US for information please contact:
HarperCollins*Publishers* Inc.
10 East 53rd Street
New York
NY 10022
USA
www.harpercollins.com

First published by HarperCollins*Publishers* 2001

© Theo Boiten and Martin Bowman 2001

10 9 8 7 6 5 4 3 2 1

ISBN 0 00711363 3

Editor: Ian Tandy
Editorial Assistant: Clara Théau-Laurent
Design: Rod Teasdale
Origination: Colourscan, Singapore

Printed and bound in Hong Kong by Printing Express

The publishers wish to thank those people who provided the pictures used in this book,
all of which were carefully selected by the authors from personal archives in the
United States, Germany, the United Kingdom, Belgium,
The Netherlands and France, to name but a few.

# Contents

# Introduction

*Battles with the Luftwaffe* provides a very rare, if not unique, insight into the air war between the US Eighth Air Force and the German air and *Flak* arms defending the *Reich* from 1942 to 1945. The authors have conducted a long and diligent search for information and photographs – many of which previously unpublished – from amongst their vast range of contacts in the United Kingdom, Germany, Belgium, the United States and The Netherlands, to name but a few. The aim has been to bring together a multitude of vivid, penetrating, personal recollections of aerial combat that are unsurpassed in the history of warfare. Here recalled, are first-hand accounts and memories of Eighth Air Force airmen, *Luftwaffe* and *Jagdverbande* pilots, *Grossbatterien* and *Luftwaffenhelfer* personnel, *et al*, often with their personal encounters identified and photographed.

During the Second World War, some of the greatest aerial battles disputed between the American Air Forces and the *Luftwaffe* took place over Germany and the Greater Reich on an almost daily basis. In 1942, there were thousands of young men in the United States Army Air Force eager to fly; they were trained to accept that daylight precision bombing in vast aerial fleets was the best method to fight an air war over Europe. It was a policy that had gained momentum in the late 1930s and when war eventually came, the American High Command saw no reason to change it. They believed that B-17 Flying Fortresses and B-24 Liberators, heavily armed so as not to need escort fighters, could, during daylight, penetrate even the strongest defences and achieve 'pickle barrel' bombing accuracy, with acceptable losses. Bombardiers using precision Norden bombsights had performed such feats in the clear skies of Texas and the southern states that a repeat performance over Europe seemed entirely feasible.

By August 1942, the few American heavy bomber groups operating in England were able to put their daylight precision bombing campaign to the test over the Greater Reich. They were led by General Ira Eaker, Commander of the Eighth Bomber Command in Britain, the man responsible for making the American daylight offensive succeed. Drawing upon their own bitter experience of the disastrous daylight bombing campaign of 1939-40, few in the RAF believed that the Eighth Air Force in England could succeed where they, and the Luftwaffe during the Battle of Britain, had failed. Eventually though, the British, notably Winston Churchill, came to accept the United States' concept of bombing by day, and it grew into a formidable 'round the clock' bombing strategy that would contribute decisively to the defeat of the *Third Reich*.

The first US heavy bomber mission went ahead on 17 August 1942. Gradually, by 1943 and into 1944, the strength of the Eighth Air Force Bomber Command was such that it was not unusual for there to be several hundred bombers and escorting fighters roving over Germany and the occupied countries at any one time. However, opposition to the US air attacks was fierce; the *Luftwaffe* and particularly several *Jagdgeschwaders* became a feared and respected enemy. Growing American presence had an immediate impact on the *Luftwaffe*. German day fighters now had to force out from the skies of Europe, the heavily armed and armoured American bombers as well as the RAF. They did this by coordinating fighter formations with closed formation attacks, particularly since the standard 8.8cm *Flak* promised no great results at altitudes above 8,000 metres.

The lethal *Flak* and fighter defences across the Channel presented the American bomber and fighter crews with the unenviable task of penetration, if the bombing war was to be pursued whilst avoiding unacceptable heavy losses. As the aerial battles of Schweinfurt and Regensburg late in 1943, and the battles of Big Week and Berlin – "Big B" – in 1944 showed, the German day fighter arm was a force to be reckoned with. When, at the beginning of summer 1944, the Eighth sought oil-producing centres in Germany, the defence against daylight high-altitude attacks increased. The co-operation of *Flak* and fighters and the operation of the *Grossbatterien* proved successful. Despite the continual loss of young men to the Eastern and Western Fronts, Germany managed to double its personnel, mainly by decreasing the personnel per battery and using the *Reichsarbeitsdienst* and some *75,000 Luftwaffenhelfer* (schoolboys) from higher schools. In Germany, all schoolboys aged sixteen had to enter their neighbourhood *Flak* school. This decision had been taken after the German disaster

at Stalingrad, when thousands of soldiers within the borders of the *Fatherland* were needed for frontline duties. In addition, approximately 15,000 women and girls, 45,000 volunteer Russian PoWs and 12,000 Croatian soldiers, were drafted into the *Luftwaffe*.

Despite all these far reaching measures, gradually, the tide turned in the Allies' favour. The US air forces had the advantage numerically and American losses were reduced thanks to the introduction of the long range P-51 Mustang, which escorted the bomber streams on deep penetration missions over the Greater Reich, to Poland, Czechoslovakia and further afield. Fortunately, also, for the Eighth Air Force, the German Me 262 jets and Me 163 Komet rocket-fighters and Hitler's V-weapons materialized far too late and in too few numbers to alter the outcome of the war. The Allied heavy bombing raids and strafing missions by the US and RAF fighter-bomber forces virtually grounded the *Luftwaffe* fighter arm until the only units able to operate up to the final defeat were the jet and rocket-powered fighters. Despite fuel and pilot shortages nearly all enemy fighter attacks on American bombers in the last two and a half months of the war in

Europe were carried out by the *Jagdverbande.*

By April 1945, the Eighth Air Force could mount bombing raids of over 1,000 B-17s and B-24s and similar numbers of escort fighters, but still the *Luftwaffe* day fighter force rose to intercept the American bomber formations. These German attackers were effectively the last generation of *Luftwaffe* fighter pilots of the war. The situation in Germany in the closing stages was so desperate that replacement pilots and crews had to be found from the bomber and reconnaissance units, and hastily trained and converted for the day fighter defence into the *Reichsverteidigung.* As the situation grew ever more desperate, young and inexperienced volunteer pilots were thrown into the battle as *Rammjäger.* Most of them came from the *Luftwaffe* fighter OTUs – the *Erganzungs-jagdgeschwader.* The concept of bringing down a large number of four-engined American bombers by ramming had first been put to *Reichsmarschall* Göring in September 1944, when it was hoped that by assembling a force of 1,500 Bf 109s, manned by young volunteer fighter pilots, the Americans would suffer such disastrous losses, they would be forced to interrupt their raids on German

cities. Although some US bombers were rammed, the plan failed and did not prevent the day fighter force from slowly but steadily bleeding to death, while the US air forces grew in strength and power.

In the final stages of the war, the Allied air forces had all but run out of targets and most of the enemy aircraft that could not take off were destroyed on the ground, out of fuel and largely abandoned. Some 747 German aircraft were destroyed on 26 April 1945 alone. The end of Hitler's much vaunted *Third Reich* came on 7 May 1945. As the victorious Allies celebrated VE Day on 8 May 1945, many were of the opinion that victory would have come much sooner if it had not been for the unquestionable bravery and tenacity of the *Jagdflieger* and the *Nachtjagd,* even though surrender stared them in the face for most of the campaign. Never must the tremendous sacrifice paid by the young American crews be forgotten either. Without their gallant contribution, victory would have been delayed and might even not have come at all. Now, many of these former adversaries' stories and photos have been brought together to provide a rare glimpse of war fought by young men on both sides of the battle.

# Chapter 1 – Round the Clock Bombing Begins

In the 1930s one of the main theories about strategic air power was that unescorted bombers could get through to a target if they were arranged properly and armed sufficiently. In America this theory was discussed and taught at the Army Air Corps Tactical School at Maxwell Field, Alabama. There a small, influential group of officers on the faculty, led by Major Harold L George, Major Donald Wilson, 1/Lt Kenneth L Walker and 2/Lt Haywood S Hansell Jr, developed a set of concepts about air power. They believed that air power could directly influence the course of wars by having strategic air forces fly long range missions, and destroy an enemy's industrial infrastructure. Furthermore, they thought that these long-range bombers, if properly equipped with defensive armament and organised into massed formations, would be capable of penetrating an enemy's defences – even in broad daylight – and striking directly at the enemy's will to resist.

As the 1930s progressed, these teachings developed into an unofficial doctrine of air power that became prominent in WWII. There were doubters. 2/Lt (later General) Curtis E LeMay, who was at Selfridge Field in Michigan in the 1930s, when the US really did not have an air force, was of the opinion that many did not believe that was the way to do it. He felt they would have to do some unescorted missions if they were going to do any bombing at all.

It could be done, yes, but you paid a price for it. When war in Europe broke out in 1939, RAF Bomber Command certainly paid a price for it. Bombing in daylight in order to see and hit their targets, and unescorted, they drifted into bombing mainly at night to keep their losses down to an 'acceptable' level. In the Battle of Britain in the summer of 1940, the *Luftwaffe* began to pay a price for it and also switched to bombing by night.

The US Army Air Corps started out bombing in daylight, with better equipment for the purpose (gyroscopically controlled bombsights for precision bombing of specific German targets) and more and better armament than RAF Bomber Command (whose Wellingtons, Whitleys and Hampdens were armed with .30 calibre guns and were not as well defended as the B-17 Flying Fortress). In 1942 American and RAF air leaders disagreed on the best method for employing strategic air forces against Germany. Initially the AAF planned to carry out massed daylight strikes against specific targets in Germany whereas the RAF, relying on the operational experiences learned the hard way in 1939-41, adopting a strategic bombing campaign based on a stream of bombers flying at night and striking 'areas' rather than precise targets. The British wanted the USAAF to join RAF Bomber Command in its night bombing offensive. The USAAF however, was not about to change its daylight precision bombing concept, which had been honed to perfection at ranges at Muroc Dry Lake in California's Mojave Desert in 1940, by the B-17B high-altitude bombers of the 2nd and 7th Bomb Groups. By using the top secret Norden bombsight, experienced bombardiers found that they could place their practice bombs within yards of the target from as high as 20,000ft – which led to claims that bombs could be dropped in a pickle barrel from such heights. Precision bombing

> *By no means had the Eighth Air Force been established to become an appendage of the RAF. That was not for the likes of General Ira C Eaker, or a young cigar-chomping, tough-talking Colonel named Curtis LeMay, or the others. The Eighth Air Force was a high-octane outfit. It was run by ambitious men and backed by an ambitious command in Washington. It had set up a large public relations staff – men from newspapers, publicity firms, advertising agencies – and made use of Hollywood celebrities. They were not attracted to the air force because they thought it was going to take directions from the English.*
>
> **Harrison Salisbury, United Press Correspondent.**

> *"I can see the target, I can see the target!'*
> *"Yes, you damn fool, and the Germans can see you too! "*
>
> **Lt Frank R Beadle, bombardier, rebuked by Col Armstrong, August 1942.**

Maj Paul W Tibbets, *Tibbets*.

*It was just past mid-afternoon when we lifted off into sunny skies. All the planes were in the air at 1539 hours. We started our climb for altitude immediately and had reached 23,000ft, in attack formation, by the time we left the coast of England and headed south across the Channel. I wondered whether or not all aircraft would make it or whether there would be aborts. However, it was a banner day with no aborts. As we departed the English coast out over the Channel, the RAF escort of Spitfire Vs joined us. Group Capt (later Air Chief Marshal) Harry Broadhurst was leading the RAF escort fighters and it was an emotional, spine-tingling event. We were off to do battle for real and fighters were there to give us protection and comfort......We caught the Germans by surprise. They hadn't expected a daytime attack, so we had clear sailing to the target. Visibility was unlimited and all 12 planes dropped their bombloads. Our aim was reasonably good but you couldn't describe it as pinpoint bombing. We still had a lot to learn......By the time we unloaded our bombs, the enemy came to life. Anti-aircraft fire, erratic and spasmodic at first, zeroed in our formations as we began the return flight. Two B-17s suffered slight damage from Flak. Three Me 109s moved in for the attack but were quickly driven off by the Spitfires that accompanied us. The only German planes I saw were out of range and I got the impression they were simply looking us over....A feeling of elation took hold of us as we winged back across the Channel. All the tension was gone. We were no longer novices at this terrible game of war. We had braved the enemy in his own skies and were alive to tell about it.*

**Maj Paul W Tibbets, 97th BG, on completing the first VIIIth BC heavy bombing raid, 17 August 1942.**

called for attacks in daylight, but the ideal conditions found in California were not often to be found in Europe, as VIIIth BC would soon find to its chagrin. Eventually, the British, notably Winston Churchill, came to accept the American method of bombing and it grew into a formidable 'round the clock' bombing strategy that would contribute decisively to the defeat of Germany. In August 1942, however, Gen Ira C Eaker, Commander of VIIIth BC in Britain, could only call upon a few B-17 Flying Fortress and B-24D Liberator bomb groups when the USAAF fully entered the fray in Europe. It had an immediate effect on the *Luftwaffe*. German day fighters now had to drive the heavily armed and armoured American bombers from the skies by co-ordination of fighter formations and closed formation attacks, particularly since the standard 8.8cm *Flak* promised no great results at altitudes above 8,000m.

Luftwaffe eye-view of B-17s straggling in formation. *USAF.*

**Below:** During his inspection tour of the VIIIth BC, Lord Trenchard, father of the RAF, inspects the tail of a 93rd BG B-24D at Hardwick on 6 April 1943. In the background is Col Ted Timberlake, the CO. *USAF.*

*Overseas – in the Philippines, Hawaii and Panama – we would have a squadron of bombers, a squadron of fighters and some observation airplanes. We did have a squadron of attack aircraft over in Hawaii. We may have had that in the Philippines. But the basic doctrine was that we would have the bombers and the fighters to escort them, and we would also have the attack airplanes to go in ahead and work over the anti-aircraft. That was the general theory. All of the historians and writers now point out the fact it was a big surprise to us when we got over to Europe in the war and found that the bombers had to have fighter escort. It was no surprise, we always expected to have fighter escorts. The only trouble was, we didn't have any fighters, and we had long since abolished the attack airplane, so we didn't have any of them either.*

**General Curtis E LeMay. (Not until January 1944 were long-range fighters available in quantity in Europe.)**

*Above:* B-17F 42-29536 *Mary Ruth Memories of Mobile,* 401st BS, 91st BG, which FTR with Lt Kenneth L Brown's crew on 22 June 1943. *USAF.*

By early August 1942, three B-17 bomb groups – the 92nd, 97th and 301st – had arrived in England. Only the 97th BG, commanded by Col Frank A Armstrong, was considered operational and had the honour of flying the first heavy bomber mission, when a dozen B-17Es attacked Rouen on 17 August. Six other Fortresses flew a diversion.

The 97th BG despatched 24 of its B-17Es on 19 August in support of the Allied landings at Dieppe. Their target was the airfield at Abbeville-Drucat in northern France, home of the infamous II./JG26, or 'Abbeville Kids', whose yellow-nosed Fw 190 pilots were among the *Luftwaffe* elite. JG26 and the American bombers would meet on many occasions in the coming months. Two of the B-17s aborted because of mechanical failures but the rest of the Group plastered the airfield, destroying a hangar and severely cratering or 'postholing' the runways. Fortunately, the *Luftwaffe* was heavily engaged over the Dieppe area and did not show. British High Command reported that 16 fighters were either destroyed or damaged as a result of the bombing strike and the airfield itself was put out of action for two vital hours. In addition, the controllers of the whole of the fighter area remained out of action until that evening. Yet despite these successes, JG26 was in action over Dieppe all day. The three *Gruppen* of JG26 flew no less than 377 sorties, against Allied aircraft, sea and ground targets. For six Fw 190s lost, the Geschwader claimed 38 aircraft shot down, plus another 11 probables.

On 21 August the 97th BG were attacked again by JG26, when 12 Fortresses were sent to bomb the Wilton shipyards at Rotterdam. None of the Fortresses were lost and the US press praised the American bombers' ability to 'destroy' six of the 25 attacking fighters. The 97th BG again escaped without loss on 24 August, when

*F*rom October 1940 until the end of the war I served with Geschwader JG26 'Schlageter' on the western Front. In May 1943 I was shot down for the first time by a Spitfire, and seriously wounded. In December 1943 I was allowed to fly again. On 31 December I brought down my sixth American Viermot, and was seriously injured again in the process. I was on operations as a fighter pilot from January 1941 to January 1944, with a few breaks in hospital. In all, I was shot down four times, twice being seriously wounded and with lengthy stays in hospital. I shot down two Spitfires and six American Viermots, all in the period from October 1942 to May 1943 plus one four-engined bomber on the 31st of December 1943, after which my flying ended.

The plain fact that I am still alive, is an incredible case of luck. During the summer of 1941, as a member of the 9th Staffel (IIIrd Gruppe JG26) in Liegcourt, I was one of the pilots who fought to ward off the British non-stop offensive, during which many of my young

Pilots of 12./JG1 at München-Gladbach, October 1942. From left: Uffz Anton Piffer; Hptfw Werth; Lt Eberhard Burath; Lt Hans Munz (KIA, 21 May 1943). *Eberhard Burath via Rob de Visser.*

comrades were killed in action. During that episode, we combatted the Blenheims, but we also encountered the Short Stirling for the first time, one of which shot me down over Bethune in the summer of '41. My Me 109F took 11 direct hits from the tailgunner. We were flying without armoured glass in front of the windscreen, and I was lucky to escape unhurt, all the bullets smashed into my cockpit to the side of me. I was only just able to make a proper landing, although the tyre on my left-hand undercarriage had been shot through; moreover, I couldn't see a thing, as the oil pump had been hit and my entire Messerschmitt was like a sardine in oil. By opening the small sliding window on the side of the cockpit hood I was just able to see enough to land properly. I flew on operations during the Dieppe raid, when I shot down my first 'Spit' (Spitfire).

In the defence of the Reich during 1942 and 1943, we were only present in the west with two Fighter Groups, 'Jagdgeschwader 2 Richthofen' and us, 'Jagdgeschwader 26 Schlageter'. In all, we could muster 240 fighter aircraft, which could only be employed in Gruppen of 25 to 30 each, as the bombers came in using different routes all the time. Our 240 fighters were dispersed from Brest to the mouth of the River Scheldt, and the individual Gruppen of our Jagdgeschwader 26 had to cover a stretch of 250 km along the Channel coast. Therefore on each mission only one, sometimes two Gruppen, could possibly be thrown against the enemy. It often happened that I took off during 1942 and 1943, for my third or fourth sortie on a day with only three or four serviceable machines, the rest having all being damaged, having crash-landed or being completely lost during the earlier sorties.

**Lt Otto P 'Stotto' Stammberger, one of the few German fighter pilots who survived the battle of attrition in the west, 1942-43, first serving with 9./JG26 and rising to the rank of Oblt and command of 4./JG26 from 26 February 1943 until he was severely injured in air combat on 13 May.**

**Above:** Fighter pilots of 4./JGI trying to relax during *Bereitschaft* (readiness) at Woensdrecht airfield beside one of the *Staffel's* FW 190A-5s, 1942-43. *Robert Olejnik via Rob de Visser.*

they hit the shipyards at Le Trait. All nine Fortresses returned safely from the raid on the Wilton shipyards on 27 August, and there were no losses on 29 August when the 97th bombed the German fighter base at Courtrai-Wevelghem in Belgium. Results appeared to be good and even the British press, which had at first been cautious of American claims, now openly praised them. On 5 September the 97th BG was joined by the 301st BG in a raid on the marshalling yards at Rouen, and all 37 B-17s returned safely.

On 6 September, Eaker mounted his largest bombing mission so far, to the Avions Potez factory at Meaulte, using the 92nd BG for the first time. The 92nd scraped together 14 B-17Es and crews, filling in with ground personnel, some of them privates. They joined with 22 B-17Fs of the 97th in the main strike while the 301st BG flew a diversionary raid on St Omer-Longuenesse airfield. A total of 30 Fortresses crossed Meaulte but

**Right:** B-17F victim of a head-on attack by the *Luftwaffe. USAF.*

only six in the 92nd BG attacked the target. German early warning radar and radio intercept services, monitoring any major increase on the American radio frequencies, were alerted and they passed the word to the German fighter control organisation. German radar could detect formations before they crossed the English coast. Fw 190s of II./JG26 were encountered continuously from the French coast to the target and the escorting four squadrons of Spitfire IXs failed to rendezvous with the bombers. JG26 intercepted the

Spitfires and shot down three. The B-17s were bounced by between 45 and 50 Fw 190s and a handful of Bf 109s. 2/Lt Clarence C Lipsky's B-17 in the 340th BS, 97th BG, was attacked by Hptm Karl-Heinz Conny Meyer, *Kommandeur,* II./JG26. It went down north-west of Amiens at 1855 hours. It crashed at Flasselles. It was the *Luftwaffe's* first American heavy bomber victory of the war. Four parachutes were seen to open. (The Red Cross reported on 17 October 1942 that Lipsky and five of the crew were PoWs.) The second Fortress lost on the mission was *Baby Doll* flown by Lt Leigh E Stewart of the 327th BS, 92nd BG, which was pursued by at least five Fw 190s. OFw Willi Roth of 4./JG26 finally shot

*Baby Doll* down at 1906 hours and Stewart crashed into the sea north-west of Le Treport. RAF ASR launches searched the area without success. Over Cayeaux, Capt Frank G Ward of the 92nd BG was attacked by six Fw 190s. One 97th BG gunner was killed, another died in hospital three days later and 2 were wounded.

On 7 September, 29 B-17s were despatched to bomb the Rotterdam shipyards. Only seven B-17s got their bombs away at the primary and two more bombed Utrecht railway station. The next bombing raid was not until 26 September, when 45 B-17s of the 301st and 97th BGs were re-dispatched to bomb Cherbourg while 30 B-17s of the 92nd BG flew two diversionary feints.

**Above:** B-17s in their combat boxes leaving vapour trails – signposts in the sky for the *Luftwaffe* – as they head for their target. *USAF.*

**Left:** B-24 Liberator going down in flames after losing its wing to *Flak* or fighters. *USAF.*

**Right:** B-24 41-23874 *Ball of Fire Jr* of the 328th BS, 93rd BG, in North Africa. This aircraft failed to return on 16 April 1943 when it crashed at St Revan, France, when it was flown by Lt franklin D Lown. *Pieter Bergman.*

The 301st BG were recalled however, because the escort fighters were not seen and cloud prevented any of the 97th BG Fortresses from bombing. On 2 October, 49 B-17s were despatched to Meaulte and St Omer/Longuenesse airfield. They returned without loss.

## Abbeville Kids

On 9 October, 84 B-17s and for the first time, B-24s of the 93rd BG, were despatched to the vast steel and locomotive works at the Camping de Fives, Lille. Also flying its first mission on this day was the 306th BG at Thurleigh, Bedfordshire. Col Charles 'Chip' Overacker Jr, the CO, led 24 crews off from Thurleigh in *Four of a Kind*, a 369th BS Fortress, flown by Capt James A Johnston. Each Fortress had a crew of nine, a second waist gunner was not thought necessary as it was believed the gun on the inside of the formation would not need to be used! The 24 B-24Ds of the 93rd BG fell in behind the Fortresses, and began crossing the coast of England at Felixstowe at 0912 hours. At about the same time III./JG26 *Kommandeur*, Hptm 'Pips' Priller, was leading his pilots from their airfield at Wevelghem. They headed north to intercept the bombers. Two of the 306th BG B-17s aborted the mission before reaching the enemy coast. Nearing the target *Flak* enveloped the formation. *Four of a Kind* was hit in the No.2 engine

**Above:** Fw I90 of II./JG26 taking off with a 250kg bomb. Lt Heinz Knocke of 5./JG1 destroyed a 91st BG B-17 by dropping a 250kg bomb in the midst of a Wilhelmshaven-bound formation of Fortresses on 22 March 1943. On 19 May, his bomb missed, but three of his *Staffel* comrades scored direct hits on three B-17s, probably the 305th BG during a raid on Kiel, all of which were ripped to pieces in the ensuing explosions. On 13 May 1943, a B-17 returned from the St Omer-Longuenesse airfield strike badly damaged by a bomb dropped by a JG26 Fw 190. *Werner Molge.*

**Above:** An Fw 190 of I./JG26 taking off. *Werner Molge.*

**Below:** JG26 aces in the spring of 1943. L-R: Willi Roth (survived the war as Lt with 20 *Abschüsse* in 5./JG26); Landa (u/k); Waldemar Radener (survived the war as Oblt and *Ritterkreuzträger* with 37 *Abschüsse* and CO of II./JG300); Gerhard Birke (KIA 17 May 1943 as Uffz whilst serving with 4./JG26, five *Abschüsse*); Kurt Ebersberger (KIA as Hptm with 27 kills on 24 October 1943); Adolf Glunz (survived the war as Oblt with 71 *Abschüsse* in 6./JG26, including 21 *Viermots*, and decorated with the *Ritterkreuz*). *Werner Molge.*

and Col Overacker was forced to relinquish the lead. As the 306th BG came off the target about 50 of the "Abbeville Kids" attacked the group from the rear and head-on.

'Pips' Priller singled out a B-17 in the 306th BG formations – *Snoozy II* in the 367th BS, piloted by Capt John Olsen. (The 367th BS was known as the 'Clay Pigeons' after an American war correspondent, writing in the *Saturday Evening Post,* said that the 367th BS reminded him of a bunch of clay pigeons. From October 1942 to August 1943, the 367th suffered the heaviest losses in VIIIth BC). Priller, who misidentified his

quarry as a Liberator, pumped cannon and machine-gun fire into the B-17 leaving Olsen and Norman Gates, co-pilot, dead in their blood-spattered cockpit. Four other crew were also dead and just three crew bailed out.

Three other bombers were lost, all of them falling to JG26. III./JG26 engaged the four-engined American bombers in combat for the first time on this day. Hptm. Klaus Mietusch, *Kapitän,* 7./JG26, led his fighters in an attack on the Liberators, which he misidentified as RAF Stirling bombers. He despatched *Big Eagle* of the 93rd BG, flown by Capt Alexander Simpson near Lille. Direct hits put No.4 engine out of action and set the bomb-bay on fire. *Big Eagle* exploded, sending Simpson and co-pilot Lt. Nick Cox into a free-fall. In the PoW camp neither knew how they got out of the disintegrating bomber or how their parachutes opened. Two others in the crew were also captured, while one evaded and reached Spain courtesy of the French Underground. Mietusch then pursued a B-17. Return fire downed his wingman, Uffz Viktor Hager, who was badly wounded, but he could not open his parachute and fell to his death. Mietusch made a second pass and damaged the B-17. It was 41-24362, piloted by 1/Lt Donald M Swenson of the 419th BS, 301st BG. Oblt Kurt Ruppert of 9th *Staffel* then repeatedly attacked the damaged Fortress. Three engines were shot up and one fell into the Channel. The loss of power caused a 1,500ft/mn descent but incredibly Swenson kept the B-17 from hitting the sea. Out of ammunition, Ruppert could only watch in amazement as the crippled Fort flew low across the waves, its crew throwing out

equipment and guns. Swenson told the co-pilot to take the controls while he went aft and ordered all the crew to take up ditching positions in the radio room. The ditching, about a mile off North Foreland, was far from smooth in the rough seas and the B-17 sank within 90 seconds. An ASR launch arrived within fifteen minutes and despite the conditions, all the crew was safely rescued and brought ashore.

l/Lt James M Stewart's *Man O'War* in the 306th BG, lost the No.2 engine, then both outboard engines began to overheat and lose power. Stewart nursed the ailing ship to the Channel and was prepared to ditch until a lone Spitfire flown by F/Lt A J Andrews of 91st turned up and guided him safely to Manston. *Ball of Fire* in the 93rd BG force-landed at RAF Northolt after being badly shot up by fighters over the target. Lt Otto Stammberger, leading the 9th *Staffel*, opened fire on the B-17s but it had little effect. Realising he was firing from too far out he closed in and scored hits on the Fortress's left wing. The bomber came from the 327th BS, 92nd BG, flown by Lt Francis H Chorak. High above the fight escorting fighters made no attempt to intervene. Stammberger attacked Chorak's B-17 again and again. By the third pass the B-17's left hand engines were on fire. Stammberger then fired at the right

*When the American Viermots came we really had to get used to their size and numbers. The first of these I brought down on 9 October 1942 over Lille. The Staffel had just landed under my command at Wevelghem, when around 0830 hours we were scrambled. We should climb into the direction of St Omer. However, we didn't gather systematically as when we were flying at a height of 3,500 to 4,000m, we already spotted quite a large pile of formidable fat bluebottles, approaching from the direction of St Omer. They were American bombers of the Boeing B-17 type. They were not flying in a tight formation, as they flew in three rows and all 'vics' obviously flew higgledy-piggledy. Up to a height of 6,000 metres, vics of Viermots were cruising along and above these I saw the vapour trails of fighter aircraft. In the meantime, the bombers had flown just past the west of Lille. Until we arrived at the boaters, the stream had turned tightly to the left and to the south of Lille and at last I got into a firing position.*

*We charged into the single vics with our fighters attacking in pairs. We came in from behind, throttled back and fired our guns. The things grew bigger and bigger and all our attacks were commenced and broken off much too early, as we were afraid of flying into the 'barn doors'. I was wondering why I didn't register any hits until I thought about the size of the lumps: a wingspan of 40m! Therefore, charge in at much closer range and so fast that nothing would happen to us anyway. Then commence firing, starting with the engines in the left wing. At my third pass, both engines were on fire, and I succeeded in hitting the right outer engine as well, which belched forth smoke, and the 'Kahn' (Luftwaffe slang for 'ship'). I plunged down to the left and towards the ground in wide spirals. At a height of some 2,000m, four or five men bailed out and to the east of Vendeville and the 'Kasten' (slang for very large aircraft) crashed. I watched this from above and then I decided to go after the others. Yet miraculously, the sky was empty! Anyway, I was out of ammo for my cannons so I backed out towards home.*

**Lt Otto Stammberger, *Staffelkapitän*, 9./JG26, describing his shooting down of B-17F 41-9018 of the 327th BS, 92nd BG, flown by Lt Francis H Chorak.**

**Above:** 41-24487 *Eager Beaver* of the 368th. 'Eager Beaver's BS, 306th BG at Thurleigh, was the longest serving B-17F in VIIIth BC, September 1942 October to 1943. It was transferred to AF Service Command 1 May 1944 and returned to the ZOI July 1944. It went to the Williamsport Technical Institute at Patterson Field, Ohio, 20 June 1945. *USAF.*

**Left:** Bombs exploding at La Pallice, one of the many U-boat bases on the French Atlantic coast. *USAF.*

outboard engine as Chorak spiralled downward in broad left turns. Five miles north of St Omer over Holque four of the nine-man crew bailed out before 41-9018 crashed east of Vendeville. Stammberger, out of ammunition, headed back to his base at Wevelghem. Three of the four B-17 crew who bailed out were captured and one evaded.

Only 69 bombers hit their primary targets and many of the bombs failed to explode. The inexperienced 93rd and 306th had placed many of their bombs outside the target area, killing a number of French civilians. Traffic control was bad and some of the bombardiers never got the target in their bombsights. During the post-mission interrogations crews revealed that they had made 242 encounters with *Luftwaffe* fighters and put in fighter claims for 48 destroyed, 18 probably destroyed and four damaged. With so many gunners firing at the same targets it was inevitable that 'scores' would be duplicated. When the heat of the Lille battle had died

**Above:** B-24D Liberators of the 44th BG bombing Dunkirk on 15 February 1943. *USAF.*

away, the American gunners' scores were whittled down to 25-38-44 and, finally, 21-21-15 (the Germans lost only one fighter). At the time the figures did much to compensate for the largely inaccurate bombing.

On 20 October 1942, Brig-Gen Asa N Duncan, Chief of the Air Staff, issued a revised set of objectives to be carried out by VIIIth BC. In part it stated,... *Until further orders, every effort of the VIIIth Bomber Command will be directed to obtaining the maximum destruction of the submarine bases in the Bay of Biscay...* On 21 October, 83 B-17s of the 97th 301st and 306th BGs, and 24 B-24s of the 93rd BG, were despatched to the U-boat pens at Keroman, about 11 miles from Lorient, while 17 B-17s of the 11th CCRC were to bomb Cherbourg. The two forces flew a long over-water flight in the Bay of Biscay to reduce the threat of *Luftwaffe* interception. However, thick cloud at their prescribed bombing altitude of 22,000ft forced all except the 15 Fortresses of the 97th BG to return to England. The 97th BG bombed the target

but just after re-crossing the French coast they were bounced by a swarm of yellow-nosed Fw 190s. The attacks were ferocious and incessant and centred upon the rear of the formation. Three B-17s – *Francis X*, flown by Lt Francis X. Schwarzenbeck in the 342nd BS, *Johnny Reb*, piloted by Lt Milton M Stenstrom and 41-24344 flown by Capt John M Bennett, both from the 414th BS, were shot down. Another six B-17s were badly damaged. The 97th now had the highest losses of any group to date.

On 7 November the 91st BG made its inaugural mission when 68 B-17s and B-24s went to the U-boat pens at Brest. Eight of the 91st BG B-17s despatched got their bombs away and the whole force returned without loss. Although Lt Julian A Harvey, pilot of *Hellsadroppin'* in the 93rd BG, crashed at Exeter after sustaining battle damage to his Liberator. Next day, 8 November, 53 Fortresses went to Abbeville and Lille. One B-17, flown by Capt. Richard D Adams of the

369th BS, 306th BG, failed to return. (Adams' B-17 was shot down by a combination of *Flak* and fighters during the group's second run on the target at Lille. Thirty Fw 190s made at least 200 attacks on the five B-17s of the 369th BS. Five men were killed aboard 41-24472, four were captured, while Adams successfully evaded and later returned to England on 24 April.) Worse was to befall the 306th BG the following day, 9 November, when 47 B-17s and B-24s were despatched to the U-boat pens at St Nazaire. Higher headquarters had decreed that the bomb run would be made from low level, some 7,000 to 8,000ft in fact. At Thurleigh, Col Overacker phoned VIIIth BC to protest. The order was not open to debate and Overacker retorted: "*If my crews have to fly the mission, I'll lead them!*". Overacker did, and all four of his squadron commanders flew too.

> *To Fly in the Eighth Air Force in those days was to hold a ticket to a funeral. Your own.*
>
> **Harrison Salisbury, United Press Correspondent.**

Three Fortresses were lost in rapid succession to the *Flak* over St Nazaire on 9 November and they all came from the 306th BG formation.

No bomber losses were experienced on the missions to St Nazaire on 16th to 18th November, when 65 B-24s and B-17s (the 303rd BG flew its maiden mission this day) were despatched to Lorient, St Nazaire, and La Pallice. For the 306th BG, bringing up the rear of the formation, it was still, however, a bloody mission. The Thurleigh Group were hit by 15 Fw 190s. The *Luftwaffe* fighters caused mayhem and casualties. Capt Robert C Williams in *Chennault's Pappy* was badly shot up and force-landed at Exeter. It never flew again. The run of ill luck experienced by the 306th BG continued the next day when *Floozy,* in the 367th BS, was shot down by a combination of *Flak* and fighters over St Nazaire. It crashed in the Bay of Biscay. Nine of Lt Ralph J Gaston's crew survived and all were taken prisoner. Later, the German fighter pilots who had shot them down visited the survivors in hospital. *Katy Bug* of the 328th BS, 93rd BG crashed at Alconbury killing four of the crew.

On 22 November, Col Curtis E LeMay's 305th BG flew it first mission, part of a force of 68 B-17s and eight Liberators, to Lorient. It was not a memorable debut. Only 11 B-17s of the 301st BG formation managed to bomb. On almost every mission bombers were hitting the target, but not in large enough concentrations to damage them seriously. LeMay was determined to alter this and decided to try and achieve greater bombing accuracy by flying a straight course on the bomb run instead of zig-zagging every 10 seconds; a tactic which had been designed to spoil the aim of the German *Flak* batteries. He put the plan into operation next day, 23 November, when VIIIth BC went to St Nazaire and its notorious *Flak* defences again.

Fifty-eight Fortresses set out from their advance base at Davidstowe Moor for the 23 November raid on St Nazaire. Bad weather and mechanical problems forced several bombers to abort, and only 36 B-17s and B-24s bombed. LeMay's 14 remaining B-17s, from the 20 despatched, flew the longest and straightest bomb run yet flown in Europe and placed twice as many bombs on the target as any other group. Despite his crews' worst fears, LeMay lost no crews over the target to *Flak* or fighters. Col LeMay was not the only one who put new tactics to the test on 23 November. On previous missions the B-17s had been intercepted from the rear where enough guns could be brought to bear on enemy fighters. However, *Luftwaffe* experiments had now proved that the frontal area of a B-17 offered very little in defensive firepower and despite the dangers of very high closing speeds this was now considered the best method of shooting them down. Obstlt Egon Mayer, *Kommandeur,* III./JG2 (who led the attacking fighters this day) and Oblt Georg-Peter Eder, *Staffelkapitän,*

12./JG2, were credited with developing the head-on attack, where the bomber armament was weakest.

The new tactic worked well. In one pass JG2 knocked down four B-17s. The 91st BG lost two bombers and the commanders of the 322nd and 323rd Squadrons, the group navigator, bombardier and gunnery officers, were among the casualties. (Two other 91st BG B-17s were badly hit, one of which, *The Shiftless Skonk* crashed near Leavesden, Hertfordshire while trying to make it home to Bassingbourn, five of the crew were killed.) *Lady Fairweather* flown by Capt Charles G Miller, of the 359th BS, 303rd BG, was shot down in flames near the target, and l/Lt Clay Isbell's B-17 in the 369th BS, 306th BG was shot down on the bomb run. Isbell and seven of his crew were trapped when the Fortress

exploded. (Determining whether an attack was exactly head-on or not when the targets were tiny dots in the distance was difficult so Mayer and Eder refined their tactics. They tailed the bombers to determine their exact course, altitude and speed, before moving out to a safe distance on one flank and overtaking the bombers, reaching a point about two miles ahead, before turning for a head-on pass).

Pin-prick raids continued to be made on the U-boat pens and airfields in France. Eaker was not helped by the decision to send three squadrons (24 Liberators) of the 93rd BG to North Africa on 6 December, but this was offset to a degree by the 67th BS of the 44th BG, at last receiving its full quota of B-24Ds. It enabled the Group to fly its first full Group mission the same day.

> *The gunners I got came supposedly from a gunnery school, but they had never been in an airplane....We had no airplanes to train with, and nobody knew how to shoot well enough to train our people. We were just terrible. We raised such a fuss about it in England in 1942 that the commanders at the six or seven AAF gunnery schools were sent over to see what all the fuss was about. We sent all of them out on a combat mission, and on their first mission four of them were shot down. That emphasized our point. The pilots that I got weren't even 90-day wonders. They came right from flying school and single-engine airplanes,, and they had never been in a multi-engine airplane until I got them in the 305th. We used three old beat-up B-17s to train crews. About all I got accomplished was to check them out so they could get up and get back on the ground without cracking up. We never flew formation until we got to England. The practice formation on the first day after we got there was a complete debacle. The next day I got them up, and on the radio got them positioned the way I wanted them. The third time we flew, we flew across the Channel.*
>
> **Col Curtis E LeMay, 305th BG CO, Chelveston, November 1942.**

> *One of the things I heard was a story from Frank Armstrong that 10 seconds in a straight line of Flak and they would shoot you down; that didn't sound right to me, since I had taken field artillery in ROTC at Ohio State. For some reason or another, I had a field artillery manual in my footlocker that I had sent over with the ground echelon. I got that out and sat down and worked out a precision fire problem with the French 75mm gun, which we were equipped with in ROTC (and which was comparable to the German 88mm anti-aircraft guns). I found out it took 300 rounds or something - I have forgotten, some big number - to hit a B-17 sitting on the hillside 25,000 yards away. That didn't sound too bad to me. In my stupidity, not knowing any better, I said, "We are going to make a straight-in run from the time we see the target until we drop the bombs off." We are going to get a bomb run, and we did. At the end of the run, we went right over the target and got the pictures, and then I took the airplane off automatic pilot and got out of there. I asked the bombardier how he did. He said, "Well, we hit the target, but I would have done better if it wasn't for the clouds." There was not a cloud in the sky; we were flying through pretty heavy Flak. But we didn't lose any airplanes. From then on we did it that way. We got accuracy where they didn't have any at all before. Actually, when you figured it out with the accuracy of an artillery piece, the enemy was firing up at you and the quicker you got through where he could shoot at you, the less rounds could be fired at you, and the less chance by the laws of probability of being hit. If you weaved around, you stayed in the vulnerable area longer. It was actually better to go straight through. We just ignored Flak – I did – right from the very start.*
>
> *We had an anti-aircraft artillery officer in our division headquarters, and every time we had a mission he had all the intelligence information out and all the guns plotted around the target. He could tell you that if you came in this way, you were going to have so many rounds fired at you, and if you came in over here, you were going to have so many rounds. The Germans knew how to lay out a defense, and it didn't make any difference from an artillery standpoint which way you came in. So we generally picked an approach with the sun at our back, or some other good approach. If a nice road ran down to the target, that was fine; it helped the crews get in and find the target. That was how we did it, not paying any attention to the artillery. We would fly right through it and come home. The fighters bothered me more than anything else, mainly because I had been in fighters for seven years, and seeing those guns winking at me out there bothered me, whereas the Flak didn't.*
>
> *Actually it is no great shakes to shoot a bomber down with a fighter if you go in there and press the attack. Of course, with all that lead flying around, it was not conducive to long life and happiness, but the fighters that did it shot bombers down.*
>
> **Col Curtis E LeMay, 305th BG CO.**

*During an attack from behind, we were under defensive fire from the bombers too long, and at least three machine gun positions fired at us from each aircraft. In addition, the escorting fighters had the task of keeping us away from the bombers. So, we had no option left but to attack from head-on. Everything went very quick in this tactic. Every second brought us 220m closer together! And of course, we didn't want to collide, but pull away over the bomber. For this pulling up and over the bomber, one needed almost the whole last two seconds (=400 metres). Our guns were adjusted to 400m. Therefore, we had two options: to fire too early, already at a distance of 600 or 500 metres, or to pull up half a second later. A very dangerous business. We didn't have one second to fire our guns. It is incredible, when one thinks of all the efforts we had to make for just one second. One thing was absolutely necessary: aim very precisely for this short moment.*

**Fw Fritz Ungar, Jagdflieger JG54 and JG26, August 1943-May 1945 (scored three confirmed kills), describing head-on tactics.**

*At first we thought we could handle the enemy fighters better than we did. We handled them quite well until they started those nose attacks on our formation and came through, breaking up the formation. Those yellow-nosed babies learned how to go through our formations. They would break us up, and we were in real trouble then.*

**Col (later General) Leon W Johnson, who would assume command of the 44th BG on 3 January 1943.**

19 Liberators flew a diversionary mission to bomb the JG26 base at Abbeville-Drucat airfield, while 85 B-17s headed for the Atelier d'Hellemmes locomotive works at Lille. Another 22 B-17s of the 11th CCRC and 306th BG took off for another diversion but the 11th CCRC were recalled. Near the French coast an abort signal was radioed to the 44th after British radar tracked oncoming enemy aircraft but the six B-24Ds of the 68th BS did not receive the signal, and they continued to the target alone. 6./JG1 came to the rescue of the Abbeville Kids and OFw Hans Ehlers and Uffz. Wloschinski each claimed a bomber (it was Ehler's seventeenth confirmed kill, Wloschinski's first). The 68th BS lost one Liberator, a B-24D captained by 1/Lt James D Dubard Jr.

The Lille force was also attacked in some strength. In one of the fighter attacks *Cherry* of the 422nd BS, 305th BG, flown by Lt William A Prentice, went down in flames 10 minutes from the target, possibly by Uffz Heinrich Schnell of 3./JG26 (KIA in Russia, 17.2.43), who shot down a bomber west of Etaples. All except the bombardier, Lt Henry J Webber and Lt Harry O Williams, who both parachuted to safety, were killed. (Both men were captured but Williams died a few days later of infection in a wound to his thigh.) Eyewitnesses credited the tail gunner, Sgt. Leaham Bryant, with shooting down the fighter as *Cherry* hurtled down. Sgt Norman E Olson was also given credit for a "probable".

On 20 December, VIIIth BC carried out its heaviest raid since Lille when 101 bombers (80 B-17s of the 91st, 303rd, 305th and 306th BGs, and 21 B-24s of the 44th BG) were sent to bomb the airfield and *Luftwaffe* servicing base at Romilly-sur-Seine, 150 miles South-east of Paris. Twelve squadrons of RAF and VIIIth FC Spitfires flew escort as far as Rouen. At this point

fighters of II./JG26, led by Maj Gerhard Schoepfel, who had paralleled the American formation waiting for the escorts to leave, attacked the B-17s of the leading 91st BG from head-on. B-17Fs 41-24452, flown by Lt Robert S English, and *Danellen*, piloted by Lt Dan W Carson, both from the 401st BS, went down immediately. Three men in English's crew died and nine men were killed aboard *Danellen*. The four other men in these two crews bailed out and became PoW. For an hour the enemy fighters attacked in relays and JG26 did not break off until the withdrawal escort appeared over the Channel. The 91st BG lost no further B-17s but it was a close thing. *Chief Sly* in the 322nd BS was hit badly in the fighter attacks and limped back across the Channel where 1/Lt Bruce Barton crash-landed at Fletching, Sussex with a seriously wounded navigator, 2/Lt Paul Burnett, who had received a bullet wound to his thigh. *Rose O' Day*, piloted by Capt Ken Wallick, was hit badly by *Flak* and fighters but thanks to Barton and his gunners aboard *Chief Sly*, together they fended off the attacks and Wallick brought *Rose O'Day* home to Bassingbourn, where he landed safely. *Chief Sly* was only fit for spare parts. B-17F *The 8 Ball* of the 359th BS, 303rd BG was also hit badly and crash-landed at Bovingdon after eight of the crew had bailed out over Maidstone.

## Three B-17s Missing

At Thurleigh three B-17Fs of the 18 ships in the 306th BG that had taken off were missing. All three were from the 367th BS. Lt Otto Stammberger, leading 9./JG26 attacking with Hptm Egon Mayer's III./JG2, saw a B-17 flip end-for-end before its tail section broke off and the Fortress fell away. It was B-17F 42-5071 flown by Lt Danton J Nygaard – a recent replacement. Fighters raked the B-17 with 20mm cannon fire shortly after the target and shells exploded in the nose, cockpit and throughout the fuselage. As the aircraft fell away from the formation it went into a flat spin and rolled over. Nygaard, who was burned on the face and arms went out of the nose hatch, followed by the bombardier, Lt John S Trost. The only other survivor was Lt Frank Leasman, navigator, who was caught under debris until the engineer freed him. With the B-17 still upside down and at about 4,000ft, Leasman climbed out of the nose hatch and then jumped up as the Fortress passed under him. For a time Leasman evaded capture after being rescued by a French girl in the Resistance, but he was

captured later. Trost successfully evaded and on 9 February he crossed the Pyrenees on foot into Spain. He eventually reached Gibraltar on 21 April and was back in London within three days.

Stammberger meanwhile, had picked out his own target. It was *Rose O'Day*, flown by 1/Lt John R McKee, one of the original nine pilots in the fated 379th BS. As Stammberger started a second head-on pass McKee's crew began baling out at short intervals. Eventually there were nine chutes. Mckee evaded capture and was back in England on 26 January 1943. The eight men in his crew who bailed out were captured. The third 379th BS loss was *Terry And The Pirates*, piloted by Lt Lewis McKesson, former squadron operations officer. McKesson and six of his crew survived. The American gunners on the raid claimed 53 enemy fighters shot down. These claims were later reduced to 21 confirmed, but in fact JG26 lost one fighter and its pilot, while III./JG2 lost two pilots. As far as the bombing went, just seventy-two of the heavies were effective over the target at Romilly.

Uffz Hubert Swoboda, a Bf 109G pilot of 11th *Staffel* JG1, made a lone attack on a B-17 formation and was hit by return defensive fire. Swoboda's guns jammed and four P-47s arrived on the scene, so Swoboda decided to ram the B-17 he had attacked. It was B-17 42-3288 *Green Fury II* of the 338th BS, 96th BG, piloted by 1/Lt Stanley P Budleski. Swoboda approached the Fortress at speed from the right and struck the rudder. The fin was also damaged and instantly *Green Fury II* dived out of control, crashing on Nordeney Island with the loss of six crew. Four men were made PoW. Swoboda bailed out and reached the ground uninjured.

Christmas 1942 arrived, and the gift for all VIIIth BC crews was a week's respite from combat missions. The heavies flew no more missions until 30 December when 77 B-17s set out to bomb Lorient. Three B-17s failed to return. New Year's Eve was party time too, and missions did not resume again until 3 January 1943, when 85 B-17s were despatched to St Nazaire. Gen Eaker abandoned individual bombing, which had been SOP (Standard Operating Procedure) from the outset, in favour of group bombing. (The lead crew concept and the "stagger formation", developed by Col LeMay, CO, 305th BG, had been tried at group level on the 30 December raid.) 21 out of the 22 305th BG Fortresses bombed and dropped most of the 105,000lbs

*The second Viermot I brought down was over Paris on 20 December 1942. I managed to shoot down a Boeing in a head-on attack, the machine turning over on its back and diving down with a jerk, and me being able to just pull up and over it. I felt certain that I must have hit the pilots; a burst of the four 2 cm cannons and the two machine guns from our Focke-Wulf into the cockpit (which was only built with sheets of glass or plastic), was guaranteed to be deadly, if we managed to score a hit!*

**Lt Otto Stammberger of 9./JG26.**

*Above:* P-47C Thunderbolt at Kings Cliffe, Northants, March 1943. *USAF.*

of bombs smack on the target. While none of the 305th BG's B-17s were lost, two were so badly shot up by *Flak* that they were left at Talbenny, Wales. Seven Fortresses in the 91st, 303rd and 306th BGs failed to return and 47 were damaged. These were the highest losses thus far.

On 13 January, when 72 B-17s went to the Fives locomotive works in Lille, the enemy fighters struck again, even though the 44th went on a diversionary raid over to the Dutch coast in an attempt to draw them away from the real raid. Singled out for attack this time were the 22 B-17s of the leading 305th BG which was forced to defend itself against upwards of 25 Fw 190s from I. and II./JG26. They flew in line astern, making all their attacks from head-on at the same altitude as the Fortresses. Most of the enemy fighters attacked singly, half-rolling into a split-S upon reaching the Fortress formation. JG26 downed the B-17 flown by Lt Conrad J Hilbinger and damaged another 10. Maj Tom H. Taylor, 364th BS CO, who in the absence of the ailing pilot Capt Allen . Martini, was flying *Dry Martini II*, with Lt Joseph Boyle in the co-pilot's seat, led the second element in the third squadron. As Taylor turned off the target, still in formation, an Fw 190 came in, weaving from side to side at 11 o'clock level. It fired a steady stream of 20mm cannon-fire as it closed, and a line of other fighters followed, with more cannon-fire. Every gun on board *Dry Martini II* opened up on the attackers. A cannon shell from the lead fighter burst through the side window of the cockpit to the left of Taylor hitting him in the chest and killing him instantly

*I don't think we had to make any change in tactics in England; there weren't any tactics there when we started because there wasn't anybody there who knew anything about it. There wasn't even a wing headquarters that could write a five paragraph field order. That's one thing I did learn down at the Tactical School; how to write a field order. I had to go up there and tell them about the five-paragraph field order so we could get some sense out of this ten feet of teletype paper that came down with the mission for the next day. They didn't even know those basics, much less anything about tactics. Everybody was learning the business from the ground up.*

**Col (later General) Curtis E LeMay, 305th BG CO. LeMay and his staff worked hard to find the best method of combating fighter attacks without compromising bombing accuracy and vice-versa. After trying "stacked up" formations of 18 aircraft, LeMay finally decided upon "staggered" three-plane elements within a squadron and "staggered" squadrons within a group. Individual bombing was replaced by lead crews, whose bombardier signalled to the rest of the formation when to bomb so that all bombs were released simultaneously.**

*Right:* Col (later General) Curtis E LeMay pictured on 13 May 1943 with Brig-Gen Hayward "Possum" Hansell (left), CO, 1st BW. *Bill Donald.*

and wounding Boyle. *Dry Martini II* immediately dropped 2,000ft. In spite of his wounds, Boyle pulled Taylor's body away from the controls and managed to level off the Fortress. The top turret gunner, S/Sgt O E Ballew, carried Taylor's body to the nose as the gunners continued to fire at the attackers. Despite incessant attacks Boyle, assisted by the right waist gunner, T/Sgt Horace L Mabry in the pilot's seat, managed to bring *Dry Martini II* home. At Thurleigh nearby, two more B-17s of the 306th BG failed to return.

In France meanwhile, changes in German fighter tactics and the disposition of units were afoot. It was announced in *Luftwaffe* circles that one of the

Americans' greatest adversaries, the pilots of JG26, were to transfer to the Russian Front where they would trade places with the Green Hearts Geschwader, JG54. However, the transfer was only partially complete when, in the spring of 1943, the growing strength of VIIIth BC increased pressure on the Jagdgeschwaders in the west, and the transfer of the remaining *Gruppen* and *Staffeln* was first postponed and then cancelled by Gen-Maj Adolf Galland. At this time the *Luftwaffe*, unhappy with the relatively small numbers of bombers being shot down, revised its tactics. On 20 December the *Luftwaffe* had made its attacks from dead ahead, or 12 o'clock level. Closing speeds of around 550mph made it

*Whilst serving as Staffelkapitän during 1943, I scored some good victories. We flew two to four sorties daily. And if we were unable to score any bomber kills, this was usually caused by their fighter escort which prevented us from getting at them. After all, we were under orders to attack the bombers and not the fighter aircraft, as the latter were not doing the German war machine much damage. At times, one was lucky to be able to attack the bombers, when the fighter escort had to turn for home and their relief had not yet arrived on the scene. Sometimes the relieving fighters weren't able to locate the bombers at all, which offered us an opportunity to get in and score kills. Even under these relatively favorable circumstances it was sheer murder to attack the American combat boxes from the rear, which we sometimes did in an effort to get more time to fire: this left us exposed to the defensive fire of the bombers for a longer time too. At a distance of some 1500m the US Viermots opened fire from all barrels. A bomber formation usually consisted of 20 machines, which flew in rows of four planes and which were sideways echelonned, and in which these rows of four bombers were stacked on top of each other, with row four and five flying in the middle. We normally opened fire at a distance of 300m and tried to close in to 30 or 40m. During all this time our fighters were subjected to the defensive fire of at least eight machine guns per bomber, which, with a group of 20 bombers, meant the concentrated firepower of 160 heavy machine guns. Each group of 20 machines also was flying echelonned to the side and higher than the leading group, so that we had to bear the full brunt of their defensive fire as well. Opening fire from behind at 300m distance, and taking us 5 to 6 seconds to overtake the bombers, these attacks were indescribable in their sheer physical and mental stress. Just imagine standing under a shower with 160 jets of water pouring out, and not getting wet!!! That of course is quite impossible, Even when we attacked with four planes in line abreast in an effort to split up the defensive fire, statistically there were still 40 guns firing at each one of us. We therefore changed tactics and started attacking from head-on, which called for incredible dexterity, a good aim and nerves of steel until the last second. After all, one could not anticipate in what direction the stricken bomber would swerve, there being four possibilities, to the right, left, up or down, and moreover, behind the bombers under attack, the other formations were flying.*

**Oblt Otto Stammberger,
Staffelkapitän, 4./JG26.**

difficult to keep targets in effective firing range for more than a split second and there was always the fear of collision at the back of the German pilots' minds. Larger attacking formations and simultaneous attacks by fighters, rather than in trail, were to be used. While they would still use the head-on approach, the angle of attack would be from 10° above the horizontal - otherwise known as 12 o'clock high, which in experiments was found to be more effective. As before, the best chance of knocking a bomber out of formation was to kill the pilots in the cockpit.

The new tactics were tried on 23 January when VIIIth BC attacked Lorient. Five bombers – all from the 303rd

BG – were shot down. Two more – one each from the 91st and 303rd BGs, crash-landed in England. Lt Otto Stammberger's *9th Staffel*, flying from Vannes with III./JG 2, were officially credited with two of the B-17 losses while 7./JG2 claimed four.

# *Chapter 2 – Gaining Momentum*

On 27 January 1943, VIIIth BC attacked Germany for the first time. Sixty-four B-17s and Liberators started the mission to the naval base at Wilhelmshaven on the north-west German coast. Having lost their way over the North Sea, 23 Liberators of the 44th and 93rd BGs wrongly identified Lemmer in Holland as Wilhelmshaven, dropping their bombs to the north of this harbour town. Wilhelmshaven was reached by 55 Fortresses. The 306th BG led the mission with Col Frank A Armstrong, CO, in the lead ship. Crews reported being attacked by about fifty fighters, including some twin-engined types. Eight bombers were claimed shot down by eight different pilots of JG1, a fighter group that clashed with the Americans for the first time on 27 January 1943. In actuality, the Americans lost three ships, one of them 41-24637, a 366th BS, 305th BG B-17 piloted by Lt Vance W Beckham. Only five men survived. The two other heavies that failed to return were 44th BG Liberators. *Spirit of 76*, flown by 1/Lt Maxwell W Sullivan and another 68th BS B-24, flown by Lt Nolan B Cargile, were attacked by around 30 enemy fighters as they left the target area of Lemmer and headed for home. During one of the numerous frontal attacks by II./JG1, a hit was scored on Sullivan's No.3 engine, setting it on fire, and he dropped from formation. Soon the fire engulfed the entire wing and the Liberator exploded over Terschelling harbour. Only one crew member survived and he later had to have a leg amputated. An Fw 190 which made a head-on attack at Cargile's B-24 clipped the wing and then the right tailfin of the B-24. Both the Liberator and the Fw 190 (flown by Fw Fritz Koch of *12 Staffel JG1*, who was apparently killed by return fire from a 68th BS Liberator) hurtled down and crashed, killing everyone on board the B-24. In all, gunners claimed 22-14-13 German fighters. Again the figures were inflated: JG1 lost just eight Fw 190A-4s and Bf 109G-ls with four pilots killed, two of which fell to American return fire.

*Luftwaffe* night fighters were now put into action against American day formations whenever the latter flew without escort. The first use of night fighters of NJG1 against American formations took place on 4 February, when 86 bombers attacked Emden, Hamm and Osnabruck. It was believed that the heavily armed Bf 110 night fighters would bolster the day fighter arm and prove effective against American day bombers. Hptm Hans-Joachim Jabs led eight Bf 110s of IV./NJG I into action against the B-17s. Jabs was a seasoned combat veteran who had his first taste of action during the Battles of France and Britain, when he served as a *Zerstörer* ('Destroyer') pilot in Bf 110s with ZG76. He quickly became one of the leading fighter pilots in the Bf 110 day fighter force, with seven aircraft shot down during the Battle of France and another 12 Spitfires and Hurricanes over England during the summer of 1940. For these excellent feats of arms, bearing in mind that the Bf 110 was clearly outdated in daylight air combat by 1940, he was decorated with the *Ritterkreuz* in October 1940 and thereupon successfully led his 6./ZG76 during the campaign in Crete. His *Staffel* became 9./NJG3 in November 1941 and on completion of night fighter training Jabs became an operational night fighter pilot. He went on to claim his first night kill in June 1942 and was appointed *Staffelkapitän* of the elite 11./NJG1, at Leeuwarden in November 1942. By the end of 1942 he had shot down four RAF night bombers.

Jabs, therefore, was well qualified to lead the Bf 110s against the American combat boxes, for the first time on 4 February. Although Jabs, OFw Grimm and Uffz Naumann claimed three B-17s shot down in the ensuing combat - among which was *El Lobo*, a 305th BG B-17 flown by Lt Cornelius A Jenkins, with five men killed - IV./NJG 1 paid dearly. All eight Bf 110s were badly damaged and two made belly landings on Ameland and

**Right:** Hptm Hans-Joachim Jabs pictured in 1944 after he was decorated with Oak Leaves to the Ritterkreuz. At this time, he was Kommodore of NJG1, his tally of *Abschüsse* standing at 45. One of these was a B-17, which he destroyed on 4 February 1943. Claims for three B-17s destroyed on 4 February 1943 were submitted by Hptm Hans-Joachim Jabs, OFw Grimm and Uffz Alfred Naumann to the NW of Ameland. All eight Bf 110s participating were either shot down or heavily damaged by return fire. *Helmut Conradi.*

near Leeuwarden. None of these aircraft would be serviceable to combat the RAF night bombers. The 305th BG lost a second B-17 when an Fw 190 slammed into *What's Cookin' Doc?* flown by Lt William K Davidson. All the crew were killed. Three more B-17s, two from the 91st BG and one from the 303rd, were lost on the mission. Fw 190s of JG1 claimed 10 B-17s shot down for the loss of these aircraft and two pilots, Oblt Walter Leonhardt, *St Kap*, 6./JG1 and Uffz Rudolf Mayer, 12./JG1.

Despite this success, losses of night fighter pilots on daylight sorties began to mount. Night fighter pilots had a habit of going in close before attacking, tactics which proved very costly when met with the heavy defensive fire of the day bombers and which soon led to the prohibition of day operations for key night fighter crews. However, German High Command refused for a long time to credit the depth of the penetrations achieved by American escort fighters and night fighters continued to be sent up on what were essentially suicide

operations. It became necessary for Gen-Maj Galland himself to take off and obtain personal confirmation before Göring would believe the situation.

The Liberators continued to fly some shallow penetration diversion missions to aid the Fortresses. Its hurried afternoon mission to Dunkirk on 15 February, the day of another maximum effort, was to prove no exception. The 'Flying Eightballs' target, found on the morning reconnaissance flight, was the *Tojo*, a German night fighter control ship which being moved up to the German Bight to fill a gap in the Ostmark area. (It is believed that the ship's name was shortened from *Togoland,* a German protectorate in Africa before WW1.) The *Tojo* was equipped with a *Dreh-Freya* early warning radar at the bow. This radar operated in the 90 to 200MHZ band and had an effective range of up to 80 miles over flat terrain. In addition, the ship was equipped with other detection devices including a *Würzburg-Riese* fighter ground control radar and heightfinding system for air raid warning radars. At

*Above:* Prior to the Bf 109, for final day fighter pilot training, *Luftwaffe* pilots flew the Arado 96, seen here at the Day Fighting School at Ingolstadt in 1942. The Arado Ar 96B was the Luftwaffe's standard pilot training aircraft throughout the war. *Peter Spoden.*

Shipdham 17 crews were hurriedly called and briefed and once airborne they met with B-24s of the 329th BS, 93rd BG, from Hardwick. They were led by the 67th BS's *Betty Anne/Gallopin Ghost*, flown by Capt Art T Cullen with the squadron CO, Maj Donald MacDonald, in the co-pilot's seat, flying as command pilot. *Little Beaver* flew on the left wing in the No.3

*Below:* For training, liaison and glider-towing duties, the *Luftwaffe* used around 50 North American NAA-57s and NAA-64 Harvards, which had been delivered to the French Air Force prior to WWII. NAA-64 (serial nr 159) was photographed at Guyancourt, France, early in 1944. *Walter Stumpf.*

position in the lead element. Just beneath them were three B-24s of the second element, with six to the right and six to the left. The formation crossed the English Channel en route to Le Havre. Cullen's navigator, 1/Lt John L Mackey, plotted a course to make the Germans believe that the Liberators were headed inland. However, they changed direction and flew straight and level up the coast of France to Dunkirk. The bomb run was exceptionally long to make certain of scoring hits, as this target required bombing of the utmost precision and accuracy, but it enabled the German gunners to put up a very accurate *Flak* barrage on the formation. Immediately after releasing bombs, the lead aircraft was hit very hard by *Flak*. No.2 engine burst into flames and No.3 was shot completely out of the wing.

For a few moments the noseless B-24 had flown on, only to fall away to starboard with the port inboard engine aflame and the right inboard ripped from its mounting. Finally, the starboard wing fell off and a huge explosion scattered debris among the formation. *Railway Express*, piloted by 1/Lt Rufus A Oliphant Jr, was also hit by *Flak* at almost the same time as Cullen's B-24. It was damaged, crippled, and slowly lost altitude coming off the target. Lt John H Diehl's B-24 spotted Oliphant slowing up for him, and another ship, *Captain And His Kids*, piloted by Capt Tom Cramer, which was also damaged by *Flak* over Dunkirk. Unbeknown to the B-24 crews the *Luftwaffe* were in hot pursuit across the Channel. Among them was Oblt Erich Hohagen, the *Kapitän* of 7./JG2. Hohagen was credited with the shooting down of Oliphant's B-24. All the crew of *Railway Express*

*We were on the bomb run. 2/Lt Paul D Caldwell, the bombardier, called out "target in view". I flew P and I for about 10 seconds, and he made a big correction to the right about 8 to 10 degrees. We flew that about ten seconds and I saw the "bomb release" light go on – and then everything flew to bits. It must have been a direct hit with 88mm under the flight deck at about the nosewheel section. It stunned me for a while and when I could think reasonably, I looked around to see that we were in a dive, no ships were in sight, no roof on the cabin – just the windshield, numbers 2 and 3 were smoking and the cowling blown off both engines and very little control on the wheel. I couldn't try the rudder because my leg was broken. When I looked over at Major Mac, he made motions to bail out. I then noticed he had a serious wound in his stomach. By this time we quit fooling with the airplane as she was on her right side and going down. Major Mac unstrapped his belt and with lots of effort on his part (it must have been agony for him) and a little pushing on my part, he went through the roof – or rather where the roof used to be. He got down all right but he died on the operating table of a Luftwaffe hospital in France. After Mac left, I went, but hit the tail of the ship, broke my leg in another place, and my arm. I heard from the Germans that Mackey was killed in the airplane.*

**Capt Art T Cullen, pilot, *Betty Anne/Gallopin Ghost*, who with three gunners, were the only survivors, 15 February 1943. Cullen was eventually repatriated in September 1944.**

perished. Three men aboard Cramer's ship also died before he could crash-land on the beach at Sandwich. The landing was made without flaps or landing gear, but those still alive on board were not injured seriously, and they soon managed to extinguish the fire in No.1 engine. Cramer's gunners claimed one of the three yellow-nosed Fw 190s that attacked *Captain And The Kids* in line astern. A subsequent attack started a fire in the No.1 engine but this was extinguished temporarily, and No.2 engine was feathered. About mid-Channel, near 8,000ft altitude, the third attack by three Fw 190s, occurred from 9 o'clock level. The left waist gunner returned fire at about 1,000 yards but the enemy fighter broke off. These three fighters had previously finished

off Oliphant's B-24. Despite all of the 'Eightballs' valiant endeavours, the raid had nothing to show for it. The *Tojo* remained afloat. (In September 1943 the ship was renamed the *Rudolf Luck*, she would keep this name until the end of the war, when she was renamed the *Svalbard* and was used as a merchant vessel once again.)

On 16 February, 77 B-17s and 18 B-24s were dispatched to bomb the U-boat pens at St Nazaire.

**Below:** Immediately after taking off from Deelen airfield on 11 March 1943, Lt Burath's Fw 190A-4 145555 of IV./JG1 crashed, most probably as a result of sabotage to his aircraft, which suffered 60% damage. *Eberhard Burath via Rob de Visser.*

*Luftwaffe* fighter controllers waited until the escort fighters turned back before unleashing III./JG2 from Brest and I./JG2 from St Brieuc. III./JG2 failed to bring down any of the B-17s but I./JG2 continued to attack the retreating Fortresses across the sea and only turned back when the Spitfire withdrawal escort reappeared. Six B-17s - two each from the 303rd, 305th, and 306th BGs - were shot down. I./JG2 and 9./JG26 made aggressive attacks on the bomber formations and each claimed three B-17s shot down. Lt Otto 'Stotto' Stammberger led 9./JG26 and he and Fw Edgar Dorre hit one Fortress. It was 42-5175 of the 367th BS, 306th BG, flown by Lt Joseph A Downing, which was crippled first by *Flak* over the target, which hit No.1 and No.3 engines, and then by repeated hits from the Fw 190s, which knocked out a third engine. Downing put his ship into a steep dive between 10,000 and 4,000ft when he found some desperately needed clouds to hide in. Stammberger saw the B-17 fall from formation, although as he was subsequently shot down, by a *Viermot* he was unable to observe the kill and it was not confirmed. About 10km west of Ploermal, Uffz E Schwarz of the 9th *Staffel* downed 42-5717 flown by Lt William H Warner of the 423rd BS, 306th BG. Four of the crew bailed out before the B-17 crashed at Ploermal - two of them evaded and two were captured. The third victory was awarded to Fw Dorre. Gunners aboard the bombers claimed 20 enemy fighters shot down but only Stammberger's aircraft (a shell smashed his cockpit and fragments hit his left hand) had to be written off. Two B-24s which collided over the Channel brought the day's total losses to eight. Thirty heavies returned battle damaged.

The increase in bomber missions did not escape the notice of the German pilots, even fresh ones like Lt Eberhard Burath of IV./JG1, who noted that, "*during February operations became more frequent. The Viermots penetrated ever more deeply over the continent.*" Burath had been posted to this unit, which was equipped with the Fw 190, at München-Gladbach, on 21 September 1942. During more than two years of training Burath learned to fly 19 different types of aircraft, including the Bf 109 and Fw 190. His flying log books had 1,112 entries for take-offs and landings, during which he had amassed 450 flying hours. He was fully qualified as an aerobatic pilot, had learned to navigate foreign territory and to fly and manoeuvre in Fighter Wings, and practiced close combat flying for up to six hours a day. What had been lacking in his training was firing practice – he had only practiced shooting at ground targets and at drogues on a handful of occasions. His combat experience would be gained with IV./JG1. His first few operational flights in the Dutch and Belgian coastal area were uneventful, but from early 1943 onwards, whilst operating from Deelen, Schiphol, Twente, Gilze-Rijen and Leeuwarden in Holland Burath's *Gruppe* was heavily involved in combating the mounting American daylight bombing offensive.

Lt Burath did not have his first contact with the American bombers until 26 February, when the Focke Wulf aircraft factories at Bremen were the target for the day. Submarine facilities at Wilhelmshaven were the secondary target if weather conditions made it impossible to attack the primary. At six air bases in

*During the usual - mostly unsuccessful - search for enemy formations I had, flying right out on the starboard wing and while continually scanning the sky, missed my formation's turn to port and had continued straight ahead far out over the North Sea. I noticed it too late and now looked for my own lot. They appeared back there and I went after them with full power. Then they grew ever larger, much too large for fighters. Can that be possible? There they were, the Viermots, 60 to 70 of them in close formation. What now? Fear comes only with experience, and that I did not have. Without thinking I turned in to the formation and attacked from ahead. Firing with all my guns I flashed right through them. Turn in, pass parallel to them ahead. In doing so I was nearly hit as a projectile, aimed with just the right deflection, came towards me like a red tomato. Nice that the fellows then still used tracer, enabling me to jink away just in time. I zoomed once more through the formation, then it was time to return to the coast which was still 100km away. What might the Yanks have thought about this 'massed attack by German fighters'? At least they had provided me with an alibi by a hit in the engine, but the 801 continued to run smoothly even on 13 cylinders (26 February 1943).*

**Above:** Lt Eberhard Burath, IV./JG1, 1943. *Jim Hamilton.*

eastern England 93 B-17s and B-24s taxied out for the mission. At Shipdham, 11 B-24s of the 44th BG, including six aircraft in the 66th Squadron, left their dispersals. They included *Sad Sack*, flown by l/Lt Robert H McPhillamey and l/Lt Wilbur F Wockenfuss and *Maisie* flown by Capt Howard Adams. As they taxied out at Shipdham, Adams' mascot, a little wooden doll of the same name, swung gently from the cabin windshield in front of him and his co-pilot. The crew had also found room for Robert Perkins Post, a *New York Times* war correspondent, the only one of seven in the 'Writing 69th' who had asked to fly with the 'Eightballs' on the mission. The Liberators were scheduled to join the 1st BW Fortresses around 0925 hours at Fakenham but a variation in predicted winds caused a delay and the 2nd BW was unable to catch the 1st BW until they were about 100 miles out to sea. The 66th BS was now positioned at the rear of the whole formation. B-17s of the 305th BG Fortresses led the formation, followed by the B-17s of the 303rd, 91st and the 306th BG. The formation, having started with 93 bombers, was reduced to approximately 73 when 20 bombers returned early with mechanical or other problems. The entire formation continued to climb until the B-24s reached an altitude of 29,000ft. At 1022 hours, a German radar installation on the island of Texel in the Netherlands located the American bomber formation. About eight minutes later, the bombers were attacked by a lone Fw 190 of IV./JG1. It was flown by Lt Eberhard Burath.

Shortly after Burath's lone effort, other Focke Wulfs joined the attack, one of which, piloted by OFw Bach of 12./JG1, claimed to have shot down a B-17. It seems likely that this was *Lucy Belle* of the 303rd BG piloted by 1/Lt Lloyd Driffin. *Lucy Belle* came under attack, but Driffin was able to evade the fighters by diving into low-lying overcast. Around 1100 hours, the bombers reached the German mainland near the North Sea islands of Baltrum and Langeoog. As the formation moved inland over Ostfriesland, the attacks intensified. Bf 109s of I./JG1 joined the attack. At Leeuwarden 30 year old Hptm Ludwig Becker, *Staffelkapitän*, 12./NJG1 and a great night fighting tactician with 44 night victories, waited to fly his very first daylight mission. Becker was known as the 'Night Fighting Professor'. Shortly before taking off from Leeuwarden in a formation of 12 Bf 110s in pursuit of the American daylight raiders, again led by Hptm Jabs, Becker was informed of the award of the Oak Leaves to his Knight's Cross, which had been bestowed on him on 1 July 1942 after his 25th night victory. At 1135 hours IV./NJG1 had taken off from Leeuwarden and intercepted the B-17s and B-24s. They returned, claiming two shot down but Becker's Bf 110 was lost without a trace.

Almost an hour earlier, Lt Heinz Knoke and 11 other pilots in I./JG1 took off from Jever-Wangerooge. They returned having shot down five B-17s and B-24s (they claimed 13 bombers!). Among the Fortress groups the 91st BG lost two and the 305th BG three B-17s. One of the latter was claimed by *Flak*. About 15 minutes from Bremen 1/Lt George E Stallman's B-17, the lowest in the entire formation, came under attack from two Bf 109s. They made several passes and the Fortress took

*Above:* An armourer of I./JG1 reloading the twin fuselage 13mm Rheinmetall MG131 machine guns of the Fw 190A-7. *Seebrandt via Rob de Visser.*

hits in the right wing and No. 4 engine, knocking the ship out of formation. A burst of *Flak* hit Stallman's B-17 as he tried in vain to catch up with the rest of the 305th BG formation over Wilhelmshaven and the crew were ordered to bail out.

As the Fortresses turned off the target the bombers performed a very steep turn and as a result, the following Fortresses had a difficult time maintaining formation. Maj Joseph J Preston, pilot of the lead plane in the 305th BG formation, said later, *This was the strongest fighter opposition so far.* Two 305th BG Forts were victims of *Flak* and fighter attacks. *Arkie*, flown by Capt Edward E Tribbett, was shot down over the town of Hooksiel, just south of Wilhelmshaven. All the crew survived. *Devil's Playmate,* flown by Lt Isaac D Benson of the 364th BS, was lost with all of the crew.

Against all odds, Capt Hugh G Ashcraft managed to bring *Southern Comfort* home with 4ft of the rudder shot away and a windmilling propeller. Over the North Sea, Ashcraft announced over the intercom *Those who want to, please pray.* Nearing Chelveston an RAF Mosquito pulled in close to look over the battered and wrecked Fortress. The "Mossie" flew so close that the American crew could see the pilot shake his head before waving his hand and flying away. The two other Fortress losses this day *Kickapoo* flown by Capt John Swais and *Short Snorter II,* piloted by 1/Lt Beman E Smith, came from the 91st BG.

*They picked me off shortly before we reached the IP. Two engines were shot out and on fire. The oxygen was shot out and there was a fire in the bomb bay. Controls, elevators, wings, etc., were also badly hit and the plane became inoperable.*

**1/Lt Robert H McPhillamey, pilot, *Sad Sack*, 66th Squadron, 44th BG, 26 February 1943.**

The Liberators too were set upon by I./JG 1. The German fighters had begun their attacks some 30 miles off the coast and they were so determined in their mission that the attacks would continue all the way into the target. *Night Raider,* also called *Heavenly Hideaway,* a 93rd BG B-24H (the first H model in the ETO) flown by Capt Beattie H Bud Fleenor, limped away from the target area with a supercharger out, *Flak* holes in its fuselage and a pair of useless tail guns which had frozen tight after only eight rounds. Fleenor's B-24 was attacked again and again.

Either Uffz Heinz Hanke of 9./JG1 in an Fw 190, or Uffz Wennekers of 2./JG1 in a Bf 109, had claimed the apparently doomed B-24 as their first victory. *Sad Sack* in the 44th BG was also shot down by one of these pilots.

Since the island of Texel, when the Liberators had first come under attack, *Maisie* had dropped behind, so 2/Lt Wayne Gotke, navigator, had spent most of the time working with position reports trying to get short-cuts filled into the flight, therefore allowing Howard Adams

*We were leading the second element and on the right wing of the group lead. Stallman's plane was to the right and below our plane. Going into Bremerhaven, we met frontal attacks by the German fighters. I fired on some six fighters coming from directly in front. I know that of the six none of them fired on us as they turned into "Split S" out of the way before getting into firing range for their sights. During a breather I saw one fighter come in below us and to the right. He was in a firing position on Stallman's aircraft. However, he was coming in too high for S/Sgt Lee "Shorty" Gordon in the ball turret to fire on him. I didn't think at the time he had hit anything, but on looking a few seconds later I saw Stallman's plane going down and saw a parachute break out of the ball turret. I knew then it was Stallman's plane as "Shorty" was the only gunner I knew who could and did wear a chute in the ball turret. Most had to come up into the plane and snap on their chute and exit through the gun port window or door. I saw "Shorty's" chute open, but we turned north to go out some distance before turning back for England.*

**Capt Ralph S Cohen, Armament and gunnery officer, flying top turret gunner in the Martini crew 26 February 1943 (Stallman and four of the crew were killed. Gordon survived and repeatedly attempted escape and finally succeeded in a "home run" on his third attempt. Exactly a year and a day after his capture, he was back in Allied territory. He became the first American airman to receive the Silver Star for escaping from captivity).**

*An Fw 190 came towards us. His wings were pure red. I could almost see the lead coming point-blank. I froze on to the trigger. His left wing dropped off - he went hell-bent into the water. But he'd fired first and hit Jung (S/Sgt Robert P Jungbluth, the radio operator) and me. I knew Jung was hurt worse than I was. I looked up and saw part of his arm hanging above the window, looked around and saw his side intact. The 20mm blast had ripped Jung's arm from his body, and the shrapnel had hit us both.' Szabo had over 80 pieces lodged in his body. Incredibly, Night Raider made it back to crash-land at Ludham, Norfolk with a badly wounded crew, no hydraulic system, punctured tyres, a 15in hole in the right tail flap and 177 .30 and 20mm cannon shell holes in the aircraft. One ground crew man said, 'This one shouldn't have come back'.*

**T/Sgt Lou Szabo, waist gunner, *Night Raider*, 93rd BG, 26 February 1943.**

***Below:*** A Bf 109G-6 or G-14 coming in to land. Note the auxiliary fuel tank fitted under the fuselage. *JaPo.*

*W*e could see the coast and opted to try for Sweden but it soon became apparent to all of us that it was hopeless. McPhillamey gave the order to bail out. At the time that all of this was happening we were flying near 30,000ft but couldn't go any higher to avoid the prop wash of the B-17s. 2/Lt Rexford W Lippert, the navigator, was killed instantly by a 20mm shell which decapitated him. S/Sgt. Robert P Garmon, waist gunner, was hit in the knee just as he bailed out. Sgt Alberto 0 Salvo, the belly gunner, was hit in the shoulder and chest, and in several other places, but managed to bail out with the rest of us. He died in a hospital shortly thereafter. After the crew was out (I thought) I started to leave as well but our engineer, Sgt. Eugene Rudiger, had passed out from lack of oxygen and was blocking the exit. I must have beaten and abused him very badly when trying to get past him. I finally made it and was about to jump when something stopped me. I thought, "My God! I can't leave the engineer." I reached back and grabbed him by the collar of his fur flying jacket and backed towards the bomb bay, falling out and dragging him with me. I saw him later on the ground and it looked like he had been through a meat grinder. I never did tell him that I had almost beaten him to death trying to get past him. I reasoned that he must have regained consciousness on the way down and pulled the rip cord.

**Wilbur Wockenfuss, co-pilot, *Sad Sack*, 66th Squadron, 44th BG, 26 February 1943.**

*I*must have opened the throttle subconsciously. I can distinguish the individual enemy aircraft now. Most of them are Liberators. They look as if their fat bellies were pregnant with bombs. I pick out my target. "This is where I settle your hash, my friend," I mutter. I shall make a frontal attack. The Yank is focused in my sights. He grows rapidly larger. I reach for the firing buttons on the stick. Tracers come whizzing past my head. They have opened fire on me!

Fire! I press both buttons, but my aim is poor. I can see only a few hits register in the right wing. I almost scrape the fat belly as I dive past. Then I am caught in the slipstream, buffeted about so violently that for a second I wonder if my tailplane has been shot away. I climb up steeply and break away to the left. Tracers pursue me, unpleasantly close. Blast all this metal in the air! I come in for a second frontal attack, this time from a little below. I keep on firing until I have to swerve to avoid a collision. My salvos register this time. I drop away below. As I turn my head, flames are spreading along the bottom of the fuselage of 'my' Liberator. It sheers away from the formation in a wide sweep to the right. Twice more I come in to attack, this time diving from above the tail. I am met by heavy defensive fire.

At the same time I open fire, pressing both buttons. The recoil of my cannons and heavy machine guns leaves my bird shaking slightly. My aim is not good. I can see only a few hits on the right wing. I swoop under the fat stomach of my opponent. The draught of his four propellers shakes me around in such a way that I think for a second that my tail assembly is torn. The combined speeds of our two approaching planes is over 1,000km/h.

*Above:* Capt Howard Adams, pilot of *Maisie*, 66th BS, 44th BG, 26 February 1943. *Jim Hamilton.*

Steeply, I pull above to the left. Tracer bullets from the guns of the Liberator follow me...For the second time I attack, this time from the front and below, and shoot until I am within ramming distance. My shots hit! I let myself fall away below. In falling away I turn my head. My Liberator is burning underneath. It turns in a wide curve to the right away from her group. We are about 8,000m high. From behind and above, once

*Right:* 44th BG crewmen at Stalag Luft III. Wayne Gotke, navigator, *Maisie*, 66th BS, 44th BG, 26 February 1943, second from left. *Jim Hamilton.*

**Above:** Lt Heinz Knoke of 2./JG1, who shot down *Maisie*, 26 February 1943. *Jim Hamilton.*

*again I attack. Strong defensive fire comes toward me. My high explosive shells hit in the top side of the fuselage and the right wing. The fire spreads along the right wing. The inside engine stops. Suddenly, the wing breaks off altogether. The body of the stricken monster plunges vertically, spinning into the depths. A long black trail of smoke marks its descent. One of the crew attempts to bail out but his parachute is in flames. Poor devil! The body somersaults and falls to the ground like a stone. At an altitude of 3,000ft there is a tremendous explosion, which causes the spinning fuselage to disintegrate. Fragments of blazing wreckage land on a farm 200 or 300 yards from Zwischenahn airfield, and the exploding fuel tanks set the farm buildings on fire. In a terrific power dive I follow my victim down, and land on the runway below. I run over to the scene of the crash. A crowd of people are there, trying to fight the fire in the farmhouse. I join in the rescue work and bring out furniture, animals and machinery from the burning buildings. Smoke blinds and chokes me, my flying suit is scorched by the flames, as I drag a fat pig out by the hind legs, squealing like mad, from the pig-sty, which is completely gutted by fire. The farmhouse and barns are saved. Strewn all over the cow field lies the wreckage of the Liberator. The explosion threw the crew out in mid-air. Their shattered bodies lie beside the smoking remains of the aircraft. One hundred yards away I find the captain's seat and the nosewheel. A little doll, evidently the mascot, sits undamaged between the shattered windows of the cabin.*

*One hour later I land at Jever. My men carry me shoulder-high to the dispersal point. That was my fourth victory, on my 164th mission… I cannot help thinking about the bodies of the American crew. When will our turn come? Those men share, in common with ourselves, the great adventure of flying. Separated for the moment by the barrier of war, we shall one day be reunited by death in the air.*

**Above:** German newspaper report of the air battle of 26 February 1943 with a photo of McPhillamey's B-24. *Jim Hamilton.*

Lt Heinz Knoke describing shooting down *Maisie* of the 44th BG, 26 February 1943. Only two men survived from the doomed B-24. Wayne Gotke was picked up after dangling between two trees about 20 feet in the air for about 25 minutes, afraid that if he unbuckled he would fall badly. At the first-aid station he saw S/Sgt. Mifflin. Also there was Lt Wockenfuss, McPhillamey's co-pilot. McPhillamey landed near a small village close to Oldenburg and was captured immediately after a couple of shots were fired in his direction. He ran into Mooney, Wockenfuss and two others of his crew at a police station in Oldenburg.

Wockenfuss said he had seen Capt Adams' leather jacket and it appeared the man had been killed. The Germans had obtained the ship's loading list from the jacket and asked me about a Robert P Post, the New York Times correspondent who was flying with us. I gave them no information whatsoever as my orders were to say nothing in the hope that if men were at large their chances of getting home would be better. The Germans asked questions about Donald Bowie, one of the gunners, and Hannan, and from that I believe these two men could not be identified. I am under the impression that all the bodies were not found, or if found, could not be identified. Positive identification of the body of Robert Post was never made. His father, Waldron K Post, continued to search for his son's grave or official verification as to the disposition of Robert long after the end of the war, but with no apparent success.

**Wayne Gotke, navigator, *Maisie*, 66th BS, 44th BG, 26 February 1943.**

On 3 January 1943, I took over the 44th Bomb Group, and we didn't receive any replacement crews until late March or April. So we had a limited number of crews. Every time we went out, while we might lose none, we might lose one or two. At dinner that night over at the club, there would be vacant seats. It was awfully hard. You didn't have to be very smart to figure out that if your force was going down all the time and you were doing the same number of missions and you were losing one and two and getting no replacements, your chances of surviving didn't look so good. As soon as the replacement crews started arriving, there were no problems at all. I don't mean to say that there were problems earlier, but you could see it in their eyes and their whole manner. Everybody did the calculations, and they knew that their chances weren't very good. When the new crews came in, it changed completely.

**Col (later General) Leon W Johnson.**

I still don't know where they came from. The thing that saved us was our system of sending down one flight after the other - for assurance. Cooper, my roommate, could hear us yelling that there were a lot of them and he got his flight down fast. The Germans scattered like a school of minnows when you toss a rock into the water.

**Capt Charles P London, 83rd FS, 78th FG, the first 8th AF fighter pilot to destroy five enemy aircraft.**

to gain and catch the rest of the formation. They fought off the fighters with very minor damage until they almost reached Oldenburg, when fighters hit them from all sides. Lt Heinz Knoke of 2./JG1 drew closer, and singled them out for the *coup de grâce*.

Bremen was the last mission of the month for the 'Eightballs'. February had been a bad month for the 66th BS, which had lost three ships and their crews.

On 4 March, 71 Fortresses were dispatched to the Hamm marshalling yards, the first US raid on the Ruhr, while 14 B-24s flew a diversionary feint. Sixteen B-17s of the 91st BG led by Maj Paul Fishburne in B-17F 42-5139 *Chief Sly II* of the 322nd BS had taken off from

**Below:** P-47D Thunderbolt *Leaky Joe* of the 361st FG. *USAF.*

*We were just approaching Brown Ridge, our half way mark across the North Sea, when I heard the faint noise of aircraft engines and hurriedly signalled astern for all boats to reduce speed to six knots so that the line of our creamy high speed wake on the water would not attract the attention of a possible German spotter plane. The noise became louder and as I listened I could hear an uneven beat and spluttering as if the engines were unhappy and liable to break down any moment. All eyes were aloft, trying to spot the aircraft -from the sound it appeared to be circling above the cloud layer right above our heads. Then we saw it - nosing down towards the sea about half a mile away to starboard with fire licking at one wing. It was a Flying Fortress. The pilot was obviously going to make a crash landing in the sea as we watched spellbound, I saw the first of the dark specks plummet from the fuselage as the crew commenced to bail out. In all ten men jumped from it -the whole crew as we subsequently discovered -but only eight parachutes opened and later we were unable to find any trace of the other two.*

*The sight of the floating parachutes broke the spell that was holding me as I followed the plane along its graceful glide to destruction; grabbing the R/T microphone I broke my rule of 'No transmission except in sight of the enemy' as I passed out the order to 'scatter and rescue.' I charged my boat towards a cluster of three parachutes which were rapidly drifting away to the Eastward and as we gathered speed I saw them drop into the water one after another. Through my glasses I could see that two were in serious difficulties and unable to cast off their parachutes. The wind was blowing them across the water like a couple of ten metre class yachts with spinnakers set. There was only one way to get them -to drive to the Eastward at top speed and having passed them to lie 'beam on' in their path and let the wind blow them against our hull. This we did and soon a couple of very waterlogged airmen were gasping and retching on our deck. Now to find the third of the bunch. Without the white of his parachute to guide us and in the failing light, it was a hard and urgent task. The tumbling sea did not promise a long life for the best of swimmers -even with a 'Mae West' around his body.*

*As we quartered around, reports of success or failure began to come in from my other boats and quickly totting up the score, I realized that this was not the only man not accounted for. After a quarter of an hour of fruitless search I was becoming desperate. Time was short and our operational orders were concise and clear -we had to be in a certain spot by a definitive time -come what may. It looked as if the unfortunate Yank - if he was still alive- would have to be abandoned, but as a last measure I moved about half a mile to the east and fired a red Very light into the air. It worked. Faint on the wind we heard a shout and knew that he was somewhere up wind of us -so steaming slowly into the west we fired a succession of 'lights' and guided by his shouts, we soon picked out a dark head occasionally showing in the water.*

*A couple of my ratings were over the side in a jiffy and between them and the aid of a length of rope enabled us to haul the three parts drowned and completely exhausted man on board. I reformed the unit and going up to full speed to make up for lost time, set a new course for the starting position for our sweep along the Dutch coastline. After my Coxswain and Bill, the First Lieutenant, had worked on the three survivors for a while, getting the salt water out of their congested lungs and finishing up with a roll of blankets and the traditional Naval medicine -a tot of rum- they were fairly comfortable, though not all the boats could report such happy results. Three of the other five died, two from injuries and one after artificial respiration had been tried for nearly three hours. I questioned an American officer named Don, who had been the Navigator and discovered that the plane had been 'jumped' by a couple of FW 190s when it got above the cloud level. The crew were all new and fresh from the States and it had been their first taste of sharp sudden death.*

**Lt Cdr Don Bradford DSC, 31 year old CO, 55th MTB Flotilla, who led his Yarmouth-based unit on an important convoy search and destroy mission off the Dutch coast, March 1943.**

---

Bassingbourn and should have formed part of a large force of 71 B-17s which were bound for Hamm, but due to very bad visibility over East Anglia and the North Sea, the Groups did not find each other. Fishburne took the decision that the 91st would continue to Hamm alone. (The 303rd and 305th BGs turned south and successfully bombed the Wilton Feyenoord shipyards near Rotterdam. The 21 B-17s of the 306th BG aborted the mission and 20 returned to Thurleigh with bombs on board. Capt William Friend's B-17 was badly damaged and set on fire by Fw Flecks and Uffz Meissner, both of 6./JG1, at 1025 hours and fell out of formation. The

*Diving away is the ace in the hole for a fighter pilot. Once the Focke Wulf could break combat and get away in a high-speed dive. But the P-47 can out-dive the FW and since, like all American planes, it is extremely well built, will hold together while catching him in the dive. What's more, a one-second burst from those eight fifties will down any fighter made. Our '47s have been in combat since April 1943. Since that time we've made a believer out of many a German pilot. We worry them and that alone is a big part of our job.*

**Maj, later Lt Col, James J Stone Jr, P-47 pilot, 83rd FS CO, 78th FG, and acting CO, 78th FG 1-12 July 1943, CO, 31 July 1943-22 May 1944.**

crew probably jettisoned the bomb load while under fighter attack: nine bombs hit two schools and two houses at Den Briel near the Hook. Four Dutchmen were killed, and between 60 and 70 children were dead or missing. The fire took hold and Friend gave the order to bail out over the sea. Seven parachutes were counted yet no survivors were ever reported.)

Fishburne's formation, having bombed Hamm whilst under fighter attack all the time, were returning over Friesland Province in northern Holland when they were attacked by Bf 110s of IV./NJG1 and III./NJG1, German units normally engaged on nightfighting duties. The B-17 gunners put up stiff resistance in the face of overwhelming odds. Hptm Jabs of IV./NJGI and his three wingmen finished off a straggler, which had repulsed at least 30 attacks before finally going down. Hptm Lütje then claimed a B-17 at 1131 hours and, shortly after, four Bf 110s had finished off another. These were probably 42-5370 flown by Lt Henderson, and *Rose 0' Day* captained by Lt. Felton. These B-17s crashed in the sea west of Texel and Den Helder respectively, at 1128 and 1134 hours. The battle raged on for another 10 minutes and 41-24464 *Excalibur,* captained by Lt Brill, finally fell victim to a Bf 110, probably flown by Lt Köstler of IV./NJG1. Brill ditched the heavily damaged bomber in very rough seas some 40 miles west of Texel and although it broke in two, the crew managed to get out safely and enter their dinghies. In a six-hour struggle with the high seas, three crew drowned before the seven survivors were picked up by an ASR Walrus. The 91st BG received a DUC for the

action this day. Maj Fishburne and Capt James Bullock, his navigator, were awarded the DFC for successfully leading and completing the mission. Lieutenants Brill and Lowry, who both drowned after ditching their B-17, were posthumously awarded the DFC. Although the American gunners claimed 13-3-4, III. and IV./NJG1 lost only a Bf 110 each. Fw 190s of II./JG1 and JG26 suffered no loss.

On 6 March the 'Eightballs' flew their fiftieth mission when 75 B-24s in the 44th and 93rd BG, flew a diversionary raid on a bridge and U-boat facilities at Brest, while 71 Fortresses headed for the U-boat pens at Lorient. All the Liberators returned but three B-17s were shot down by III./JG2. Two days later the Liberators set out on another diversion mission. This time 20 B-24Ds headed for the Rouen marshalling yards as 67 B-17s attacked another marshalling yard, at Rennes. Three squadrons of RAF Spitfires and, for the first time, the 4th FG's P-47C Thunderbolts, escorted the bombers. Twenty-four year old 1/Lt James E O'Brien from Monongahela, Pennsylvania, a pilot in the 68th BS, led the 'Eightballs' in *The Rugged Buggy* (with Lt.-Col. James Posey, the future 44th BG CO, aboard), but he was forced to return to base when one of the gunners passed out through lack of oxygen. Capt Clyde E Price of the 67th Bomb Squadron in *Miss Dianne* took over the group lead and l/Lt Bob W Blaine moved up to the deputy lead. (The ill-fated 67th BS, which, having begun missions from England with nine crews, was now down to just three of its original crew.) Fw 190s of II./JG26, led by Oblt

*We were hit by Fw 190s as well as by Flak, amidship. Needless to say, with oxygen and hydraulic lines damaged, fire was inevitable. The bail-out bell was sounded. The ship was well aflame. Due to the nose attack, the flight deck personnel did not make it out. I assisted Sgts Iris Wyer and Duane Devars out the right waist window, and also checked on Sgt Fleshman, but he was already dead. [Devars and Wyer were captured a day or two later.] I bailed out of the right waist window and upon hitting the ground, saw Lt Morton P Gross, the bombardier, coming down. His whole abdomen was ripped open and he died in my arms, with the German soldiers looking on. Lt Gross told me to take his watch and give it to his mother, but the Germans took the watch away from me.*

**S/Sgt Kenneth L Erhart, gunner, *Miss Diane*, shot down 6 March 1943.**

Wilhelm-Ferdinand 'Wutz' Galland, brother of Gen-Maj Adolf Galland, led fighters in a tight turn to go *von Schauze auf Schnauze* (snout to snout). *Miss Dianne* and Blaine's B-24 went down immediately. Only three gunners survived from Price's ship, which crashed in flames at Totes at 1404 hours with the bombs still in their racks.

Blaine's ship had been singled out by Uffz Peter Crump. Crump had fired a long burst at the B-24 from long range and could clearly see a number of hits in the cockpit area. He dived away in a split-S, then saw to his horror that he was immediately in the way of Blaine's jettisoned bombs. Crump managed to miss them in a tight turn but lost sight of his target and could not say which of the falling aircraft was his kill. (Blaine's B-24 crashed at Barentin at 1405 hours. There was just one survivor.) He saw one of the doomed Liberators crash in a patch of trees north of the Seine, but without a witness Crump would not be awarded confirmation of his victory. Instead, it went to OFw Willi Roth. The Spitfire escort, which had its hands full with Maj Josef 'Pips' Priller's III./JG26, finally showed up in time to prevent further losses. Even so, two Liberators barely made it back to Shipdham, and *Peg*, a 93rd BG Liberator, which was attacked by Oblt Johannes Naumann of II./JG26, limped back across the Channel and crashed at Bredhurst, Kent.

On 12 and 13 March, the Liberators again flew diversions for the Fortresses. Then on 18 March, Gen. Ira Eaker ordered a maximum effort; 73 Fortresses and 24 Liberators, the highest number of bombers so far, to attack the Bremer Vulkan Schiffbau shipbuilding yards on the Weser, a few miles north of Bremen. The yards were ranked the fourth largest producer of U-boats in Germany. At Jever at 1412 hours, operation orders for I./JG1 arrived telling the Bf 109 pilots to intercept and attack a formation of heavy bombers approaching the coast of Germany. Lt Heinz Knoke and his comrades had been practising for a few days previously on bombing the tight formations of American bombers from above with 100Ib bombs. This idea had been

thought of by Lt Dieter Gerhardt late in February 1943. In the early morning of 18 March, Gerhardt and Knoke made a practice flight off Heligoland with each dropping four 100lb bombs on a sack which was towed by a Ju 88. Gerhardt's third bomb scored a direct hit and the idea became a reality. However, the *Alarmstart* (scramble) on 18 March gave the pilots of 2./JG1 too little time to arm their fighters with bombs and so Knocke decided to attack with guns only on this occasion.

At 25,000ft Knoke made contact with the American formation in the Heligoland area and he led his flight in close formation in head-on attack on the Liberators. He opened fire on a B-24 flying low right in the 93rd BG formation. It was *Hot Freight*, flown by l/Lt Howard E 'Tarzan' Kleinsteuber, which immediately caught fire and fell away to the right like a crippled beast. Knoke pursued it, attacking from the rear, then from head-on. Suddenly, at 1514 hours, *Hot Freight* exploded, hurling wreckage through the sky. Sgt Louis A Webb was the only survivor. Knoke hurled his Fw 190 into a power dive to escape the flying engines and debris and only just managed to miss the falling fuselage of the doomed Liberator, which fell into the sea 10km south-east of Heligoland. It was Knoke's fifth victory. In his diary Knoke says that his friend Dieter Gerhardt's first Liberator 'went down a few minutes before'. In fact, he claimed it at 1537 hours off Heligoland. (Possibly *Eager Beaver*, a 93rd BG B-24D, which although badly hit and seen to drop from formation with a smoking engine, made it back to England.) Gerhardt was shot down moments later attacking a second *Viermot*. Though he managed to bail out he died of his wounds in his dinghy. Maj. John 'The Jerk' Jerstad, who led the 93rd BG, reported that they were under attack from fighters for one hour and 45 minutes. Vegesack was officially described as 'extremely heavily damaged'. The bombers had dropped 268 tons of HE smack on the target and later photographic reconnaissance revealed that seven U-boat hulls had been severely damaged and two-thirds of the shipyards destroyed.

On 22 March, when 84 Liberators and Fortresses attacked U-boat yards at Wilhelmshaven, Lt Heinz Knocke tried aerial bombing for the first time. He carried a 500lb bomb on the underbelly of his Bf 109G and he dropped it in the midst of a formation vic of Fortresses. Knoke observed a wing break off one of the

*We were all pretty flat. We had been working hard, no sleep, and so forth. Everybody was just tired out, and then all at once, "bang," everything was back to normal again. I didn't figure out what happened for two or three months: the crews could do simple arithmetic, and at the rates we were losing crews and getting replacements, the last B-17 would go off on a mission 30 days later. The men had concluded, "We are not going to make it. We might as well get shot down today as tomorrow; let's go." It was that simple.*

**Col (later General) Curtis E LeMay, CO, 305th BG, spring 1943.**

*We were coming home from Wilhelmshaven when the ship was badly shot up by German fighters. Shortly after several attacks on us, the ship was shot up so badly that we all had to bail out, in spite of the fact that we were out a bit over the North Sea. We all came down in the vicinity of Alte Mellum Island, but into the water. Sgt. Klug, the left waist gunner, and I were the first two picked up by a ship headed for Heligoland. Apparently, all others drowned, or died of exposure in that frigid water before rescuers found them.*

**Lt Robert J Walker, navigator, *Maggie*, flown by Capt Gideon "Bucky" Warne, 67th BS, which was damaged by *Flak* over the target area, 22 March 1943 and shot down by Oblt Sommer of I./JG1 (his second victory.) *Cactus*, flown by l/Lt Virgil R Fouts, 506th BS, whose crew were flying their first mission, was shot down into the sea off the coast of Holland, by Lt Pancritius of 8./JG1; his third 'kill'.**

B-17s. It was *Liberty Bell* of the 324th BS, 91st BG, piloted by Capt Hascall C McClellan, and it scattered the two others. All 11 men in McClellan's crew perished when the B-17 crashed 18 miles off Heligoland. l/Lt Jim O'Brien and Maj Francis McDuff 68th BS CO, led twelve Liberators of the 44th BG in *Rugged Buggy* behind five B-24s of the 93rd BG. Col Ted Timberlake, who was leading the 93rd in *Teggie Ann*, narrowly escaped death when a 20mm shell entered the cockpit and missed him by only a few inches. When the Liberator returned to Hardwick there were no less than 368 holes in the aircraft. Jim O'Brien described the mission as 'hot as my first' and later counted 29 separate holes in *Rugged Buggy*.

Shortly after noon on 28 March, 103 B-17s and 24 B-24s set out to bomb the Rouen-Sotteville marshalling yards but the Liberators were recalled early because of poor weather. The Spitfire escort at first failed to rendezvous with the Fortresses and the B-17s flew a triangular course in mid-Channel which allowed the *Luftwaffe* ample time to intercept them. When the Spitfires finally arrived they had to return low on fuel, leaving the B-17s to fly on alone to the target. The Second *Gruppe* JG26 and 12./JG2, tore into the unescorted B-17s and though they damaged nine of the Fortresses, only one was shot down. 42-29537 of the 324th BS, 91st BG, flown by Lt John A Coen, was shot down by Lt Georg-Peter Eder of 12./JG2. Eder was injured by return fire from the B-17s but was able to force land his badly damaged Bf 109 at Beaumont-Le-Roger.

Three days later, on 31 March, 102 B-17s and B-24s took off to bomb the wharfs and docks area at Rotterdam but four of the six bomb groups which set out were recalled because of strong winds and thick cloud. *Ooold Soljer* and *Two Beauts* in the 303rd BG were lost in a mid-air collision. 33 heavies hit the dock area. Many of the B-17s, blown off course by strong winds and bad visibility, missed their objectives completely and killed 326 Dutch civilians when their

**Left:** Maj Jim O'Brien, CO, 68th BS, 44th BG. *Jim O'Brien.*

109G-4s and Fw 190A-4s of JG26 began attacks on the formation. JG26 made repeated frontal attacks, sometimes by four and six fighters at a time.

*Dry Martini III,* the lead plane in the 364th BS, 305th BG, was attacked by a swarm of enemy fighters. Cannon shells smashed through the windshield, and Martini was temporarily blinded. His co-pilot, Lt Boyle, was wounded and momentarily knocked unconscious. The B-17 dropped 1,000ft before the two pilots could bring the Fortress under control. One engine was out and they were alone, easy prey for the fighters - or so JG26 thought. They massed for the *coup de grace,* but although they riddled the airplane and in particular the right wing and left aileron, they could not bring the aircraft down. (Investigation later showed that the right main wing-spar had been all but shot through.) Incredibly, not only did *Dry Martini III* make it home to Chelveston, with 160 cannon and bullet holes, the 305th BG gunners claimed 25 enemy fighters destroyed, six probables and five damaged. *Dry Martini III*'s gunners alone were credited with the destruction of ten enemy fighters, a record for a bomber crew on a single mission. Pronounced beyond repair *Dry Martini III* never flew again and instead was used as a "hangar queen".

Lt Herschel B Ellis and his crew in the 422nd BS went down in their flaming Fortress. Ellis and seven others of his crew bailed out and were captured but the bombardier and ball-turret gunner were killed aboard the aircraft. *Available Jones,* flown by Lt Morris M Jones of the 364th BS was also shot down. The third 305th BG B-17 lost was flown by Lt Harold P 'Neill of the 366th BS. Two of the crew were killed, the rest were made PoWs. *Holy Mackeral!* flown by Lt Ercil F Eyster of the 359th BS, 303rd BG, was the fourth B-17 lost. Six of the crew were KIA and four were taken prisoner. Two of the B-17s lost were claimed by Hptm. 'Wutz' Galland of II./JG26, while Oblt Karl Borris of 8th *Staffel* claimed a third. A fourth was awarded to Maj Walter Oesau of JG2. At 1433 hours, the Spitfire escort reappeared to provide withdrawal support, but six of their number were shot down in a seven minute battle without loss to the *Luftwaffe.* In all, American gunners claimed 47 German fighters destroyed. The real losses were two JG26 pilots killed and one wounded. After the raid, photographs smuggled back to England by the French Resistance showed that the Renault works had been severely damaged. For its action this day, the 305th BG received a Distinguished Unit Citation.

On 5 April, 79 B-17s and 25 B-24s were despatched to Belgium to bomb the ERLA VII aircraft and engine repair works at Mortsel, near Antwerp. (During the

bombs hurtled down into the streets of Rotterdam. JG1 intercepted the returning 305th BG formation and made one pass before their fuel was expended. Uffz Peter Crump of 5./JG26 attacked *Southern Comfort* and it caught fire between the No.1 and No.2 engines. Hugh Ashcraft managed to fly the B-17 to England where the crew abandoned the Fortress safely. It crashed at Wickham Bishops. B-24D *Satan's Chariot* of the 409th

BS, 93rd BG, flown by l/Lt Bill F Williams, was shot down by Oblt Otto Stammberger of Fourth *Staffel,* II./JG26, his fourth victory. Williams crashed into the sea shortly after 1245 hours, 60 miles off Ostend. There were no survivors.

Bad weather grounded the Eighth until 4 April, when 97 B-17s headed for the Renault works in the Billancourt district of Paris. Most of the 81 tons that landed square on the factory were released by 18 B-17s of the leading 305th BG formation, led by Maj. Tom McGehee in *We The People,* flown by Capt Cliff Pyle. Before the last group had left the target the whole area was blotted out by a thick pall of smoke reaching to 4,000ft. Unfortunately, the groups in the rear of the formation were not as accurate as the 305th had been and many bombs fell outside the target area causing a number of civilian casualties. North of Paris I./JG2 and the operational *Staffel* of JG105, both led by Spanish Civil War veteran Maj. Walter "Gulle" Oesau, Kommodore, JG2 made the first interception of the B-17s. They made several head-on passes before the Fortresses reached the Rouen area where 50-75 Bf

war, 4,000 Bf 109s were in fact repaired at this factory.) 18 B-17s of the 306th BG led the mission, with Lt Col Jim Wilson and Capt. John Regan in *Dark Horse* at the head of the formation. Brig-Gen. Frank Armstrong, CO, 1st BW, flew aboard this aircraft as an observer. The 368th BS flew Lead, the 423rd High and the 367th 'Clay Pigeons' Squadron flew Low. 21 bombers returned early with mechanical problems leaving 83 heavies to continue. The leading 306th BG was the first to feel the weight of head-on attacks by Fw l90A-4 and A-5s of JG26 and II./JG1, which continued all the way to the target. III./JG26 had taken off to intercept the Fortresses in the Ghent area. Just before 1510 hours the *Kommandeur*, Hptm Fritz Geisshardt and his Stabs Flight encountered the B-17s. Geisshardt attacked a B-17, coming in from the right and to the side and from above. He went charging in again from the same direction, but was hit in the abdomen by return fire from the B-17s. He was able to make a wheels-up landing in his Fw 190A-4 on the airfield at Ghent at 1515 hours, but died from loss of blood early the following morning. (Geisshardt had been decorated with the Knight's Cross with Oak Leaves for his 102 confirmed victories.) At around the same time *L'il Abner,* flown by Lt. Clarence Fischer, was hit by *Flak* over Ghent en route to the

target and finished off by Maj "Pips" Priller. The crew managed to bail out before the Fortress exploded at Wilrijk. It was Priller's 84th victory. Lt Kelly Ross's aircraft was badly hit on the way into the target by cannon and machine gun fire from Hptm. 'Wutz' Galland. After the No.2 engine was shot out Ross gave the order to bail out. All except the tail and waist gunners survived. It was Galland's 38th victory, which crashed 4km NW of Zandvliet, Belgium.

The Fortress piloted by l/Lt William H Parker was shot down at 1538 hours by OFw Adolf 'Addi' Glunz of 4./JG26 who claimed it as his 32nd of his eventual 71 victory tally. Only three of the crew bailed out before the crippled bomber spun in near Ainteloord, 50 kms north of Antwerp. At 1535 hours, north of Antwerp, Oblt Otto Stammberger, *Staffelkapitän*, 4./JG26, found a faltering B-17 squarely in his sights. It was *Montana Power* flown by 2/Lt Robert W Seelos of the 368th BS, which, after having lost its No. 1 engine to *Flak*, had dropped from formation during the bomb run. Stammberger raked the B-17 from head-on with a burst from his four cannon and two machine guns. Stammberger had to pull up quickly because the Fortress suddenly nosed downward. He watched the survivors bail out and saw the pilotless ship carry on for

a short time before finally crashing at Kalmthout. It was his fifth victory. Seelos came down on the edge of the town of Wuustwezel, Belgium, and was captured. He eventually ended up at Stalag Luft III. Seven of his crew managed to evacuate the doomed ship but the top turret gunner (a waist gunner) and Lt Murray, were killed. In a bomb group reputed for its high turnover rate, Murray had the shortest tour of all in the 306th BG – a matter of

*My fifth victory, a B-17, fell over Antwerp on 5 April. Three days later, on 8 April, I downed a Spitfire south of Dieppe and on the 17th of that month I engaged a Spitfire south of Le Treport, but was unable to close in for the kill due to further dogfights developing. I saw a white contrail heading in the direction of England, but received no confirmation of my claim. On 21 April, I shot up a Ventura to the north of Abbeville and left it on fire, it dived into the low clouds; I didn't see it back and the kill was therefore not confirmed.*

**Oblt Otto Stammberger,
*Staffelkapitän*, 4./JG26.**

hours only. Kramarinko and S/Sgt William E Baker evaded capture and together reached Spain, only to be caught and handed over to the Germans.

*Dark Horse* was hit by cannon fire from an Fw 190 attacking head on during the bomb run. Lt Col James Wilson, 306th BG CO, managed to bring the Fortress home safely to Thurleigh aided by Capt Robert Salitrnik, the lead navigator. Salitrnik had been critically wounded when he was hit in the leg by fragments from a can of *.50* calibre ammunition which exploded when hit by 20mm fire from an Fw 190 during a head-on attack. (Salitrnik received four pints of plasma on arrival at Thurleigh and was out of shock the next day but developed gas gangrene on 15 April and died the next day.) Well aimed bombing was not possible because of the persistent fighter attacks, which forced many bombers off course. This serious situation was aggravated by problems with the Norden bombsights in the 303rd (and 44th) BGs and the 82 B-17s that got their bombs away consequently dropped most of them on Mortsel - where over 3,000 houses were destroyed, killing 936 inhabitants and injuring 1,342. Only four bombs hit the ERLA VII works, which killed 229 workers, with another 78 missing. The ERLA Werke however suffered little damage and within a few weeks,

aircraft and engine repairs were back to the normal level.

On 13 April, P-47Cs of the 4th FG were joined by the 56th and 78th FGs for the first time when they became operational with P-47C-2 Thunderbolts. A *Rodeo* (fighter sweep) by one squadron from each group was flown to St Omer in the Pas de Calais with the aim of luring the 'Abbeville Kids' into combat, but the *Luftwaffe* fighters did not show. Two days later the two new groups met the *Luftwaffe* for the first time. On the evening of 15 April the 4th put up 12 P-47s, led by Maj Don Blakeslee and the 56th and 78th each put up 24 aircraft. They tussled with 15 Fw 190A-4s of II./JG1 over Ostend and three Fw 190s were claimed destroyed. In fact the German unit suffered no loss, although OFw. Hutter of 5./JG1 force-landed with battle damage at Woensdrecht. Two 334th FS, 4th FG P-47s and their pilots fell victim to OFw Ernst Heesen of 5./JG1, his 26th and 27th victories. A third "Jug" crashed in the North Sea as a result of engine failure, the pilot being rescued by ASR.

On 16 April, the first mission since Antwerp, 59 Fortresses bombed Lorient for the loss of a single B-17 and 18 Liberators bombed Brest. The 44th BG had eight B-24s damaged but the heaviest fighter attacks by JG2 seemed to be aimed at the 93rd BG, which lost four B-

24s to Fw 190s attacking from the rear of their formation at the target. 1/Lt Frank Hodges and his crew in *Liberty Lass* were the first to go down, followed by the crew of *Ball of Fire Jnr,* flown by Lt Frank Lown (Hodges and Lown were captured and sent to Stalag Luft III). Capt Bud Fleenor and crew (who had crashed at Ludham on 26 February) in *Missouri Sue* went down in the Channel after the bombardier had bailed out over France. *Judith Lynn* was the fourth B-24 lost and Lt Packer nursed the crippled *Yardbird* back to England and crashed at St Eval.

---

*It was like firing into a feeding frenzy of sharks.*

**S/Sgt. Donald J Bevan, gunner, *Unmentionable,* flown by Lt Warren George Jr, one of ten B-17s of the 306th BG shot down, 17 April 1943. Everyone was calm and stayed at his post until George finally told the crew over the intercom: *All right, I guess we better bail out.* Eight of the crew were captured. George and T/Sgt. Warren A MacGregor, engineer, were KIA.**

**Left:** Fighter leaders (left) Oblt Eugen Wintergerst (St Kpt 9./JG1 KIA 4.9.43 S of Dunkirk), discussing with Hptm Hans Philipp, Kommodore of JG1 (on right) at the entrance to the Ops tent at Deelen in April 1943. By the time of his death in action on 8 October 1943, ObstIt Philipp had accumulated an amazing 206 victories in air combat (25 in the West) during the course of over 500 sorties. *Eberhard Burath via Rob de Visser.*

**Below:** Oblt Rolf Strohal, technical officer of Stab I./JG1 relaxes on the wing of his Fw 190A-5, Deelen airfield, April 1943. The black and white stripes painted on the engine cowling, were applied to the Staff Flight's I./JG1 Fw 190s for a short period during the spring of 1943. *Eberhard Burath via Rob de Visser.*

**Above:** B-17F 41-24488 *Banshee,* 367th BS, 306th BG which FTR from Bremen on 17 April 1943 with Capt William 'Wild Bill' J Casey's crew. Five men were KIA in fighter attacks. Five others, including Casey, bailed out and were made PoW *Richards' Coll.*

**Left:** Two mechanics working on the armament and BMW801 engine of one of 9./JG1's Fw 190A' s sometime mid-1943 at Deelen airfield. *Haspel via Rob de Visser.*

*B*y this time the bombardier was on the bomb sight and we were settling down on our bomb run. And then the Flak began to come up at us. It came up so thick and fast that it looked as though we had run into a thundercloud....At the same time we were hit by fighters coming head-on into us. Just before our bombs went away our No.4 engine was hit and oil started pouring all over the place. Vibration caused by the windmilling propeller seemed to be about to shake the ship to pieces. When the bombs finally went, none of us felt them give the ship the jar they usually give it, as we were already bouncing around like a stovepipe hat in a March gale.

The sky was literally swarming with fighters. The pilots made old Queenie hurl herself around the sky in evasive action dodging the oncoming pursuits until we must have looked like a small plane doing acrobatics. The pursuits came in so fast that at times the navigator and I had to be content with taking shots at every second or third plane making a pass at us. And the way we were thrown around in that nose from the evasive action made us feel like a pair of dice.

All this time I was trying to navigate us out of that place by the fastest route possible. I'd get a check point and then grab my gun and start spraying lead out like a hose. They had every kind of plane in the Luftwaffe up there trying to knock us down. Bombing was excellent. As the English say, we really pranged the target. Not one of our bombs was off the target area.

**Navigator, *Queenie*, 303rd BG, Bremen, 17 April 1943.**

***Left:*** Capt Pervis E Youree, 423rd BS, 306th BG pilot. On the 17 April 1943 mission to the Focke Wulf plant at Bremen when the 306th BG lost 10 B-17s, Youree brought *Old Faithful* home 200 miles at wave top height after fighters put out two engines and shot the aircraft almost to pieces and he crash-landed at RAF Coltishall, Norfolk. Youree completed his combat tour on 29 June 1943, the Thurleigh group's 50th mission. *Richards.*

Next day, 17 April, a record 111 bombers set out for the Focke Wulf factory at Bremen. Intense fighter attacks by an estimated 105 fighters of III./JG54 and JG11 were encountered on the bomb run and 15 Fortresses were shot down, 10 of them from the 306th BG, while the 401st Squadron, 91st BG, lost all six of its Fortresses. 39 B-17s suffered battle damage, two men killed and four WIA. Gunners claimed 63 enemy fighters shot down.

On 1 May, 56 bombers in two waves attacked St Nazaire. On 4 May, 65 bombers hit the Ford and General Motors plants at Antwerp, accompanied for the first time by P-47s of the 4th and 56th FGs who provided fighter escort up to 175 miles. Meanwhile, more than 30 B-17s and B-24s flew diversionary feints towards the French coast. These succeeded in drawing over 100 German fighters away from the main force, which returned without loss. Bombing results, however, were disappointing on 4 May. It was not until 13 May

*O*n 13 May I was shot down myself by a 'Spit' at a height of 8000m, and was forced to bail out of my burning plane. One-third of the parachute canopy was consumed by fire and I was very fortunate to escape alive!! My skull was fractured, but otherwise I was in one piece!

**Oblt Otto Stammberger, *Staffelkapitän*, 4./JG26, who was shot down by a 331 Squadron Spitfire. He had to exit his Fw 190 when the fuel tank exploded, but his parachute failed to open fully and he was seriously injured on landing. He would not return until October.**

that the bombers went out again. In mid-afternoon, 97 B-17s of the 1st BW attacked the Avions Potez aircraft factory at Meaulte. For its first mission, the 4th BW put up 72 B-17s (from the 94th, 95th, 96th, and 351st BGs, which had arrived in England in April) for a strike on St Omer-Longuenesse airfield. It was hardly an auspicious beginning. The 96th BG lost a B-17 when it crashed into the wash at the start of the mission and the Group failed to bomb the target due to a misunderstanding in the formation leaders. The straggling 351st BG formation of 14 B-17s abandoned the mission mid-Channel. Three B-17s in the 1st BW failed to return. A 305th BG ship captained by Lt Harold C Pierce of the 365th BS, was shot down by *Flak* with the loss of five crew. Maj "Pips" Priller JG26 CO and Lt Hoppe of 8th *Staffel*, put in claims for the two 91st BG B-17s shot down. Both came from the 323rd Squadron. *Vulgar Virgin*, flown by Lt Lawrence J Stark, crashed and exploded at Abbeville with the loss of eight crew. 42-5406, flown by Lt. Homer C Biggs Jr, was lost with seven crew. Six men were taken prisoner from the two Fortresses. Eleven B-17s, including one badly damaged by a bomb dropped by a JG26 Fw 190, returned with battle damage.

Next day, 14 May, 196 bombers made simultaneous attacks on four targets. The principal attack was made by 115 B-17s of the 1st BW and 21 B-24s of the 44th BG on the Krupp shipyards at Kiel. Meanwhile, 15 B-17s of the 96th and 351st BGs bombed Wevelghem airfield, and 42 Fortresses of the 94th and 95th BGs, the Ford and General Motors plant and locks nearby at

*I* am making a 90° turn and going down. They're Huns lads! Give them hell! Here we go! Tallyho! OK lads. Stay in pairs now.'

**Col Arman 'Pete' Peterson, CO, 78th FG, on the first P-47 bomber escort mission, 14 May 1943. A sweep on 16 May gave Peterson his first victory. He was KIA on 1 July 1943 in combat with I./JG1 over Goeree, Holland. Fw. Martin Lacha claimed the victory.**

*Right:* B-17F 42-29673 *Old Bill*, 365th BS, 305th BG. On 15 May 1943 pilot l/Lt William Whitson, helped by gunner Albert Haymon and bombardier, l/Lt Robert W Barrall, nursed this aircraft back to Chelveston after 20mm cannon fire from fighters over Heligoland had riddled the Fortress and shot out the Plexiglas nose, killing navigator 2/Lt Douglas Van Able and injuring Barrall. Whitson and Barrall were each awarded the DSC and the rest of the 11-man crew (which included a photographer) received eight Silver Stars and seven Purple Hearts. 'Old Bill' was the creation of British artist and 'Stars and Stripes' cartoonist Bruce Bairnsfather, who painted the nose of the aircraft with the WW1 soldier. *Bill Donald.*

Antwerp. The fourth raid was to be made on a power station at Ijmuiden, Holland, by 12 B-26 Marauders of the 322nd BG at Rougham, near Bury St Edmunds.

Large numbers of Spitfires and P-47s escorted the bombers but they could not prevent heavy losses at Kiel. The 44th BG crews, flying in the rear of the formation behind the slower B-17s had been briefed to bomb from 21,000ft but constant zigzagging over the North Sea put them over Heligoland Bay at 18,000ft. As they turned into the strong wind for bombing they were down to 160mph, almost stalling speed. The 44th's cargo of incendiaries had required a shorter trajectory and a 2 mile longer bomb run than the B-17s. Flying a scattered formation the B-24s were exposed to fighter attack.

Altogether, five B-24s were shot down at Kiel. Worst hit was the 67th BS, bringing up the rear of the formation, which lost three Liberators in quick succession. The first to go down was 1/Lt William Roach and his replacement crew flying in *Annie Oakley*. There were only two survivors. *Miss Delores*, flown by Lt Bob Brown, was hit by *Flak* over the target and also went down. Only six men got out. The third 67th BS Liberator lost was *Little Beaver*, piloted by Capt Chester L "George" Phillips (KIA), which was shot down after leaving the target. Only four men from the 11 man crew survived after three explosions rocked the ship.

Eight other 44th BG B-24s were damaged, and twelve men were wounded. *Margaret Ann* returned to base with one gunner mortally wounded and three seriously

*Sid Banks, bombardier, and I in the nose of the plane, were aware at first of an order to bail out, which we did by going out through the nose door hatch. On the way down I saw two chutes, one on each side of me. The one between me and the coastline was Banks. I never knew who the other one was. I came down in the Baltic about 10 miles from shore. Later, I found out that both Douglas B. Myers, co-pilot, and Swanson (the last one out) came down on land.*

**2/Lt Richard L Schiefelbusch, navigator, *Wicked Witch*, 506th BS, 44th BG, flown by Capt. John W "Swede" Swanson, 14 May 1943. *Flak* had damaged the No.2 engine before the target but Swanson maintained formation and was able to salvo his bombs. As the group turned off the target *Wicked Witch* was finished off by enemy fighters making head-on attacks.**

*The bomb bay doors opened and the 44th let go its clusters of matchstick incendiaries. These only created more confusion. The clusters did not hold together for more than 200ft before breaking up. As soon as they hit the slipstream they were all over the sky in a negative trajectory, flying back through the formation and bouncing off wings and propellers. Nothing worked better for the Germans at this point as the formation scattered to avoid these missiles. Meanwhile, we had dropped our own clusters of bombs and had plenty of trouble. The cockpit smelled of gasoline and our unspoken thoughts as Howell and I looked at each other were fire and explosion. We had now separated from the rest of the group after leaving the target and I noticed at least two other stragglers off to the right. One was Capt. "Swede" Swanson of the 506th Squadron (flying Wicked Witch).*

*There was plenty of company joining us. FW 190s were in formation on the left and Bf 109s off the right wing. "Mac" McCabe in the top turret kept yelling through his oxygen mask to dip the wing so he could hit them with his .50s. Not knowing what else to do, Howell and I were just trying to keep the ship flying. We had been through this before and somehow fate had brought us through. In the past, we had outlasted German fighters until they turned back over the North Sea but now we were practically standing still in a 100mph headwind on a 285° heading with lots of German soil still underneath. There must have been two Jerries sitting off our tail end pumping a steady flow of cannon and .30 calibre bullets into us. I heard several .30s zing into the cockpit and bounce off the armour plate seats. Mixed in with these .30s were some incendiary bullets which made a good mixture with the intense gasoline fumes and pretty soon we had a roaring furnace in the bomb bay. My first knowledge of fire was the intense heat all over the cockpit. I leaped out of my seat, breaking my oxygen hose in the process. I pulled open the top hatch directly in front of the top turret to get out, saw the whirling propellers and antenna wires and thought better of it. I stuck my head out of the hatch and my steel GI helmet, which we wore before the introduction of Flak helmets, blew right off in the slipstream. If there was any time to take a second guess, it was then that I decided on some other exit.*

**Maj Jim O'Brien, 68th Squadron, commander 44th BG, flying in the co-pilot's seat of *The Rugged Buggy*, flown by Lt Malcolm "Mac" Howell, 14 May 1943. O'Brien was captured along with most of the crew and made PoW. In Stalag Luft III he received a letter informing him that "Mac" Howell had been killed. In four months beginning January that year, O'Brien's squadron, the 68th lost nine Liberators with only four survivors from the 90 men in them. O'Brien wrote; *No friends left it seems.***

wounded. *Ruth-less,* piloted by Lt Frank Slough in the 506th was very badly damaged but made it back, although Slough finally had to crash-land in Northern Ireland because Shipdham was so congested that it could not take any more aircraft in trouble. III./JG54 lost seven Bf 109s by return fire. (Next day, 15 May, this *Gruppe* was further decimated during B-17 raids against targets in the German Bight, losing eight aircraft. Two very experienced *Ritterkreuzträger,* Hptm Fink and Lt Rupp, were among those KIA.) Meanwhile, the 14 May attack on Wevelghem airfield by the Fortress had fared better. It was so heavily damaged by bombs dropped by the 96th and 351st BGs that III./JG26 was forced to move to Lille-Nord. On the bombers' return east of Ypres they were attacked *en masse* by fighters. II./JG26 shot down two B-17s of the 351st BG. Both *The Annihilator,* piloted by Capt William P Forsythe of the 510th Squadron, and Lt Clifford J McCoy's B-17 in the 508th BS, crashed at Courtrai. *Flak* bracketed the 94th and 95th BGs at Antwerp and the Fw 190s and OFw Bach of II./JG1 applied the *coup de grâce* to 42-3115 of the 95th BG, captained by Lt. J E McKinley, who had already been badly shot up in an earlier fighter attack. It spun out of formation at only 2,500ft and crashed on North Beveland Island at 1315 hours, near Kats village. All the crew were killed. Oblt Sternberg of JG26 claimed a second (possibly a 94th BG ) B-17 over the Scheldt estuary. A 78th FG P-47 (one of three Thunderbolts lost) and a Spitfire were also shot down by pilots of JG26 but the German unit lost two pilots to return fire from the bombers. Hptm Karl Borris, Kapitän of 8th *Staffel,* who was forced to bail out at 22,000ft after coming off worse against a bomber, was fortunate to survive when his parachute failed to open properly. A fourth Fw 190 was shot down by the 78th FG. The day's missions cost 12 B-17s and B-24s. 67 fighters were claimed shot down. The Marauders returned safely, but missed their target at Ijmuiden completely.

On 15 May, 193 B-17s bombed targets at Emden, Heligoland and Wilhelmshaven. Next day, a fighter sweep by 11 P-47s of the 4th, 56th and 78th Fighter Groups over northern Belgium resulted in combat action. They met 30 fighters of JG1 in the Vlissingen area being led by the Geschwaderkommodore, Maj. Hans 'Fips' Philipp, an ex-JG54 *Experte,* who had assumed command of JG1 on 1 April. Philipp claimed a P-47 as his 205th *Abschuss** at 1312 hours, followed one minute later by another 'Jug' shot down by Oblt Koch as his 16th kill. (Philipp was KIA on 8 October 1943 during air combat with B-17s and escorting fighters over Nordhorn, Germany, after having claimed a B-17 for his 206th and final victory.) Col Arman Peterson, 78th FG CO, destroyed one Fw 190 and two more fell to the guns of his Group. There was only one victim, Hptm Dietrich Wickop, *Kommandeur,* II./JG1, who had 13 victories to his name, including three B-17s.(*Luftwaffe* pilots were on a points system which converted to various awards. An *Abschuss* or shoot-down of a *Viermot,* or *4-mot* (four-engined bomber) earned three points, while a *Herausschuss* or separation, was worth two. A pilot who finished off an already shot up four-engine bomber, was awarded one point for *endgültige Vernichtung,* or final destruction. Decorations

*We came under very heavy fighter attacks in the target area and were quite vulnerable because of our spread out bombing formation. Just prior to dropping our bombs, I saw an Fw 190 peel off at us from about 1 o'clock and slightly high and as the puffs of bursting 20mm self-destroying ammo came toward us, it became apparent that the line of fire would put the successive bursts right into our cockpit. Purely reflex action alone caused me to hit the wheel in a dive to try to get below the line of fire, but unfortunately the bursts did not quite clear the plane, but hit the top turret directly behind the cockpit. The resulting explosion tore the top turret canopy completely off, and the shrapnel severely wounded T/Sgt Adam Wygonik about his head, neck and upper body. The inside of the turret and the gun barrels were pitted from the force of the shrapnel. Either the force of the explosion or Wygonik must have reflexively dumped his seat lever as he immediately fell out onto the flight deck. T/Sgt Alan Perry, radio operator, immediately sized up the situation, left his own oxygen supply and attempted some first aid at Wygonik, who was bleeding profusely from his head and body wounds – and no oxygen supply. Perry snapped Wygonik's chest pack onto his harness and put his hand around the ripcord ring, insomuch as Perry intuitively concluded that Wygonik would die before we got back to England and medical attention. He intended to roll Wygonik out of the ship as we were still over the target area – and the possibility of immediate medical attention.*

*Perry was suffering from lack of oxygen and returned to his oxygen supply to keep from blacking out but when he was able to turn back to Wygonik, Adam was gone! Apparently, or intentionally or otherwise, Adam had rolled off the flight deck, onto the catwalk in the open bomb bay. The bay doors were still open as we were on the bomb run. No one could say for sure that Adam's chute had opened since all attention was on fighting off the attacking aircraft. We had no way of knowing whether Adam reached the ground dead or alive, though the odds seemed stacked against his survival due to the severity of his wounds, the resultant loss of blood and the fact that he was without oxygen even longer than Sgt Perry.*

*The plane, as we came away from the target, was severely damaged with one engine smouldering, loss of top portions of one vertical stabilizer and rudder, multiple hits from 20mm fire including the blown-away top turret canopy. Unable to maintain position in our formation, I dove towards a group of B-17s that were ahead and below us in a shallow dive toward the coast, and managed to hold position behind and below their rear flight. This protected our top with their bottom and rear turrets. After the fighter attacks broke off, we flew pretty much back to England*

1/Lt John Y Reed, pilot *Scrappy,* 66th Squadron, the sixth and final 44th BG loss, 14 May 1943. Reed nursed the B-24 back to Shipdham where the crew bailed out after Reed and 1/Lt George W Winger, co-pilot, set course on autopilot for the North Sea before they too bailed out. *Scrappy* had to be shot down by RAF Spitfires. (Wygonik landed in the target area and was soon picked up by German soldiers. Later, his right eye was removed at hospital in Vienna before he was eventually repatriated.)

*Then things began to happen. Three of them started at us. Our top turret gunner picked out the leader and let him have about 50 rounds from each gun. The co-pilot saw black smoke pour from the nacelle and the plane go into a spin.*

*Despite the temperature of 20° below zero. I was sweating like mad. I had on a pair of winter flying boots and nothing else except regular dress, which was wringing wet. Two more fighters came in from the nose. I could see them firing their cannons, so I pushed forward on the stick with all my might. We went down like a streamlined brick and they whizzed past us, barely missing the top of our wing. One of them took along several of our slugs with him, because our tracers were seen to go through his fuselage. When I pulled out of that dive, our top turret gunner was thrown from his turret, as was the tail gunner. All the other members of the crew were thrown about a bit. But the Jerries had missed us and that was the important thing.*

*Just as we were approaching the target, four more fighters attacked us from dead ahead. One of their cannon shells hit our left wing. A moment later the co-pilot announced that the No.3 engine was out.*

*"Want to feather it?" he asked.*

*"Hell, no!" I yelled.*

*Feathering a propeller over enemy territory is like writing the boys at the mortuary for space on their slab. All of the fighters see that you are crippled and immediately set upon you for the kill. We had only three half-hearted attacks from then on to the coast, and those pilots must have been very green, or else I had become hardened to it all by that time. Off to our left, I saw one Me-109 do a slow roll and then head for home. His manoeuvre meant, "Well, boys, it's all over for this time. See you soon."*

**44th BG pilot, Kiel raid, 14 May 1943.**

were awarded after points totals were reached. For instance, one point earned the recipient the Iron Cross Second Class and three, the Iron Cross First Class. Forty points were needed for the Knight's Cross, although this varied in practice.)

On 16 May, the 322nd BG's new CO, Col. Robert Stillman, was called to a conference at HQ, Elveden Hall, near Thetford. He was informed that reconnaissance photos of the P.E.N. electricity generating plant at Ijmuiden on the Dutch coast, the target attacked by the Marauders on 14 May had shown no damage and was still in full operation. Col Stillman was informed that VIIIth BC wanted the target to be attacked again the next day. On 17 May, 159 B-17s would also be despatched to bomb Lorient while 39 B-24s were to attack Bordeaux. Col Stillman could not believe they were serious, stating that to attack the same target so soon could mean enemy defences would be

ready and waiting for them. Gen Newton L Longfellow, VIIIth BC, was adamant that the attack should go ahead and although he sympathised with Col. Stillman's point of view, threatened him with the loss of his command if he refused to obey orders. Upset at the thought of sending his crews back to the same target so soon after their harrowing first mission (where they suffered a number of casualties and lost Lt Howell and his crew in a crash near the base), Col Stillman returned to Rougham Field near Bury St Edmunds. The order for the mission arrived at 0036 hours on 17 May asking for a maximum effort raid, flying the same route as on 14 May. Lt Col Alfred Von Kolnitz, the 322nd BG's Chief Intelligence Officer, was alarmed that the same route was to be flown, as he expected heavy enemy opposition. He wrote a memo to Col Stillman, ending it: *For God's sake, get fighter cover!*

The crews alerted for the mission were from the 450th and 452nd Squadrons, who, with four exceptions, had

**Above:** B-26 Marauder goes down in flames. *USAF.*

not flown the first mission. One of these was Col Stillman, who was determined to lead. The 322nd could field 11 B-26 Marauders for the mission, with the 452nd aircraft leading. Although the crews were confident of a second success, they all expected to meet stiff opposition and many were convinced they would not return. Col Stillman was also convinced that the mission was going to be a disaster, but was determined to do his duty and ensure that the target was knocked out this time. As he left the Intelligence Section after the mission briefing, Lt Col Von Kolnitz said, *Cheerio.*

Stillman answered: *No, it's goodbye.*

Trying to cheer him up, Von Kolnitz said: *I'll see you at one o'clock.*

*It's goodbye,* replied Stillman firmly.

At 1050 hours the Marauders began taking off. At 1147 hours and 33 miles off the coast of Holland, Capt Stephens in the 452nd flight, aborted due to power failure to the top turret and one engine not giving the correct boost. Off course, the remaining B-26s crossed the Dutch coast 25 miles from Noordwijk and headed toward Rozenburg Island, in the Maas River Estuary, the most heavily defended area in the Netherlands. They were showered by 20mm cannon shells. The lead aircraft took direct hits, which severed the flight controls and killed Lt. Resweber Stillman's co-pilot. As a result of the loss of flying controls, the Marauder snap rolled and Stillman saw the ground coming up to meet him. His

plane crashed upside down, but amazingly, Stillman, Sgt Freeman and Sgt Willis, were all pulled from the wreckage alive. The two sergeants survived the first mission and had now been lucky again.

The following flight, which was two miles to the south, also encountered heavy fire from the ground. Lt Garrambone's aircraft was hit, he lost control and the aircraft crashed into the Maas river. Lt Garrambone and three of his crew survived. Believing that they were approaching the target area, pilots and navigators looked for the landmarks they had noted on the mission briefing. As they were way off course there were none, and they were flying somewhere between Delft and Rotterdam. Capt Converse now led the first flight and taking evasive action to avoid *Flak*, collided with Lt. Wolf's aircraft, which was leading the second element. Both B-26s went down, but four gunners survived from the two aircraft, one being Sgt Thompson, the fourth veteran of 14 May. Debris hit *Chickersaw Chief*, causing the pilot, Lt Wurst, to crash-land the B-26 in a field near Mieje. Sgt Heski, top turret gunner, lost a foot in the

**Left:** M/Sgt Joseph H Giambrone paints the 25th bomb mission symbol on the nose of the *Memphis Belle* of the 324th BS, 91st BG at Bassingbourn after the *Belle's* 25th mission, to Lorient, on 17 May 1943. Although the *Belle* was not the first Fortress to achieve 25 missions, it nonetheless served Hollywood and the AAFs' publicity machine well. Capt Robert K Morgan, pilot of all 25 missions in this aircraft, is far right. His girlfriend, Miss Margaret Polk of Memphis, Tennessee, was the inspiration for the name. *USAF via Tom Cushing.*

*Y*ou can't be here. You're dead, we saw you crash. I've already reported you and your entire crew dead.

**Lt Col Purinton's reaction on seeing Col Stillman walk into the Stalag Luft III. Of the 60 airmen shot down in enemy territory, on 17 May '43. 22 survived as prisoners of war. Whilst a prisoner of war, Col Stillman surmised that the mission was a disaster and one factor had contributed to its failure. When Capt Stephens aborted at the start of the mission, he climbed to 1,000ft. Col Stillman did not blame him for this, as it was standard operating procedure for the B-26, in order to allow the crew to bail out, if necessary. However, Stillman was convinced that in so doing, Capt. Stephens had unwittingly exposed his aircraft to enemy radar, thus alerting the Germans to the presence of the rest of the force. As a result of the 17 May disaster, the 322nd BG was stood down and the Marauder programme was put on hold temporarily. It was deemed suicidal to fly the B-26 at low level, so it was used at medium level instead. The 322nd BG moved to Andrews Field, near Braintree, Essex, as a part of this strategy and resumed operations on the last day of July 1943. Col Glen C Nye, the man who had nursed the 322nd BG in the early days of its existence, before Col Stillman, had been given command.**

crash and was the only serious casualty.

This left only Lt F H Matthew and Lt. E R Norton of the third element of the lead flight, in the air. Lt Norton's co-pilot was his twin brother, J A Norton. These two aircraft joined the second flight to make a more effective force to bomb the target. Unfortunately, the second flight was as lost as the first and had no idea where the target lay. Forty-five miles into Holland, the remaining aircraft decided to turn for home. Lt Col Purinton, who was leading the second flight, asked his navigator, Lt Jeffries, for a heading. Jeffries answered: *270 degrees,* followed by *Hold it a minute, I think I see the target, Yes, there it is!*

Bomb doors were opened and Purinton's co-pilot, Lt Kinney, sighted and dropped the bombs on what they thought was the target. In reality, it was the gasholder in the suburbs of Amsterdam. All aircraft dropped their bombs when Lt Kinney dropped his, but they were heading directly towards the 'real' target at Ijmuiden. There they encountered more heavy *Flak* and Purinton's plane was hit, but he managed to ditch two miles

offshore. Jeffries was killed in the crash and a German patrol boat picked up the rest of the crew. Lt Jones' aircraft was the next to be shot down and crashed. Lt Aliamo was the only survivor. The Norton brothers, now flying at 250mph. to try and make it home, were shot down west of Ijmuiden. Their tail gunner, Sgt Longworth, was the only survivor of their crew.

Only Lt Matthews and Capt Jack Crane now remained, at some distance apart. They survived the coastal *Flak* and raced for England. Their troubles were not over. When the Marauders crossed the coast on their inbound flight, 26 Fw 190s of II./JG1 were sent out on a combat alert from Woensdrecht, southern Holland, and were vectored to meet the bombers. At 1218 hours, they saw Matthews' and Crane's aircraft flying low and fast over the North Sea and they attacked. Crane asked the top turret gunner and engineer, George Williams, *Come up front, George, there is something wrong with the rudder.* Williams checked the rudder cables and repaired a damaged section with some safety wire from the rear of the turret. As he returned to the turret, the aircraft

was peppered with bullets and he saw the port engine in flames. He called to Crane but there was no reply. The plane started to lose altitude, levelled off and then dived into the sea. Williams and Sgt Jesse Lewis, tail gunner, scrambled to safety out of the camera hatch, climbed into a liferaft, and watched the Marauder sink in about 45 seconds. The time was 1224 hours, and they were 80 miles from England. They spent five days in the raft before being rescued and returned to England, and to the 322nd BG. Lt Matthews' plane was shot into the sea at 1230 hours. There were no survivors. Fw Niederreichholz of Stab II./JG1 and OFw Winkler of 4./JG3 were the victorious *Jagdflieger* on this occasion.

At Rougham, the estimated time for the Group's return was 1250 hours. On the control tower balcony, Gen Brady from 8th BC, and other watchers, were growing apprehensive. At 1305 hours, an RAF listening post reported that it had intercepted a German radio transmission, which said that it had shot two bombers into the sea. By 1330 hours, it was decided that no aircraft were still airborne and that a disaster had

*Suddenly through the haze and mist we saw a break in the coastline. Although it wasn't very plain, it stood out well enough to be recognised as the estuary that curves crazily from the Bay of Biscay to Bordeaux, some 30 miles inland. When we reached the IP on the bombing run a few minutes later, it was the bombardier's baby. He took over. It was the finest piece of precision bombing I ever hope to see. The locks collapsed, water gushed out of the basin into the river; there were hits on the bottleneck of the railroad yards, strikes on the aero-engine factory. It was beautiful!*

**Ed Mikolowski, lead navigator, *Suzy Q*, 44th BG, Bordeaux mission, 17 May 1943. "Gentleman" Jim DeVinney flew lead bombardier.**

**Right:** Bf 109G-6 '*Kanonenvogel*' ("cannon bird") of III./JG53 'Pik As' tipped onto its nose in a taxiing accident. In 1943 the '*Kanonenvogel*' had, in addition to a 30mm MK108 engine-mounted cannon and two 13mm MG13ls atop the 1, 475hp Daimler-Benz DB 605 liquid-cooled engine and two extra 20mm Mauser MG151/20 cannon fitted under the wings for combating the American *Viermots*. *Fritz Müller via Detjens.*

**Inset:** Another improvement in the armament of the *Reichsverteidigung* fighters, introduced in the summer of 1943 was *Wurfgranaten* or 21cm rocket-launchers for the unguided W Gr. 21 *Dodel* missile, two of which were fitted under the wings of the Bf 109 and Fw 190. II./JG26 first tested these in battle, but they were too cumbersome for single-engined fighter aircraft and it was decided to equip the *Zerstörer*, or heavy twin-engined fighter units, with the rocket devices instead. The tubes of the 21cm rockets are clearly visible, together with a streamlined and jettisonable under-belly fuel tank on this Bf 109G-6 of III./JG53 which is being calibrated in early 1944. *Fritz Müller via Detjens.*

occurred, with all 10 B-26s being lost.

The Fortresses and B-24s did not come through unscathed on 17 May either. Six B-17s attacking Lorient failed to return, five of them being shot down by III./JG2 from Vannes. *Avenger II*, a B-24 of the 44th BG developed engine trouble on the Bordeaux raid and crash-landed in Gijon, Spain. It brought the total losses for the day to 17.

Two days later, on 19 May, 102 B-17s hit Kiel and 64 B-17s bombed Flensburg. A smaller force of B-17s flew a diversion. The Flensburg force returned without loss but the Kiel force lost six Fortresses, three of which were ripped to pieces by bombs dropped from above by Fw Fest, FW Führmann, and Uffz Biermann of 5./JG11. Lt Knoke's bomb failed to hit a *Viermot*, but he brought down a B-17 by his cannon and machine guns at 1217 hours near Husum. On 21 May, 98 B-17s attacked

Wilhelmshaven and 63 Fortresses bombed Emden.

With the increase in attacks on the north German coast on 23 May III./JG26 flew to Cuxhaven-Nordholz to reinforce JG1, II./JG27, III./JG54 and JG11 against the American attacks. On 27 May only 11 bombers hit St Nazaire, but on the 29th 147 bombers managed to drop their bombs on the U-boat pens there. It was the last raid by the 8th that month. In June 1943, Gen Ira Eaker was able to send the 1st and 4th Wings on two-pronged attacks against north German targets at Emden, Kiel, Bremen, Wilhelmshaven and Cuxhaven on a single day. On 11 June, the B-17s set out to bomb Bremen but the target was covered with a solid layer of low cumulus clouds down to about 5,000ft and they also partially covered Wilhelmshaven. Some 168 B-17s bombed Wilhelmshaven while 30 bombed the secondary target at Cuxhaven. About 20 fighters attacked the low groups in

*The 21 May was a great but also difficult day. At 10.30 we were directed against a 4-mot formation, but did not find it and landed at 11.13 at Schiphol. At 12.21 we took off again against the returning formation. This time the directions were correct. We caught them about 100km north of Ameland as they were heading in a north-westerly direction for home. I was wingman to Hptm. Schnoor. We drew past them and attacked from ahead. From too low, I got the B-17 flying on the outside right into my sights at an impossible angle. Leading by three lengths, I pressed all the firing buttons; no effect observed. After landing I was incredulous as Hptm Schnoor congratulated me for my first Abschuss. At this time I had been thinking of something entirely different. On breaking off from the enemy formation I had observed an Fw 190 crashing into the sea and a parachute above it. I had started my stopwatch, noted the course and where this would have crossed the coast. Oblt Munz, my old room mate from München-Gladbach, was missing. I wanted to search for him. I took off as soon as my aircraft was ready. First to the noted place on the coast, then the reverse of the course I had noted and starting the stopwatch. When the time had elapsed I scanned the sea to right and left. Then I saw something yellow, a rubber dinghy, but to my horror empty and bouncing about on the rough sea. Low over the water I searched around the dinghy in tight circles. Only white spumes, no other colours. 'Man, Hans, where are you?' Nothing. The red warning light urged me back. 68 minutes. A rescue seaplane was called and the position given. I took off once more and met with the rescue-Wal at the old position. We searched until I had to return. 73 minutes. It had got dark and the seaplane also had to abandon the search. This loss hit me hard. Had he seen us during the search? What despair when we turned away! Six weeks later he was found on the beach at Sylt - 'a better man I never knew.'*

**Oblt Eberhard Burath, *Gruppen* Adjutant I./JG1, one of the German fighter pilots airborne, 21 May. (30 year old Oblt Hans Munz, *Staffelkapitän*, 1./JGI, was washed ashore on 27 June 1943 and buried at Westerland. Burath's B-17 claim of 21 May 1943 has not been identified as several of the 12 B-17s shot down by II./JG27 (five *Abschüsse*) and I./JG1, whilst returning from raids on Emden and Wilhelmshaven crashed into the North Sea.)**

**Above:** End of a Thunderbolt. *USAF.*

the 4th BW but it was the 1st BW that suffered the greatest onslaught. They were attacked by fighters for over an hour. The units involved were 6./JG11 (five *Abschüsse*) based at Leeuwarden, and III./JG26, from Nordholz, flying new Bf 109G-4/R6 and –6/R6 "gunboats" with MG151/20 cannon in large underwing gondolas. During the bomb run the leading 303rd BG formation was bracketed by a severe *Flak* barrage. Col Chuck Marion, the CO, lost two engines and following aircraft had to manoeuvre violently and reduce speed dramatically to avoid a collision. Just at that moment the *Luftwaffe* took advantage of the now scattered formation and made repeated head-on attacks. B-17, 42-5430 *Pappy* of the 303rd BG was rammed by an Fw 190 that failed to pull out in time. The 379th BG, flying only its second mission, bore the brunt of the attacks, losing six B-17s. The 1st BW lost eight B-17s in all and the 4th BW, one Fortress. 62 B-17s returned damaged. The American gunners claimed to have shot down 85 enemy fighters. In actual fact, only seven German fighters were destroyed or damaged and two pilots injured.

On Sunday 13 June, 102 heavies attacked Bremen while a smaller force bombed Kiel. Both forces were unescorted,

*A fighter pilot must possess an inner urge to do combat. The will at times to be offensive will develop into his own tactics. I stay with the enemy until either he's destroyed, I'm out of ammunition, he evades into the clouds, I'm driven off or I'm too low on gasoline to continue the combat.*

**Col Hubert M Zemke, CO, 56th Fighter Group.**

the short-ranged P-47s being used instead, during the morning and afternoon, on two diversionary sweeps off the Belgian coast. In the morning the 56th FG (which had claimed its first victory the day before) came upon 10./JG26. Over Dixmuide Col Hubert 'Hub' Zemke, the CO, claimed two of the Fw 190s and Lt Robert Johnson got a third before the German pilots knew what had hit them. (Only one Fw 190 was lost. Ogfr Heinrich Zenker was killed in the P-47 attack and ObFw Karl-Heinz Bocher was wounded.) In the afternoon 44 Thunderbolts of the 78th FG flew their sweep over Ypres and St Pol. II./JG26 shot down two of the P-47s for no loss.

The B-17s, meanwhile, had headed for their targets in north-east Germany, hoping that their two-pronged

attack on Kiel and Bremen would split the *Jagdflieger*. It failed, almost all the German fighters forsaking the 1st Wing's attack on Kiel, which lost four B-17s, to concentrate on the 76 B-17s of the 4th Wing heading for Bremen. Leading the 4th Wing this day was the 95th BG with Brig-Gen Nathan Bedford Forrest III, from HQ 402nd PCBW, riding in the co-pilot's seat of the command aircraft flown by Capt Harry A Stirwalt. Forrest was the grandson of a very famous Confederate cavalry general in the American Civil War, whose motto had been *To win – git there fustest with the mostest*. On Forrest's instigation, the 17 B-17s of the 95th BG's main formation (seven more flew in the Composite Group formation) were flying a hitherto untried "flat" formation, wingtip to wingtip, supposedly to be able to concentrate firepower ahead, below, above and to the rear more effectively. The Kiel force was attacked before they crossed the enemy coast. Among them were 6./JG11 (with five *Abschüsse*) and 32 Bf 109Gs and Fw 190A5s from Nordholz led by Hptm Kurt Ruppert, adjutant of III./JG26. The Bf 109Gs and Fw 190s attacked the Fortresses just after the bomb run. Many of the Fortress gunners were unable to return fire as their guns, which were lubricated with a new type of oil recommended by Forrest, had frozen. A massive diving frontal attack

*Above:* All eight crew members of Maj Lewis Gordon Thorup's crew of B-17 42-29708 *Shackeroo!* of the 333rd BS, 94th BG, who were rescued by MTB 245 after ditching in the North Sea after a German fighter attack during the mission to Kiel on 13 June 1943. It was one of nine Fortresses of the 94th BG lost on this raid. CO of this 22nd MTB Flotilla boat, was Lt Douglas Hunt RNVR (second from left). Col Thorup commanded the 447th BG. 31 March–30 June 1945. *Douglas Hunt DSC.*

raked the lead aircraft with cannon fire from one end to the other and Stirwalt's ship fell out of formation and spiralled down. All 13 men aboard bailed out but only Lt Willard Brown, group navigator, survived. A strong offshore wind carried Forrest and the 11 other crewmen to their deaths in the Cold Baltic Sea. Forrest was the first American general to be lost in combat in Europe.

Ruppert's *Gruppe* singled out the six B-17s of the Low Squadron of the leading 95th BG and made a rear pass, shooting down four Fortresses at a stroke. Hptm Kurt Ruppert's Fw 190 was hit by return fire and he was forced to bail out. He tried to open his parachute too quickly and the speed of his descent ripped his old hemp harness, throwing Ruppert to his death. At the time of his death Ruppert had twenty-

one kills to his credit. Two more 95th BG B-17s were lost from the High Squadron, and three more from the Composite Group formation brought the group's total losses to 10. The 94th BG was also hard hit, losing nine Fortresses, including *Shackeroo!*, Flown by Maj Lewis Thorup, whose crew was rescued by MTB 245 after 11 hours in the open sea. All told, the 4th BW lost twenty-two B-17s. Gen. Eaker referred to the Kiel mission as a *great battle* and said that he *was satisfied with the results obtained.* Brig-Gen Frederick L Anderson, CO, 4th BW, said: *It was a privilege to lead such men, who but yesterday were kids in school. They flew their Forts in the face of great opposition like veterans.*

## "REMEMBER KIEL"

*Following a thoroughly depressing and sad de-briefing during which he listened to the accounts of the surviving crews in silence, Col Kessler, his eyes brimming with tears and very obviously distressed, could only murmur, to no one in particular, "What's happened to my boys? What's happened to my boys?"* Capt John Miller, 412th BS Operations Officer, 95th BG, and pilot of the severely damaged Fortress *T'Ain't A Bird,* recalling the stunning impact upon his group commander at the news that 102 flight crew members were MIA, 13 June 1943.

*We had taken a beating, a heavy beating. Before the debriefing we received a drink or two of Scotch Whiskey instead of coffee and a spam sandwich. This was a first. All I wanted to do was to go off somewhere quiet to cry or get drunk. I did both.*

**Sgt Arlie Arneson, waist gunner, *T'Ain't A Bird,* 13 June 1943.**

47

# *Chapter 3* – **Blitz Week and Beyond**

On 22 June 1943, the 8th made its first large-scale attack on the Ruhr, when 182 heavies bombed the chemical and synthetic rubber plant at Hüls. Once again elaborate diversionary measures were put into operation with two planned 'spoof formations' making feints over the North Sea. Unfortunately one of the diversions, a formation of 21 B-17s of the 100th BG (making its theatre debut this day), was delayed because of ground mists and other problems and played no major part in the proceedings. The 381st and 384th BGs (which were flying their maiden missions) fell behind schedule and failed to rendezvous with Spitfire and Thunderbolt fighters which were to escort them to the Ford and General Motors works' at Antwerp. This lapse placed the 41 B-17s at the mercy of Fw 190s of JG26, which had refuelled after an earlier raid by RAF medium bombers, Bf 109s of II./JG1 and the ERLA factory protection *Schwarm*.

Maj Pips Priller, leading his *Geschwader*, led the first JG26 attack from the front before the Fortresses reached the target. The Fw 190s made one pass through the bomber ranks in flights of six to eight and shot three B-17s of the 381st BG out of formation. Priller's victim was 2/Lt Earl R Horr, whose Fortress crashed near Terneuzen. One 381st BG B-17F, 42-30016, was claimed shot down between Yerseke and Krabbendijke by both Fw Adolf Glunz of JG26 and Uffz Niki Mortl of the ERLA *Schwarm*. The B-17 flown by Lt. Martin L. Shenk, had suffered a runaway propeller on No.2 engine staggered across the target and, although badly shot up, he managed to make it back to crashland at Framlingham. 2/Lt John J Martin's B-17 went down pursued by OFw. Johann Edmann in the Stabsschwarm, who was hit by return fire from the Fortress and he crash-landed near Woensdrecht with severe injuries. Only one man survived aboard Martin's B-17. Hptm Wutz Galland and the 2nd *Gruppe* reached the Fortresses as they were leaving the target and they attacked from the rear. They made repeated

*Below:* B-17F of the 366th BS, 305th BG over the Hüls synthetic rubber plant, the most heavily defended target in the Reich at this time, near Recklinghausen on the edge of the Ruhr, 22 June 1943. The Hüls force severely damaged the plant and smoke rose as high as 17,000ft. Production was curtailed for a month and was not resumed for five months after that. Sixteen B-17s were lost, ten of them shot down by 1st *Gruppe* JG1, which also recorded 11 *Herausschüsse*. Five Fw 190s were damaged for no loss. *II.Gruppe* shot down one B-17. *III.Gruppe* shot down one B-17 and suffered one WIA while about 10 Bf 109s were damaged in emergency landings after running out of fuel. *USAF.*

**Above:** B-17F 42-30037, 546th BS, 384th BG, flown by I/Lt Lykes S Henderson, is inspected by German officers after being shot down on the Villacoublay, France, mission on 26 June 1943. *Hans Heiri-Stapfer.*

attacks and were out of ammunition when the P-47s of the 4th and 78th FGs finally arrived to provide withdrawal support. The Thunderbolts claimed seven fighters and a Bf 109 for no loss but JG26 lost no further Fw 190s, although two pilots were wounded. II *Gruppe* claimed four B-17s and was credited with three. However, Lt Jobe of the 381st BG brought the crippled *Little Chuck* back and crash landed at North Foreland. Two 384th BG B-17s failed to return. *Salvage Queen*, flown by Lt Fred G Disney, ditched in the Channel with the loss of seven crew, and the other crashed at Goes in Holland. Four of 2/Lt Robert J Oblinski's crew were killed. All in all, 16 heavies failed to return from the main raid on Hüls.

On 25 June, 275 B-17s were despatched to bomb targets in north-western Germany. Cloud hampered bombing at Hamburg, the main objective, and split up the formations and scattered some of the groups in the sky - an open invitation to fighter attack. The 1st BW lost 15 Fortresses, including six in the 379th BG, four of which were credited to I./JG26 from Rheine, which intercepted the 1st BW south of Emden. Three B-17s of the 4th Wing also failed to return. 61 B-17s were damaged. I./JG1 from Schiphol; III./JG1 at Leeuwarden; III./JG26 from Nordholz; III./JG11 at Oldenburg and 12./JG54 were other units involved in the air battle of

25 June. JG1 shot down three B-17s. *Gruppenadjutant*, Oblt Hardt of III./JG1, was killed bringing down a B-17, three pilots were wounded and another was MIA. The American gunners claimed 62 enemy fighters shot down though the real score was 12 lost and six damaged (all Bf 109G-6s; five pilots of III./JG1 were killed or injured, whereas 9./JG26 suffered three pilots missing. 12./JG54 lost another pilot KIA near Wesermünde).

Cloud interfered on the 26th also, when in the early evening, 165 B-17s of the 1st BW bombed Triqueville airfield and an aircraft factory at Villacoublay in the Paris area, while 81 Fortresses of the 3rd BW bombed Le Mans airfield. Five B-17s – all from the 384th BG – were shot down by Fw 190s, including one Fortress which fell to the guns of Maj 'Pips' Priller, Kommodore of JG26, between Dieppe and Le Treport on the return. JG26 also intercepted the 49 P-47s of the 56th FG near Forges, France as the Jugs arrived to provide withdrawal escort for the bombers. Five P-47s were shot down without loss to JG26, and a sixth came down in the sea off Scratby. Lt Robert Johnson had a fortunate escape when an Fw 190 which pursued him and pumped 20mm shells into his Thunderbolt, HV-P *All Hell,* was forced to break off out of ammunition. With a wave and a shake of the head, the German pilot rocked his wings in salute and broke off, perhaps thinking that the stricken

P-47 would never make England anyway. Johnson, fortunately, did, putting down safely at Manston.

On 28 June, 191 B-17s of the 1st and 4th BWs (the latter fitted with long range tanks for the first time) journeyed to St Nazaire and a smaller force of 50 B-17s from the 303rd, 379th and 384th BGs, headed for Beaumont Le Roger airfield further inland. Units of JG26 at Vendeville and Vitry took off to intercept but soon landed when the bomber formations passed out of range. The German controllers waited until the Spitfire escort had turned back and then sent III./JG2 into the fray. Hptm Egon Mayer's *Gruppe* claimed nine Fortresses for the loss of one Fw 190 and its pilot. Four of the bomber losses were from the 351st BG, one was from the 91st and the 95th BG lost three. 57 B-17s of the St Nazaire force returned with damage and three dead crewmen.

During July in an attempt to bring more firepower to bear on the B-24 and B-17 formations, both the Fw 190A and Bf 109G had their armament increased substantially. The Bf 109G-6/R6 now carried three MG

*The days passed with defensive patrols, sea reconnaissance and repeatedly alarms without contact with the enemy. But on 1 July there was something new in the sky; In the vicinity of Hoek van Holland we met up for the first time with Thunderbolts. From a distance they looked disconcertingly similar to the Fw 190. What they were able to fire from their eight squirters I frequently came to feel later on.*

**Lt Eberhard Burath, I./JG1. (Col Arman 'Pete' Peterson, CO, 78th FG, was shot down and killed by Fw Martin Lacha of I./JG1 during the 1 July dog fight between I./JG1 and the 4th and 78th FGs. Peterson's 'Jug' crashed near Ouddorp on Goeree-Overflakkee.)**

151 cannon in addition to its two MG 151 13mm machine guns and the Fw 190 now carried two Rheinmetall MG FF-M20 cannons in addition to its two MG 15s. During July also, the Fw 190A-6, equipped with two MG 151 20mm cannon in place of the MG-FF-M, became operational in the *Jagdgruppen*.

On 10 July, 185 B-17s of the 1st BW headed for airfields at Caen and Abbeville, while 101 B-17s of the 4th BW went to Le Bourget airfield. Fighter cover was provided by 18 squadrons of Spitfires and eight squadrons of P-47s. Bombing by the 1st BW was largely ineffective, while none of the 4th BW B-17s found their target because of cloud. Three B-17s were lost on the return. Two of these were from the Le Bourget attack force, while *Exterminator*, a 412th BS, 95th BG Fortress flown by Lt James R Sarchet, was shot down by Lt Helmut Hoppe 4th *Staffel* CO, JG26, near Fecamp, west of Rouen in his first pass. The Fortress crashed at Elbent with six crew dead. Two crew evaded and two were captured. Wutz Galland's 2nd *Gruppe* continued to attack the bombers for 10 more minutes until low fuel forced them to break off.

Despite continuing losses the addition of more groups allowed Eaker to send a record 322 bombers to Hanover on 17 July. On 24 July, a week-long series of heavy bomber raids (later called 'Blitz Week') went ahead, beginning with a raid by 208 B-17s on Heroya and

*Another Independence Day, quite unlike any other I can remember. A German aircraft factory deep within France got a look at some American fireworks in the form of several hundred 500lb bombs. Our own crew went today as spares and had to return just short of France. Today we have been heavy hearted because Lt B's crew did not return.*

**Extract from a 381st BG gunner's diary 4 July 1943. In Lt Olef M Ballinger's crew, three men evaded, four were KIA, and three became PoW. The diarist himself flew one more mission, his 5th and Air Medal mission, on 8 July, and went MIA on 14 July with *Widget* and Lt Robert J Holdem's crew.**

*It was mid-morning, 14 July 1943. Our formation was approaching Paris to bomb nearby Le Bourget airfield. Each "Fort," including ours, 42-3190, carried 16 500lb bombs. At my fight waist gun position, I felt the ship take a forward hit. Smoke filtered back to the rear. "What the hell is going on up front?" I yelled to Earl Porath, back-to-back with me at his left waist gun position. Through my own open gun port, I could see German fighters continuing the attack on the front of the ship, diving from above or zooming up from below like a swarm of angry hornets.*

*The ship began to fall out of formation. I squeezed off a couple of ineffective bursts from my .50 calibre Browning machine gun as the fighters flashed by at such speed that it was nearly impossible to track them through my gunsight for more than a fraction of a second. Those German pilots were smart veterans. I could hear and feel Porath's ".50" firing behind me and Jeff Polk's twin ".50's" blazing away from his ball turret below me. In the tail of the ship, Ossie Asiala's guns added to the racket. But I couldn't hear firing from any of our forward guns.*

*The smoke was getting heavier. The ship went into an abrupt dive, then levelled again and seemed to move erratically as if the pilot were taking evasive action. I realised that the German fighter attack had ended. I listened on the intercom for some word from the cockpit. Silence! We were in deep trouble. A horrible thought came to me. Had they all been killed up front?*

*The ship went into a shallow dive and it was hard for me to hold my footing. Porath yelled, "Here they come, Looie!"*

*German fighters were closing on us, not head-on or diving but rather parallel to us, as if in escort. I could even see the pilot of one fighter looking at us. I was amazed by this tactic but didn't stop to think about it. My enemy was out there at practically point blank range. Instinct took over and I began firing. So did Porath, Polk, and Asiala. Parallel to us, with their fixed wing guns at right angles to us they were totally defenceless. I saw two fighters in flames and one of them exploded as it fell. Others may have been hit but I wasn't sure.*

*Then all hell broke loose! Other German fighters raked the ship. Wires and control cables dangled like spaghetti. I listened for the bail-out order. Silence – again. She went into a steep dive. I was torn loose from my gun and flipped against the bulkhead. Porath slammed against me. Polk had gotten out of the ball turret and then he too, fell against the bulkhead. As I lay pinned there, I couldn't see out of the ship and thought, "Oh my God, we're going straight into the ground." I lost all hope. "This is it," I said to myself.*

*Unbelievably, the steep dive angle was lessening and I dimly wondered if the ship was still airworthy and who was at the controls. Capt Harrison, I hoped. She began to pull out and levelled off. We staggered to our feet, heading for the door to jump. I struggled to hook my chute buckles as I got to the door. Porath was shaking his head "No!" and pointing out the window. The ground was rushing up to meet us. We braced ourselves. We were going in!*

*She nosed up gently as she bellied into a wheat field. The tail touched first and we heard a tearing, crunching sound. Someone yelled, "The bombs!" We looked toward the bulkhead. The ball turret had torn loose and was pushed up through the floor. It seemed an eternity before we slid to a halt. There was no fire. Almost no sound. We had ridden her in!*

*We forced the door open, jumped into the wheat field and everyone scattered. Ossie and I paired up. We saw Porath and Jim Curtis, the engineer and top turret gunner running together toward a wooded area. Polk and Charlie McNemar, our radio operator/gunner, ran together in the opposite direction. They all appeared in good shape. I don't remember seeing Capt. Harrison and our co-pilot, Lt David Turner, or our bombardier and navigator. I would wonder about their fate for many months.*

*It was Bastille Day, 14 July 1943, in German occupied France. Ossie and I were alone in a French wheat field, belly landed behind enemy lines – with a full bomb load.*

**Sgt Richard H Lewis, recounting in his book *Hell Above and Hell Below* of the demise of B-17F 42-3190, 332nd BS 94th BG, shot down by Oberstleutnant Egon Mayer, Kommandeur, III./JG2, on 14 July 1943. (The 94th BG lost four B-17s, the total losses for the Le Bourget strike.) Harrison elected to crash-land the Fortress to save the engineer, whose parachute had been burned in the fire aboard the aircraft. Harrison, his co-pilot, and the engineer, managed to escape with the help of the French Underground. They walked across the Pyrenees into Spain.**

**Above:** B-17F 42-3190, 332nd BS, 94th BG, shot down by Oblt Egon Mayer *Kommandeur,* III./JG2 on 14 July 1943. *Harry Holmes.*

**Left:** 12 July 1943. Uffz Walter Stienhaus (left) II./JG3, the centre of attention from his comrades as well as from a Propaganda film unit on return from a mission on the Eastern Front when he scored his 5th *Abschuss.* Prominent in the middle and proudly wearing his *Ritterkreuz* is 31 year old Maj Kurt Brändle, CO of II./JG3, who had claimed more than 150 *Abschüsse* by this time. II./JG3 was transferred to the *Reichsverteidigung* on the western front in early August 1943. Brändle was killed in combat on 3 November, only moments after getting his final two kills, both P-47s over the North Sea to the west of Amsterdam. At the time of his death, his score stood at 180 combat victories in over 700 operational sorties. Helmut Henning via Rob de Visser.

*W*e were doing about 450 kmh now and were coming down slightly, aiming for the noses of the B-17s. There were about 200 of us attacking the 200 bombers but there was also the fighter escort above them. We were going for the bombers. When we made our move, the P-47s began to dive on us and it was a race to get to the bombers before being intercepted. I was already close and about 600ft above and coming straight on: I opened fire with the twenties at 500 yards. At 300 yards I opened fire with the thirties. It was a short burst, maybe 10 shells from each cannon, but I saw the bomber explode and begin to burn. I flashed over him at about 50ft and then did a chandelle. When I had turned around I was about a 1000 feet above and behind them, and was suddenly mixed in with American fighters.

Straight in front was a Thunderbolt., as I completed the turn, and I opened fire on him immediately, and hit his propwash. My fire was so heavy his left wing came off almost at once and I watched him go down...We flew south, ahead for a few seconds, preparing for another strike at the bombers and then, coming from above, I saw them. I called a warning: "Indianer über uns!", and as they came in behind us we banked hard left. There were 10 P-47s and four of us and we were all turning as hard as we could, as in a Lufbery. I was able to turn tighter and was gaining. I pulled within 80 yards of the P-47 ahead of me and opened fire. I hit him quickly and two of the others got one each, so that in a minute and a half three of the P-47s went down...

*Staffelkapitän* Oblt Georg-Peter Eder's 7./JG2, combat report, 14 July 1943. Eder's bomber victim was *Windy City Challenger* of the 422nd BS, 305th BG (which crashed at Lieuesant, south of Paris), part of the force of 116 B-17s of the 1st BW attacking Villacoublay air depot between 0811 and 0815 hours. Seven of Lt John H Perkins Jr's crew were killed and four were taken prisoner. (The other 1st BW force of sixty-four B-17s, which attacked Amiens/Glisy airfield at 0742 hours, was the only one of the three forces sent out early this day to have escorts. Bf 109Gs of 3./JG27 and II./JG2 attacked shortly before the target was reached and a 3./JG27 Bf 109 shot down *Widget* of the 535th BS, 381st BG flown by Lt Robert J Holdem, the only loss to the Amiens force.) Three P-47s were lost – one from the 4th FG, two from the 78th FG and one battle-damaged Thunderbolt was abandoned off Newhaven, pilot saved (three P-47s alone were claimed this day by Maj Wutz Galland, II *Gruppe* CO). (The Villacoublay air depot strike force lost three B-17s, bringing total bomber losses for 14 July to eight. At Villacoublay the hangers housing the Fw 190 repair facility of Luftflotte 3 were destroyed, along with 70 Fw 190s.)

**Above:** *Staffelkapitän* Oblt Georg-Peter Eder, 7./JG2. *Bill Donald.*

**Below:** Eder's bomber victim on 14 July 1943 was *Windy City Challenger* of the 422nd BS, 305th BG which crashed at Lieuesant, south of Paris. *Bill Donald.*

Trondheim in Norway. One B-17 failed to return and 64 were battle damaged. Next day, 25 July, 218 bombers attacked Hamburg, devastated the night before in the great RAF Bomber Command fire raid and Kiel. Cloud cover and the huge smoke pall from the still burning fires at Hamburg caused 59 B-17s of the 92nd, 305th and 306th BGs to abandon their strike altogether. The Hamburg force was intercepted by III./JG26 as the leading B-17s approached the Elbe estuary and three Fortresses were shot down. Over Hamburg and beyond JG11 took over and finally, over the North Sea, the stragglers were

attacked by II. and III./JG1 from Rheine and Leeuwarden. II Gruppe shot down two B-17s and III Gruppe destroyed another. Maj Karl-Heinz Leesmann, Gruppenkommandeur, III./JG1, crashed into the sea after an attack on a B-17. His body was washed ashore on 16 August. Altogether, 15 B-17s - seven of them from the 384th BG - were shot down and 67 returned battle damaged. The Kiel force lost four B-17s and 50 returned damaged, two of which crashed on landing. JG1 and 11 accounted for most of the 19 bombers that failed to return with 15 Abschüsse.

**Above:** B-17F 42-29670 *"Thundermug"*, formerly of the 333rd BS, 94th BG, was transferred to the 544th BS, 384th BG. It was one of seven in the Group lost on 25 July 1943 when it went MIA with Lt Kelmer J Hall's crew. Two men were KIA, eight were PoW after the B-17 crashed at Hamburg. *Richards.*

*W*hen the fighters hit us, the wing swelled up like a balloon and then burst into flames, and we went into a dive. I didn't give the order to bail out because I thought I might pull out of it. I got it under control only 150ft above the water, just in time to ditch. We tied our dinghies together and then started worrying. We were a long way from home and closer to Germany than any other land. We were afraid the Germans might pick us up. We not only watched Kiel burn that night, but we actually sat out there in the water and had a grandstand view of the RAF bombing the German coast. We could see the Flak bursting and the fires started by the RAF blockbusters. About noon the next day a British plane spotted us. He dropped three big dinghies and then hung around to protect us from possible attack by a Ju 88 that hovered in the distance. Soon another RAF plane joined him, then three more, then three Forts joined up. It looked like the combined Allied air force above us. One of the RAF planes dropped a launch by parachute. It was a sight to see that boat come parachuting down, settling right beside us. It was all closed, with the hatches sealed.

We opened it up and there were sleeping bags, food, water, gasoline and directions for running the thing. I had an idea I might get the boys to head for New York...

**Lt John P Keelan, pilot, B-17 42-30206 *Happy Daze*, 410th BS, 94th BG, ditched in the North Sea, 25 July 1943 returning from the raid on Kiel. One crew member was KIA. On 26 July, an airborne lifeboat dropped by a 279 Squadron Warwick from Bircham Newton near to the ditched crew who steering westward, were picked up by fishermen who delivered them safely to an ASR motor launch.**

***Below:*** On 25 July 1943, Lt John P Keelan and crew of B-17 42-30206 *Happy Daze*, 410th BS, 94th BG, ditched in the North Sea returning from the raid on Kiel. One crew member was KIA but on 26 July an airborne lifeboat was dropped by a 279 Squadron RAF Warwick from Bircham Newton near to the ditched crew and the other nine men returned safely to England. *Dick Vimpany.*

*On 26 July (after my 54th scramble without enemy contact) I caught, having been separated from my own bunch, a straggling B-17 with the last of my fuel in the tank. There was not enough left for overtaking and an attack from ahead. Flying at the same level, I did a steep turn to starboard and fired a well-aimed burst at him from the cockpit right through to the tail. I would not liked to have been at the receiving end. Then I saw two Me 109s who must have given him the rest. I got myself an emergency bearing from Borkum. Everyone was shouting for bearings - and 'with God's help and my brakes' I managed to stop my 190 at the field's edge on the perimeter track. That's how I imagined a landing on an aircraft carrier. The take-off afterwards was equally hair-raising, just clearing the hangar roofs with the tailwheel almost touching the tops. It got more hairy as the week went on.*

**Lt Eberhard Burath, I./JG1. On 26 July, 146 bombers attacked Hanover and Hamburg and again JG1 and JG11 accounted for most of the 24 bombers shot down. II./JG1 alone claimed seven *Viermots* destroyed for the loss of two aircraft (both pilots safe).**

*On 28 July, the commander wanted to observe from a distance how an attack from ahead should really be carried out and I was to take his place as the leader. We overtook a formation (B-17s of the 95th BG) entering the north of Holland, then Hptm Schnoor sheered off to get a good view from above. Now it was my turn. Far enough ahead, about 3km, then right wing down to give the signal and a 180° turn to face the centre of the formation. Good. So far and I am approaching from dead ahead. A glance to the side - and I am struck dumb - way ahead of the others, I am hurtling all alone at the 4-mots. Now good night! Instead of spreading the defensive fire evenly to all, the Yanks concentrate on the lone cheeky one and the tracer comes flying at my breast. I make myself very small, get the B-17 I was aiming for briefly into my sights, and press the trigger. Then it rattled into the kite like at a fireworks. 'Curtains and exit!'*

*Smoke! Sheer off. The prop stops, but fortunately no fire. Handy that the Dutch have such nice fields. I select a convenient one and approach, somewhat too fast, the kite refuses to sit down, I pass the end of the field, a pity that the Dutch have so many canals, I pass over them with the nose into the opposite bank, tail up and ready for a somersault.. But then my guardian angel gives the port wing a tiny nudge, my kite turns 180° on its nose and slaps neatly down, potatoes rain down on the fuselage and then a wonderful calm after the storm. I thank my guardian angel and crawl out of the cockpit into the potatoes. The machine looks quite sound, only 20cm shorter at the nose. I was soon collected from the nearby village of Buitenpost. I did not even get a rebuke, my comrades had taken too wide a turn; only later on, when the escorting fighters were there, everyone thrust ahead in an attack as it was none too healthy at the rear. So ended my role as Gruppen commander.*

**Lt Eberhard Burath, I./JG1. Burath's victim was *Spook III*, flown by 2/Lt Francis J Reagan of the 336th BS, which was finished off by *Gruppenkommandeur* Hptm Emil-Rudolf Schnoor, his third victory. *Spook III* ditched in the North Sea with the loss of all 10 crew. It brought the 95th BG's losses for the day to three. Lt James F Rivers' B-17 in the 334th BS crached at Hoehausen and all the crew were taken prisoner. *Exterminator*, flown by 2/Lt Fred D Hughes of the 412th BS, crashed at Lathen, Germany and all crew were made PoW. Five other B-17 victories were claimed by pilots of JG1.**

**Above:** Dortmund airfield, January 1944. Maj Emil-Rudolf Schnoor, Kommandeur, I./JG1 (second from right) looks on as his Fw 190A-7 is serviced by his mechanics. The 'Winged 1' painted on the engine cowling became the official emblem of JG1 after the death of its Kommodore Maj Hans Philipp on 8 October 1943 when he was shot down and killed by P-47s near Nordhorn. Philipp had 206 victories, including 177 on the Eastern Front. *Köhne via Rob de Visser.*

**Left:** Maj Emil-Rudolf Schnoor, Kommandeur of I./JG1 gets strapped into the cockpit of his Fw 190A-7 at Dortmund airfield, January 1944 . *Seebrandt via Rob de Visser.*

*W*hen we sighted the bombers off to our left we made a 90° turn and picked them up near Winterswijk. One straggling bomber was observed flying below the main formation in a dive, trailing black smoke and being attacked by about five E/A. I peeled my flight down and to the rear of the straggler. This would be about 1,000ft below the main formation at about 21,000ft. All E/A sighted us and took evasive action to the extent that I was unable to close, although I did fire a burst with improper deflection. The E/A was in a diving attack from the rear on this straggler. I initiated my attack from the port side rear of the fighters, swinging in behind them to the right and broke sharply downward to the rear. I followed them in the climb, attempting to get a deflection shot. When he broke downward I found I was directly beneath the bombers and saw a number of ball turret gunners firing at my flight. I broke down and to the rear, and pulled up to starboard side of the bombers about 1,000 yards out and at about their level.

Looking up, I observed six E/A flying parallel to the bombers and about 1,000ft directly above me. They failed to see us and did not take any action, so after they passed I made a climbing turn to the left to come up to their level and behind them. At this point I missed my second element and found myself alone with my wingman. In our pull up we missed the original six E/A sighted but sighted a single E/A ahead on same level at about 1,500 yards. I dived slightly below, opened full throttle, and closed to about 400 yards. I pulled up directly behind the E/A and opened fire. Several strikes were observed on E/A, his wheels dropped and he spun down trailing a large volume of dark smoke and flame.

I continued parallel to the bombers and sighted two more E/A about 2,000 yards ahead. I used the same tactics, closing to 400 yards astern, pulled up and opened fire on port aircraft. Observed strike reports and E/A billowed smoke and flame, rolled over and went down. I was closing so fast that I had to pull up to avoid hitting him. I observed my wingman, F/O Koontz, firing at the second aircraft but did not see the results. Both of these aircraft were Fw 190s.

After this second engagement, we were about two miles ahead of the bombers still well out to their starboard side. About this time I observed one E/A, an Me 109, peeled to starboard to attack the bombers head-on, and I followed closing to 500 yards before opening fire. Two bursts were behind but the third burst caught him and he spun down, trailing smoke and flame, some 1,500 yards ahead of the bombers.

**Maj Eugene P Roberts, 84th FS, 78th FG, P-47 *Spokane Chief*, describing the first 'hat trick' of kills on 30 July 1943, to become the first US pilot to score a triple victory in Europe.**

On 26 July, 92 heavies bombed rubber factories at Hannover and 54 others attacked shipbuilding yards at Hamburg. 24 aircraft were lost, mostly to enemy fighters.

After stand-down on 27 July, the 8th despatched just over 300 bombers on the 28th in two forces to bomb German targets, but bad weather interfered with the mission and only 49 bombed the Fieseler aircraft works at Kassel, with 28 hitting the Fw190 factory at Oschersleben. JG1 and 11, shot down the majority of the 22 bombers lost, I./JG26 claiming two B-17s on the return leg over Holland.

After Burath's lone attack on B-17s of the 95th BG, 4th FG Thunderbolts came to the bombers' rescue. The Jugs, which provided withdrawal support on the 8th AF's first fighter penetration of German airspace, engaged an estimated 45 enemy fighters over northern Holland. For just one fighter lost, P-47C 41-6238 of the 336th FS, 4th FG, shot down by Hptm Hermichen of I./JG26 to the west of Rotterdam, the Thunderbolt pilots claimed nine fighters destroyed. In fact, 1 and 11 *Jagdgeschwadern* lost 20 Fw 190s and Bf 109s with three pilots killed and eight injured, I./JG26 another three Fw 190A-5s.

On 29 July, 168 B-17s of the 1st BW were despatched to bomb the U-boat yards at Kiel and 81 Fortresses of the 4th BW attacked the Heinkel aircraft factory at Warnemünde. Some 39 B-26 Marauders attacked targets in Holland and France. The 4th BW lost four Fortresses and the 1st BW lost six B-17s. Four of the 1st Wing's losses came from the 306th BG, whose crews had had little or no sleep at all since flying to Kassel the day before. The 306th BG was intercepted by III./JG26 from Nordholz. Thanks to radar, the *Luftwaffe* unit had an hour's warning of the bombers' approach making it possible to mass and make contact with them at Heligoland Island. The Third *Gruppe* attacked the unlucky 13 B-17s of the 306th BG (five had aborted) all the way across Schleswig-Holstein to the target. Newly promoted Capt George E Paris Jr of the 369th BS, which had now flown 42 consecutive missions without loss, was leading the 306th BG this day. Just before the target, the first of more than 100 attacking aircraft hit the small formation in a vicious head-on pass. It would appear that 1/Lt Keith Conley, a 22-mission veteran, was the first to go down. Oblt Paul Schauder, 9th *Staffel* CO, was credited with the kill. All 10 crew were reported to have bailed out but two men were later reported killed in action.

Next to go was 1/Lt Donald R Winter's crew from the

*T*hey were so terribly tired...they had to get up at 1.30 this morning and I doubt that some of them had slept at all, The maintenance crews are tired too and they can't keep the planes in shape for so much combat... It's all a vicious circle resulting in poor flying by the pilots, poor bombing by the bombardiers, and high losses, There is a human element to this thing that Bomber Command seems to fail to consider.

**Maj Thurman Shuller, flight surgeon, 306th BG, late July 1943.**

same Low Squadron. A wing came off and four of the crew were killed. OFw Heinz Kemethmüller of 7./JG26 was credited with this victory. A few minutes later, F/O Carl D Brown's B-17 in the 376th BS exploded with the loss of all 10 crew, and F/O Berryman H Brown's Fortress from the same squadron went down after losing two engines. Hptm Hermann Staiger, 12./JG26 CO, was credited with the destruction of both bombers. Two of Berryman H. Brown's crew were killed, including S/Sgt Eric G Newhouse, waist gunner, who had left his native Austria in 1938 as a boy of 15 to escape the Nazi persecution of the Jews, finally arriving in the USA. Officially, the 306th BG was credited with the destruction of three Bf 110s and three Fw 190s. (JG26 lost one Bf 109G-6 and three were damaged.) JG11 claimed eight Fortresses.

On 30 July 186 B-17s went to Kassel. The bombers' route took them over Woensdrecht airfield, the scene of an ineffective attack by 11 B-26 Marauders that morning (an attack on Courtrai-Wevelghem was abandoned). Parts of I./JG26 took off from Woensdrecht and intercepted the bombers. Two B-17s were shot down, by Lt Gohringer of Stab I./JG26 (a 388th BG B-17, 42-30208, flown by F/O E Pickard), south of Antwerp, and Fw Christof of I./JG26 over Flanders, at 0825 and 0835 hours, respectively. The latter's claim, his ninth victory, was B-17F 42-30290 *Lucky Lady II*, flown by 2/Lt Carmelo P Pelusi, of the 338th BS, 96th BG, which had jettisoned its bomb load and had two engines knocked out by *Flak* over Belgium. It exploded and came down near Tielrode. Five crew were killed while five bailed out and were taken prisoner. (F. Christof was KIA just over two

hours later when he was shot down by 1/Lt Kenneth G Smith of the 335th FS, 4th FG over Schouwen.) The Fortresses carried on to the target, where 134 bombed. Waiting for them on their return were the fighters from all four of the Jagdflieger defensive zones. Near Apeldoorn II./JG26 attacked, sending two B-17s down in flames for the loss of three Fw 190s. One of the B-17s was 42-3100 flown by Lt. Guerdon W. Humason with Maj Robert F Post, 532nd BS CO, 381st BG, aboard, which came under attack from five Fw 190s. Its final destruction was credited to Maj Wolfgang-Ferdinand Galland, II *Gruppe* CO. Three engines were put out of action and four crewmen bailed out before the doomed B-17 descended into cloud near Ascheberg. One of the men was almost certainly killed when he hit the tail. Six men remained aboard as Humason brought the aircraft in for a crash landing at Deelen, where it was strafed by at least one of the Fw 190s. Post suffered a broken leg and lost an eye as a result of the strafing and he was repatriated in 1944.

Hptm Johannes Naumann, 6th *Staffel* CO, was credited with the destruction of a 91st BG B-17 5km south-east of Est. His victim was 41-24399 *Man O'War*, flown by 2/Lt Keene C McCammon of the 323rd BS, which crashed at Opijnen. Eight of McCammon's crew were killed and two were taken prisoner. (Naumann's *Staffel* lost three Fw 190s and one pilot KIA to return fire from the B-17s.) Fw. Crump claimed a YB-40 near Arnhem but no B-17 "gun ships" were lost this day. Uffz Wiegand's claim of a 379th BG B-17 west of Eupen was upheld (the group lost three B-17s this day, including one Fortress which crash-landed at Alconbury) and Flg Hans-Walter

Sander claimed a 96th BG B-17 at St Trond; most likely *Dry Run II*, flown by 2/Lt Andrew Miracle, also of the 338th BS. The nine-man crew and photographer Sgt Bruce, who called themselves *The Miracle Tribe*, lived up to this name, 2/Lt Miracle putting the crippled bomber down in the North Sea where all 10 men were picked up by ASR. Altogether, 12 bombers and six US

**Above:** A badly wounded gunner in the 379th BG is given immediate medical treatment by the side of his Fortress. *USAF.*

fighters were lost.

Some 107 fighters of the 4th, 56th and 78th FGs arrived on the scene in an attempt to prevent further losses. (They carried auxiliary tanks for the very first time this day, which greatly enhanced their range and undoubtedly contributed to the severe German fighter losses.) The US fighters claimed 24 enemy fighters shot down, including three, the first triple victory in the ETO by Maj Eugene Roberts of the 78th FG. Capt Charles London, also of the 78th FG, was credited with downing two fighters.

The 78th FG lost its second CO within a month when Lt Col Melvin F McNickle was shot down at 1030 hours. Whilst severely injured, he was made PoW near Ravestein in Holland. His wingman, Lt Byers, was shot down and killed near Elden in Holland a few minutes before his CO went down. (One of these was probably claimed by Hptm Hermichen of I./JG26, who destroyed a P-47 at 1015 hrs in the Dordrecht area). At least 24 *Luftwaffe* fighters were lost over Holland. JG1 lost eight Fw 190 A-4s and A-5s destroyed with another three severely damaged when their pilots crash-landed their Bf 109G-6s after being damaged in air combat. JG2 lost seven destroyed; JG11 one Bf 109G-6 destroyed with another five G-1s and G-6s between 15 and eighty per cent damaged. JG26 had four write-offs and JG54 lost another four. In all, eight Bf 109s and 16 Fw 190s were

**Left:** On 30 July 1943 near Apeldoorn II./JG26 attacked, sending two B-17s down in flames for the loss of three Fw 190s. One of the victims was 42-3100 of the 381st BG flown by Lt Guerdon W Humason with Maj Robert F Post, 532nd BS CO, aboard, which came under attack from five Fw 190s and whose final destruction was credited to Maj Wolfgang-Ferdinand Galland, II *Gruppe* CO. *Ron Mackay.*

# BLACK SUNDAY IN BULGARIA

Bulgaria became an ally of the Third Reich on 1 March 1941. Until 1940 the Bulgarian Air Force was equipped with obsolete aircraft such as the He 51, Ar 65, PZL 24B and the Czech-built Avia 534-BN biplane. In 1940-41 the Bulgarians bought 18 Bf 109E fighters from Germany. These 18 aircraft were based at Baltschik and Sarafowo (near Burgas) to protect the Black Sea coast and the German military installations in the area. On 1 March 1941, Bulgaria joined the Axis Pact, but did not take part in the war between Germany and Yugoslavia. At this time all aircraft of the Bulgarian Air Force were organised in regiments, corresponding to a German Geschwader. There were five regiments, including the 6th Royal Bulgarian Fighter Regiment at Marno pole, an airfield near Karlovo east of Sofia in southern Bulgaria. At the beginning of 1942 the regiment consisted of three flights of Avia 534s under the command of Polkovnik (Lt Col) Vasil Vulkov. When Bulgaria declared war on Britain and the USA on 13 December 1941, these states were not able to take offensive action against the country. Throughout 1942, air activity over Bulgaria remained very limited. Occasional flights, mainly with two or three aircraft, dropped leaflets or agents, mainly over Macedonia to organise resistance among the population. Ammunition was also dropped over Serbia to Tito's partisans. All this took place mainly at night.

The first contact Bulgarian fighters had with the Americans was on Sunday 1 August 1943, when the USAAF mounted *Tidal Wave*. On this day the oil refineries of Ploesti in Romania were the targets for 177 B-24Ds of the 8th (44th, 93rd and 389th BGs on TDY – temporary duty – from England) and 9th AF (98th and 376th BGs) flying from North Africa. Malfunctions and accidents en route reduced the effectiveness of the Liberator force and navigational errors caused severe problems in the target area, forcing some groups to bomb each other's assigned targets. In Bulgaria Col Vulkov (who was executed as "peoples enemy" in February 1945) put his four airfields on readiness to catch the B-24Ds heading for Ploesti. Sixteen Avias from Karlovo and six Bf 109G-2s from Marno pole, took off to try to intercept the Liberators. At 1225 hours at two airfields near Sofia, six Avias of Oblt Marin Petrov's Squadron 612 at Wraschdebna, and four Avias of Lt Rusi Rusev's Squadron 622 at Bojouriste, also took off to intercept the B-24Ds, in the Osogovska Mountains. The Bulgarian pilots were only able to sight the rear echelons of the 389th and 44th BGs heading north-east at 15,000ft, too high for the Avias (as their oxygen supply and radio equipment had been removed to obtain more speed), to reach them.

Some 167 B-24Ds actually attacked their targets, dropping 311 tons of bombs on the Ploesti refineries. Coming off Ploesti the B-24s were low, so low that when they

**Above:** Another European country to become an ally of the Third Reich, on 1 March 1941, was Bulgaria. The slow and lightly armed Avia 534 biplane fighters engaged B-24s for the first time on 1 August 1943, two pilots claiming to get into firing position against the big American bombers. *Todor Walkow.*

**Above:** During 1940-41, Bulgaria purchased 18 Bf 109E fighters from Germany and based them at Baltschik and Sarafowo (near Burgas) to protect the Bulgarian Black Sea coast. *Todor Walkow.*

**Below:** B-24 Liberator over the inferno at Ploesti, 1 August 1943. *USAF.*

**Below:** Red I, Steaua Romana at Campina burning 1 August 1943. *USAF.*

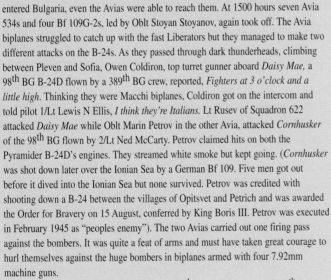

**Above:** Oblt Stojan Stoyanov was in the thick of the action from 1 August 1943 and ended the year of fighting against the Americans as Bulgaria's leading fighter ace with nine confirmed victories. *Todor Walkow.*

**Right:** The Bf 109F (above) and G-2/G-6 (below) formed the backbone of the Bulgarian fighter force, 1943-44. *Todor Walkow.*

entered Bulgaria, even the Avias were able to reach them. At 1500 hours seven Avia 534s and four Bf 109G-2s, led by Oblt Stoyan Stoyanov, again took off. The Avia biplanes struggled to catch up with the fast Liberators but they managed to make two different attacks on the B-24s. As they passed through dark thunderheads, climbing between Pleven and Sofia, Owen Coldiron, top turret gunner aboard *Daisy Mae,* a 98th BG B-24D flown by a 389th BG crew, reported, *Fighters at 3 o'clock and a little high.* Thinking they were Macchi biplanes, Coldiron got on the intercom and told pilot 1/Lt Lewis N Ellis, *I think they're Italians.* Lt Rusev of Squadron 622 attacked *Daisy Mae* while Oblt Marin Petrov in the other Avia, attacked *Cornhusker* of the 98th BG flown by 2/Lt Ned McCarty. Petrov claimed hits on both the Pyramider B-24D's engines. They streamed white smoke but kept going. (*Cornhusker* was shot down later over the Ionian Sea by a German Bf 109. Five men got out before it dived into the Ionian Sea but none survived. Petrov was credited with shooting down a B-24 between the villages of Opitsvet and Petrich and was awarded the Order for Bravery on 15 August, conferred by King Boris III. Petrov was executed in February 1945 as "peoples enemy"). The two Avias carried out one firing pass against the bombers. It was quite a feat of arms and must have taken great courage to hurl themselves against the huge bombers in biplanes armed with four 7.92mm machine guns.

After this encounter Ellis saw *The Witch,* a 98th BG B-24 flown by a 389th BG crew captained by 1/Lt Julian T Darlington, and *Prince Charming,* another 98th BG B-24 flown by a 389th BG crew, captained by Capt James A Gunn. These, and a third B-24, were flying along together and Ellis joined them for mutual support. They now became targets for the Karlovo Bf 109Gs, which came upon the scene. They had taken off in two sections with an interval in between. This resulted in each section having its own battle with different groups of bombers. One section, led by Lt Krastev, now discovered the small group of four bombers. Krastev singled out *The Witch* and shot out the No.4 engine and the Liberator began to fall behind. Gunn throttled back to try to help his friend but Lt Peter Bochev struck and white smoke and flames streamed from *Prince Charming,* which exploded. Several burning

parachutes came out of the Liberator but only S/Sgt Stanley Horine, the rear gunner, was able to save himself with his parachute. Three of Darlington's gunners bailed out as *The Witch* dived for the ground and the pilot was able to crash-land in a mountain-side wheat field. All of Darlington's crew survived. Krastev, meanwhile, had got over Skopjie in Macedonia during the course of this fight and he had to make an emergency landing through lack of fuel.

Meanwhile, the other section led by Oblt Stoyanov, discovered 18 to 20 enemy bombers not far from Michailowgrad and attacked the last machine from behind. But the Bulgarian fighters were fired at by the entire formation and they had to break off immediately. Stoyanov then attacked head-on. He flew about 10km in front of the bomber group, turned 180° and approached the formation out of the sun. The distance between them decreased very rapidly and Stoyanov opened fire on the leading aircraft with all his guns. The Liberator dropped its nose and went down. After this attack Stoyanov made three attempts against another B-24. It was *Pudgy* of the 93rd BG, piloted by Lt Milton Teltser. Both of *Pudgy's* port engines caught fire and it crashed killing five crew. (Teltser and four others were captured by the Romanians.) As Stoyanov's ammunition was almost exhausted, he ordered his wingman, Lt Iw Bonev, to take over the lead. Bonev opened fire on another B-24 and two engines caught fire.

Five Liberators were claimed shot down by Bulgarian pilots, including two credited to Stoyanov. (However, only four B-24Ds fell over Bulgaria and two of these were *Exterminator* and *Let 'Er Rip,* both from the 93rd BG, which collided in cloud). These were Oblt Stoyanov's first two confirmed victories in a series of nine, which would make him Bulgaria's top-scoring fighter ace in WWII. All attacks except the first one had been carried out from behind and below. (44 B-24Ds were lost. Three B-24s crashed into the sea. Eight B-24Ds were interned in Turkey, while 19 landed in Cyprus, Sicily and Malta. Of the 92 that returned to North Africa, 55 were battle damaged.) At least 33 Liberators were downed by *Flak* and 10 by fighters (I./JG4, IV./JG27, and Bulgarian and Rumanian units) for the loss of 10 German and 15 Romanian fighters.

destroyed. 10 Jagdflieger were killed and two were MIA. Another nine fighter pilots were injured. Two of these fighters, both of JG26, were shot down by Spitfires escorting the B-26s in the early morning attack on Woensdrecht airfield. The remaining 22 *Luftwaffe* fighters lost were all victims of the fierce dogfights with P-47s and in attacks with the B-17s. The next day, 31 July, VIII<sup>th</sup> BC announced a three-day stand-down from combat. In a week of sustained operations, about 100 aircraft and 90 combat crews had been lost.

On 12 August, 243 heavy bombers were despatched unescorted to targets in the Ruhr. Some 25 bombers were shot down. 10 of the losses were claimed by JG1, when all three *Gruppen* made contact with a formation of about 300 B-17s over the Ruhr area after intense *Flak* over Solingen had disrupted the formation. II./JG1 lost one

pilot killed and 12 fighters were damaged by return fire. Eleven other bombers lost were claimed by I. (six) and II./JG26 (five).

Over 300 bombers were sent to attack targets in Holland and France on 15 August. This was part of the *Starkey* deception plan created to make the Germans believe that an invasion of the French coast was imminent, to relieve some of the pressure on Russia and halt troop movements to Italy. Strikes against enemy airfields in France and the low countries continued on 16 August, then early that evening base operation staff throughout eastern England waited for their orders for the morrow; the anniversary mission of the 8<sup>th</sup> AF. Eaker and his planners had conceived a most ambitious and daring plan to simultaneously attack aircraft plants at Schweinfurt and Regensburg. The *Luftwaffe*'s

operational fighter strength on the western front was showing a significant increase and Regensburg was the second largest aircraft plant of its kind in Europe - the largest being at Wiener Neustadt, near Vienna. The original plan to bomb all three plants on one day, 7 August, had been disrupted by bad weather so the plan had been modified to bomb each target when the opportunity arose. On 13 August, Wiener Neustadt was bombed by B-24s of VIIIth BC and on 14 August by B-24s of the 9<sup>th</sup> AF, both forces flying from North Africa. Production at Regensburg was estimated at 200 Me 109s a month, or approximately 25 to 30 per cent of Germany's single engine aircraft production. It was estimated that the total destruction of the Regensburg plant would entail a nine month delay in production. Immediate results would be felt in operational strength, it was hoped, between one and a half to two months. The double strike was a bold move as hitherto, the campaign against the German aircraft industry had been waged within reasonable striking distance from the British mainland.

Brig-Gen Robert Williams, CO 1st BW, would lead his force to Schweinfurt while Col Curtis E LeMay would lead the 4th BW to Regensburg. To minimise attacks from enemy fighters it was decided that Le May's B-17s would fly on to North Africa after the target. The 1st BW, meanwhile, would fly a parallel course to Schweinfurt to further confuse the enemy defences and return to England after the raid. (Not enough 1st BW Fortresses were equipped with "Tokyo tanks" and could not make the 725 mile trip.) Despite the planning Eaker and his subordinates knew the B-17 crews would have a running fight on their hands but hoped that the fighter escort would keep losses down. Four P-47 groups were scheduled to escort the Regensburg force but only one group rendezvoused with the bombers as scheduled. The overburdened Thunderbolts could not possibly hope to protect all seven groups in the 4th BW. The long, straggling formation stretched for 15 miles and presented the fighter pilots with an awesome responsibility. Fortresses in the rear of the formation were left without protection at all. Fw 190s of JG1 and JG26 began their attacks 30 km east of Brussels.

In the 90 minutes preceding the bomb run, 17 Fortresses were shot down. The first Fort to go down was 42-30389 *Dear Mom* of the 331st BS, 94th BG, which went down after a frontal attack by Maj Borris, *Kommandeur*, I./JG26, crashing at Lummen, Belgium, with the loss of six of the crew. Even Bf 110 night fighters were employed to pick off stragglers: Hptm Von Bonin, *Kommandeur*, II./NJG1, and leading a vic of three Bf 110s, is known to have destroyed B-17F 42-30063 *Picklepuss* of the 100th BG, which crashed at Schmalgraf near Kelmis at 1140 hours, with the loss of six of the crew.

The 385th BG lost three bombers while others, so badly shot up, would barely make it over the treacherous snow-covered Alps. The bombing was extremely accurate

**Above:** On parade at Bassingbourn in front of *Delta Rebel No 2*. This B-17 failed to return on 12 August 1943. *USAF.*

*A*lmost disinterestedly I observed a B-17 pull out from the preceding 95th BG drop back to a position about 200ft from our right wingtip. His right 'Tokyo tanks' were on fire and had been for a half hour. Now the smoke was thicker. Flames were licking through the blackened skin of the wing. While the pilot held her steady, I saw four crew members drop out the bomb bay and execute delayed jumps. Another bailed from the nose, opened his parachute prematurely and nearly fouled the tail. Another went out the left waist gun opening, delaying his opening for a safe interval. The tail gunner dropped out of his hatch, apparently pulling the ripcord before he was clear of the ship. His parachute opened instantaneously, barely missing the tail and jerked him so hard that both his shoes came off. He hung limp in the harness whereas the others had shown immediate signs of life, shifting around in their harness. The Fortress then dropped back in a medium spiral and I did not see the pilots leave. I saw the ship though, just before it trailed from view, belly to the sky, its wing a solid sheet of yellow flame.

**I Saw Regensburg Destroyed by Lt Col Beirne Lay Jr, who flew in Lt Murphy's *Piccadilly Lily* in the 100th BG formation, as an observer on the mission. Lay was one of Gen Eaker's original seven officers.**

*A*nd then our weary, battered column, short 24 bombers, but still holding the close formation that had brought the remainder through by sheer air discipline and gunnery, turned in to the target. I knew our bombardiers were grim as death while they synchronised their sights on the great Me 109 shops lying below us in a curve of the winding blue Danube, close to the outskirts of Regensburg. Our B-17 gave a slight lift and a red light went out on the instrument panel. Our bombs were away. We turned from the target toward the snow-capped Alps. I looked back and saw a beautiful sight - a rectangular pillar of smoke from the Me 109 plant. Only one burst was over and into the town. Even from this great height I could see that we had smeared the objective. The price? Cheap. 200 airmen.'

*I Saw Regensburg Destroyed*
**by Lt Col Beirne Lay Jr.**

*W*e had to do some unescorted missions if we were going to do any bombing at all. It could be done, yes. On the first Schweinfurt mission, for instance, I flew clear across Germany without any fighter escort and destroyed a target. But you paid a price for it.

**Gen Curtis E LeMay.**

*W*e came off the target and re-grouped. I looked around at the group and there wasn't much of us left. In my squadron we started with six ships; two three-ship elements, and being in the lead ship I saw all five of them go down. Out of 18 aircraft we had six left. Lt Jeffries said, "That's the government's half, now for ours."

**Henry C Cordery, co-pilot 306<sup>th</sup> BG Schweinfurt 17 August 1943.**

**Above:** ObFw Adolf "Addi" Glunz of 4./JG26. On 17 August 1943 he shot down B-17 41-24564 *Patches* and 2/Lt Douglas Mutchler's crew of the 305<sup>th</sup> BG NW of Diest. *John Elearts via Bill Donald.*

**Below:** 2/Lt Douglas Mutchler's crew. L-R standing: 2/Lt Wendell D Luce, bombardier; 2/Lt William D Bagwell, navigator; 2/Lt Edward L Carter, co pilot (KIA); Douglas Mutchler (KIA. Kneeling: Sgt Edwin W Grundman, tail gunner; T/Sgt Anthony L Buckley right waist; Sgt Meyer Baker, left waist: T/Sgt Whitney Simon, radio operator; Sgt Carlton I Boberg, engineer (KIA). *John Elearts via Bill Donald.*

and might well have had something to do with the presence of Col LeMay, exponent of high-level bombing technique, in the first wave. Six main workshops were hit, five being severely damaged. A hangar was partially destroyed and storerooms and administrative buildings wrecked. Thirty-seven Bf 109s at dispersal were damaged if not wrecked and all production at the plant came to an abrupt halt. Although unknown at the time, by way of a bonus, the bombing had destroyed the fuselage jigs for a secret jet fighter, the Me 262.

The surviving 128 B-17s, some flying on three engines and many trailing smoke, were attacked by a few fighters on the way to the Alps. LeMay circled his formation over Lake Garda near Verona to give the cripples a chance to rejoin the wing. Red lights were showing on all four fuel tanks in every ship and it was a ragged collection of survivors which landed at intervals

up to 50 miles along the North African coast. Altogether, the 4<sup>th</sup> BW had lost 24 bombers, with the 100th BGs nine losses being the highest loss of all.

The 4<sup>th</sup> BW encountered so many fighters en route because the 1<sup>st</sup> BW had been delayed by thick inland mists for three and a half hours after the 4<sup>th</sup> BW had taken off. This effectively prevented a two-pronged assault which might have split the opposing fighter force. The delay gave the *Luftwaffe* time to refuel, re-arm and re-deploy to forward bases in Holland after dealing with the Regensburg force. 13 *Jagdgruppen* (250 fighters of JG1, JG2, JG11, JG26, ZG 26 and I./NJG1 – twice as many as against the Regensburg force) were hurled against the Schweinfurt force from the moment it crossed the mouth of the Scheldt on their way in. Attacks on the Schweinfurt force cost 36 Fortresses. III./JG1 alone was credited with 12 *Viermot* kills for the loss of five Bf 109Gs

*It was indescribable. This was the first time I had any thoughts that we were in for a fight. I will always remember the tail gunner reporting formations of B-17s flying into positions behind to protect our rear. We thought we weren't going to have the attacks on the tail like we had been getting on our last two missions. Then all of a sudden, "Oh my God!" the Germans were letting go air-to-air rockets, straight into our group. I was fortunate in that one went right past my window. The rocket landed right in the wing of the lead plane right by a gas tank. I watched it burn and it wasn't long before the entire wing was on fire. The pilot dropped back and the stricken crew bailed out. Eventually, the B-17 blew up. It was a terrible sight to see.*

**Bill Rose, pilot, 92<sup>nd</sup> BG, 1<sup>st</sup> BW, Schweinfurt 17 August 1943.**

**Right:** Bill Rose, pilot, 92<sup>nd</sup> BG. *Bill Rose.*

**Above:** The *Rüstsatz R3* or auxiliary 66 gallon (300 litre) drop tank for long-range missions, and the 21cm rocket launchers can clearly be seen in this view of a III./JG53 Bf 109G-6, in Italy early in 1944. Lt Fritz Müller, (who survived the war with 16 *Abschüsse* in III./JG53 and another six while flying the Me 262 jet fighter in III./JG7 and *Erprobungs Kommando* 262) is seen mounting the cockpit, aided by his First Mechanic on the right. Between 1942 and 1944, 23,000 aircraft were constructed of the Bf 109G 'Gustav' series, the most important of which was the G-6. *Fritz Müller via Detjens.*

*We've flown this far for Uncle Sam, from here we fly for "U.S." us.*

**Capt McLoughlin, pilot, 92nd BG, 1st BW, Schweinfurt, 17 August 1943.**

*The first Schweinfurt was a matching of excessive efforts. We, for our part, put up a maximum all-out effort in an attempt to deal the Hun a telling blow and at the same time prove to one and all the decisive nature and the viability of the daylight programme. The Germans, on the other hand, felt themselves pricked at their sensitive heartland with their major industries threatened and the morale of their population in the balance. So they put up everything they had to stop the Yankee thrust and make it so costly it would not be repeated. The result. was a mixed bag. Our effort fell far short of expectations but nonetheless achieved some of its purposes. But the losses suffered were certainly unbearable and could not be borne by us on a sustained basis.*

**Col Maurice 'Mo' Preston, CO, 379th BG, who led the 103rd Provisional Combat Wing, to Schweinfurt, 17 August 1943.**

**Above:** A lone B-17 of the 381st BG making its way home. *USAF.*

(four pilots were severely injured). Worst hit B-17 groups were the 381st and 91st, which lost 11 and 10 B-17s respectively. The 91st led the 1st BW strike on Schweinfurt with Lt Col Clemens L Wurzbach, the CO, and Col Cross of Wing HQ, flying lead in *Oklahoma Oakie*. Brig-Gen Robert B Williams, the Task Force commander, also flew in the 91st formation. 27 B-17s in the 1st BW were so badly damaged that they never flew again.

Altogether, 60 B-17s were MIA (almost three times as high as the previous highest, on 13 June, when 26 bombers were lost). A further 60 Fortresses had to be left in North Africa pending repairs, so in the final analysis 147 Fortresses had been lost to all causes on 17 August. The *Luftwaffe* lost 27 fighters on 17 August, as against claims by the B-17 gunners and escorting fighters of 288 German fighters destroyed! The almost non-existent maintenance facilities in North Africa ruled out any further shuttle missions. Gen LeMay and the 4th BW earned the following accolade from Gen Frederick

*My crew and I were now 10 nervous wrecks and we didn't sleep much that night. In fact we slept fitfully for about the next year. Nightmares continued most nights until 1945. The battle has affected everyone, myself included, morally and in other ways, for the rest of our lives. Like the terrible battles of World War One, when 24,000 men could be, and were lost on a single day, the nightmare would not and never will go away.'*

**Bill Rose, pilot, 92nd BG, Schweinfurt 17 August 1943.**

L. Anderson at Wing Headquarters, Elveden Hall; *Congratulations on the completion of an epoch in aerial warfare. I am sure the Fourth Bombardment Wing has continued to make history. The Hun now has no place to hide.*

The heavies were stood down on 18 August, while 54 B-26 Marauders of the 322nd and 386th BGs were despatched, to targets in Belgium and Holland. 32 out of a formation of 36 386th BG Marauders successfully bombed Woensdrecht at 1032 hours without loss. This forward fighter base was largely destroyed in another B-26 raid, by the 386th and 387th BGs, on 3 October 1943, and again, by the 387th BG on 9 October. Due to the persistent Allied raids against coastal fighter bases like Woensdrecht, Schiphol and similar airfields in Belgium and France, the *Luftwaffe* abandoned the use of these forward fields by the end of 1943, thus losing their vital ability to respond early to incoming forces of Allied bombers bound for the Reich.

The Fortresses' stand down meanwhile, was brief, as on 19 August, 125 B-17s of the 1st BW were despatched to bomb the airfields at Gilze-Rijen and

Flushing, while 45 Fortresses of the 4th BW were sent to bomb the airfield at Woensdrecht. None of the force briefed to bomb Woensdrecht was able to bomb because of bad weather over the target and one B-17 was lost. Some ninety-three B-17s of the 1st BW force, however, were successful at their targets. 38 B-17s bombed Gilze-Rijen between 1802 and 1814 hours, while 55 Fortresses bombed Flushing at 1756 hours. Four 1st BW B-17s were lost - three of which were claimed by JG26, which had a tough time fending off Spitfires (10 squadrons of Spitfires were airborne this day) and Typhoons which were airborne to protect B-25s and B-26s attacking Amiens and Poix, and, later, the Fortress formations attacking the Dutch airfields. The B-17s were also supported by a force of 175 Thunderbolts, the P-47s of the 4th and 78th FGs being used as penetration support and the Thunderbolts of the 56th and 353rd FGs, serving as the withdrawal support.

P-47s and Spitfires shot down three of JG26's fighters, while one Fw 190A-4 crashed out of fuel, and two Bf

*Above:* The wartime grave of Maj Wilhelm-Ferdinand 'Wutz' Galland, *Kommandeur*, II./JG26, who was killed in a surprise attack by Capt Walker 'Bud' Mahurin of the 56th FG west of Maastricht on 17 August 1943. At the time of his death, 'Wutz' had flown 186 combat sorties, during which he had accumulated 55 victories, including eight American *Viermots* and 37 Spitfires. Two months prior to his death, Maj Galland had been awarded the *Ritterkreuz*. *Otto H Fries.*

*Above:* An almost daily sight from 1943 onwards: vapour trails of American bomber boxes heading into the hostile skies over the Third Reich stand out against a clear blue sky over the Friesian Island of Terschelling. Note the *Freya* early warning radar to the right of the lighthouse, which formed part of 'Tiger', the *Himmelbett* GCI night-fighting station on the island. *'t Behouden Huys.*

109Gs were shot down by return fire from the B-17s attacking Gilze-Rijen and Flushing. Oberst "Pips" Priller, CO of the *Geschwader* and OFw Grunlinger, each claimed a 305th BG B-17 but it is possible that these were one and the same aircraft as the Chelveston group lost one B-17 (42-29807 *Lady Liberty*, flown by Lt Ralph R Miller of the 364th BS, with eight crew KIA and two taken prisoner) this day. Hptm Mietusch III./JG26 CO, was credited with a 303rd BG Fortress north-west of Breda. The 303rd BG lost two B-17s. 42-3192 *City of Albuquerque*, flown by Lt James Nix of the 358th BS, crashed at Raamsdonkveer in Holland, with the loss of four crew. 42-5392 *Stric Nine* of the 427th BS, flown by 2/Lt Lauren H Quillen, crashed into the North Sea with the loss of six crew. Uffz E Schwartz of 8./JG26 claimed a B-17 of the 388th BG but it was not confirmed. In fact B-17F 42-30068, flown by 2/Lt B Howe, was hit by *Flak* which set his No. 4 engine on fire and he dropped out of formation. He was then attacked by enemy fighters near Haamstede and went down.

The Schweinfurt losses were still having a mighty effect on the B-17 groups and for three days no Fortress

missions were flown. Then, on 24 August 110 B-17s of the 1st BW were sent to Villacoublay airfield, with a dozen more B-17s flying a diversion. The 4th BW put up 42 B-17s for a raid on other airfields. Some 166 P-47s flew escort and only one bomber was lost on the day's missions. The Jugs claimed six enemy fighters for no loss to themselves. The Fortresses were out again on 27 August, when 224 B-17s were sent out on the first of the raids against V-weapon sites and 187 B-17s got their bombs away on Watten. The heavies were escorted by 173 Thunderbolts, one of which was lost while they claimed eight enemy fighters shot down. Four B-17s were lost. A 92nd BG B-17 came down in the sea and the crew was rescued. The 303rd and 305th BGs each lost one B-17 apiece, while *Fast Woman*, a 508th BS, 351st BG Fortress, piloted by Lt William A Suit, was shot down by Oblt Walter Matoni of 5./JG26 3km north-west of Dunkirk. *Fast Woman* crashed at St Omer. OFw. Addi Glunz of 4./JG26, was credited with shooting down *Augerhead*, piloted by Lt William Monahan of the 303rd BG, four days later during the raid on Amiens-Glisy airfield. Two other B-17s of the 91st BG also

failed to return.

Shallow penetration raids remained the order of the day for the B-17 groups throughout September as VIIIth BC was not yet strong enough to mount raids deep into the Reich. On 2 September, airfields in north-western France were bombed. During the morning of 3 September the heavies pounded Romilly-sur-Seine and other targets in France. JG2 attacked the Fortresses of the 4th Wing near Paris and before the IP two JG26 *Gruppen* singled out the 1st BW targeting Romilly. North of Paris Lt Helmut Hoppe, 4th *Staffel* CO, made a head-on attack against a 92nd BG B-17. 2/Lt Ralph Brule's Fortress in the 407th BS pulled away from the formation and went down. Four crew were captured while six evaded. The 1st BW lost three more B-17s, OFw Addi Glunz claiming one of them east

*I*t's a remarkable thing what goes through your mind when you bail out. I recalled the time I had signed on at 17. My mother had been very upset and had said, "You'll probably end up getting shot down." I also thought about my friend Curtis, who belonged to a fighter group near London. We were going to meet that coming weekend for a birthday party for an English friend at High Wycombe. I drifted down, heading for a little town. I had seen some German parachutists who had bailed out over London and they had slammed into the sides of buildings. I thought how ironic it would be if I did the same, in this, a small town of only about 30 buildings. There was little I could do but I was glad that I wasn't heading into the water. As it turned out, I came right over the top of the buildings and landed on a "kwelder" behind a dyke near Ouderdom. I had missed landing in the water by only a hundred feet. It was raining at the time but my appearance did not bother five contented cows, which looked up once and then continued grazing! I noticed a group of people coming towards me. I got out of my parachute, gathered it together, and walked over to meet them. One of the group was a policemen so I raised my arms to show I had no weapons. I handed over my parachute to the civilians and gave away my escape and emergency ration kits. One of the Dutch people later made a wedding dress from my parachute and another used part of it for a christening robe. I asked a young Dutch lad about half my age if there was any chance of escape. He said the area was heavily defended and the Germans would arrive shortly. The Germans lost no time in getting to the scene. I was taken to the café of Jan van der Laan and taken prisoner. It was quite a shock to have a fully fledged German officer walk up to me brandishing a .38 pistol in my stomach and my blood turned to water.

**Orlo Natvig, radio operator, *Local Girl*, 91st BG, shot down at Geefsweer, northern Holland by a Bf 109 after a raid on Emden, 27 September 1943. 2/Lt William G Peagram, pilot, remained at the controls while eight crew bailed out over the coast near The Ems River. Peagram and Melvin Peters, waist gunner, who went on firing to the end, were found dead in the wreckage. Larson, engineer, and Cosgrove, navigator, drowned when the cords of their parachutes became entangled in the "botschuttings" or "flounder fences"; a device of twigs and branches to catch flat fish. Norman Eatinger, bombardier, was rescued by a Dutch fishing boat.**

**Left:** A German soldier and local Groningers pose by the wreck of B-17F 42-3111 *Local Girl*, 324th BS, 91st BG, came under Bf 109 attack and exploded over Geefsweer village, in Groningen Province after returning from a raid on Emden 27 September 1943. Lt Bill Pegram and three of his crew perished. *Pieter Bergman.*

**Below:** German soldiers and two Dutch policemen, van Klaveren (left) and Max van Diederhoven, inspect ammunition clips from *Local Girl. Ab A Jansen.*

**Above:** Two elderly German soldiers guard the cockpit area of *Local Girl* at Geefsweer, 28 September 1943, the day after the Fortress exploded over eastern Groningen. *Ab A Jansen.*

**Above:** Two Me 410s (9K+Vv and 9K+Ww) of *Erg. (Ergänzungs) Gruppe* KG51 *(Jagd)* flying in close formation. Note the clearly outlined rearward-firing gun blisters, and the red/yellow *Reichsverteidigung* band around the rear fuselage. *Lorant via Punka*.

of Paris and Fw Mayer claiming another near Melun airfield. Their victims were either 381st BG or 384th BG machines.

At the end of September 1943, apart from the single-engined Bf 109 and Fw 190 day fighters, B-17 and B-24 crews now faced over 150 Bf 110Gs and Me 410A-1/B-1s in five *Zerstörergruppen*. The P-47D, with the installation of a 108 gallon belly tank, could escort the bombers as far as Duren on 4 October when 282 bombers hit Frankfurt, Wiesbaden, and Saarbrucken. The P-47s helped keep losses down to 12 B-17s. However, on 8 October, when more than 350 bombers attacked Bremen and Vegesack again, the several attempts to reduce the effectiveness of the *Jagdgruppen* in north-western Germany failed. A diversion mission by 55 B-24s to Vegesack was flown and the 1st and 3rd BWs approached Bremen from two different directions in an attempt to fool the German controllers. However,

**Right:** This Bf 110 F or G packed a hard punch with an auxiliary gun pack fitted under its belly for combating the American bomber Pulks. Coded M1, the pack contained two MG 151 20m cannon.Japo.

War was raging on all fronts and for the German Wehrmacht there were shortages everywhere. My fighter unit, II./JG3 'Udet', was based north of Taganrog on the Sea of Azov. In Hamburg, after highly effective 'windowing' by the RAF to confuse the night fighter radar, it had rained phosphor for the first time - which had been predicted by no weather forecast. A number of fighter units was hastily transferred from the east to the west as a kind of 'flying fire brigade'. We also were part of these units and we were not particularly pleased about it, for that which confronted us in the west was a combination of material quality, flying skill and -numbers. In short, there it meant biting into wholemeal bread!

After re-equipment of the Gruppe with new aircraft (from Me 109 G2 to G4 and G6 which, instead of the light 'squirters' with calibre 7,65, now had 13mm guns mounted over the engine – which did not improve their flying quality due to the bulges on the fuselage – they in fact had the opposite effect), our unit was transferred from Uetersen/Schleswig-Holstein to Schiphol. A beautiful airfield with all mod-cons, comfortable quarters for the three Staffeln and private accommodation (partly with Dutch families). So far a spring-like life without end after the spartan conditions on the Russian front. But the snag was the reason of our sojourn in the hospitable Holland.

In Russia we had been accustomed to throw ourselves with gusto at the rear of any formation of the Ivans and to help ourselves as independent hunters. At first we thought it would be similar here in the west - and lost quite a few feathers in the process. The 'Fat Cars' (Luftwaffe slang for four-engined Allied bombers) flew nicely in formation, making their firepower almost impenetrable. Our stout Gruppe had soon shrunk to the size of a strong Staffel. Soon we attacked the 'Fat Cars' only from head-on, which meant of course that the chances of scoring hits were reduced considerably for both sides. In any case, operations in the west for German fighters soon became sacrificial journeys. Mistakes by the leadership and weather conditions, as well as the limited range of our worthy Me 109s, turned out to be fatal over Holland, that land of damp and frequently inclement weather.

One morning, on 18 October 1943, a thin layer of low cloud began to form over Schiphol when suddenly all three Staffel, including the staff flight (in other words

We are currently based in Holland near Amsterdam. At first, we assumed that there was little trade for us here, but lately we have been flying and fighting so hard that a couple of days leave wouldn't do us any harm. Flying here in the Channel zone is a completely different thing than the enjoyable days we had in Russia. All of us would readily go back. Life really was better there. I had managed a few kills in Russia already, whereas over here, one gets shot down. Whereas the flying there was more or less leisurely, with us seeking out the combat and having more freedom of tactics, I readily compare the flying here with the way infantrymen attack. Unwaveringly, we commit to the attack in our birds, despite the defensive fire that is hurled at us in great quantity and might. We usually encounter four-engined bombers, the first time I saw these beasts, I was flabbergasted. In neater formations than one sees at the Reichs Party Days, they crossed the skies over Germany undisturbed. We poor little devils can achieve so little against them and are often filled with unbounded anger, when we can't hit them decisively. In the few weeks we have now been here in the West, we have suffered severe losses. My Chief has been shot down twice already. The Tommy is not only superior in numbers, but also in quality. So, against these odds, we are in a difficult position. I managed to shoot down a Thunderbolt, and the day before yesterday, I knocked down a Viermot, but unfortunately without any witnesses to confirm my claim. I therefore doubt if I will get this Boeing Fortress II confirmed. Getting at these big 'mills' at all is damn hard, due to the fabulous defensive fire they pour at you. Well, we'll rock this baby anyway.

**Uffz Uwe Micheels, II./JG3, 6th *Staffel*, at Schiphol, writing to his brother Jürgen on 8 October 1943. Uwe Micheels was KIA 10 days later, 18 October.**

*Right:* B-17s of the 388th BG crossing Bremen on 8 October 1943. The target is obscured by smoke pots. *USAF.*

these ruses and feints, and the use of airborne *Carpet* radar jammers aboard some of the B-17s for the first time, were not enough to prevent the loss of 27 B-17s and three B-24s. P-47s, before they had to return, low on fuel, took on Geschwaderstab JG1 over Nordhorn and accounted for Geschwaderkommodore Maj Hans Philipp, a 206 victory ace Oberst Walter Oesau, previously Jagdfliegerführer 4 Brittany, and forbidden to fly operationally, assumed command two days later. Oesau, in turn, was KIA on 11 May 1944.

On 9 October, 352 B-17s and B-24s attacked targets in East Prussia and Poland in its longest mission to date. 28 bombers failed to return. Next day, 10 October, 274 B-17s set out on a direct course for Münster, with 39 Liberators flying a diversion. The B-17s' direct route was planned so that the 216 P-47s could escort the bombers all the way to the target. However, when the 352nd FG turned back as planned at 1148 hours, their place, which should have been taken by the 355th FG, went unfilled as the latter group remained fog-bound in England. At 1453 hours, just nine minutes from the

*Above:* March 1944 and the strain of continuous combat is clearly visible in Oberst Walter "Gulle" Oesau's face. Oesau had shot down 10 aircraft in Spain and was the third German pilot to reach 100 victories, 26 October 1941. After a brief spell on the Eastern Front, he had returned to the West to lead JG2 and on 10 October 1943, JG1. Oesau was one of the *Jagdwaffe*'s most experienced fighter leaders when he was shot down and killed in air combat with P-38 Lightnings to the south-west of St Vith, Belgium on 11 May 1944 in his Bf 109G-6. At the time of his death, his score stood at 127 aerial victories, including 14 *Viermots*. He was one of the men the *Reichsverteidigung* could ill afford to lose at this crucial stage of the war. *Helmut Conradi.*

the entire Gruppe)were ordered to take off. The last ones only just managed to get off the ground and the assembly became a problem because of the increasing fog. Well, with some difficulty we managed to form up and the fighter controller in Deelen (beneath more than a metre of reinforced concrete) directed us 'most strategically' northward over the good old North Sea towards a supposedly plotted US bomber formation of B-24 Liberators, which in spite of a long search we never found. Time passed and our tanks got emptier. Auxiliary tanks (drop-shaped below the fuselage) had long been requested - but had not yet turned up. Having achieved nothing, we were soon forced to turn back towards the coast and the picture which presented itself to us there was anything but encouraging. All of Holland, Belgium and northern Germany were covered in a continuous sheet of low cloud. As we crossed the coast according to our calculated timing, the red lamp (fuel warning: maximum remaining fuel for 20 minutes) had come on in almost all the aircraft. That can turn out to be fun! And it did, too.

Penetrating that in formation would be catastrophic. So the Staffel commanders decided to give the pilots a free hand in the means of finding their way back to mother earth or, as a last consequence, to use their parachutes. What then occurred bordered onto despair, for no one was inclined to abandon his aircraft and bail out. As already remarked, some 10 minutes of the red light and no sign of mother earth! So throttle closed and a first attempt to penetrate the clouds. Instrument flight down to zero on the altimeter. I had a horrid feeling in the pit of my stomach; I would have preferred the worst of dogfights! Ease open the throttle and up out of the murk. Then again in another place where the clouds were a little lower, down in another attempt to get sight of the ground. Again at altimeter indication zero up and, close to despair a final attempt. Now I was determined: either down to ground contact (including the possibility of a crash) or up again and the undesired bailing out.

The altimeter was already just below zero - when suddenly a cow rushed past my port wing. I was through - ceiling between 10 and 15m! To my left a hill with houses, of which only the lowest were visible. Everything else completely flat. My engine was still running and with sight of the ground my normal attitude to life returned. White dots were visible on the completely flat plain. I assumed them to be stones and thought the ground would be firm. That was my mistake. I wanted to land my aircraft without damage and extended the undercarriage. To be on the safe side I landed not far from the houses. It turned out to be a landing like on raw eggs and I already thought to have saved my aircraft, when suddenly the undercarriage collapsed and the 109 made an elegant somersault. at which the fuselage broke off just aft of the cockpit. Complete silence about me. There I was, upside down and hanging in my straps. First thought: does it or doesn't it catch fire. It didn't, and that is why I can now write this account.

After about 20 minutes there was a knock on the cockpit window and I was asked how I was, to which I replied that I had fared better. They were two soldiers from the air signals unit on the island of Urk. A doctor followed them who asked in the North German dialect if I was wounded. "No, I am not, but get me down from here," I replied in like jargon. The Me 109 weighs three or four tons and help was required to move this weight. After an hour enough had collected and I was dragged out into the fresh air. The assumed stones turned out to be mussels, mussels of the shallows around Urk. And mussels lie on soft ground. A belly-landing would have been much more elegant.

Followed by spectators, the signallers took me to their quarters and Amsterdam-Schiphol was informed. In the evening, some sweet Urk maidens consoled me about my misfortune. A Boeing B-17 lay in the shallows. We inspected the big ship and I made comparisons between the armament of the American bomber and that of our Ju 88 or He 111. That made me thoughtful. How were we to confront the like in the long run? And that was only the beginning.

The following day a Fieseler Storch of the fighter Gruppe at Schiphol picked me up. We flew to Groningen where a comrade who had not fared so well lay in hospital. Result. of the grandiose effort: Three total losses, two wounded and only one had landed by pure chance on an airfield. And all that without contact with the enemy. A total success for the other side!

**Lt Gerhard Thyben, pilot, 6./JG3 autumn 1943. Thyben survived the war as *Ritterkreuzträger* with oak leaves with 157 *Abschüsse*.**

*S*ince two months I am on operations with the 9th Staffel of Jagdgeschwader 54 Grünherz (Green Heart). We fly the Me 109G-6 which is equipped with four guns. We are stationed in Schwerin. This morning we flew with two Me 109s to Gardelegen with special orders to operate from there whenever an enemy reconnaissance aircraft is reported. Gardelegen is 130km west of Berlin. We had taken off on such a mission on 8 October at 1453. Uffz Erich Kolodzie (we call him Gandhi) is my section leader, I am still the new one. In my eight weeks on operations I have still not experienced contact with an enemy. Gandhi takes account of my inexperience and shows me all the tricks. The most important is: To see! One has to spot the smallest speck in the sky at once, however far away it is. It will grow quickly and then open fire.

I remain at his side whatever our manoeuvres and our eyes scan the sky without pause. We are seeking a single aircraft, the reconnaissance one, which is to photograph the results after a bombing raid. It could be a Spitfire or a Mosquito. We have good weather, clear visibility, only occasional fair weather clouds. Since the beginning of October enemy air activity is increasing, which had been impossible during September due to bad weather. Apart from us two, a section (two aircraft) of Me 109s had taken off from two other airfields, because one could never know the route of the reconnaissance aircraft beforehand. We know his probable target, but not the route he would take.

We had flown on a westerly course from Gardelegen, climbing to 6000m height. It is important to remain below the condensation level in order not to be spotted by the enemy. Above a certain level the engine exhausts turn to ice, these are called condensation trails. That commences at varying levels, depending on weather conditions. Absolute radio silence has been ordered for this flight because the enemy monitors our frequencies. Using the radio emissions he can then fix our position. There is a wonderful silence in our earphones. But only superficially, our nerves are tense. We are dependent entirely on ourselves, on our eyes. Unceasingly we search the airspace around us, over, below, to all sides.

Now - - - today we were unable to catch the reconnaissance aircraft, but for me there is an unforgettable experience yet to come. Our westerly course has taken us over Holland, close to Amsterdam. For a moment I think back to Schiphol, the airfield of Amsterdam. Until the middle of August we had been stationed there and had then been moved to Schwerin. Everyone of course has his own memories of such a time. But I was suddenly wrenched out of my dreams: In front of me I can clearly see a four-engined B 17. We follow it. For the first time I see an enemy aircraft in the sky. Seconds later Gandhi flips over on his back and dives steeply downward. I follow at his side. At 1610 we land at Bergen/Holland. While our aircraft are being refuelled for our return to Schwerin I have but one question for Gandhi: 'Why did you not shoot the Boeing down?' Gandhi, in his quiet, merry way replied grinning: 'Which one?' 'Didn't you see him, we were very close?' 'Correct, the first one was huge. The three beside him were a little further off, in front of them 20 Boeings and high above us about 20 Spitfires.' I am still the "new one" and have much to learn, especially: To see.

**Fw Fritz Ungar, *Jagdflieger*, IV./JG54/26 1943-45, recalling one of the sorties early in his flying career, 8 October 1943.**

***Above:*** Fw Helmut Notemann of II./JG3 at Schiphol airfield in October 1943, posing for the camera in full flying gear on his Bf 109G-6, ready to be scrambled. *Helmut Henning via Rob de Visser.*

*T*his was the most frightening of all the missions I flew. I still get scared and have weird dreams about that day. We did not have complete air supremacy and our fighters did not yet have long-range belly tanks. They could not follow us on long-range missions. We lost eight out of 19 aircraft. The Flak was unbelievable and the Luftwaffe must have had every one of their planes attacking us. The loss of so many friends was overwhelming. I got a '109 and it went down smoking and burning.

**Gus Mencow, lead navigator, 520th BS, 390th BG, Münster, 10 October 1943.**

target, the fighter attacks began. First to attack were the single-engined fighters, which paused only when the *Flak* opened up at the approach to the target. They resumed their attacks again after the *Zerstörer* waded in with rocket attacks to add to the carnage. Worst hit were the unlucky 13th Wing comprising the 95th, 100th and 390th BG. It took just seven minutes to tear the 'Bloody Hundredth' formation apart, losing a dozen B-17s, while the 390th lost eight out of 19 despatched, and five out of the 20 95th BG B-17s despatched also failed to return.

12 B-17s were claimed by JG26, seven of which were confirmed. Only the intervention of the 56th FG prevented further losses. Lt Robert Johnson destroyed two fighters to become an ace and was joined by Maj David Schilling and by Capt Walter Beckham of the 353rd, both of which downed their fifth fighters on this mission. In all, 30 B-17s were either shot down or written off in crashes. 14 were claimed shot down by JG1 and 11, with another eight *Herausschüsse* and two P-47s shot down, one by Oblt Knoke - his 18th victory. The Americans claimed 180 fighters shot down, 105 claims being submitted by the 13th Wing alone. (The *Luftwaffe* had lost 25 fighters, including three JG26 fighters, nine Bf 110s and Me 410s, and seven Fw 190s and Bf 109s of JG1, with four pilots killed in this *Geschwader*.)

No bomber missions were flown between 11 and 13 October. On the afternoon of 13 October, Maj Gen Frederick L Anderson, Commanding General, VIIIth BC, and his senior staff officers, gathered at High Wycombe for the daily Operations' Conference. On 1 October 1943, British Intelligence sources had estimated that despite round-the-clock bombing of aircraft factories and component plants, the *Luftwaffe* had a first-line strength of some 1,525 single- and twin-engined fighters for the defence of the western approaches to Germany. American sources put the figure at around 1,100 operational fighters. In reality, the *Luftwaffe* could call upon 1,646 single and twin-engined fighters for the defence of the Reich; 400 more than before the issue of the *Pointblank* directive, although

*You know, every time we take off on a combat mission, it is with mixed feelings, because it never turns out to be a pleasure trip. It is so depressing when one realises that our 'comrades from the other side' are far superior to oneself, and to know that when one engages the Viermots, sooner or later one gets shot down. During the only short period we've been here, our Staffel has already lost two pilots killed and two wounded. One had a hand shot clean off and from the other he lost a couple of fingers. The second injured pilot lost an eye. So, our Staffel, nominally on strength with 12 planes, has only four or five serviceable kites left. In the beginning, the Gruppe operated with 30 to 35 machines. Nowadays, only 10 to 15 can be scrambled at any one time.*

*On the other hand, we have gained fame here on the Channel coast. Not a single Gruppe has chalked up such great combat results in this theatre, and such a thing simply is impossible without incurring losses. All this results in our frame of mind being that of a lost bunch. We call ourselves the 'Last Knights' and indeed, it is a great thing to see how everyone gets at our adversary and fires doggedly. I do admire my 'Chief', who has already been shot down twice here, who almost always gets back to base with his machine shot up and still rushes in and, with his thick Westphalian skull, approaches his adversary to point blank range to make sure of the kill. One can only say, 'Hats off'. I am always satisfied with the hits I register and then make it back home. I must add that there is no choice but to get at them regardless of own losses, in an effort to prevent them from wreaking more destruction than they already do. One feels so impotent and can only watch powerless when facing such an opponent. In Russia, we would have completely destroyed any formation. Over here, any formation destroys us. How can you win! Sometimes, I fly as Schwarm (Flight) leader. That usually is the task of a very experienced pilot, but one has to have this first. I am responsible for the safety of three men, who I lead into combat behind me. How could I ever do that? A hundred or more enemy aircraft in the sky (I am not exaggerating) and I should cover my 4th man's tail? Only the other day, my wingman got shot down. You know, the most sacred commitment for a flight leader is the one to his wingman. I am hanging in the middle of a Pulk with my men behind me, enemy fighters appear, I look around and see my wingman, but no angry enemy. When I finally believe to have got away reasonably unscathed, my wingman is gone. I assume he has fled from the scene one way or the other, but when I touch down at base some time later, he is missing. Only that night, whilst I have been reproaching myself severely, one reports that he is in hospital in Aachen. The poor fellow's eye has been removed. Things like that easily get on one's nerves.*

*Tonight, we will celebrate 'Daddy's' birthday, 'Daddy' is our boss. There's only five of us pilots left now. Didn't we have a great time in the early days in Russia when there were still 16 of us. When I think of it, I feel tears welling up in my eyes. I never write such letters, but I have to get these thoughts off my chest and you are the only one I can confide in. Here, we don't discuss such things. The boss only talks about it in ruthless jokes, obviously trying to suppress his weaker side and his compassion. Still, he can't hide the fact that it has made a deep impression on him too, today he turned 27, but looks 37. It is a privilege to meet such men, who make one keen to get on with the job and who one admires.*

*But isn't being a fighter pilot a great thing! Speedily dashing through the skies and then plunging into the action. My dear, it makes one's heart shout with joy! Sometimes, it also trembles, but only occasionally. Do you know the saying: "Enjoy the war, because the coming Peace will be dreadful!" Every day, we repeat this with a sadistic pleasure. The boss is very good at it, which helps him to keep his bunch of men together as best he can.*

**Uffz Uwe Micheels, fighter pilot, II./JG3, 6th *Staffel*, at Schiphol, writing to his girlfriend Ilse, 11 October 1943. He was KIA one week later.**

**Below:** Gus Mencow (third from right), lead navigator, 520th BS, 390th BG, Schweinfurt, 14 October 1943.

**Above:** B-17Fs of the 91st BG at Bombs Away. The B-17 bottom left is 42-5714 which failed to return with 2/Lt Robert M Slane's crew on 14 October 1943. The aircraft crashed at Nancy, France, Eight men were made PoW, one evaded, and one was KIA. *USAF.*

*We got 15 planes over Schweinfurt. One was lost to a combination of Flak and fighters. Other groups did not fare so well. The Flak was extremely thick but fortunately the Luftwaffe concentrated on other groups. When we got back to base and learned of the high losses it turned out to be a sad day. The week was just too much for all of us and Schweinfurt put the finishing touch. We felt convinced that getting through the war was impossible but somehow we carried on.*

**Gus Mencow, lead navigator, 520th BS, 390th BG, Schweinfurt, 14 October 1943.**

only about a third of this force was ready for immediate use, the remainder being reserves or temporarily unserviceable. The Allies' figures confirmed their worst fears. The decision was taken therefore to attack the ball bearing plant at Schweinfurt for the second time in three months to deliver a single, decisive blow against the German aircraft industry and stem the flow of fighters to the *Luftwaffe*. Mission. No. 115, to Schweinfurt, went ahead on 14 October. Anderson hoped to launch 420 Fortresses and Liberators in a three-pronged attack on the city of Schweinfurt but the weather and aborts took their toll even before the bombers reached the continent. Of the 60 Liberators scheduled to make the mission, only 29 succeeded in forming up and these were redirected on a diversion towards Bremen. Ultimately,

of 320 B-17s and B-24s dispatched to Schweinfurt, only 229 were effective.

Schweinfurt soaked up 482.8 tons of high explosives and incendiaries but losses were high. The 1st BD lost 45 B-17s and the 3rd BD lost 15 Fortresses. Worst hit of all the groups was the 305th BG, which lost 13 of 18 despatched. Maj Johannes Seifert, Kommandeur, II./JG26, shot down 42-29952 at Limmel, Maastricht, with the loss of five of the crew. At least six other 305th BG B-17s were shot down by Fw 190s of I./JG1, over the Dutch-German border, and by Bf 109s and Fw 190s of II. And III./JG1. Next highest loss was the 306th BG, with 10. The 92nd BG lost six and a seventh was written off in a crash-landing at Aldermaston. The 379th and 384th BGs each lost six B-17s in combat and three crews from the latter group had to abandon their aircraft over England, making nine in all. The 303rd BG lost two aircraft, including one which crash-landed after the

crew had bailed out near Riseley. The 91st, 351st and 381st BGs each lost one B-17. In the 3rd BD the 96th BG lost seven, the 94th six and the 95th and 390th, one apiece. The 100th, 385th and 388th BGs suffered no loss. Of the bombers returned to England, 142 in both divisions were damaged as a result of fighter attacks and holed by *Flak*. Sixty Fortresses and 600 men were missing. Five B-17s had crashed in England as a result of their battle-damaged condition and 12 more were destroyed in crash-landings or so badly damaged that they had to be written off. Of the returning bombers,

121 required repairs and another five fatal casualties and 43 wounded crewmen were removed from the aircraft. The losses were softened by claims of 186 enemy fighters shot down (the actual figure was about 35).

However, only 88 out of the 1,222 bombs dropped, actually fell on the plants. Production of the Kugelfischer plant, largest of the five plants, was interrupted for only six weeks and the German war machine never lacked for ball bearings throughout the remainder of the war. As in many other German

*Above:* B-17s of the 306th BG weave through heavy *Flak* over Schweinfurt on 14 October 1943. The Group lost 10 Fortresses, second highest loss in the 1st BG. *Richards.*

industries dispersal of factories ensured survival for the German ball bearing industry and careful husbanding of resources meant that some forms of machinery needed less or no ball bearings at all. Four days after the raid, Gen 'Hap' Arnold confidently told gathered pressmen: *Now we have got Schweinfurt!* However, the bombers had to return to Schweinfurt again and again before the end of hostilities. It was only when the city was finally overrun by US armoured divisions that America could at last confirm that it had 'got Schweinfurt.' In recognition of the heavy losses and the 305th in particular, the "Rainbow Division" presented the German flag, captured at the Kugelfischer plant, to the group at Chelveston shortly before it returned Stateside.

---

*The entire works are now inactive. It may be possible for the Germans to eventually restore 25% of normal capacity, but even that will require some time*

**Brig-Gen Orvil A Anderson, Chairman of the Combined Operational Planning Committee.**

---

*The Schweinfurt raid may well go down in history as one of the decisive air actions of the war and it may prove to have saved countless lives by depriving the enemy of a great part of his means of resistance.*

**British Chief of the Air Staff, Air Marshal Sir Charles Portal.**

# *Chapter 4* – **Reichsverteidigung**

The losses and a spell of bad weather restricted VIIIth BC to just two more missions in October. One of these, on 20 October, when 212 B-17s bombed Duren and Woensdrecht airfield, nine B-17s were lost. Four were claimed by JG26. ObstLt "Pips" Priller claimed a 96th BG B-17 south-east of Arras-Cambrai and Lt E Burkert of 9./JG26 claimed a second 96th BG B-17. B-17F 42-3439 piloted by 2/Lt Charles F Gerger of the 413th BS, crashed 3km south-east of Utrecht, Holland, in the village of De Bilt – with the loss of five crew. Gerger and three others were captured while one man evaded. *Shack Rabbit II*, flown by 2/Lt Robert E. Grimes and crew of the 339th BS, on only their fifth mission, crashed 3km south of Venray, southern Holland – with the loss of four of the crew. Grimes and the bombardier evaded, while four men were captured. Hptm Peter-Paul Steindl and Hptm Klaus Mietusch III./JG26 CO, each claimed a 358th BS, 303rd BG B-17. *Charlie Horse* flown by 2/Lt William R Hartigan, and 41-24629, flown by Lt John W Hendry Jr, both

**Below:** Frank Walls poses in his co-pilot's window of *Shack Bunny*, 551st BS, 385th BG. This B-17F and Lt Lyle V Fryer's crew, was lost over France on 20 October 1943 on the mission to Duren, Germany. All the crew were PoW. *William Nicholls.*

*Those Schweinfurt missions were unbelievable. I know that I was fortunate enough to receive the Medal of Honor for 15 minutes of fighting, over Ploesti and they fought for about five hours over Schweinfurt. I don't remember anyone getting a Medal of Honor out of that. I think that I would rather do five Ploesti raids than one Schweinfurt.*

**Gen Leon W Johnson, who earned the MoH for his leadership of the 44th BG at Ploesti on 1 August 1943. The medal was presented at a ceremony at Shipdham on 22 November 1943, by which time he commanded the 14th CBW.** *USAF.*

crashed at Cambrai. Three men in Hartigan's crew evaded, six were captured and one was KIA. Within Hendry's crew, eight men were captured and two KIA.

After Schweinfurt, desperate attempts were made to improve the range of the few Thunderbolts in the ETO. The 200 gallon flush ferry tank provided for the early P-47C and D models was unsuitable for combat and there were not enough 75 gallon drop tanks available. A British-made 108-gallon tank made of pressed paper could be used under the fuselage or two could be fitted beneath the wings, increasing radius of action to 350 and 445 miles respectively. The tanks, first used on 12 August, caused a number of problems, including the inability of an aircraft with tanks attached to climb above 20,000ft. In 1942 the 8th AF had lost all its P-38 Lightnings when they went to North Africa with the 12th AF. The decision must have been bitterly regretted for it was not until 15 October, the day following the Schweinfurt disaster, that the Lightning re-entered combat in England when the 55th FG at Nuthampstead became operational on the P-38H. The 'H' had a combat radius of 400 miles. During early November 1943 individual squadrons of the 20th FG, which had been busy working up on the P-38H at King's Cliffe since August, flew missions as a fourth squadron in the 55th. They would not fly their first full Group mission until 28 December 1943. Eaker knew that his deep penetration missions were finished without a proven long-range escort fighter. *At this point nothing was more critical than the early arrival of the P-38s and P-51s,* he said. The P-38 Lightning was not the total solution for long-range fighter escort duties. That would only come

with the introduction of the P-51B Mustang, but when this magnificent fighter finally entered combat, on 1 December 1943, it was as a tactical fighter with the 354th FG, 9th AF. The first 8th AF group to receive the Mustang was the 357th FG at Raydon, Essex. They flew their first escort mission on 11 February 1944, and in March that year P-51Bs would fly to Berlin and back for the first time. The Mustang was the straw that would break the back of the *Jagdgruppen* (the twin-engined fighters of the *Zerstörergruppen* in particular were no match for the P-51), but for the time being the bomber crews were, for the most part, still very much on their own against the *Luftwaffe*.

Still the long-range missions persisted. On 3 November, 566 B-17s and B-24s were despatched to Wilhelmshaven. Seven bombers were lost in a fierce air battle with elements of JG1, JG11, JG26 and ZG26 over the German Bight. German losses were relatively high, III./JG1 alone lost eight Bf 109s, including two *Staffelkapitäne*, to escorting P-47s and P-38s. Two days later 323 B-17s bombed Gelsenkirchen and 104 B-24s hit Münster. Three B-24s and eight B-17s were lost, including one in the 92nd BG and two in the 388th BG. Near Gelsenkirchen the Ist *Gruppe*, JG26 made a pass at the 1st BD formation during which Fw. Aherns of 3./JG26 claimed the 92nd BG machine. It was 42-30007, the lead aircraft, piloted by Capt John O Booker and Maj Wilson P Todd, which had been hit by *Flak* just past the target. Todd had only just assumed command of the 327th Squadron. Eight parachutes were seen. Intervention by P-47s then scattered the enemy fighters, shooting one Fw 190 down and forcing two others to

*Above: Bf 109G-6 26058 flown by Maj Brändle on his fatal mission, 3 November 1943, at Schiphol airfield only days before his death. Fw Helmut Henning, Brändle's First Mechanic, is at the controls of the aircraft. Note the so-called clearview Erla-Haube (or 'Erla cockpit canopy', named after the Erla aircraft repair unit at Brussels). Helmut Henning via Rob de Visser.*

crash land. The IIIrd *Gruppe* of JG26 meanwhile, mixed it with the 3rd BD Fortresses and their P-47 escorts of the 353rd FG. The 353rd shot down two of the Bf 109G-6s and two others force-landed with combat damage. In return, JG26 claimed a P-47 and Hptm Hermann Staiger, 12th *Staffel* CO, claimed a 388th B-17. The Knettishall Group lost two B-17s to enemy action (Group records contend that all three losses this day were attributable to *Flak* - a third crashed in England after receiving battle damage over enemy territory). B-17 42-30789, flown by 2/Lt W J Bramwell, was hit in the No.1 engine just before the target and pulled out of formation and dropped its bombs. When last seen the No.1 propeller was feathered and the engine was on fire. *Pistol Packin Mama*, flown by 2/Lt R M Walker with crew only on their third mission, fell behind just after bombs away with the bomb bay doors still open. Walker left the formation from 27,000ft with the No.2 propeller feathered and No.3 engine smoking. While the crew was bailing out, S/Sgt R B Feese, the ball-gunner's chute caught on the tail section of the B-17 and he was carried down with the aircraft.

On 11 November, JG26 was successful in its interception of the bombers during the 3rd BD attack on Münster. A failure of PFF aircraft caused the 95th, 96th,

100th and 388th BGs to turn back before the enemy coast, leaving just the 61 unescorted B-17s of the 94th, 385th and 390th in the 4th and 13th CBWs to continue to the target. Four B-17s were lost, three of these were from the 94th BG, which was flying as the low group, and one from the 385th BG. The Fw 190s of the IInd *Gruppe* JG26 took off from Epinoy and attacked the Fortresses repeatedly from 00.00 hours and 0600 hours claiming four B-17s of the 94th BG. Three of the claims were upheld, but one, claimed by OFw Addi Glunz of 5./JG26 was not. His intended victim, *Lil' Operator*, flown by Lt. Johnny Pyles - whose crew in the 410th BS was on only its third mission - disappeared into the undercast in a vertical dive, but Pyles brought the Fortress under control, levelled off at 15,000ft and applied full rudder to keep it on course. Three and four engine throttles were dead so Pyles decided to shut down

the No.3 engine, which was windmilling. Then Ervin Smith, ball turret gunner, called up on the interphone to say that the undercarriage was in the "down" position. Amazingly, Pyles brought *Lil' Operator* home to Rougham on two engines, a wing and a prayer. Next day, on leave in London, the B-17 crew watched a British newsreel showing an "American Flying Fortress *shot down over Münster.*" As the crew watched the frame showing the large "square A" on the tail and the lowered undercarriage, they jumped up out of their seats as one man, startling their fellow cinema goers with cries of "Hey, that's us!" Pyles was lost on 26 November with a new crew on its first mission when an Fw 190, probably flown by Oblt Fritz Falke of 8./JG26, who was most likely already dead, flew straight into Pyles' B-17, hitting between the No.2 engine and the fuselage. The tail broke away during the explosion and the rear gunner managed

to bail out. He was the only survivor.

Glunz's other claim for a B-17 of the 94th BG south-west of Dordrecht was, however, confirmed. A second 94th BG B-17 fell to the guns of Hptm Johannes Naumann, 7th *Staffel* CO, who had a B-17 confirmed north/north-west of Breda. These two B-17s were 42-39812 *Casey Jones*, flown by Lt Richard W Ralls of the 332nd BS, which crashed at Tilburg, Holland killing nine of the crew, and 42-39855 *Ole Bassar*, piloted by Lt Paul J Kane of the 331st Squadron, which crashed at Fijnaart, Holland with the loss of three crew. The seven others were taken prisoner. Oblt Leuschel, 8th *Staffel* CO's victim, which he hit south-west of Numansdorp and crashed near this location, was also confirmed. It was 42-39868, flown by Lt Robert B O'Hara of the 331st BS. Seven of the crew were killed and three taken prisoner.

On 13 November 1943, 272 B-17s and B-24s were

*Left:* III./JG11 fighter pilots posing in front of *Wulf Hound*, autumn 1943. During 1943 and 1944, coded DL+XC in KG200, *Wulf Hound* toured the *Reichsverteidigung* fighter bases to give the *Jagdflieger* an opportunity to have a close look at their feared opponent. *Coen Cornelissen*

Oldenburg, 25 miles west of Bremen. Lamma and four of the crew were lost. B-24H 42-7503 *Miss America* of the 577th BS, flown by Lt. Frank Marfia, is believed to have been damaged by enemy action and went down in the North Sea on return after running out of fuel. All 10 crew perished. B-24H 42-7483 *Big Dog*, flown by Lt Isaac Marx of the 578th BS, was hit by *Flak* just before the target and made its way back over Holland. It was attacked north of Zwolle by OFw Heitmann of 4./JG26 who sent it crashing to earth. As the doomed B-24 hurtled down all the crew bailed out successfully. JG26 were also credited with a 355th FG P-47 destroyed. Oblt Wolfgang Neu, 4./JG26 CO, was credited with shooting down a 96th BG B-17 north-east of Arnhem. B-17 42-37830 of the 413th BS, piloted by 2/Lt Henry E Marks Jr, crashed with the loss of seven of the crew. JG11 lost four fighters on 13 November, II./JG26 another four aircraft.

For the first two weeks of November 1943, England was blanketed by thick woolly fog and airfields were lashed with intermittent showers and high winds. When the bad weather front finally lifted on 16 November, VIIIth BC struck at targets in Norway. The 1st BD attacked the molybdenum mines at Knaben and the 3rd BD attacked a generating plant at Vermark in the Rjukan Valley. Both targets were connected with the German heavy water experiments, which were designed to give

*A*s we approached our rendezvous I could see the rear of the bomber formation under attack from German fighters. I picked out a pair of twin-engine Me 110s below me and led the flight down behind them. The 110s saw me coming and pushed over into a dive in hopes of escaping. That tactic didn't work any better for the 110 against P-47s than it did for the lighter German single-engined fighters. I closed in behind them rapidly and opened fire on one at about 700 yards range. Normally, I would wait until I got a lot closer before shooting, but in this case I was going so fast that I had to hurry the shot. From 300 yards away I could see both engines on fire. Then suddenly I was right on top of the 110. I just barely had time to push the control stick forward and duck below the burning German fighter. In a flash I could see oil from the 110 spattering on the left wing of my P-47, and then I could smell its smoke, which must have been sucked into the cockpit through my heater system. Now that's close — too close!'

**'Gabby' Gabreski, 56th Fighter Group, on becoming an 'ace', 26 November 1943, claiming two Bf 110s of ZG26 destroyed.**

*A*ircraft 215 was hit in its number two engine when two Fw 190s attacked the low squadron at 10.45. It fell out of formation and dived for cloud cover. Enemy aircraft followed but P-47s went to the rescue. The plane was then seen from time to time flying below the formation. At 10.48, one chute was seen to open and at 11.03 hours, nine more chutes were seen. At 11.05 hours, it hit the ground and exploded. During its last few minutes in flight, fire had spread over the entire left wing.

**Eyewitness in the 100th BG formation describing the last moments of B-17G 42-31215, flown by 2/Lt George W Ford on his first mission, claimed by OFw Addi Glunz of 5./JG26 who with his wingman, attacked from 6 o'clock low, at 1103 hours, near Beauvais, 26 November 1943. Glunz had also shot down a 78th FG P-47 at 1040. Three of Ford's crew evaded, two were KIA, and five were made PoWs.**

*Above:* B-17G 42-37762 *Champlain's Office*, 545th BS, 384th BG, on its belly at the naval airbase at Zwischenahn, near Bremen, 26 November 1943, one of the 25 heavies lost from the 633 aircraft dispatched. *Champlain's Office*, flown by 2/Lt Charles A Zituik, was badly damaged by fighters before reaching the target and was then 'escorted' by three Bf I09s. Zituik circled Zwischenahn aerodrome, where eight of the crew bailed out. Seven men came down safely, but ball turret gunner, Sgt. Robert H. Rimmer Jr's opened 'chute caught a jackscrew in the bomb bay. Repeated attempts by 2/Lt Frank Pelley, bombardier, to pull him back on board, failed, and Rimmer was smashed to death against a hangar on the airfield which the Fortress narrowly missed during the crash-landing, at 1202 hours. The nine survivors were taken prisoner. On board the Fortress, the Germans found the secret radio codes for 26 and 27 November 1943, and an intact H2S navigation radar set. *Coen Cornelissen*.

directed to bomb targets at Bremen but bad weather caused many in the 1st BD to abandon the mission during assembly, only 143 of the heavies were successful. The mission cost 16 bombers, three of which were B-17s. The 93rd BG suffered the day's highest loss, losing five B-24s. Next worst was the 392nd BG, which lost four Liberators. B-24H 42-7540 *Crew Chief*, of the 576th BS, piloted by Lt John Harris, took off in heavy overcast, became lost and failed to find the formation. When the B-24 let down through the overcast on the return it was hit by *Flak* and the crew evacuated the ship, while Harris and co-pilot Louis Kearns put the bomber down south of Rotterdam. B-24 42-7561 *Mac's Sack II*, piloted by Lt Ralph Lamma of the 579th BS, encountered Flak and fighters, which left engines 1 and 2 burning. Lamma had no alternative but to order his crew out before the B-24 went into a spin near

*Right:* The crew of 42-37762 (pictured in front of B-17F *Cherry*) who belly-landed at Zwischenahn airfield near Bremen on 26 November 1943 Kneeling, L-R: Sgt Clarence R Lehmann, tail gunner; Sgt Florian S Protasiewicz, left waist gunner; S/Sgt Lewis E McNatt Jr, radio operator; Sgt Robert H Rimmer Jr ball turret gunner (KIA 26.11.43); S/Sgt Anthony J Roberto, engineer. Standing, L-R: 2/Lt Richard C Teevan, co-pilot; 2/Lt Baradi, pilot (did not fly on the 26.11.43 mission); 2/Lt Rodney R Helms, navigator; 2/Lt Frank A Pelley Jr bombardier. *Coen Cornelissen.*

**Above:** Fortresses of the 96th BG releasing their bombs on the Focke Wulf factory at Bremen, 26 November 1943. *USAF.*

**Left:** L-R Alvar M Woodall, top turret gunner; Harold L Morris, ball gunner; and John R Ward, all from Lt Forrest T Poor's crew, 551st BS, 385th BG. Woodall and Morris were KIA flying in *Mary Ellen III,* one of three 385th BG Fortresses MIA on the mission to Emden, 11 December 1943. Eight others were PoW. *William Nicholls.*

the Nazis the atomic bomb. Five days later the heavies were sent to Gelsenkirchen again and on 26 November, 633 heavies (the largest formation so far assembled by VIIIth BC) bombed targets as far apart as Bremen and Paris. Twenty-nine B-17s and five fighters were lost. Almost all the heavies lost came from the main raid on Bremen. German claimants came from II./JG27, IV./NJG1 (attacking stragglers over northern Holland) and ZG26 *Zerstörer.* On 30 November, the last raid of the month, 381 B-17s and B-24s were briefed to bomb Solingen in the Ruhr but only 80 heavies got their bombs away when cloud prevented the 1st and 2nd BDs from continuing to the target.

Next day, 1 December, 299 heavies were sent out to Solingen again. This time, the raid was more successful and 281 sorties were deemed effective, although the 3rd BD was prevented from bombing because of the weather. The 1st BD lost 19 B-17s and the 2nd BD, five B-24s. Four of the B-17 losses were from the 384th BG and five came from the 91st BG. Four B-17s were claimed by JG26 and two were confirmed as 384th BG machines. Four days later, 5 December 1943, 548

*O*n 5 December 1943, I was still in bed after a heavy night of drinking when there was an alarm. Approach of a 4-mot formation from out to sea on Bordeaux. Wearing my best trousers and shoes, I ran to the dispersal, assigned instructors and the senior pupils to a combat formation and off we went. The directions were good and we caught the formation, which had turned away without dropping its bombs over the coast. Without bothering with tactical ideas I attacked the formation from behind, to starboard and above. The manoeuvre from ahead seemed to offer little chance of success with this inexperienced lot. I placed myself behind a B-17 and was able to put a good burst into his starboard wing between the engines; it was sufficient for this one. While breaking off there was a bang in the fuselage behind me and the radio went dead. My lot scattered and was not seen again.

Well out over the Bay of Biscay I attacked again and then set course for the coast. A glance at the instruments - holy smoke - the oil pressure went. Save the remaining oil for the landing. Ignition off, prop feathered, flaps to take-off. The heavenly silence of a glider surrounded me as I slowly glided towards the coast. Will it suffice? The altimeter wound inexorably down, the coast appeared. Only 1000m left. No, it won't do. So, make the coast with the last of the oil. Or so I thought! The propeller would not unfeather, probably shot up. One blade was pointing downwards. Ditch? The sea had white spumes on it and waves. You'd go under like a U-boat. Landing on the beach? Would not the prop in this position cause a somersault., possibly in the shallows and you'd drown? So, as closely as possible to the beach and then jump, the very first one. I had always been good at theory. Checklist recited, then ready for the reality. Headset unplugged, straps released, cockpit cover jettisoned, knees drawn up. It was so nice sitting in the silently gliding aircraft. 500m... 450m... at 400m you must get out. I had to summon up all my courage. At 400 m I stuck the stick forward and to the left. The machine disappeared below me and I continued on my own through the air. Right elbow drawn in, my hand to the left, I have the handle, pull - nothing! I continue to fall and stare at the handle in my right hand, the ripcord hangs from it, still nothing! Before I have time to get really scared there is a hard jerk and I hang in the harness like a dead pig. Before I have time to think I'm in the water. The parachute sinks onto the water and remains standing like a spinnaker. Release the straps and away from the 'chute. Another snag! A buckle is caught on my right leg. I sail away with a strong bow wave. Stop! It is pulling me to the west, out to sea! I pull myself up along the lines and the 'chute collapses with me beneath it, wrapped up in the lines like a parcel -such bodies, when found, were called 'parachute mummies'. Being an old North Sea flyer (in IV./JG1), I fortunately had on me my 'Texas belt.' for such emergencies. Clasp knife out, it slips from my wet hands, but it hangs on a cord and can be retrieved. Cut loose, at last the straps release and I am swimming. 'Clear for boat manoeuvre.' Inflate lifejacket, but only the collar, otherwise you cannot get into the boat. Inflate rubber dinghy. With a swish the yellow horseshoe inflates, secured with a line - I have to think of Hans Munz (Oblt Munz, St Kapt 1./JG1, probably drowned on 21 May 1943), he must have forgotten that – after a brief tussle I am in it.

Uff! What now? Fire a red, reload pistol, orientation. There is the coast. Why wait? Start paddling. I paddle with my hands with my back to the shore. It's getting cold; after all, it's December. After some shivers I no longer feel the cold water through my thin trousers. Off to the north I see a large rubber dinghy with a sail drifting out to sea. Shot-down Yanks. Then there are rifle shots from the shore, the boat lowers its sail and remains drifting. Now some figures are running along the shore in my direction. I hope they don't start shooting at me. There is a throbbing in the air, a seaplane comes along and lands near the Yanks. They have not seen me. Fire another red. Cock the pistol, which is loaded. I can't do it with my frozen fingers, they are weak like sausages, my knees won't help either. Well, the next time then, if there is another one. With gnashing teeth I watch the flying boat take off. I continue paddling towards the shore but I'm getting so tired. Just 15 minutes! I slide down the boat and lay my head on the bulge. Then I'm startled. Had you not read in reports of polar expeditions that men always go to sleep before freezing to death? Up then and onward! How long have I been drifting? Two hours? With the last of my strength I reach the surf at last. Turn around, Florida surfer, the last breaker flings me from the boat into the knee-deep water, then onward on all fours.

An officer is riding towards me into the breakers, but his horse seems to misunderstand this and lays down in the water. Hands drag me to my feet, I look up and see wild looking faces; black hair, black eyes, shaggy beards, many-coloured turbans. Are these the doorkeepers of hell? Have you gone that far? I want to walk but cannot. Two men carry me to a car, drive me to a fisherman's hut; I am no longer fully conscious. I feel them taking my clothing off me, wrapping me in a blanket, than shoving me with my backside almost into the fireplace. After a while I mutter the word 'cognac'. A resolute woman shouts 'nix cognac, you kaput'. Well, then I'll do without. After an hour some mulled wine did it as well. As my brains began functioning again I realised that soldiers of the Indian 950th Regiment, who were guarding the coast here, had saved me. In the evening, having recovered my strength, I strolled, slightly tipsy and wearing the overcoat lent my by Obstlt Kappe, through the village, and casually accepted the salutes of the Indians. To this day I drink a strong grog on the 5th December of each year.

**Oblt Eberhard Burath, (who became St.Kpt. in EJG West – "Reserve Fighter Wing West" at Azaux, France, in September 1943) who claimed one of the 3rd BD B-17s lost on 5 December 1943. Worst hit was the 94th BG, which lost three B-17s. The 385th and 388th BGs lost two Fortresses each. In the 388th BG formation 2/Lt P A Todd in *Ole Bassar* fell out north of the target with No. 1 engine feathered and was reported shot down by Fw 190s. Eight of the crew were KIA, and two, including Todd, PoW. 2/Lt C D Willingham, co-pilot, bailed out safely and evaded capture. The second 388th B-17 MIA was flown by Lt Robert W Moyer, who returned with a crippled aircraft and ordered the crew to bail out over England. The 390th BG lost one B-17 when out of fuel, *The Bad Penny*, flown by Lt N M Palmer of the 571st BS, crashed in the sea off the Kent coast. Seven men died.**

bombers set out to attack targets in France again but bad weather completely disrupted the mission. Just over 200 Fortresses of the 1st BD were briefed to attack targets at La Rochelle and Paris but none of the B-17s were effective. The same was true of the 2nd BD's attempt to bomb targets at Cognac-Chateaubernard and St Nazaire, while the 3rd BD fared no better at Bordeaux-Merignac air depot. Only two B-24s of the 389th BG bombed the target and just one B-17, in the 96th BG, was successful at Bordeaux. For this wasted effort, eight heavies were lost.

The 390th BG suffered another loss on the 30 December 1943 mission to Ludwigshafen, when *Sarah Jane* flown by 2/Lt Campbell C Brigman Jr, of the 571st BS failed to return to Framlingham. *Sarah Jane* was shot

**Right:** Alvar Woodall, top turret gunner (KIA 11 December 1943). *William Nicholls.*

*I* started my flying training in Stettin-Altdamm on 30 June 1941 at the A/B flying school. On 8 August 1943, I went via Reims to Paris to the Schlachtgeschwader 101. At Orly we flew the Me 110, the HS 129 (or the 'Flying Coffin') and the Potez 63. Schlachtgeschwader 101 did not become operational and we became ZG76. I flew my first operational sortie under Oblt Richter in an Me 110 from Orly to the coast but it was uneventful. We were transferred to Frankfurt-Eschborn. The Me 110 was equipped additionally with a pair of rocket launchers under the wing (these rockets were compressed air shells, we called them 'Dödel'), each weighing about 120 kilos (250lb). Our Gruppe had a bad time in Eschborn. Several crashes on training flights and during final approaches with wrecked aircraft and dead crews. There was one day I shall never forget. It was shortly before Christmas 1943 and some of my comrades already had visits from their wives and brides. A training flight under the command of Oblt Richter with 16 Me 110s had been ordered and I was to lead one of the sections. During take-off my Me 110 lost its cockpit roof and I therefore abandoned take-off. Furious about this, I accused my mechanic of negligence. But for me it turned out to be a 'lucky day'. We never saw any of the aircraft or their crews again. They had flown into a mountain and all were dead.

From Eschborn we operated against Viermot attacks around Mannheim, Hannover-Wunstorf and as far as the North Sea coast. At that time the enemy flew in tight formations and were covered by strong fighter escorts. An approach to within effective range, say about 500m, was almost impossible. We managed to shoot some down, but whose rocket shells had scored the hits was impossible to say.

**Fw Walter Ibold, day fighter pilot, ZG76.**

*A* t the IP another group cut in front and we experienced severe prop' wash. The last report on the intercom was the pilot saying 'We're going over.' Unfortunately, *Satan's Sister* could not take the strain and she broke in two at the radio room. Lt. Slentz, our bombardier, took off like a football fullback and plunged headlong through the Plexiglas nose — without a parachute. Lt. Bassler, the navigator, and the sole married man in the crew always put on his chest 'chute at the first sign of Flak or fighters; he went through the nose after Slentz, coming within inches of the inboard propellers which were still revolving at full power! Jim Neal, the right waist gunner, put his 'chute on and went back to check the radio room. He opened the door, took one step and found he had involuntarily bailed out! Parizo, the other waist gunner, went to the ball turret to extract Sgt. Brincat, put on his 'chute, opened the waist door and promptly 'froze.' Brincat tried in vain to budge Parizo but the

*T* his was an all out effort to blast it off the map. There were more planes in the air than I have ever seen before. We were in formation and well on our way when I looked back all I could see were bombers all over the sky; high, low, left and right. It always gave a man chills to know that many planes were gong into the Flak after you. We were told that it took time for the ack ack gunners to line up on the first planes. We were somewhat relieved and luckier to be in the lead group. The Flak over the target was very heavy and there were a few ships hit. Just after the target and on our turn for home we met our first enemy fighters. Keith Kent, our bombardier, said over the intercom, 'Those guys are blinking their landing lights at us. Immediately, "Ace" Conklin, our co-pilot yelled, "Those aren't lights, they're wing guns." Then, as if by impulse, every single .50 calibre gun in the formation opened up. We felt like sitting ducks up there as fighters swept through our formations. Reluctantly we admired those enemy pilots making a pass through our formation in the face of so many guns firing at them. We often discussed how the German fighter pilots had the guts to fly through a formation of B-17s with all of our guns firing at them at the same time. It took some kind of courage.

Our group was not hit but those on our right and left were. We saw six B-17s go down. It's rough to think that 60 men were involved and we would try and count the chutes as they bailed out, or at least those that could get out. This was our Air Medal mission. If you completed five missions the Air Medal was awarded, These first five were tough with heavy Flak and rough targets. It was hard to believe that we had to do 20 more to go home.

**Larry Goldstein, radio operator, *Worry Wart*, 388th BG, Bremen, 16 December 1943.**

**Right:** S/Sgt Larry Goldstein, radio operator, *Worry Wart*, 388th BG. Goldstein.

latter's vice like grip and his extra weight (180lbs to Brincat's 110lbs) held him in position. Brincat gave up and bailed out of the right waist gate. For me it was a case of up, down, up and over...The tail section was whipped round like an autumn leaf from a tall oak tree in a high wind. By this time, although I was scared as hell, I did not know what had happened, but there was no noise of any kind. I released my Flak jacket and finding my chest 'chute snapped it onto my harness. I

then pulled the release on my escape hatch — nothing happened; then struggling to escape, I banged the door with my shoulder and it finally blew out with Yours Truly following....

**Bob Scalley, tail gunner, one of only four survivors from Lt. Arthur W. Carlson's crew of *Satan's Sister*, 388th BG, Ludwigshaven, 30 December 1943.**

*Below:* Lt. Arthur W Carlson's crew that went down over Ludwigshaven, 30 December 1943. Back row, L-R: Lt. Carlson (KIA); Lt. Benjamin H Scoggin co pilot (KIA); Lt. John R Bassler navigator (PoW); Lt. Edgar F Slintz, bombardier (KIA). Front row. T/Sgt Harold L Hawkins, engineer (KIA); S/Sgt James A Neal, waist gunner (PoW); T/Sgt Danny Letter, radio operator (KIA), S/Sgt Robert E Scalley, tail gunner (PoW); S/Sgt Charles H Parizo, waist gunner (KIA), S/Sgt Frank S Brincat, ball turret gunner (PoW). *Larry Goldstein.*

*Crew 45-25*

The airfield was very well laid out with a very long runway and well built dispersals. A few days before Christmas, on a beautiful winter's day with sunshine but very poor horizontal visibility, we were suddenly ordered into the air. Our 3rd *Staffel* had five Bf 109G-6s at readiness and, having started our engines and taxied out of the revetments, my aircraft was on the left of the start line as no. 5. Being the 3rd *Staffel*, we had to wait until the other two had taken off and we had a little time during which I checked all my instruments etc., during which I heard some dull sounds in rapid succession which I had never heard before. On looking up I saw to my horror the Marauder bombers, which we had been sent up to intercept, dropping their loads on our airfield. We would have liked to have taken off at once to avoid the bombs, but we had to await the departure of the 1st *Staffel*, which was taking off from the other side of the airfield towards us. During that time the 1st *Staffel*'s dispersal was hit by a carpet of bombs, causing many explosions and smoke. At last the green Verey light appeared, the take-off order for our *Staffel*. For once in exemplary alignment, we got away and none too soon, for another hail of bombs came down just to the left of where the first aircraft had been standing. A third shower coming from the right fell into the middle of the field and the last of these bombs exploded beneath me just as I had become airborne and was about 5 to 10m up in the air. The effect was disastrous. A number of

splinters penetrated the wings from below, tearing considerable holes which looked very funny. The coolant went away in a white stream and it became clear to me that any further participation in the action was out of the question. So: back to the ground. For that I had to change from my northerly course to west and then east in order to reach the runway. After some difficulties I was able to get the undercarriage down, which the lights confirmed, but it was an almost totally blind approach through the smoke from the engine. As a result, I did not land on the runway but beside it on the grass, which turned out to be lucky for me for the runway had been completely destroyed by the bombs. While I was braking hard, the good old 109 passed very close to several bomb craters and came to a stop after a short run. I don't know what became of this 109, it was probably a total loss. As the airfield had been made unusable for some time by the bombing, the Gruppe was transferred on one of the following days, about 23 or 24 December, to Denain.

**Joachim Foth, a fighter pilot with 3./JG3, a high-altitude fighter unit in the *Reichsverteidigung*, late 1943, describing being on the receiving end of a Marauder raid on his *Gruppe*'s airfield, Vendeville near Liege, a few days before Christmas 1943.**

*I* was a guard at the V-1 building site and its workforce Ivrench de Roche near Abbeville in Northern France. The building sites were attacked daily by British and American fighters, fighter-bombers and reconnaissance aircraft. This in order to discover what was being built, then to keep an eye on the progress and to hinder it, as the workers, composed of many nationalities and mostly prisoners, threw away their tools and dispersed at each attack and so delayed its building. Being the best gunner of our unit, I was number one on our aircraft machine guns with a double magazine. Towards midday, 20 December 1943, I managed to hit an attacking aircraft, its engine stopped and the machine made a belly landing about 1km behind our position. The pilot was uninjured.

Next day, 21 December 1943, again about midday, the 'duty reconnaissance aircraft' again made its appearance. I had just had a wash in our earth bunker and was stripped to the waist when we got the alert. I only put on my steel helmet and rushed to my gun. We came under attack by a number of fighter bombers. The second aircraft coming in killed my second gunner with a shot through the head. I had to reach over the barrel in order to place a fresh magazine drum on the gun and in doing so I burnt my left upper arm on the hot barrel. Unfortunately the burn was just where SS soldiers had their blood group tattooed. Of course, during the attack, with the next aircraft coming in, one did not bother about such a minor injury. I succeeded in hitting the attacker and flames came out of its engine. In a quick reaction the pilot pulled up his machine in order to bail out. Before he had landed with his parachute the aircraft had crashed and exploded just behind us. I saw both pilots during an interrogation in the afternoon. Unfortunately I spoke no English, but the pilot who had bailed out and had a bullet lodged in his left leg, opened his iron rations and we smoked one of his cigarettes. Both pilots were taken to the camp for pilots at Oberursel near Bad Homburg the next day. Unfortunately my aircraft recognition was not very good at this time. All that mattered was to shoot down if possible any attacking enemy aircraft, whether Spitfire, Mustang or Hurricane. So I cannot say what types these were. (After I was taken prisoner of war by the Russians; on 19 May 1945, the burn on my upper left arm caused me no end of difficulties during my five years of Soviet captivity. I was taken for an SS criminal who had abused women, murdered children and burnt villages, and now, fearing recognition and punishment, had obliterated the tattooed blood group, leaving the scar of a burn.

**19 year old Martin Hoffmann. For his two confirmed kills, Flieger Hoffmann was decorated with the E K II 24 December 1943. He was allowed to join the *Luftwaffe* for pilot training after having turned 18 in October 1943, and over the next year, he passed through the various stages of pilot training, before he graduated to the Fw 190A and was posted to JG105 at Schonering, near Linz/Austria, October 1944.**

***Above:*** Martin Hoffmann was credited with shooting down two Allied fighters attacking the V-1 building site at Ivrench de Roche near Abbeville, France 20 and 21 December 1943, with a ground-mounted MG15 machine gun. Hoffmann is pictured, aged 19, with the rank of Flieger (AC2), January 1945. *Martin Hoffmann.*

down by Fw Heinrich "Jan" Schild of 2./JG26, the bomber crashing near Vimy in northern France. Eight of Brigman's crew evaded capture, two did not. JG26 claimed five other B-17s shot down. Confirmed kills went to two other JG26 pilots. South of Florennes, Belgium, *Woman's Home Companion* of the 360th BS, 303rd BG, piloted by Lt William C Osborn, was caught straggling

behind the main formation by Fw-Fhj Gerd Wiegand and Fw Hager of 4./JG26. Wiegand left the kill to Hager, whose first victory this was. (Wiegand was credited with shooting down two 353rd FG P-47s this day, the 353rd replied by destroying two Bf 109Gs for the loss of another P-47.) Five of Osborn's crew were captured, three KIA and two evaded.

Lt Karl "Charlie" Willius, 2./JG26 CO, accounted for a 100th BG B-17 at Soissons. The 100th BG lost two B-17s by the time it reached the English Channel after the target. The first, *Laden Maiden*, in the High Squadron, was piloted by Lt. Marvin Leininger and Albert Witmyer. It was reported to fall behind and go down in flames after being followed by three Fw 190s.

***Above:*** 'Unser Lustiger Charlie'. Fw Karl Willius showing how to engage the enemy. 2./JG26, Wevelgem, Belgium, in late 1941. Note an Fw 190A-1 in the background. After being shot down on 8 April 1944, Willius' body was not recovered until 1967, when it was discovered still in his Fw 190 15ft down in the Pieperpolder near Genemuiden. *Lisette Arend-Willius.*

Only the navigator, Leonard McChesney, and the bombardier, Charles Compton, survived. Both evaded capture and returned to England by 17 April 1944. The eight crew who died were buried in a common grave near the small hamlet of Liry, five miles east of Cernay Durmois, where *Laden Maiden* crashed. All 10 men aboard *Heaven Can Wait* bailed out after an enemy fighter attack damaged the radio room with its 20mm cannon, starting a fire, probably in the oxygen tanks. Both the pilot, Francis Smith and the co-pilot, James Law, were taken prisoner. The rest of the crew, on its fifth mission, successfully evaded, spending some comfortable time in Paris. *Heaven Can Wait* crashed just north of Les Rosiers, 3km south-east of Monthois.

Another 100th BG B-17, piloted by Lt Dean Radtke, barely made it back after being hit by sustained *Flak* in the target area. It was then attacked by two Fw 190s south-west of Abbeville, where a number of 20mm shells riddled the left wing and nose. One shell entered the navigator's compartment and struck the co-pilot, Lt

Robert Digby in the head, killing him instantly. Shell fragments struck Radtke, wounding him in the face, head, and in the neck beside his jugular vein. One fragment completely closed his right eye and splinters from the instrument panel were driven into the muscles of his right leg, rendering it useless. The explosion also ripped the oxygen mask from his face and stunned the engineer, Russell Pinner, who was hurled against the turret controls. Upon regaining his senses, Pinner thought first to escape, as he was certain that the plane had been blown apart. Through the smoke, he could see the pilot and co-pilot slumped over the controls. Blood was spattered over the shell-pitted compartment. The windows were shattered and broken.

At this time, Radtke regained consciousness and saw Pinner about to leave. He yelled to him and the engineer returned to his station. Radtke then called the rest of the crew and reassured them. Most of the crew were never aware that Digby had been killed or that Radtke himself was severely wounded. Lt William Agnetti, bombardier,

was called up, he moved the co-pilot's body to the navigator's compartment, then returned to assist Radtke. Due to the loss of one engine and severed control cables, the B-17 lagged behind the formation. Radtke doubted whether he could remain conscious long enough to bring the B-17 home but with fingers useless because of severe cuts, he skilfully used the butts of his hands to manipulate the controls and fought his way back into position in the formation. Radtke got the crew safely home to Thorpe Abbotts where he made a perfect landing. In all, six B-17s of the 100th BG returned with battle damage. Altogether, 17 B-17s and six B-24s were lost. One of the Liberators that failed to return was credited to Oblt Walter Matoni of 6./JG26, who destroyed a B-24 15km north-west of Soissons.

Next day, 31 December, when VIIIth BC completed its second year in England with all-out raids on airfields in France, 25 bomber crews and four fighter pilots would not return to their bases to celebrate New Year's Eve. On the other side of the Channel JG26 also enjoyed mixed fortunes. Two of its pilots were killed and three were wounded. Lt Vavken of 7./JG26 added to JG26's overall score, with a confirmed victory over a 96th BG B-17 5km north of Ault. His victim was 42-31121 flown by 1/Lt Ralph A Woodward of the 338th BS, one of the Fortresses attacking ball bearing factories outside Paris. Three of Woodwind's crew were killed. OFw Addi Glunz of 5./JG26 was also credited with the destruction of a B-17 between Lorient and Auringes.

*I destroyed my sixth Boeing, over Bordeaux, but once more had to bail out myself. I landed in the canopy of a tree 20m high and injured both my legs.* Oblt Otto "Stotto" Stammberger, *Staffelkapitän*, 2./JGr West at Bergerac, 31 December 1943, his 104th and penultimate combat sortie of the war.

On this day, 11 January 1944, when 291 Fortresses were dispatched to Oschersleben and Halberstadt, it was reported that fighter opposition was the heaviest since the Schweinfurt mission of 14 October 1943. (In August 1944 the 1st BD received the Presidential Unit Citation for this raid.) Altogether, 42 Fortresses and two fighters were lost. *Zerstörer* of ZG26 destroyed 20 *Viermots*, III./JG1 (operating from Volkel), II./JG27 (from Eelde),

**Oblt Eberhard Burath began the New Year with a different unit. A few days after his narrow escape on 5 December 1943, he had received a new operational posting, this time to II./JG1 at Rheine, where he became *Staffel* Officer of the 4th *Staffel*. He noticed too that the war had changed.**

*The Reich's defence had meanwhile become much tougher. The 4-mot formations were coming with strong long-range fighter escorts which made it very difficult for us to get even near them. Even old hands were hunted just like the young ones. Dummy attacks made us rush back and forth between Fehmarn and the Swiss border. Frequently we only just managed to reach the enemy formation with our last drops of fuel and then had to land. The "4-mots" had now stopped using tracer ammunition. On attacking we went through a flickering curtain of defensive fire, now anything might happen. On the further side another such flickering curtain; once through there, one was safe. On our own side large formations were put together for defence against attacks on Berlin. The great battles took place in the area around Hannover-Brunswick-Magdeburg; a great deal of metal fell from the skies there.*

*After the quiet of the festive season we got really busy at the beginning of January. On 5 January 1944, they sent us to Cuxhaven but we made no contact with the enemy; again at noon and also without success. But on 11 January we came upon a huge "buch" of them in the area of Paderborn en route Berlin. In a 'snake-bite' attack, pulling up from below, I got a B-17 in my sights and was able to send a good burst through the fuselage; pulling up I was still behind her and continued firing. That was too much for her and it was my third Abschuss.*

and probably elements of JG11, were also successful against the combat boxes. JG26, a constant thorn in the side of the B-17 crews, claimed 12 B-17s. Three of the *Jagdgeschwader's* claims were for two 92nd BG B-17s and a 482nd BG Fortress (all of which were confirmed), while eight more (seven of which were upheld) were for B-17s of the luckless 306th BG from Thurleigh. 22 B-17s of the 92nd BG had left Podington on 11 January, when, because of poor weather conditions, a recall had

been sent out after the mission was despatched, but the message was not received. Continuing in alone, the 1st BD was jumped by over 200 enemy fighters just past the Dummer Lake. On the return, near Heerde in Holland, the Fortress piloted by 1/Lt William B. Lock of the 326th Squadron went down with two of the crew dead. Three men evaded and five were taken captive. Also lost was the B-17 piloted by 2/Lt Joseph A Tryens of the 325th BS. All ten crew were captured after

bailing out. Oblt Matoni of 6./JG26 and Uffz. Georgi of 7./JG26, were credited with these two kills.

As already mentioned, the 306th BG, which was one of the groups that went to Halberstadt, was among the worst hit (the 91st lost five B-17s and the 381st lost eight), losing five Fortresses over the continent and two more were written off in crash landings in England. In addition, three of the Group's B-17s were severely damaged, eight seriously damaged and four were

classified as slightly damaged. The 306th put up 20 B-17s in the main group and the composite group, led by Capt Dennis Sharkey flying with a High Squadron from the 92nd BG, had 14 more B-17s from Thurleigh. Col George L Robinson, the 306th BG CO, led the 40th CBW. Two of the 306th BG B-17s returned early and the rest proceeded to Halberstadt.

At just after 1320 hours Fw 190s of I. and II./JG26 came upon the 306th BG formation high and rolled

through the formation. In under eight minutes they knocked eight B-17s out of the 306th BG formation. One of the first fighters through the formation (Oblt Beese, 1./JG26 CO) went between Col. Robinson's lead ship and the 482nd BG PFF (Pathfinder) B-17 flying on its wingtip, and shot away the tail of the PFF Fortress. No chutes were seen from it. B-17F 42-30782 and 1/Lt Willard D Reed, an experienced 368th BS pilot, was lost off Robinson's left wing when it was hit hard in the

**Right:** Engine fitter of I./JG1 fastens the engine cover of the C.O. HpTm Schnoor's Fw 190A-7 before take-off, Dortmund, January 1944. *Seebrandt via Rob de Visser.*

**Below:** Mud-spattered Fw 190A-7 WerkNo. 430352 *Schwarze 3* ('Black 3') of II./JG1 at Dortmund, January 1944. *Seebrandt via Rob de Visser.*

leading-edge of a wing and the extensive damage caused the B-17 to go into a spin. A raging fire ensued and the B-17 broke up in the air and went down at Nijverdal. Five of Reed's crew died. 2/Lt Donald W Tattershall's 369th BS B-17 had the tail shot off and was last seen near the Zuider Zee. It crashed at Diepenveen, Holland. Only the radio operator survived.

2/Lt Ross McCollom was on his second mission for the 367th BS, flying in the Low Squadron. His right wing was struck by another B-17 in the formation, causing some damage. McCollom rang the bail-out alarm but regained control. Almost immediately, the B-17 was hit by three elements of Fw 190s from head-on. Only the bombardier, 2/Lt Lloyd G Crabtree, survived, the bomber crashing at Epe. *Arch Bishop*, piloted by 1/Lt George Campert, a veteran 367th BS pilot, was knocked out of formation during the fighter attack and was last seen flying beneath the formation. None of the crew survived when this aircraft crashed at Heten/Raalte, Holland. 2/Lt Perry Cavos and his crew also went down at Heten/Raalte, probably after colliding with Campert's aircraft. From the five 306th BG B-17s to go down, 50 airmen were lost. 43 of these men were killed. Only one 4./JG26 Fw 190A-6 was lost during this one-sided air battle over central Holland, the pilot, Uffz Voigt, bailed out successfully. The *Luftwaffe* lost 39 aircraft on 11 January 1944.

Lt Kenneth F Dowell's 369th BS B-17 was hit by Fw 190s which set fire to his No.3 engine. Dowell was unable to feather it and lost his electrical system so that the alarm bell did not sound when he hit the bail out switch. Dowell put his B-17 into a dive to escape, with flames screaming out of the battered engine. It burned so furiously that it fell off the wing of the B-17. At 4,000ft the Fortress became more manageable, the fire was out and the pilot continued on toward England. While in the dive a Bf 110 flew along with them, spraying them with machine gun fire. Incredibly, Dowell got the B-17 home on three engines and crash-landed at RAF Great Saling. Lt Charles J Kinsey's B-17 was hit by a 20mm shell which hit the base of the pilot's window, wounding Kinsey in the leg and ending his combat flying. Kinsey still managed to put the badly shot up Fortress down at RAF Foulsham in Norfolk. Lt Bill W Casseday crash-landed his 369th BS B-17 at Horsham St Faith near Norwich, where it was declared a total loss. (This Fortress was most probably claimed as "destroyed" by Oblt Martin Drewes, St Kpt 11/NJG1 and his radio /radar operator, Uffz Handke who claimed two B-17s shot down on 11 January 1944.) Only eight Fortresses returned to Thurleigh unscathed.

On 21 January 1944, 795 B-17s and B-24s set out to bomb V-weapon sites and other targets in the Pas de Calais and at Cherbourg. Some of these aircraft bombed targets of opportunity while some combat boxes remained in their target areas too long identifying targets. (One target reportedly required 10

**Right:** Bf 110G-2 *Pulkzerstörer* being serviced at München-Riem airfield, early spring 1944. The G-2 was armed with a 37mm cannon under the fuselage and two MG151 20mm cannons in the nose. *Albert Spelthahn.*

*On one occasion, it must have been on 5 January 1944 near Hannover, our group had been scattered and had suffered some losses. I flew into a formation of bombers, the Viermot I attacked was streaming smoke, but I had to return to Wunstorf as quickly as possible with my starboard wing badly damaged by return fire. During this attack my radio operator sang a song. I shall never forget it. Then we were transferred to Nördlingen, the Geschwader staff was at Ansbach. Our Kommodore was Obstlt Rossiwal. One day, after returning from a sortie, he had to leave his aircraft at Stendal. After it had been repaired my radio operator Helmut Schmale and I went by train to Stendal. We took off and headed in the direction of Ansbach, but came into contact with the enemy on the way. My starboard engine was put out of action by enemy fire, and I had to complete the flight and landing on one engine. The flaps stuck, I touched down too far down the runway, ran into a ditch and we turned over on our back. We suffered a slight concussion, otherwise we had a lucky escape. Transfers followed to Vienna-Seyring, then to Nowidwor in Slovakia. Meanwhile we had taken over the Me 410 in Prague. During this time I flew some 25 to 30 sorties with two Viermots confirmed shot down, two Mustangs damaged in air combat and three other indecisive combats. I was shot down twice, once I had to bail out by parachute, the second time I had to crash-land near Ingolstadt with a hard belly landing. Helmut and I had been lucky again. On our first sortie over Hungary there were Viermot formations flying in from the south. During my first attack I was able to*

*finish off a Boeing, it was already damaged. On our return flight we were chased by two Mustangs. They came closer but did not fire, they had probably exhausted their ammunition. One of them flew in a curve to dead ahead of my Me 410, the pilot waved and I instinctively pressed my firing button. He burst apart. I could weep even today when I think about it.*

*We handed over our Me 410s after our operations over Slovakia (in July 1944) and proceeded to fly some training sorties in Me 109s at Bonn-Hangelar. Then we received news that there were brand new Me 109Gs ready for us at Bremen and we travelled up to collect them. Once again, my luck held. At take-off, I suffered an engine failure and belly-landed my Me 109G beyond the airfield. The next day I flew back to Hangelar in another 109.*

**Uffz Walter Ibold, Bf 110 and Me 410 Zerstörer pilot, ZG76, in the**
*Reichsverteidigung, 1944*

**Below:** Me 410B-1/U-2 of ZG26 which crash-landed at Königsberg/Neumark airfield, summer 1944. The Me 410B-I/U-2 was armed with forward-firing 13mm machine guns instead of the usual 7.9mm guns and an additional pair of MG151 20mm cannon in the underfuselage weapons bay. *Petrick via Punka.*

runs before the group dropped its bombs!) A total of 628 escorting fighters were to shepherd the bombers and protect them from *Luftwaffe* fighter attack. However, the delayed runs and constant circling of some of the groups meant that the escorting fighters became low on fuel and had to withdraw, leaving some of the attacking bombers vulnerable to fighter attack. Bombing was also hampered by the poor weather, with heavy cloud over most of northern France, and fewer than half the bombers dropped their bomb loads on the assigned targets. The 44th BG was assigned two targets. The 66th and 68th Squadrons were to bomb the V-1 site at Escalles-Sur-Buchy in the Pas de Calais, while the 67th and 506th Squadrons were to bomb military

installations at Agathe D'Aliermont. Normally, this would have been a relatively easy "milk run", as it was so close to the English Channel. However, it was to turn out to be very costly in men and machines for the 'Flying Eightballs'. V-1 sites were notoriously difficult to hit and the bombing altitude for the attack was at 12,000ft. Conditions therefore favoured the attackers. Once again, it was the 'Eightballs' old enemies, the "Abbeville Kids" of JG26, that rose to meet them. The Liberators flew on towards their targets and at 1420 hours Hptm Karl Borris, CO of I./JG26, and his 15 fighters took off from Florrenes to look for American bombers.

Over Poix Borris saw what he was hoping for, an unescorted *Pulk* (herd) of Liberators. He immediately

gave orders for his fighters to attack the Liberators from the rear, where the seven Liberators of the 68th BS had drawn the unenviable "tail-end Charlie" position in the formation. It was here that the JG26 pilots had the richest pickings. Such was the speed and surgical method employed by the attackers that four of JG26's pilots claimed all their five victories simultaneously, at 1530 hours. They were subsequently confirmed. Four of the victims were from the unlucky 68th BS bringing up the rear. The 66th BS lost *Queen Marlene*, piloted by 2/Lt Martin E. Spelts, while attacking Escalles-Sur-Buchy. At 1514 hours this aircraft was seen to wing over and dive down, no chutes. It hit the ground and exploded. This loss occurred during the first attack by

---

*7 January 1944 was a particularly turbulent day. I took to the air for flight nr. 754. At that time, the Second Gruppe of JG27 was stationed at Wiesbaden-Erbenheim for Reich Defence duties. I took off with the 4th Staffel at 1111hrs against a reported enemy force. In the area of Saarbrücken, at about 8m, we encountered a formation of 150 B-17s with strong fighter cover, coming towards us about 500m lower. Above and beside us, Lightnings and Thunderbolts circled about dangerously close by. So careful now and jettison auxiliary tanks, for a dogfight with the escort was unavoidable. Our main target was however, according to orders, the bombers. We flew our first attack as usual from ahead, hurled ourselves upon the leading formation with all guns blazing, saw here and there flashes from some of the bombers, and were through them. Their tracer accompanied us briefly and we turned in for the second attack. It was always difficult to re-establish some sort of formation after an attack. Everyone knew that on his own he would have no chance against the escort. We therefore always endeavoured to stay together at least as a section to guard each other's backs.*

*While I was looking around for an Me 109 of our formation, there was a banging inside my machine and I saw a Lightning diving away below me. My cockpit filled with smoke and the controls no longer did what they should. So - bail out! The first two parts went well. The cockpit roof jettisoned right away and I got clear of the uncontrollable machine. At what height was I? I knew that the tops of the clouds were at around 3000m. So I restrained myself from pulling the rip-cord right away, for it could get unpleasant without oxygen. So I allowed myself to fall and pulled about a few hundred metres above the clouds. The opening jerk of my parachute caused the fur boots to take leave of my feet and I watched them disappearing as small dots into the clouds. I was worried about my parachute which, probably through turbulence, collapsed twice before it steadied itself. Meanwhile I had passed through the clouds and saw a large white snow covered field. Now my feet were cold and I was glad to be able to wrap them in my parachute after landing successfully at about 12.20. Only much later did I realise that now I had been shot down for the sixth time.*

**22 year old fighter pilot Fw Hans-Eberhard 'Hardy' Blume, who had joined 4./JG27 in the *Reichsverteidigung* in May 1943, a unit in which he fought against the Americans until July 1944.**

**Below:** Bf 109G-6 'cannon bird' of Hptm Fritz Keller, *Gruppen Kommandeur*, II./JG27, with OFw Müller, (left) and Fw Blume, Wiesbaden-Erbenheim, early spring 1944. Note the IInd *Gruppe* symbol on the nose. *Hans-Eberhard Blume.*

I./JG26 and the pilot is believed to have been hit, because the aircraft was not visibly damaged.

In the 68th BS formation only three Liberators would return to Shipdham.

B-24 42-7514/O piloted by 1/Lt Gary M Mathisen of the 68th BS was also hit fatally by the fighters of JG26 and was seen to nose up and over the formation with the waist position burning profusely. Nobody reported seeing any parachutes but three men did survive, though one of these, probably Sgt Leo M Tyler, ball turret gunner, was seriously injured. He died later. When 2/Lt Donald R Hoeltke, the bombardier, hit the ground, he was immediately surrounded by troops with about 18 bayonets shoved at him. There was no possibility of him evading capture. Hoeltke was later sent to Stalag Luft I, Barth and he remained there until the end of the war. B-24 42-7501/P, piloted by 1/Lt Frank W Sobotka, was also hit by JG26 and the bombs were dropped immediately. The stricken B-24 was observed to circle off to the left and begin burning, apparently under control.

The five B-24s of the 44th BG that were shot down by JG26, on the fateful 21 January mission, were claimed by Oblt Artur Beese (two), Lt Leberecht Altmann, Lt Georg Kiefner, and Uffz Hans Ruppert. To make matters worse for the 'Eightballs', *Liberty Belle*, flown by 1/Lt Keith Cookus of the 67th BS, who was leading the

**Above:** A Bf 110 attacking a formation of 91st BG Fortresses, January 1944. *USAF.*

**Above:** B-17G 42-39867 piloted by Lt Frank E Valesh of the 351st BS, 100th BG, which he put down at Eastchurch on 24 January 1944 after being hit by *Flak* over France after the mission to Frankfurt was recalled. Repaired, this Fortress was later assigned to the 349th BS and named *Boeing Belle*. It survived the war. *USAF.*

*Our squadron was flying the low element of the flight and our ship was in the position known to all as Purple Heart corner. Upon approaching the target, we got a call from the lead ship saying, 'We missed our target, go around. Go around.' As we approached it a second time, Lt Spelts called the bombardier (on this particular mission the navigator and bombardier were replacements and I did not know them) and told him we were on course and he should open the bomb bay doors and take over the ship. The bombardier replied, 'I have the aircraft, thank you, Sir. We are on target. Bombs away'. At about that moment, I saw about five or six Fw 190s, or as we called them, Goering's Yellow Bellies, closing in on us. I yelled "Fighters, Fighters at 6 o'clock low!" The sound of their gunfire rang through the aircraft from the underside. The ball turret gunner, Sgt Reedy, screamed, 'I'm hit, I'm*

*hit!' The fighters passed on and made a curve to the right, and returned from above, again fired at us, killing our top turret gunner, Sgt Hites, and our co-pilot, Lt Smith. Next, I heard someone who I assumed was our radio man, Hall, yell, 'Hydraulic fluid is spraying over my face!' Then navigator, Lt Rodgers, said, 'I'm hit! The bombardier is dead. My God, we're going down!'*

*Lt Spelts' voice then came through the interphone with, 'Abandon the...'. That was all – our intercom had gone out. I then looked back into the waist positions and saw the two gunners, Gooden and F P Hall, putting on their chutes. I rotated my turret to gain access to the rear section and fell backward out of the turret; I grabbed my chute with my right hand and opened the lower escape hatch with my left. While I was snapping my chute to the right harness ring, it happened! The ship did a rollover – and I presume there was an explosion because I blacked out.*

*T*he target area was cloud covered when we arrived and we were on our third run, trying to get a good visual drop from about 12,000ft when we first saw the German fighter formations. They made the first pass from off our right wing, then climbed ahead to make the next from about 11 o'clock, high. They must have raked us with several 20mm hits. One exploded directly on the nose, killing the bombardier and navigator, and turning their compartment into an instant inferno. We think the co-pilot, Lt Curtis, was killed by that very same blast. Another round must have gone off either on, or very near, the top turret I was manning, blowing off the Plexiglas dome and sending shrapnel into my left chest and arm. I grabbed the seat release cable and dropped to the flight deck. The right wall above the radio station was on fire and Rosenblatt, the radio operator, was putting on his chute. He yelled that we had other fires in the waist area and had been ordered to bail out by the pilot. A quick glance forward showed the pilot, Howington, fighting the controls and was apparently unharmed. I snapped on my chute, opened the door to the nosewheel compartment, and dropped down to be hit by heat and flames blowing back from the nose area. I stepped out on the catwalk, thankfully noting that the bomb bay doors were open and the bombs had been jettisoned. Just then Rosenblatt dropped down from the flight deck. I took one final glance into the cockpit. The pilot was looking back and motioning with one hand for us to jump.

I actually jumped with the intention of free-falling for 2,000 to 3,000ft before opening my chute as we had been instructed to do many times while in training. But that falling sensation was such a shock to my system that I could not have been more that 20 to 30ft beneath the plane when I changed my mind and gave a hearty yank on that cord. I wanted to know – and immediately – whether or not that chute was good! It was, and the heavy jerk of the canopy's opening was welcome relief.

**Sgt Archie Barlow, engineer, *RAM IT-DAM IT/ARIES* 68th BS, 44th BG, flown by Lt Hartwell R Howington (KIA). Barlow and three others escaped and eventually returned to England**

**Left:** *RAM IT-DAM IT/ARIES*, 68th BS, 44th BG, which was shot down by JG26 21 January 1944. Mike Bailey.

When I came to, I was falling free from the aircraft. My chest pack was hooked to the right ring only. I frantically tried to hook the left ring but the harness was too tight. I decided to pull the ripcord anyhow, but the chute didn't open! I clawed at the cover and managed to open it, and reeled the chute out by hand. It finally opened with a loud crackling sound — and I felt like I was going right through the harness. I blacked out again, momentarily, this time, and when I came to again, I saw pieces of the Queen Marlene falling around me.

Luckily, I landed in a newly ploughed field and I didn't appear to have any serious injuries. The left side of my face was bleeding – shrapnel, I imagine, but nothing serious – burns, cuts. However, I had lost my partial dental plates and my flying boots were gone. Before I could get to my feet, two Frenchmen ran to me, felt my arms and legs for broken bones and being assured that I was OK, they ran up a small rise to see what happened to the airplane. I followed them and saw the remainder of the ship burning. I did not see any parachutes or anyone else around. There were German military trucks racing to the site of the crash. At that time, it was the policy of the German Army to go to the site of the crash and search an area one mile in diameter. When I saw the Germans, I ran back, buried my chute and raced off in the opposite direction to where I met a French farmer with a cart loaded with boughs. I crawled under the wood and hid.

**S/Sgt Richard A Mayhew, tail turret gunner, sole survivor, *Queen Marlene*, 21 January, successfully evaded capture and returned to duty 29 May 1944. He was sent back to the US for skin grafts and treatment.)**

*W*e were attacked by Me 109s while circling to find our target. Both engines on the left side were shot out, putting us in a steep left turn and rolling our plane over on its back. With both Frank (Sobotka) and me on the controls, we managed to right the plane, but couldn't pull it out of the flat spin it went into. The rudder controls were gone and the instrument panel was shot out. Frank immediately hit the alarm bell switch alerting the crew to bail out. After a few seconds, I spotted only four chutes descending. The mess in our cabin, due to the rolling over, was unbelievable. Our chest chutes, usually stowed behind our seats, had ended up in the radio compartment. I retrieved the chutes, putting Frank's in his lap and buckling mine on. Sgt Clair Shaeffer was strapped in the top turret, obviously dead, and our radio operator, Sgt Tom Capizzi was putting his chute on as well. Frank was yelling at us to jump. Capizzi and I stood at the edge of the bomb bay, so I jumped and apparently Capizzi froze up. He and Frank rode the plane down. I have no idea what had happened in the waist or nose sections of the plane, but I know I was the last one out. We were so low at the time I jumped that my chute only oscillated once before I hit the ground. I came into contact with the Underground about three days after landing. The only information they could give me about my crew was that Abe Teitel, the bombardier, was alive and Frank Sobotka's dog tags were found in the wreckage of the plane.

**Lt Milton L Rosenblatt, co-pilot, B-24 42-7501/P, 68th BS, 44th BG. Teitel and Rosenblatt escaped and subsequently returned to England. 1/Lt Fred Butler, navigator, S/Sgt Charles W Shockley, left waist gunner, S/Sgt August F Smanietto, and S/Sgt Ross J Andrew, right waist gunner, were made PoW.**

*I was new to this crew. I flew only two times with them before going overseas with them. Therefore, I was not well acquainted with the crew. This was our very first combat mission. We came under heavy fighter attacks by Fw 190s and Me 109s. They eventually knocked out three of our engines and we could no longer stay in the air. Our co-pilot, Lewis W Rhodes, was killed on the very first pass by the enemy aircraft. Our pilot, Alfred A Starring, was wounded as well, probably also on that first attack. As our co-pilot was already dead, Starring found it impossible to stay in formation especially with two engines out. When later attacks knocked out the third engine, we were on our way down. At this time, the waist gunners went forward and jumped out through the bomb bay but I opened the rear hatch and went out from there just as the plane went into its final spin. We must have been quite close to the ground by then as my parachute had barely opened a few seconds before I hit the ground. Our navigator, Weldon H Maneval, must have jumped from the front end at about the same time as I did, with his parachute opening but not quite quickly enough, and he was killed by the impact with the ground. I was taken prisoner and spent 16 months in Stalag Luft 6 and Robert A Mitchell, our right waist gunner, survived PoW camp but found that he had tuberculosis when he returned home after the war.*

**Robert C Schild, tail gunner, Victory Ship (so called because of its code letter "V"), the 68th BS, 44th BG's fourth loss, piloted by 1/Lt Alfred A Starring. Victory Ship was hit by JG26 and engines one and two were set on fire, but the pilots managed to keep in formation. But when the enemy made following attacks, this B-24 went down in flames. Seven parachutes were seen to open.**

*Above: Victory Ship*, 68th BS, 44th BG. *Mike Bailey.*

formation attack on Agathe D'Aliermont, was hit severely by *Flak*. Cookus managed to nurse the shattered Liberator back across the Channel where it was written off in a crash at Manston. Two of the thirteen men aboard were killed. Three men who bailed out over France were taken prisoner.

The bombers were stood down for two days following the 21 January missions, but resumed again on 24 January when 857 heavy bomber crews were briefed to attack aviation industry plants and marshalling yards at Frankfurt. Bad weather during assembly though resulted in all except 563 bombers being despatched. The 2nd BD Liberator force was recalled before being despatched and at 1020 hours all groups were recalled due to worsening weather en route. All except the leading combat wing in the 3rd BD, at the German border and decided to select a target of opportunity and turned for home as instructed. Two B-17s were lost this day, both from the 95th BG. Fighter attacks over Belgium claimed *Lover Boy*, piloted by 2/Lt Clay A Burnett, and *Roarin' Bill*, flown by 2/Lt Charles H Mowers.

The weather remained bad and the next heavy bomber mission was not flown until 28 January when 54 B-24s were despatched to France. 43 Liberators bombed their

*The end of my operational flying came on 24 January 1944 when we were scrambled from Bergerac-sur-Dordogne. Temperature was -17°C, and with the throttles fully open I chased after my Staffel. I was only just airborne and flying at a height of 3m, when the engine stopped with a jolt due to frozen oil. I crashed into a house on the edge of the airfield, fortunately the aircraft did not catch fire: 150m beyond the house the remains of the aircraft came to rest with me sitting on top of the full fuel tank! I had suffered a double fracture of the base of the skull, plus several other fractures of the skull and injuries to both eyes, but the rest of me was still intact! This was the last time I flew in the war. I was no longer fit for flying duties. I spent the rest of the war on the ground, as Adjutant for special duties, as ground controller, etc. I arrived back at my Geschwader only two days before the Invasion, and was among the last men moving out of our airfield, after the machines had taken off to a new 'drome. I know from the reports of my comrades, that after the American long-range fighters, the Thunderbolt, Mustang, and also the Lightning, entered the fray, it was no longer possible to get at the bomber 'Pulks' without suffering grievous losses.*

**Oblt Otto "Stotto" Stammberger, *Staffelkapitän*, 2./JGr West.**

targets and all of the aircraft returned safely to their bases. The following day the bomber crews were assigned targets at Frankfurt and they were not so lucky. Of the 863 heavies despatched, 24 B-17s and five B-24s failed to return. Once again the *Luftwaffe* seized upon lapses in the bomber formations, which began to go awry soon after crossing the coast at Dunkirk when

navigational errors and radar problems caused several combat wings to fly most of the mission without fighter escort. The Fw 190s of the *1st and 2nd Gruppen* of JG26, took off at 1010 hours and were vectored east to Namur where they intercepted the B-24 formation. While some of the enemy fighters moved on to seek out B-17s in the 3rd BD formations, the 7th *Staffel* remained with the Liberators and near Trier they singled out the 44th BG formation. Lt Waldi Radener later claimed one of the Liberators but this was not filed. Uffz Kurt Stahnke singled out another Liberator – it was Pinder's – and the German scored hits near the bomber's right wingtip.

Luckily for the 'Flying Eightballs', 20th FG P-38 Lightnings appeared on the scene and the fighter pilots of JG26 were forced to break off their attacks and seek cover in the clouds. The Lightnings shot down three of the Fw 190A-6s, losing one of their number to Gefr. Manfred Talkenburg of the 8th *Staffel*. The 'Eightballs' were not yet safe. 8./JG26 *Staffelkapitän* Oblt Rudi Leuschel stayed with the Liberators and shot down B-24 41-29157 flown by 1/Lt George H Maynard in the 66th Squadron.

Some of the other pilots in JG26 found other targets further afield. Oblt Kurt Kranefeld of I./JG26 shot down a 385th BG B-17 south of Maubeuge at 1245 hours and Oblt Wolfgang Neu CO, 4./JG26, did likewise. Five minutes later, 8km south-south-west of Le Cateau, Fw Heinz Gomann was credited with shooting down a 388th BG B-17. It was *Mary Ellen*, piloted by 1/Lt F P Hennessey, that had been hit by *Flak* over the target and was trying to make it back flying on the deck. (Hennessey and navigator, 2/Lt C Richardson, bailed out and evaded capture, returning to England on 22 March

1944. Four of the crew were captured and three crewmembers were killed.) Gomann also received confirmation for the shooting down of a 389th BG Liberator into the sea west of Calais at 1348 hours. It was *LA City Limits* flown by Lt Boyd L Dout. All 10 crew perished. Hptm Karl Borris's claim for a B-17 east of Bonn, and Fw Josef Zirngibl's claim for another B-17 were also confirmed but three other claims by JG26 pilots for two more B-17s were not. A claim by Lt Wilhelm Hoffman of 8./JG26 for a 95th BG B-17 shot down 2km north of Lutrebois at 1330 hours was confirmed. The 95th BG lost two B-17s this day: 42-3545 of the 334th BS, which was flown by 2/Lt Andrew Rozentinsky and crashed at Brussels, and *Spook No.5*, flown by 2/Lt. James D. Higgins of the 336th BS and crashed at Ziegfeld. In addition to these victories pilots of JG26 were also credited with the destruction of four fighters.

*Below:* Oblt Waldemar Radener, in Fw 190 A-8 'Brown 4' leading 7./JG26 from Coesfeld-Stevede on 4 May 1944. Note the rows of *Abschuss*-symbols on the tail unit of 'Waldi' Radener's aircraft, whose tally at that time stood at 20 kills. A few days later, on 11 May, he rammed a B-24 in air combat over France while flying 'Brown 2' and was wounded. Barely recovered, he was shot down by a Mustang on 15 June and was severely injured before bailing out. He survived the war scoring 37 *Abschüsse*, including 17 *Viermots*, in the *Reichsverteidigung*, and was decorated with the *Ritterkreuz* on 12 March 1945. *Werner Molge.*

*We were over France and about an hour from the target, with all bombs on board, we were jumped by a flight of fighters and were hit immediately. Shells hit just behind me and made very large holes in the waist section. No.4 engine was hit and put out of action. So were the controls to the tail section. So the pilots could only control flight with the three remaining engines. With the possibility of getting back to England now so slight, the decision was made to head for Switzerland. The bombs were salvoed, but even then with the trouble of trying to steer with the engines, we continually lost altitude across France. We did finally cross the Swiss border but by then we were less than 1,000ft. We were shot at and hit by (Swiss?) ground fire, and No.2 engine was put out of commission as well. Not being able to gain altitude over the rising terrain of Switzerland, we had to circle back to abandon ship. Only the three of us got out – all from the rear – because we were so low by that time that the others did not have time to get out and open their chutes.*

**S/Sgt Derise L Nichols, tail gunner, B-24 41-29157 flown by 1/Lt George H Maynard, 66th BS, 44th BG Seven of the crew, including Maynard and his co-pilot John E Norquist, perished, while the navigator, ball turret gunner, and Nichols, bailed out and were taken prisoner.**

**Left:** Fw Heinz Gomann, pilot, 8./JG26 at Stevede airfield in 1944. On 17 August 1943, whilst still an Uffz, Gomann attacked an American *Viermot* but was hit by return fire and had to bail out of his Fw 190. His parachute became entangled with the tail unit and only after a prolonged struggle was he able to free himself. Gomann was admitted to hospital with slight wounds. He went on to claim 12 *Abschüsse* in III./JG26 and survived the war as the longest-serving pilot in his *Gruppe*, having been in action since 1942. *Walter Stumpf.*

**Right:** Lt Thomas H Gunn, 323rd BS, 91st BG, flew B-17G 42-37938 *Betty Lou's Buggy* safely back to Bassingbourn on 19 April 1944 after sustaining heavy damage from Bf 109s at the FW assembly plant at Eschwege near Kassel. Fighters holed the left wing fuel tank, put a turbo out, damaged an engine, knocked out the elevators and left aileron and exploded shells in the nose, cockpit, bomb bay and fin. Gunn could only control direction by using the engines and had to apply full right aileron to keep the B-17 level. Only the co-pilot, and navigator were wounded. Robert D Smith, tail gunner, inspects the damage to the fin of *Betty Lou's Buggy* caused by a cannon shell which severed the rudder controls. The Fortress was repaired and survived the war, only to be cut up for scrap at Kingman, AZ, in December 1945. *USAF.*

*The day was much the same game as before, with about 200 4-mots in the area of Hannover. The huge fighter escort left us largely alone as long as we flew in a close formation. But as soon as our lot was dispersed after the first attack, everyone had a whole bunch after him. Once I was chased by 16 Thunderbolts to the Harz. The sole means of escape was dodging away at tree-top level. A few days later, on 8 February, they came from the south. I wanted to land at Liege (or Maastricht) with the last of my fuel, but found the runway blocked against enemy airborne landings and had to put my kite down in a field south of Liege, as low clouds barred my way over the Eiffel to Aachen.*

*Two days later they turned up again. It turned out to be a memorable day. I had taken off as wingman to an experienced OFw and we were approaching a 4-mot formation near Brunswick. First the OFw attacked alone and set a B-17 on fire. You must manage that too, show him! I approached very close from behind and with satisfaction watched my burst strike the starboard wingroot. Flames shot out. But the aim of the gunners of the neighbouring aircraft was not bad either. It thundered into the fuselage behind me and suddenly my aircraft went vertically downwards. With sudden dismay I found no pressure on the stick and the trim brought nothing either. Nothing but out. Cockpit cover away, and I was stuck like a stamp on the armour plating of my seat; right arm out, it was dragged backward by a ton weight. I must have had a terrific speed from 7000m. I pressed my head out to the side and I must have had nostrils like a snorting stallion. My left hand grabbed the windscreen and pulled and pulled. One grows in strength in an emergency. Suddenly I am out, the air around me screams and stops my breath, tears the jacket from my body, pulls one of my boots off and tumbles me about like a Ping-Pong ball.*

*'Don't pull, don't pull!' I shout to myself. I am too fast, too high and the sky is full of Yankee fighters, I have seen them myself firing at us in our parachutes. So down, down. Now I am slowing up, I am quietly lying, head down and looking at the sky beyond my flapping trouser legs. Stay calm! Cloud base was at 2000m, then you can pull. 4000m freefall; not bad at all. Now I am approaching the clouds. No fighters in sight. Pull. I*

*already know the jerk. As I am hanging something black rushes past me, my boot. Into the clouds, the big prize question is, where do you come out? Then it gets darker below me, land in sight. Oh ho, nothing but woods. So far all had gone well, now I'm going to land in the trees. Luckily a fresh wind, I drift quickly to the edge of the wood, float low over a village, call cheekily to the people in the street below me who look startled up towards me. A freshly ploughed field appears, looks likely for my landing. Then I am down, on my stomach, the lock is covered in dirt, won't release. The 'chute drags me across the whole field on my stomach. I look like a pig after a mud bath. There is still snow everywhere. I pull a gauntlet over my right sock and set off for the nearby village. At the first house I call to a woman on the first floor; startled she slams the window, probably takes me for a Yankee Negro. Reacting to my good German she then lets me in and smothers me with her mothering instincts. A wash, fried potatoes with a fried egg in the warm room. Then suddenly there were shouted orders outside, 'two men to the back door, don't let him get away!' The door flies open and I stare at several shotgun muzzles. The Landwacht (country guard) wants to make a capture. My front-flyer's ID card pacifies them. 'We have a first-aid man with us, you must be wounded.' 'Why?' I ask incredulously. 'But you crept through the snow on your left foot and your right hand, We have followed your tracks.' 'My glove instead of my boot!' Great laughter. They arrange for transport to the airbase of Helmstedt. Thank you, guardian angel! You must have dragged me out of the machine, I would never have managed it on my own.*

*I had sprained my right shoulder somewhat on getting out of the aircraft and with my arm in a sling I was given a few days leave. In the overcrowded train an old woman offered me her seat. 'Sit down, Herr Leutnant, you are wounded.' I felt quite ashamed.*

**Oblt Eberhard Burath, II./JG1, Rheine, 30 January 1944. Four weeks after sustaining his shoulder injuries, Burath re-entered the fray again, or, as he put it, the party continued. Sorties over Rothenburg, Hamm. Dogfight with Thunderbolt over Wesendorf, over the airfield of Rheine. At 0845 to Oldenburg, at 1005 to Kassel, at 1445 again to Rheine. They chase us across Germany's skies.**

# Chapter 5 – Strategic War

Early in 1944 the *Luftwaffe* was still a force to be reckoned with, especially when one considers its day fighter *Geschwaders* of conventional fighters could and did, shoot down dozens of B-17s and B-24s on a single mission. Despite a highly effective fighter shield of long-range P-51 Mustangs - which could accompany the bombers to their targets and back again - the USAAF was, on occasion, powerless to prevent German fighters causing carnage on a large scale as the bombers flew even deeper and in greater numbers to the far flung targets of the *Third Reich*.

Operation *Argument* was the first battle involving the mass use of bomb groups of the Strategic Air Forces (USSTAF). Gen Carl 'Tooey' Spaatz and his subordinate commanders, Maj Gen Jimmy Doolittle (8th AF) and Maj Gen Nathan F Twining (15th AF), planned to make a series of co-ordinated raids on the German aircraft industry, supported by RAF night bombing, at the earliest possible date. Good weather finally permitted 'Operation *Argument*', to take place during the week 20-25 February, which quickly became known as 'Big Week'.

On 20 February, 1,028 B-17s and B-24s and 832 fighters in the 8th AF attacked 12 aircraft plants in Germany for the loss of 25 bombers and four fighters. Three Medals of Honor (two posthumously) were awarded to B-17 crewmen. The 15th did not take part because it was committed to supporting the Anzio operation. Next day, 21 February, 924 bombers and 679 fighters bombed aircraft factories at Brunswick and other targets. The 15th was grounded by bad weather. This time the 8th lost 19 bombers and five fighters but

60 German fighters were claimed shot down. Two of the B-17s lost were from the 95th BG, which succumbed to fighters of JG26. 42-30634 *Liberty Belle* piloted by Lt John P McGuigan of the 412th BS, crashed into the Zuider Zee with the loss of six crew. The rest were captured after bailing out. 42-3462 *San Antonio Rose*, piloted by 2/Lt Morris R Marks of the 336th BS, crashed into these waters with the loss of eight of the crew. Two men were captured and made PoW. These two B-17s were shot down by OFw Addi Glunz, 5th *Staffel* CO and Uffz Loschinksi of 7./JG26.

JG26 were active again on 22 February when the 8th bombed targets in Germany and Holland - with the loss of 41 bombers, while 118 bombers of the 15th AF bombed the Messerschmitt assembly plant in Regensburg, for the loss of 14 aircraft. Hardest hit in the 8th AF was the 1st BD, which lost 38 B-17s (the 2nd BD lost the other three bombers this day). JG26 pilots claimed seven B-17s shot down and all came from the 91st or 384th BGs, which lost five and four B-17s respectively. OFw Addi Glunz claimed two B-17s shot down and a third forced out of formation in the first combat sortie of the day. That same afternoon he claimed two more Fortresses and a Thunderbolt. Glunz received confirmation for three B-17s and the P-47, taking his tally to 58 victories.

On 23 February, bad weather kept the heavies on the ground but 102 bombers in the 15th AF destroyed 20 per cent of the ball-bearing works at Steyr, Austria. Next day, 24 February, 114 B-17s and B-24s of the 15th AF returned to Steyr. Seventeen bombers failed to return.

**Right:** Fw 190A-7 340283 'Gelbe (Yellow) 6', of 3./JG1 was lost in combat with American *Viermots* on 8 February 1944. Fw Gerhard Giese perished when his aircraft crashed near Charleville. It is seen here being topped-up at Dortmund airfield. *Seebrandt via Rob de Visser.*

**Full page:** Fw 190s of 3./JG1 taking off from the snow-covered airfield at Dortmund in early 1944. *Köhne via Rob de Visser.*

*Right:* Stab II./JG26 Fw
I90 revving up its engine.
*Werner Molge.*

Meanwhile, 238 Fortresses attacked Schweinfurt, losing
11 B-17s, while 295 B-17s struck at targets on the
Baltic coast with the loss of five Fortresses. Some 239 B-
24s headed for the Messerschmitt Bf 110 assembly plant
at Gotha. *Flak* was heavy over Holland and the B-24s
encountered repeated attacks by the *Luftwaffe*. The
arrival of three Thunderbolt groups just after 1200 hours
was unable to beat off attacks by over 150 fighters and
five of the 445<sup>th</sup> BGs 28 Liberators were shot down in
almost as many minutes. The German fighters continued
to attack all the way to the target and four more 445<sup>th</sup>
BG B-24s were shot down. P-51s and P-38s took over
from the flagging Thunderbolts near Hanover and
covered the Liberators as they neared the target.

Some confusion arose in the Liberators' ranks at the
IP when the 389<sup>th</sup> lead navigator suffered oxygen
failure and veered off course. The bombardier slumped
over his bombsight and accidentally tripped the bombs.
Before the small 445<sup>th</sup> formation reached the target its

On 22 February 1944 we received our new Me 109s and wanted to give them a try-out. But it turned out differently. Suddenly there was a report of an American formation flying in the direction of Regensburg. So it was action stations and we took off. The Americans came in at about 6,000m high. They first dropped bombs on Prüfening and then it was Obertraubing's turn. We attacked from behind with all guns firing and the Americans' projectiles came at us like out of a watering can. I had damaged a B-17, continued with further attacks and finally shot it down 15km south-west of Straubing. Three men bailed out. The machine crashed close to a wood.

When I returned to the airfield the barracks and hangars had been hit by bombs and the field had many craters. I was able to make out a strip between the craters and made a smooth landing. The hangars were damaged, my quarters and the mess completely destroyed. A gruesome scene greeted me close to where I parked my machine. An American had come down by parachute, he had dropped onto a metal structure which had cut him open from between the legs to his head, into two halves.

**Lt Heinrich Freiherr von Podewils, fighter pilot, I./JG5, 22 February 1944.**

**Right:** Lt Heinrich Freiherr von Podewils, early 1944, when he served as fighter pilot with I./JG5 in the *Reichsverteidigung*. Heinrich ended World War Two with three confirmed victories in JG5. Heinrich Freiheir von Podewils.

*Luftwaffe fighters made attempts to penetrate our formations but our 'little friends' kept them at a distance and, when the opportunity prevailed, dove in for a 'kill'. Using our thick vapour trails as a screen, the Germans often struck from below and from behind to shoot up any lagging bomber. Bending south-eastward toward Gotha, the white, snowy earth looked cold and lifeless; only the large communities, rail lines and an autobahn stood out in relief. Fighter attacks became more persistent. By the time we reached our IP (Initial Point) to start our bomb run, the sky about our three squadrons was full of busy P-38s and P-51s fending off the*

*Germans. They dove past the lead ship in pursuit of Messerschmitts and Focke-Wulfs making head-on attacks. Our gunners got in a lot of shooting, too. The staccato of the turrets' twin fifties vibrated throughout the airplane. It was real scary.*

**Maj Myron H Keilman, deputy lead pilot, 392nd BG, 24 February 1944.**

**Below:** 457th BG Fortresses braving the *Flak* at Schweinfurt, 24 February 1944. *USAF.*

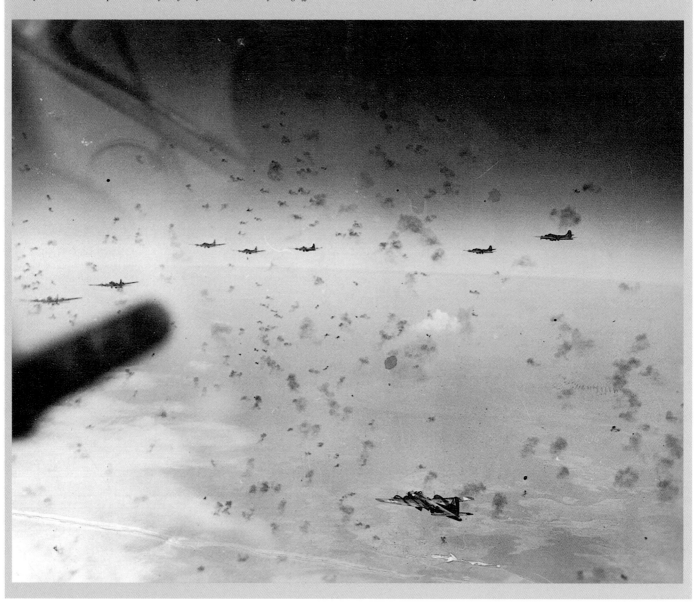

10th and 11th fell victims to the German guns. By now the 445th consisted of only 14 Liberators; three having aborted before entering Germany. Another B-24 was shot down just after leaving Eisenach. The 13 remaining B-24s, realising that they had veered off course, continued alone. They arrived over the target at 1325 hours and executed an eight minute bomb run. Some 180 500 pounders dropped from 12,000 ft and inflicted heavy damage on the Messerschmitt plant. A further 171 B-24s dropped another 468 tons of assorted bombs from varying altitudes and directions. The 445th's 13th B-24 was shot down moments after 'bombs away'. The 392nd BG released 98 per cent of its bombs within

2,000ft of the aiming point. Intelligence sources later estimated that six to seven weeks' production was lost. Only 13 Liberators in the 445th BG returned to Tibenham and six 389th Liberators were also lost. Both the 445th and 392nd BGs were later awarded Presidential Unit Citations for their part in the raid.

On 25 February, the USSTAF brought the curtain down on "Big Week" when 1,300 8th and 15th AF bombers and 1,000 fighters were despatched to aircraft plants, ball bearing works and components factories throughout the Reich. The 1st BD caused heavy damage to the Messerschmitt plants at Augsburg and the ball bearing plants at Stuttgart were also bombed. The 2nd

BD bombed the Me 110 components plant at Furth and considerable damage was caused to the Bf 109 plants at Regensburg by the 3rd BD and 176 bombers of the 15th AF. The latter hit the aircraft plants an hour before the England-based force arrived over the city. Output at Augsburg and Regensburg was severely reduced for four months following the raids. The 8th lost 31 bombers while the 15th AF lost 33 bombers. 13 of the B-17s lost by the 8th AF came from the 1st BD, which attacked the Me 410 assembly plant at Augsburg. The 306th BG lost three B-17s, two of which were credited to JG26. At about 1120 hours, on the way in, the Group was greeted by accurate and unexpected *Flak* from Saarbrucken.

*T*he bombs were smack 'on target' but the battle wasn't over. No sooner had the wing left the target's Flak than we were accosted by German fighters again. Strung out in trail and with some planes slowed down from Flak damage, our three squadrons became vulnerable to vicious attacks. For the next hour and more, Messerschmitt, Focke Wulf and Junker fighters worked us over until our fighters could fend them off. As deputy command pilot, I frequently changed off flying formation with the airplane commander to keep occupied and not have to watch the Jerries

press their blazing gun attacks. The inter phone was alive with excited calls of enemy action. Head on passes and tail attacks; in singles and in 'gaggles'; rockets, 20mm cannon, and even some cables were thrown at us. Seven of our B-24s were shot down. Many of us were shot up, but it was not all one-sided. The gunners of the 22 airplanes that returned accounted for 16 German fighters.

**Maj Myron H Keilman, deputy lead pilot, 392nd BG, 24 february 1944.**

***Above:*** Bombs away over Germany during 'Big Week', on 20 February 1944. *USAF.*

***Right:*** On the 10 February 1944 mission to Brunswick, 29 B-17s and eight escorting fighters were lost to the ferocious German defences. Five Fortresses came down in the Netherlands, including B-17G 42-37950 *Dinah Mite*, 731st BS, 452nd BG, piloted by 2/Lt. Thomas F Sharpless, which force-landed north-east of Urk in the recently reclaimed land in the eastern Ijsselmeer (Zuider Zee), the Noordoostpolder. During the following months, the wreck was visited illegally many times by local inhabitants. *Coen Cornelissen.*

This split the Group wide open and, before it could properly reform, two diving attacks by German fighters took a 368th BS BS B-17 on each pass. F/O James R Coleman, his crew and 1/Lt Joseph M Gay Jr's B-17 were shot down near Charleville by Hptm Klaus Mietusch, III./JG26 CO, and Oblt Schauder 10th *Staffel* CO. OFw Addi Glunz claimed a 390th BG B-17 and two 96th BG B-17s were also claimed by pilots of

*Left:* Extensive battle damage to *Dinah Mite's* tail. Three of Sharpless' crew were taken prisoner, seven evaded capture. *Coen Cornelissen.*

*Right:* The *Jagdwaffe* lost 23 pilots killed and 17 missing in the great air battles of 10 February 1944, plus six pilots injured. One of the young fighter pilots posted missing was Uffz Ingomar Feldmann of III./JG54, seen here with his Bf 109G at Orange airfield, France, in 1943. Feldmann went missing in the Steinhuder Lake area. *Coen Cornelissen.*

*Bottom right:* B-17F 42-31363 *Vapor Trail,* 368th BS, 306th BG, at Thurleigh with wing tip damage after a collision. *Vapor Trail* and I/Lt Rene C Fix's crew FTR from the mission to La Rochelle on 27 March 1944. They were hit by *Flak* approaching the target, and Nos.3 and 4 engines were knocked out. Fix ditched in the Bay of Biscay where the crew took to their dinghies. Fix and his co-pilot, 2/Lt. Weldon B Frantz, stayed in the water for a long time putting cold patches over the holes of one dinghy. As darkness fell they were spotted by a German three-engined amphibian which took them to Bordeaux where all 10 crew were hospitalised for several days before being sent to PoW camps. *Richards.*

JG26. The intensity of the battles of 'Big Week' can be judged by total losses of some 226 bombers.

Less than a week after Big Week, the USAAF launched its first attack on 'Big-B' - Berlin. The 3 March attack by 748 heavies was aborted because of bad weather and 79 bombers attacked targets of opportunity at Wilhelmshaven. Next day, 4 March, the heavies were briefed to bomb Berlin again but bad weather forced the B-24s to abort early, leaving 502 Fortresses and 770 fighters to continue to the target. Severe weather en route resulted in a recall and 219 B-17s hit targets of opportunity while 30 B-17s in the 95th and 100th BGs defied the elements to drop the first American bombs on the Big City. The B-17s were stood down on the 5th while the Liberators attacked targets in France. On 6 March, the 8th despatched 730 B-17s and B-24s and 801 P-38, P-47 and P-51 escort fighters to targets in the suburbs of Berlin. US fighters claimed 81 enemy fighters shot down and the bomber gunners claimed 97 destroyed (the *Luftwaffe* actually lost 64 fighters destroyed and two damaged beyond repair). The 8th

lost (a record) sixty-nine bombers and eleven fighters, while 102 bombers were seriously damaged. Worst hit of all the bomb groups was the Bloody Hundredth with fifteen B-17s shot down.

Some 100 Fw 190s and Bf 109s of JG1, JG11, and III./JG54 were the first to attack the incoming bombers, between 1200 and 1230 hours, between Osnabruck and Hannover. JG3, the *Schwarmstaffel,* I./JG302, II. and III./ZG26, the *Einsatzstaffel Erla,* ZG26, and even 16 night fighters of NJG5 and IV./NJG1, totalling at least 134 aircraft, unleashed their might north of Magdeburg at 1235, attacking for over one hour without a pause. On the way back, elements of JG1, JG11, JG2, JG26, JG300 and IV./NJG1 – 85 fighters in all – intercepted the badly battered bomber formations just to the east of the Dutch-German border, at around 1430 hrs. Among the German losses on 6 March 1944 was Hptm Hugo Frey, the 28 year old St Kpt of 7./JG11, who was shot down and killed in his Fw 190A-6 "White 1" at Erm-Sleen, Holland. Frey was one of the *Jagdwaffe's* foremost *"Viermot"* killers, among his 32 victories

were 26 B-17s and B-24s. In the hour before he was killed, probably by return fire, Frey claimed his final four B-17s destroyed.

Groups were stood down on the 7th before they resumed the daylight offensive against Berlin again on 8 March. A total of 623 bombers were sent to bomb the VKF ball-bearing plant at Erkner in the suburbs of Berlin, escorted by 891 fighters. Of the force, 539 heavies got their bombs away over the German capital, which once again was heavily defended. The leading 3rd BD lost 23 Fortresses, 16 of them from the leading 45th CBW, which came under mass enemy fighter attack. Six B-17s were lost from the 96th BG, and five each from the 388th and 452nd BG formations. JG26 claimed seven of the 45th CBW's missing Fortresses (and two US fighters, for the loss of one Bf 109G-6). The 1st BD lost five B-17s to fighter attacks and *Flak.* Nine B-24s and 18 fighters were lost. The heavy bomber gunners claimed to have shot down 63 enemy fighters, while the escorts claimed a further 79 for the loss of eighteen of their own. In fact, only 27 *Luftwaffe* fighters were lost on 8 March. Despite the continued high losses, the 8th AF attacked Berlin again on the 9th. A total of 361 B-17s bombed Big B while 165 Liberators visited Hanover, Brunswick and Nienburg. Weather conditions kept the *Jagdwaffe* on the ground and for once the enemy fighters were noticeable by their absence. The 800 escort fighters returned without claiming any enemy fighters and the B-17 groups lost six

**Above:** B-17 42-31329, 334th BS, 95th BG, which crash-landed at Oberriet-Kriessern, Switzerland, on the mission to Augsburg, 16 March 1944. Five of Lt James W Reed's crew were interned and five were made PoW. *Hans Heiri Stapfer.*

**Left:** Lt Wilhelm Hofmann, 8./JG26 CO, was credited with the destruction of B-24 *My Ass'am Dragon* of the 44th BG north-west of Gevelsburg, 15 March 1944. *Mike Bailey.*

**Right:** During spring 1944, many *Tagjagd Experten* fell victim to American escort fighters. Here Lt Karl Willius, St Kpt of 2./JG26 is climbing into the cockpit of his Fw 190A-8 at Florennes, Belgium in 1943. Note the national flags painted beneath his cockpit, denoting the countries over which Willius had seen action (Holland, Belgium, France, England and Russia). After claiming a 44th BG B-24, 8 April 1944 on his 371st combat mission (as his 11th *Viermot* kill and his 50th combat victory), 'Charlie' was hit by a Thunderbolt of the 357th FS, 361st FG, flown by 1/Lt Alton B Synder and was killed when his Fw 190A-8 'Black 5' exploded near Genemuiden, Holland. His widow Lisette received a posthumous *Ritterkreuz* on 9 June 1944. *Lisette Arend-Willius.*

of their number over Berlin while the B-24 groups lost two, all to *Flak*.

Smaller scale raids on targets in France and Germany followed the early March strikes on Berlin, and on 15 March 344 bombers were despatched to aircraft component factories at Brunswick. Some 157 of the attacking force were Liberators, 145 of which successfully bombed their targets. At Lille and Florennes, the Ist and IInd *Gruppen* of JG26 were ordered to take off at 1100 hours and fly to Rheine to wait for the American bombers returning from Brunswick. Two Fw 190A-6s collided on take off and once airborne, the 7th *Staffel* was bounced by Spitfires of 401 Canadian Squadron, which were escorting some B-26 Marauders. Lt Wilhelm Hofmann, 8./JG26 CO, was credited with the destruction of a B-24 north west of Gevelsburg. It

was *My Ass'am Dragon*, of the 44th BG flown by 1/Lt David R Talbott. The other Liberator lost was *Pocatello Chief*, of the 392nd BG piloted by Lt Bert D Miller, which crashed at Hiddenhausen, Germany. Lt Karl "Charlie" Willius, CO of 2./JG26, claims to have pursued a damaged 392nd BG B-24 out over the North Sea and shot it down 50 miles east of Great Yarmouth, Norfolk, at 1630 hours. However, the only other loss this day was a 100th BG B-17, which exploded at the target.

On 16 March 1944, 740 B-17s and B-24s went to targets at Augsburg, Ulm, Gessertshausen and Friedrichshafen. Gunners claimed 68 enemy fighters. 23 bombers were lost.

After a stand-down on 17 March, the heavies were out again on 18 March, when 738 B-17s and B-24s were despatched to targets at Oberpfaffenhofen, Lechfeld,

*O*n 16 March 1944, we were again in action. So far, we had only encountered enemy bombers. The cities of Friedrichshafen, Augsburg and Munich were attacked. We were sitting in the machines, but then there was a snow storm and we had to get out again. After half an hour there was a large gap in the clouds with blue skies, so we took off with 24 Me 109s, first the Kommandeur and then I, then two more making it a flight. That made six flights. All aircraft with drop-tanks. As the field was very wet, we did not get airborne until the last 100m from the boundary. The Americans were already on their return flight and we still had to climb to 7000m. After some time we saw the hindmost formation with forty Boeings at 6000 metres. So overtake and attack from head-on. The rear defences of the enemy formations were too strong as each bomber had two or even four machine guns facing rearwards. That made at least 80 guns. Our speed was 700km/h from above and the yanks flew with 350 km/h. So full concentration at this speed, then fire, the others fired too, then through them and straight ahead in order not to offer a target to the tail gunners.

My Major Gerlitz pulled up right away and by the time I reached him his undercarriage was hanging out of the Me 109. I told him about that on the radio. He was able to retract the undercarriage again. Then off for another attack. At this closing speed it was impossible to tell whether one had scored any hits. Above and at 10,000m we saw fighters and thought they were our own. The second attack worked like the first. So off for a third, but then the Thunderbolts came from above and Gerlitz dived away instead of staying to fight. I was his wingman (Katschmarek) and had to follow. We dived with four machines and suddenly a Thunderbolt which was much heavier than ours and therefore faster in a dive, was sitting behind the Kommandeur. I wanted to fire with all guns, a cannon and four machine guns, but failed to look behind: I got a burst from behind, the projectiles struck the armour plate at my back and the engine. I throttled back and the Yank passed quite close to my Me, I could see him quite clearly in his brown leather flying suit as he looked at me.

**Above:** B-24 41-29331/F *Blondies' Folly* of the 755th BS, 458th BG which was lost with 2/Lt. Neil A J Peters' crew on 16 March 1944 when it was shot down by JG26 over France on the mission to bomb aviation industry targets in southern Germany. At Vitry the Liberator was shot out of formation by 11th *Staffelkapitän*, Lt. Peter Reischer, and near Reims the crippled bomber was finished off in three attacks by Uffz. Heinz Gehrke, who was on his first combat sortie. *Blondies' Folly* remained airborne however, before finally ditching in the Channel with the loss of eight crew KIA and two PoW. Alone now, Gehrke's Bf 109G-6 was jumped by P-47s of the 356th FG, who shot him down after the German made the fatal error in trying to dive his way out of trouble, always a fatal mistake in combat with the Thunderbolt. The P-47s shot the Bf 109 to shreds and Gehrke bailed out, landing with nothing more serious than a strained back. SW of St Dizier-Worms another B-24, *Ballsafire* of the 700th BS, 445th BG, was shot down by Hptm. Staiger 12th *Staffel* CO. Five of Lt. Richard A Raroha's crew were KIA and five PoW. P-47s of the 56th and 78th FGs shot down and killed five pilots of JG26 and wounded two more. (Peter Reischer committed suicide on 18 December 1944 after losing his nerve going into combat). *Mike Bailey.*

When he had passed I wanted to open the throttle and fire but the engine stopped. So down, but I did not want to bail out as I reckoned to be no more than 1000m over the Alb near Ulm. The instruments were dead. Coming from a great height one has no feeling for speed. I wanted to land near a village but was much too fast, then there was another power line. Now way up ahead there was a forest, but it is dangerous to land amongst the thick trees. There were three birches in a meadow and I aimed for these, one has but seconds to think. I hit one birch with the engine and the other two with the wings. The trees broke like matchsticks and the Me 109 was flung into the air. The machine turned over and fell upside down into the 30cm deep snow.

I was probably unconscious for a short while. As the cockpit was at a slant, I was able to release the cover, then I undid my harness and fell out with my parachute into the snow. I was able to stand up, passed my hand over my face and noticed that I was bleeding profusely. But I felt no pain. I scanned the sky

**Below:** Lt Heinrich Freiherr von Podewils posing with his Bf 109G early in 1944. Heinrich Frhr. *von Podewils*

*as the Yanks fired at pilots on the ground, not a very gallant thing to do. It was quiet. The aircraft lay on its back, the wings snapped upwards, the torn-off engine a few metres off, also the guns. The tail hung on a tree stump. I took my parachute, map and first-aid kit and wanted to walk to the village I had flown over. It was very heavy going in the snow. After a quarter of an hour I gave up, I saw no village, no road, so back again. By now, the Me 109 was being guarded by the Landsturm, the last resort in civilian dress with rifles, and the women were praying for the dead pilot. When I told them that I had been in the machine they did not want to believe me. They relieved me of my parachute and we walked along a path to the village of Radstetten and went to see the Burgomaster. My head had only suffered a cut and this was attended to with a sticking plaster. The first thing I did was to phone my airfield at Herzogenaurach and heard that my Kommandeur, Major Gerlitz, was dead. He had bailed out a few kilometres from me and, as he must already have been below 1000m, his parachute had failed to open fully. My presentiments before the flight had now turned out to have*

*been only too true. The Burgomaster gave me a meal, beer and Schnapps. Then I was taken by horse-sleigh to Urspring. Then to Ulm by train, where I was picked up by a car of the town commandant, a Colonel decorated with the Ritterkreuz. I had to tell the Colonel about the air battle, aided by some Kirschwasser (Schnapps).*

*Towards 6 pm I was taken to the train for Nurnberg which was overcrowded, but I got a seat together with my 'chute. Everyone in the compartment wanted to know what had happened. I told them and there was more Schnapps, it must have been home-brewed Schnapps for there was no longer any to buy. At one o'clock in the night I arrived in Nürnburg together with three other pilots and we were driven to Herzogenaurach and we fell into bed. On 17 March I heard that of our 24 aircraft 17 had been shot down and only seven had returned home.*

**Lt Heinrich Freiherr von Podewils, fighter pilot, I./JG5, 16 March 1944.**

**Below:** Wreckage of B-24 41-28742 *Old Glory*, 579th BS, 392nd BG, which was damaged by *Flak* over Friedrichshafen, 18 March 1944 and crashed 1500m NW of Hardt, near Schramberg, Rottweil with the loss of all but one of 1/Lt Dallas O Books' crew. *Jim Marsteller.*

*The left waist, gunner, Norm Willig was laying on the floor and Robert Hampton in the ball, was not moving. Fire was streaming past the waist window. The right outboard engine was feathered. Another fire was between Daniel Jones in the nose turret and me in the tail turret. He was screaming, 'Help me Pappy, get me out Pappy.' Things were happening so fast, I was only reacting to the flames, when enemy fighters came in*

*from all directions putting round after round into our ship. I screamed over the intercom to Lt Dallas Books, the pilot, 'Bank left and head for Switzerland!' His response, 'hang on, we'll be OK.' Again, the fighters came through what was left of the formation. The oxygen system failed and I became light headed. Our ship was streaming flames and slowing down, not able to keep up now, as more rounds came smashing through the ship.*

*On the intercom I heard the co-pilot, Capt John Slowik screaming and cursing the German fighters as more rounds came through Old Glory. The ship started to pitch and dive, then the oxygen tank next to my head exploded, blowing me out the waist window. I awoke to find myself' falling, and instinctively pulled the ripcord. Pieces of the plane were falling around me, but I didn't see my ship, or my crew, or my friends, ever again.*

S/Sgt Chester C Strickler, tail gunner, B-24 41-28742 *Old Glory*, 579th BS, 392nd BG, flown by l/Lt Dallas O Books, which was damaged by *Flak* at the target, Friedrichshafen, 18 March 1944. The 392nd suffered its heaviest single mission loss, losing 15 aircraft and crews and nine other ships damaged by fighters and *Flak*, all totalling 154 casualties. Strickler, who became a PoW, was the only survivor on Books' crew. He died aged 85.

**Above:** German villagers turn out to look at the remains of *Old Glory. Jim Marsteller.*

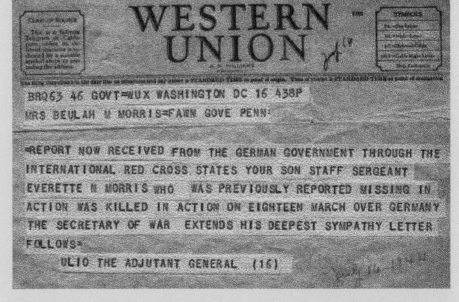

**Above:** Telegram informing the Morris family of the death of their son Everette, engineer gunner, *Old Glory*, 18 March 1944. *Jim Marsteller.*

*A*ccording to the reports reaching our base, we anticipated that we were in for something turbulent. Our Gruppe took off at 1304 and we flew southward. Lt Kapp led our section, in which I was pair-leader with Uffz Wilken as my wingman. In the area Ulm/Augsburg a large formation of B-17s crossed our course. It was evidently on its return flight, for it was no longer in its usual formation. Also, the formation was flying at a relatively low level. We made a wide sweep to get at it from ahead. Our superior height soon brought us into the right attacking position. We passed though the formation, firing with all our guns as usual, were able to observe strikes by the flashes of our projectiles as they hit, but without recognition of their effect in the seconds of time available. We dived away to escape the fire of the Boeings. Our section had become two pairs which had lost sight of each other after the attack. Only now did we notice that the sky was filled with 'fiddles' (enemy fighters). The escorting Lightnings had evidently not noticed us yet. We swept around in order to get at the formation again from behind and had to try to gain some height in the process.

Suddenly I spotted a Lightning behind Wilken, warned him and turned into it. It flew through my steady fire and broke off, trailing smoke. More, I was unable to observe as there were bangs in my machine. So we had been spotted after all. The usual white coolant smoke indicated my now little remaining time in the air, which had already been limited as we had jettisoned our auxiliary fuel tanks before commencing our attack. I had to concentrate on getting out of the Lightning's field of fire, which must still be in my vicinity. I put my aircraft into a shallow turn and got my 'white 5' as closely as possible to the ground, for I could not risk a dogfight as the Lightning had a smaller radius of turn and better visibility. I tried to confuse this unpleasant adversary by suddenly throttling my engine, with success, for he passed over me, but unfortunately there was another one whom I was unable to see and he scored some more hits on me. I stayed close to the ground and decided on a belly landing as a last resort, for which the ground appeared suitable. As I had not yet got down to landing speed, I pushed the aircraft down onto the soft ploughed field and seemed to slither along forever. I then got out of the cockpit, saw three Lightnings approaching, flung myself down behind a small rise in the ground, and watched the final destruction of my machine. A Flak battery nearby took me in, informed my unit and took me to Krumbach for the journey home.

**Fw Hans-Eberhard 'Hardy' Blume, 4./JG27, 18 March 1944. (A total of 113 P-38s of the 20th, 55th and 364th FGs were airborne this day and five were MIA). Blume served in 4./JG27 against the Americans until July 1944, after which he briefly served with 2./JG27. During September 1944-March 1945 he served as a fighter pilot instructor with 5./JG104, when he was posted back to front-line duties with 9./JG53. During his career as a fighter pilot, he was credited with six confirmed victories in air combat, including a B-17 and a B-24. He was forced to bail out three times, and survived a total of seven belly-landings.**

# ME 410 *HORNISSE* ('HORNET')

*I*ntended as the successor to the failed Me 210, the Me 410 Hornisse or 'Hornet' was developed by Messerschmitt during 1942, both in a fast bomber and a bomber destroyer versions. Of the latter type, the Me 410Al/U4 was designed as a specialised bomber killer, fitted with a single 50mm BK 5 cannon in the undernose weapons bay (recognisable by the barrel extending some 3ft in front of the nose). Normal armament of the Me 410A-1/U2 Zerstörer variant consisted of two forward-firing 7.9mm machine guns and two 20mm cannon, with provision for an extra pair of 20mm cannon being fitted in the bomb bay, plus two 13mm machine guns in rear-firing remote-control turrets fitted to both sides of the mid-fuselage. The second main Zerstörer production variant was the Me 410A-2 which carried extra heavy forward armament, the machine guns being removed and replaced by a pair of 30mm cannon. Operational conditions further led to various 'Rüstsätze' or 'Field Conversion Containers' with different mixtures of cannon armament being constructed and fitted in the aircraft's weapons bay. For breaking up the American combat boxes, it was also fitted with four underwing tubes for launching unguided rockets, or Dödels. In early 1944, the Me 410B series were introduced, differing mainly from the A series in that it was powered by 1,900hp DB603G engines instead of the 1,750hp DB603A in the A series. With its heavy armament and a crew of two, the Me 410 reached a top speed of 388mph (624.4kph), a service ceiling of 32,800ft, and had a range of 1,450 miles which in theory made it an ideal bomber destroyer aircraft. Two Geschwader, ZG26 and ZG76, were equipped with the Me 410 during the course of 1943, operating against the 8th and 15th AFs over Germany, Austria, Hungary and Czechoslovakia. II./ZG1 and III./ZG26 retained their Bf 110Gs until the summer of 1944. These elderly Zerstörer were also heavily armed, with two 30mm and four 20mm cannon and four 21cm rocket launchers firing forward, plus two 7.9mm machine guns in the rear cockpit for rear defence.

Although on paper the heavily armed *Zerstörer* were ideal bomber destroyers, the raw practice in the *Reichsverteidigung* proved totally different. The Bf 110, Me 210, and Me 410 were very vulnerable when encountering American P-38, P-47 and P-5l escort fighters. Against only few successes, losses to these American fighters in II./ZG1, ZG26 and ZG76 soared during late 1943 and the first half of 1944. Against this, only few operational successes were had by the *Zerstörer*, notably on 29 November 1943, when six B-17s of the 95th BG fell foul of a frontal rocket attack by six Me 410s of ZG26 during a raid on Bremen, on 16 March 1944 (some 18 B-17s and B-24s destroyed by Bf 110 and Me 410 *Zerstörer* in the area of Augsburg) and on 10 April 1944 (25 *Viermots* claimed destroyed by Ju 88 and Me 410 aircraft between Poznan and Rostock). On 16 March 1944, however, ZG76 lost 26 out of 43 aircraft destroyed in air combat, plus ten further *Zerstörer* being wrecked in crash-landings. The unacceptably high losses to American fighters finally led to ZG26 and ZG76 being withdrawn from the front in July and August 1944, subsequently converting to the Bf 109 and Fw 190.

**Above:** Me 410B-I of Stab Third *Jagddivision* at Le Mans airfield, France in 1944. *Dressel via Punka.*

**Left:** Hungarian Me 210Aa-1 crews being briefed for an operation against the 15th AF at Ferihegy airfield, south-east of Budapest, during spring 1944. Me 210 ZO+14 has its wingtips painted yellow. *George Punka.*

**Right:** Two Hungarian *Zerstörer* crews mounting their Me 210's for a mission. The 1,350hp Daimler Benz DB601F liquid-cooled engines gave the Me 210Ca-1 a top speed of 288mph. *George Punka.*

**Above:** A German ally which operated the Me 210 was the Hungarian Air Force. Their 210s were licence-built aircraft, constructed by the Danube Aircraft Factory at Horthyliget, 1943-early 1944. Some 270 *Zerstörer* were built, mainly Me 210Ca-1s, virtually identical to the Messerschmitt-built Me 210A-2. The Hungarian Air Force took 160 of these aircraft on strength, the *Luftwaffe* taking the remaining 110 aircraft. Two Hungarian Air Force units, the 5/1. Night Fighter Squadron, better known as 'Owl Squadron' (equipped with 12 Me 210s), and the Air Force Experimental Institute Combat Squadron (with 18 Me 210Ca-Is on strength) were employed against 15th AF formations when these started bombing Hungarian cities on 3 April 1944. Only ten days later, the 13th, saw the Hungarian *Zerstörer*'s finest hour, when the two units were scrambled to intercept American combat formations bombing targets in and around Györ and Budapest. In fierce air battles, Owl Squadron lost nine Me 210s and three crews killed, the second *Zerstörer* unit losing four aircraft. The Hungarian *Zerstörer* crews claimed four P-38 Lightnings and five B-24s destroyed. The outcome of the 13 April 1944 air battles was that the Hungarian Me 210s were withdrawn from the day battles with the American combat boxes and their escorting fighters, and they were transferred to the fast bomber and ground attack role. The rear-firing remotely controlled 13mm MG131 machine gun fitted to the side of the *Zerstörer* can clearly be seen but the pilot's cockpit has not yet been fitted with Revi-sights. *George Punka.*

**Above:** Bf 110 at Munchen-Riem airfield, April 1944. *Albert Spelthahn.*

*T*he Zerstörer's fight against all odds in the Reichsverteidigung is vividly illustrated by Fw Fritz Buchholz's story. Serving as a flying instructor before being posted to II./ZG26 in late 1943, Buchholz was to fly the Zerstörer version of the Me 410 on daylight missions against the American bomber formations:

*There came the day when Göring remarked, at some airfield in north Germany, that he would make use of the instructors from the flying schools if the rate of success in shooting down enemy aircraft did not improve. In accordance to this reasoning I was, together with about 10 other instructors, posted to ZG76 in the Reich Air Defence. There they were baffled by this new fangled and wasteful idea and, after some checking back, directed us to the Zerstörer school at Bad Aibling. Here we were rushed through our training in a special course…I was then posted with two other instructors via the Replacement Gruppe Braunschweig to II./ZG26 (of Hptm Eduard Tratt) at Hildesheim. My joy to have achieved my dream of becoming operational at last soon received a damper. We former instructors did not feel welcome in the community of this suicide commando. Some bright spark had had the absurd idea to convert the Me 410 to a single-seater. By dispensing with the radio operator, the radio gear and the rearward guns, they thought to make the machine so fast that attacks from behind no longer needed to be considered.*

*What a deadly error! The proponents of this idea soon found that the extra 20km/h was not enough to make up for the experienced eyes of a rear gunner and the moral effect of having the guns. To place the meanwhile despised aircraft in the hands of us instrument flyers crowned it all. I flew my first sortie on 11 February 1944, led by Hptm Tratt; as newcomer at the tail-end of course (incidentally a wonderful feeling). Our formation consisted of 12 aircraft. We met up with a bunch of Me 110s and went onto SW course trailing long condensation trails. For Hptm Tratt our retarded progress due to the slower Me 110 soon got too boring and he increased power in order to make sure of catching the 'Fat Cars' on their way home. Meanwhile I had moved up to nr. 4; the others had taken their leave because of 'lame horses' etc. I had no radio contact, only concentration on keeping good formation (Hptm. Tratt was very critical in this respect) and awaited the things to come. Vibration in the starboard engine tore me from my dreams. I went spiralling down (full power on the port engine and idling with the starboard), trailing white smoke. The white snowscape offered no means of orientation. So I 'got myself a ticket' (a pinpoint fix) at the railway station of Bad Kreuznach and swindled myself to Wiesbaden-Erbenheim on one engine and a red light. In the evening my kite was serviceable again. Flying control did not want to allow me to take off for Hildesheim because of snow showers and clouds covering the Taunus hills. I showed them my instrument rating and my last piece of chocolate helped to secure permission for take-off. I took off at 1630 hours, pulled up and flew above the clouds in the direction of home. After my calculated time had elapsed, I went down through a fortuitously discovered gap in the clouds. I was swallowed up by the dark and the Mittelland Canal became my saviour, enabling me to find Hannover and the railway line to Hildesheim. In a two-seater with radio operator this flight would have been easy. The single-seater made it punishable carelessness. I was cured. Hptm. Tratt was already back with two or three Lightnings shot down. His wingman was down on his belly at Hanau.*

*After further more or less successful operations with and without 'Dödel' (rocket launchers fixed under the wings) we were re-equipped at Oberpfaffenhausen with new aircraft mounting a 5cm*

cannon. The BK 5 weighed some 1600kg and made
the 410 very clumsy, supposedly had a recoil of seven
tons, had a magazine of 21 rounds which were
mounted in a ring around the breech and were fed by
compressed air. After this re-equipment we were
moved, because of enemy fighter cover, to
Königsberg/Oder. From there we operated, partly with
fighter escort, against all attacks on the Reich from
the Baltic to Bavaria and Silesia. The BK 5 was a
dangerous weapon with its high-explosive mine
ammunition. Bombers hit with it burst like a balloon.
[Lt Frös of 2./ZG26 is known to have destroyed three
B-17s during April 1944 with this weapon] but, due to
its fast and far-reaching trajectory and telescopic
sight, there was the temptation to commence an attack
too soon. Apart from that, it mostly jammed after the
first or second shot, and this could not be rectified
during flight. The successes did not reach the hoped
for expectations. Added to which we lost the most
successful Zerstörer commander, Hptm Tratt. He was
shot down during a daring single-handed attack on a
bomber formation over Nordhausen. (On 22 February
1944 whilst his tally stood at 38 aerial victories,

**Above:** Air-to-air shots of Me 410s are rare. Here, five V./KG2 aircraft are seen in training formation somewhere over Germany. V./KG2 was re-named II./KG51 in January 1944 and became operational as bomber interceptors. Planned as multipurpose replacements to the Bf 110, the Me 210 and 410 *Hornisse* were plagued by persistent structural problems and proved failures in air combat. *OKW via Punka.*

including three Viermots. Ritterkreuzträger Eduard Tratt was the most successful
Zerstörer pilot of the war; to his aerial tally must be added 26 Russian aircraft
destroyed on the ground, plus 24 tanks, authors.) Oblt Prokopp, the only witness, was
some time later, while flying beside me, rammed by a Thunderbolt and killed.

Lt Dassow (posthumously awarded the Ritterkreuz and one of the most successful
Zerstörer pilots in the Reichsverteidigung during 1943, who was killed in action on 25
August 1944 whilst serving as St.Kpt. of 8./JG6 and with twenty-two combat victories
to his credit, including 12 Viermots, authors), dissatisfied with the poor results with his
BK 5, had eight 2cm cannon mounted in the nose of his aircraft. It was a pleasure to
see his successes with that lot. With that 'watering can' missing was impossible. Re-
equipment of this sort might have resulted in a reprieve for the already doomed Me
410, for the losses were out of all proportion to the successes.

When the bomber formations got the idea to drop their bombs through a complete
cloud cover and the Zerstörer units were unable to take off due to bad weather and the
lack of instrument flying training, a six-seater Junkers W34 crew trainer was quickly
obtained and I had to instruct the flight leaders in instrument flying in between sorties.
On occasion it also happened that I led the formation through the cloud layers and
then handed over to the formation leader. When however the 'Red Indians' had got
onto our formation, all closed up wingtip to wingtip and a change of position was no
longer possible. Then it was mostly course east, descending fast, full throttle and
avoiding clouds whilst speeding towards home. Many comrades were shot down under
such circumstances. In view of the burning comrades who were no longer to be helped,
I frequently pulled back the stick and swung myself sidewards into the clouds. Using
the direction indicator of the airfield radio beacon I then got home along the shortest
route. My instinct for self-preservation was not of course welcomed by the Gruppe, but
I had damned little inclination to go to the dogs because of the inability of others in
instrument flying, especially as I had seen far worse examples.

On 29 June 1944 for example, we were directed to a bomber formation in the area of
Dessau. We flew at 8,000m, when suddenly I saw the bombers below me flying at
6,000m and called: 'Fat cars to starboard' and turned on my guns. For a while nothing
happened. Suddenly the tails rose and in an almost vertical dive and an impossible
angle for firing we went through the formation in the direction of home. I pulled up
again, followed by eight others, and tried to get at the bomber stream from head-on.
Due to the lengthy overtaking process the enemy fighter relief came along and
prevented a second attack. I dived into cloud with the others and landed under Flak
fire at Magdeburg-East. (The Me 410 was unknown to the gunners.) At the evening
debriefing I was the whipping boy because a) I had not reported: 'Fat cars below us',
(which for me, due to the known height difference, was obvious) and b) had broken off
the second attack. The fact that the commander of the Gruppe with about 20 aircraft

had gone home after the botched first attack (without fighter defence) was played
down.

On 13 June 1944 we were directed onto a bomber stream consisting of Liberators
flying on a south-east course over the Baltic. Having made out the bombers, we flew
on a parallel course within sight of the formations, even though no 'Red Indians' were
to be seen, until east of Frankfurt/Oder. From base we received the report: 'No Red
Indians over home garden fence (base).' Missing was the addition: 'Hanni (height)
8,000, course south-east.' After a few minutes we were attacked by 20 Mustangs. I was
forced to bail out and my parachute opened over the military exercise area at Reppen.
That evening 12 Me 410s had to be struck off the list of available aircraft. The
Liberators were able to bomb the aircraft factory at Posen undisturbed.

Our engineers had fitted the valuable aircraft clocks with a hinge and a nail in order
to enable pilots to pocket the timekeepers before baling out. I have never seen a clock
which had been saved by this method. In August 1944 we converted to Fw 190s and
were renumbered II./JG6. After 18 take-offs (including circuits and gunnery training)
we transferred, on 21 August 1944, to the invasion front near Rheims with 40 brand
new machines fitted with the under-wing Dödel (rockets) and four wing cannon. On the
5th sortie of the Gruppe, on 25 August, 16 Fw 190s were lost within minutes in a fight
with Lightnings. [Capt Lawrence E Blumer, 367th FS, shot down five of these aircraft.]
Of the entire Staffel led by Lt Dassow no one returned. According to the combat
reports nineteen Lightnings had been shot down.

For the 6th sortie I could take off with only four aircraft. From this fight against
fighter-bombers in the area of Le Havre only Oblt Friedemann returned. I landed by
parachute on a bridgehead west of the Seine. An SS car took me as far as Juvincourt.
Here they were all ready to leave and had prepared to blow everything up. I took an
abandoned Fw 190 ('Black 5') which was to be blown up as there were no pilots left
on the airfield. I took off without parachute or helmet for Liege. As the undercarriage
could not be retracted I stayed at minimum level. Abeam of Namur the engine gave up
with seized pistons and I slipped the kite over the banks of the Maas into the foliage.
Fortunately the engine made itself independent in the process and prevented a quick
fry-up. I was rescued from the wreckage by Belgian farmers (fortunately not partisans),
taken to a chemist, bandaged and then collected by German soldiers with a horse-
drawn carriage.

This sacrifice of a Fighter Gruppe within five days was the result of an over-hasty
conversion. No overtired Zerstörer could become a perfect fighter pilot in so short a
time. It would probably have been better to have left us for a while in the Reich
Defence to get accustomed to the new machine. Later on I was posted as instructor to
EJG1, where I trained fighter pilots until the end of the war.

*I* take over the 4th Staffel on 1 March 1944. During the three months of my command 36 pilots went through my hands; three times the normal establishment. An entire Schwarm (Flight) led by an old hand, was shot down over the Moselle. When we heard in the morning that three Wings of bombers were formatting up over England we went off our breakfasts, in spite of the temptations of steaming fried eggs. Even the 'old hands' suffered from nerves. Before the take-off everything was smothered in cigarette smoke with some of the men unapproachable. Only Major Bär, now again in command of the Gruppe, remained calm. One day he accompanied us to the restaurant of the Spa Hotel in Wiesbaden, all of us in flying gear. We were applauded on entry and they set up a table for us. But we did not feel very heroic about it. After the air battles we had to grasp the first glass of cognac with both hands, otherwise we would not have raised it to our mouths, they shook so much; it flowed until late in the night.

On 23 March again a major battle over Brunswick during an attack on Berlin. At 1033 I shoot down my 5th B-17. The losses are huge. (28 heavies, and four fighters). On 29 March, after an alarm scramble, we climbed, spiralling through a small gap in the clouds upwards, to find Thunderbolts waiting for us. Auxiliary tanks away, thousands of litres scattered over the town, then they chased us apart. I dived back into the clouds with my wingman, a very young lad, beside me. Suddenly the stick grew soft as butter. Too late I look at the instruments, the pointers are all awry, the horizon too. I try wild control movements. Nothing responds, I lose altitude fast. At 1000 metres I jettison the roof, 500m, out! I only need to release the straps to fall like a stone out of the machine which must have got into a flat spin on its back - I pull the ripcord straight away and emerge from the clouds in flurrying snow just above the ground. A gust drives me towards some houses, I haul on a bunch of lines to increase my rate of descent, but too late. I strike a laundry post in the parson's garden with full force and remain dazed under the 'chute. Then voices rouse me. 'Beat him to death, the gangster, hang him, the dog!

Hallo, they mean you; I'm wide awake again and shout at the people, who had collected around me with clubs and shotguns, in my best German dialect as I crawled out from under the silk. Then they saw my armband, not with a swastika but with 'Deutsche Wehrmacht' on it. (More than one man in my situation had been killed.) 'Oh, that's a German one.' They seemed quite disappointed. But I could understand their impotent anger at the bombers. One hour later I reported back to the airbase commander at Helmstedt, who treated me like an old friend. Against that, Oblt Stark (the Gruppen Adjutant) greeted me in Rheine with the subtle words 'do you actually want to live forever?' I did not find that very friendly. When Bär obliged him by taking him along in an open-cockpit trainer a few days later, he threw him around so violently that it turned even our stomachs as we watched them from the ground. Stark's own, including its contents, came up several times; I grinned with satisfaction. He deserved it.

**Oblt Eberhard Burath, II./JG1.**

**Right:** Fw 190A-6's of *Sturmstaffel 1* lined up at Dortmund airfield, January 1944. Note the barrels of the four MG151 20mm cannon with which these aircraft were armed, the absence of the normal twin MG131 nose armament, and the variety in camouflage painting. Having been established in October 1943 with heavily-armoured Fw 190A-6s, this special bomber-destroyer unit conducted independent operations against the American combat boxes until April 1944 with Fw 190A-6, A-7, and A-8 aircraft, when it was incorporated into IV.(*Sturm*)/JG3 as 11./JG3. Their special tactic was to attack the American bomber boxes in a tight, massive formation from behind -therefore the extra armament to the Fw 190s. *Seebrandt via Rob de Visser.*

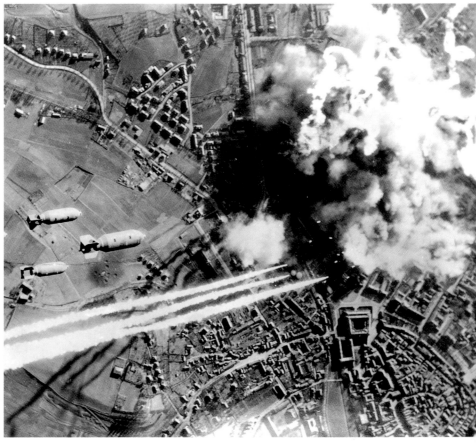

**Above:** Bombs dropped by B-17s of the 452nd BG hit the Ju 88 plants at Augsburg, 16 March 1944. *Sam Young.*

Landsberg, Memmingen, Munich and Friedrichshafen. A total of 43 bombers and 13 of the 925 fighters dispatched were lost. The fighters claimed 13 victories, while the bomber gunners put in claims for 45-10-17.

On 1 April, 246 B-24s headed for the chemical works at Ludwigshafen. Thick cloud over France forced all except fifty-four B-24s to continue to the target while 162 B-24s bombed targets of opportunity at Pforzheim and Grafenhausen. Some thirty-eight bombers in the 44th and 392nd BGs veered off course and bombed a Swiss town in error. The incident led to America having to pay the Swiss thousands of dollars in reparations. It was not

until 8 April that the cloudy conditions abated and allowed the 8th to assemble in force. Some thirteen combat wings, consisting of 644 bombers, were dispatched to aircraft depots throughout western Germany, including 192 bombers, which attacked Brunswick. A total of thirty-four heavies were shot down during the day's missions. Thirty of these were Liberators, of which eleven were from the 44th BG and six were from the 466th BG. The majority of the losses came down in the area of Brunswick due to persistent fighter attacks.

On Easter Sunday, 9 April, 104 Liberators headed to

*I was terribly distraught that the group lead radioed in the clear that because of weather we would bypass Stettin and bomb an alternative target. I knew the Germans monitored our frequencies and to alert their defences of our imminent arrival seemed sheer stupidity at the moment, though I don't recall actually encountering any enemy fighter attacks or anti-aircraft fire over the target – whatever its name. On reflection I suspect that Col Vandevanter, the Command Pilot as well as Group Commander, was using a codename to mislead the enemy. If so, it worked.*

*We were flying left wing (low) in the second element in the low squadron, not a good position because of the stratus clouds the group was struggling to climb over at about 28,000 or 30,000ft. Being the lowest ship in the group we were dragged through the tops of several cloud layers made worse by dense contrails from the planes ahead and above us, and by other groups ahead of us whose contrails were sometimes at right angles to our heading as they climbed, creating a false sloping horizon and making us feel we were in a turn when we weren't. Very uncomfortable, near-vertigo intermittently for a few seconds. To avoid running into other planes in the clouds I pulled to the left 10 or 15 seconds then continued to climb straight ahead with all aboard keeping a lookout for other aircraft.*

*Suddenly I noticed a small break in the cloud layer below us to my left and was surprised to see for perhaps two seconds a squadron of six twin-engine German fighter-bombers about 500ft below heading in the opposite direction, apparently unaware of our presence, though, of course, I couldn't be certain. I called out their location to the crew and told the co-pilot that if the German squadron should attack our lone airplane, we would dodge them by re-entering the cloud layer a few feet below. I then called the navigator and suggested he tune nearby Malmo, Sweden, on the radio compass in case we needed a safe haven from the German fighters since the clouds seemed thickest to our right (north). "It's been tuned for five minutes!" was his quick reply.*

*Happily, the Germans didn't attack and in a few minutes we were between cloud layers, sighted the group a short distance ahead, quickly caught up and proceeded to the new target. The trip home was uneventful till letdown when we broke up into squadrons and widened our disassembly pattern because of hazy conditions over East Anglia. Suddenly our squadron met another squadron head-on, with no time to manoeuvre. How we missed each other will forever be a mystery.*

**Lt Bryce S Moore, pilot of B-17 *Esky* (after the trademark character on the front of *Esquire* magazine), 551st or "Green" Squadron, 385th BG, Stettin, 11 April 1944, his 26th and next to last mission, and longest 10 hours and 30 minutes.**

*Day after day they came with masses of fighters; Thunderbolts, Mustangs, Lightnings, we could take our choice. Our feet hardly touched the ground. Even when we had arrived at our ceiling, they were well above us. Even so, they were reluctant to attack a closed formation. The 4-mots had allocated 'gun ships' at the most exposed positions. They threw an unearthly fire at us. It was more of a killing than a battle. Each landing was a frightening thing. They circled our airfields at low level and fired at everything which did not look out.*

*On 8 April - operations west of Magdeburg, on 9 April - to Fehmarn, this time Liberators over the Baltic. On our first approach we already had the fighters on our backs. On a hunch I look round to see the yellow Easter egg of a Thunderbolt cowling close behind me. As he pressed the trigger, I kick full into the left rudder, the shower from his eight squirters just strikes my starboard aileron. Then I dive, vertically, so as to remain below his line of fire, the speed mounts up, he gives up, not getting me into his sights. After pulling out close to the ground I still have 800 kph on the clock, have to pull up over Lubeck-Blankensee to get rid of my speed. Then a neat landing. Major Bär also comes down there, takes a look at the damage and advises not to take off again with the damaged aileron. At 1600 it's repaired and I fly to St. Ormede near Geseke, where the Gruppe had been transferred to a few days before.*

**Oblt Eberhard Burath, II./JG1.**

*On 10 April, my 69th scramble without enemy contact, but on the 11th again a full programme. I had my 6th Abschuss of a 4-mot in the old battle area over Brunswick. My guardian angel is again doing overtime during the attack; with a 40 hour week I would have been dead long ago. Someone is firing tracer, I can see it coming from the port bow, it's coming straight for my belly. But no, but no! There was a flash at the end of my prop, saved. This time we land at Fassberg, the next day after a tussle with fighters over Saarbrucken at Erbenheim. Then a whole Combat Gruppe is transferred there. On 13 April we come across a large bunch east of Frankfurt. Where are the fighters? We can see none, something must have gone wrong with the escorts. At them! First attack from ahead. I believe I have aimed well. Several go down. Who had shot down whom? The old game. The main thing is that they are down and no longer dropping bombs. A second attack, this time from the rear. Startled, as huge pieces of cladding are flying towards me, I snatch up the nose, Abschuss? I was not credited with it. Never mind! Who cares today? Towards evening on the same day we again meet fighters, Mustangs and Lightnings over Darmstadt records my log book, 38th dogfight, with next on 15 April, 70th scramble without enemy contact. On 29 April, I am involved with a formation with fighter escort. My reflector sight became unserviceable, how am I to aim? I broke off, but with a guilty conscience. Had I chickened out? On 1 May, again against Mustangs over Rhein-Main, then I went down with influenza. Before I was able to fly again I got my posting to JG51 at Brest-Litovsk/Terespol. I reported my departure to Ihlefeldt at Lippstadt. That was on 5 June 1944, the day before the invasion. Thank you, guardian angel!*

**Oblt Eberhard Burath, II./JG1, who went on to score a seventh confirmed kill whilst serving with III./JG51 on the Eastern Front, surviving the war in the rank of Oberleutnant. During his time in JG1 and EJG West during 1943-44, he had been credited with six *Viermot* kills. Between January and April 1944, the *Luftwaffe* day-fighter arm lost over 1,000 pilots, which included the core of experienced fighter leaders. The main aim of the American strategic bombing offensive during these hard-fought four months – the destruction of the *Tagjagd* arm – had been all but achieved – the arm was about to collapse.**

*As a youngster I had stood on the edge of dove fields at daylight on frosty mornings and watched the doves coming to feed. They came in at great speed, dipping and darting, and were laughingly called "blue whistlers". As soon as one was spotted, everyone had a go at him, but sometimes he made it through and flew out on the field. It was a sad sight when one of those proud, beautiful birds crumpled up and pitched to earth. As the B-17s flew through the maelstrom of Flak, I knew exactly how that poor dove must have felt. The guns were larger, and so were the birds, but it was the "dove field" just the same.*

**Ben Smith Jr, radio operator, *Chick's Crew*, 303rd BG, 18 April 1944, Berlin, his first mission.**

the aircraft assembly plant at Tutow. On 13 April, overall command of the Combined Bomber Offensive and the 8th AF officially passed to Gen. Dwight D. Eisenhower, newly appointed Supreme Allied Commander.

On 22 April, the American heavies were late taking off for a raid on the marshalling yards at Hamm. Five B-17s of the 3rd BD were lost on the raid. In the 1st BD, *Thru Hel'en Hiwater* and *Nero* of the 303rd BG, and *Just Nothing* of the 91st BG also failed to return. Four B-24s were also lost at the target to *Flak* and fighters although the US fighters claimed 22 *Luftwaffe* fighters for the loss of 15 of their own. On the homeward trip worse was to follow. First though, the *Luftwaffe* was on the look out for stragglers that had been hit and damaged by *Flak* at the target. One was the aptly named B-24 *Flak Magnet* of the 753rd BS, 458th BG, flown by 1/Lt George N Spaven Jr At the target an AA burst had peeled back a large section of top-fuselage and its skinning now flapped wildly in the

slipstream while inside, fuel spewed from three ruptured main fuel cells. The crew worked feverishly to stem the fuel leaks, jettison the 500lb bombs still aboard and keep *Flak Magnet* airborne, but they could not prevent the crippled Liberator from dropping out of formation. They were now completely alone and a target for any *Luftwaffe* fighters.

At Stormede Maj Heinz "Pritzel" Bär, CO, II./JG1, with OFw Schumacher flying wingman, took off in their Fw 190s to intercept the badly damaged Liberator. Bär was a veteran with 199 victories. *Flak Magnet* would be his 200th. Bär saw the bombs fall from the Liberator and dived on the B-24 from 5 o'clock. He expected return fire from the Liberator's tail turret but Herman Peacher had bailed out when

*Below:* On 16 April 1944, Maj Schnoor, Kommandeur I./JG1 had a narrow escape when his Fw 190A-7 'White 20' touched trees in low-level flight and crashed as a result. *Seebrandt via Rob de Visser.*

**Right:** Hewett dead-sticked his Jug down between the Steinhuder and Dummer lakes: he came to a rest only inches short of a very large hardwood tree and was taken prisoner. Note the three victory symbols and Hewett's personal nose art; his black Labrador retriever dog 'Clarkie' carrying a Dornier Do 217 bomber in its mouth. *Dr Jan Heitmann.*

**Below:** P-47D Thunderbolt 42-74702 of the 361st FS, 356th FG, at Martlesham Heath, Suffolk. Capt. Sidney Hearst Hewett flew this aircraft in combat during early 1944, and finally was shot down in air combat with six Bf 109s/Fw 190s on 4 May 1944.

**Below:** B-17s of the 91st BG taxi out at Bassingbourn, May 1944. Aircraft at right is *Little Patches*, which survived the war. *USAF.*

*Right:* Bf 109G-6s of JG51 at the snow-covered airfield of Bobruisk, early 1944. In May 1944, 2., 7. and 12./JG51 were withdrawn from the Eastern front to the *Reichsverteidigung*. *Stipdonk via Rob de Visser.*

*Right:* B-17F 42-3040 *Miss Quachita*, 323<sup>rd</sup> BS, 91<sup>st</sup> BG and 2/Lt Spencer K Osterberg's crew, FTR from Gütersloh, Germany, its 18<sup>th</sup> mission, on 22 February 1944, when it was shot down by Maj Heinz 'Pritzl' Bär, Kommandeur, III./JG1, in an Fw 190. He is seen here looking over the wreckage at Bexten, near Saltzbergen, where the B-17 crash-landed. Two crewmen were KIA. The other eight were made PoW. *Miss Quachita* was deemed repairable by a German salvage team, but she was strafed and destroyed by US fighters before the Germans could retrieve the bomber. The top scoring NCO pilot in the Battle of Britain, Bär scored his 200<sup>th</sup> victory two months later, on 22 April 1944. He ended as the top scoring jet ace of WW2, with 16, and eighth overall on the list of *Experten* with 220 confirmed victories. Bär was killed in a light aircraft crash in 1957. *USAF.*

*D*usk fell as we were coming home from a raid on Hamm. It was almost impossible to see. Suddenly, I saw tracers shooting past from the rear. Our ship sort of shuddered as machine gun bursts hit us. I looked out and saw three black Junkers 88s peeling away from us. Our No.2 engine started to burn. Later, three crewmen bailed out over England. As we came in flames were still shooting out of the engine and there was a big fire in the bomb bay. While we were still rolling 70 to 80 mph, three jumped out but no one was hurt. 1/Lt Don Todt, navigator, and two others went up through the top hatch and rolled out over the wing. It was a miracle they were not killed.

The enemy fire had severed the gasoline line and it was dripping into the bomb bay which already was burning like an inferno. Sgt George Glevanik sat down on the catwalk and held the ends of the line together with his hands. That was all that kept us from blowing up.

**Capt William G Blum, 448<sup>th</sup> BG, Command Pilot, Hamm, 22 April 1944. Blum was KIA on 9 September 1944.**

fuel had engulfed his turret. In fact by now none of the guns aboard *Flak Magnet* were manned. Bär looked through his Revi reflector sight and blasted the bomber with cannon and machine gun fire and the No.2 engine burst into flames. Spaven tried doggedly to keep the B-24 airborne but the odds were just too great. From the shattered cockpit, Spaven and his co-pilot Lt Robert L Zedeker could see Bär's Fw 190 peeling off to the right as he swept round for a frontal attack. Releasing his seat harness, Zedeker hoisted himself clear, yelling at Spaven, "Let's get the hell outta here!" Bär's next burst shattered the instrument panel, killing Spaven in the process. Zedeker was saved by the back of his armoured seat and he scrambled out of the doomed bomber. 2/Lt Peter

Kowal, navigator, followed. *Flak Magnet* dived steeply, exploded, and crashed near Hoetmar. The victorious Bär landed at Stormede to a rapturous welcome. He climbed out of his Fw 190, "Red 23", and was helped from his flying suit to celebrate his 200th victory.

The 11 B-24 groups of the 2nd BD meanwhile, sped back to England as darkness descended. They were still over the North Sea at the official blackout time of 2138 hours. Unbeknown to the crews, they were being chased by several Me 410A-1 *Hornisse* (Hornet) intruders of II *Gruppe,* Kampfgeschwader (KG)51 *Edelweiss.* Led by 5th Staffel commander, Maj Dietrich Puttfarken, the Me 410's had taken off from Soesterberg, Holland, to infiltrate the returning bomber stream. (A few days

earlier, in the early hours of 12 April, 10 intruders had penetrated airspace over East Anglia and a Me 410A-1 of KG51 had shot down a B-17 flown by Lt Donald M MacGregor of the 413th Squadron, 96th BG while on approach to the 390th BG base at Framlingham). The attackers were aided in their approach by the American formation, which turned on their lights as darkness descended. It was so dark that the KG51 fighter crews incorrectly identified their targets as RAF Halifaxes! There was no mistaking the outcome however. One of the first victims was *Cee Gee II*, of the 735th BS, 453rd BG, at Old Buckenham, which was credited to Lt Nommining of II./KG51 who blasted the Liberator 15 miles off the east coast. 1/Lt James S Manse, whose B-

**Above:** Fw 190A-7 of I./JG1 taxiing at Dortmund airfield early in 1944. *Seebrandt via Rob de Visser.*

24 was named in honour of his daughter Carole Gene, and his co-pilot, Lt Robert O Crall sacrificed their lives so that their crew and companions might bail out from the flaming B-24. As *Cee Gee II* crossed the coast the fuel tanks exploded, blowing three crew members out, while five others were able to jump. Since the interphone system was gone, Munsey was unable to determine whether all his crew had jumped and with complete disregard for his own safety, he remained at the controls until he no longer had sufficient height to bail out. Bob Crall, although ordered by Munsey to *get his butt* out of the airplane, said, *Well I'm staying with it too.* Munsey and Crall died together and they share a common headstone at Cambridge Madingley cemetery. (Munsey was posthumously awarded the DSC on 13 July 1944.)

In an instant, a 448th BG B-24 flown by 1/Lt Cherry C Pitts fireballed, plunged into the sea and vanished beneath the waves with all 10 crew.

In the night's confusion, 12 Liberators crashed or crash-landed in Norfolk and Suffolk as a result of KG51's actions. 38 American crewmen were killed and another 23 injured. Hptm Viner of the 4th *Staffel*, and Lt Loness of the 5th *Staffel* were credited with a B-24 apiece. Fw Zorn of 6./KG51 was credited with a Liberator and a B-17 (sic), and Uffz Leonim, also of the 6th *Staffel*, was credited with three B-24s, one of them west of Orfordness. Fw Volg of 6./KG51 shot down a B-24 south of Norwich. (Ten miles south-east of Norwich at 6,000ft two 458th BG Liberators, one piloted by 1/Lt Teague G Harris Jr, which crashed near its base at Horsham St Faith, and the other, flown by 2/Lt Charles W. "Red" Stilson, which crashed on the south-western side of Norwich, were reported hit by fire from the

*W*e didn't know that Me 410 night fighters had followed us back to England because it was full dark and they were apparently using clouds as cover. However, the English anti-aircraft batteries knew they were there because they showed up on radar. So a situation developed where English AA batteries were firing at the German night fighters who were firing at the American bombers who were firing at the German fighters. It was mass confusion on a grand scale and no-one could say who caused damage to which planes.

The first plane to attempt to land at Seething was Peggy Jo of the 714th Bomb Squadron. Following standard procedure, it turned on its landing lights as it approached Seething, which was the signal for the tower to turn on the runway lights. With its landing lights on the plane it made an excellent target and the German fighters simply followed the runway lights, and fired at a point between the two landing lights of the plane. The bomber's starboard engine was set afire, forcing the pilot [1/Lt Melvin L Alspaugh] to pull up so the crew could bail out, and the bomber crashed at Worlingham just beyond Seething.

The second plane to come in was the Vadie Raye and she was on fire. Most of the crew had bailed out but the pilots, Capt Alvin Skaggs and Capt William Blum, brought the plane down on the main runway, then swerved it off and into the field so it wouldn't block the landing of the following planes. The remainder of the crew got out and ran to safety just before the Vadie Raye exploded. The explosion and fire produced dense smoke which blew across and greatly reduced visibility on the main runway.

The third plane to come in [The Ruth E K Allah Hassid] landed safely, but was strafed as it rolled up the runway. The crew got the plane to the end of the runway, but because of the strafing, they abandoned it there and ran for the safety of a revetment. Our plane, Ice Cold Katie, was the fourth plane to land and as we came in on our final approach we could see the smoke from the Vadie Raye but, because of the smoke, we couldn't see the plane stopped at the end of the runway. We experienced some strafing as we rolled up the runway, and it wasn't until we passed through the smoke from Vadie Raye that we were able to see the plane blocking the runway ahead. The pilots were able to stop Ice Cold Katie just short of that plane and, because of the strafing, we left the plane and ran for the relative safety of a revetment.

The fifth plane to come in [Tondelayo] got down safely but as it passed through the smoke from Vadie Raye, it found two planes blocking the end of the runway and was not able to stop before slamming into the tail of Ice Cold Katie, forcing it into the plane in front. When the pile up stopped the crew of this plane jumped out and ran for the revetment. One of the gunners somehow caught his parachute in something as he jumped out of the waist window and the ripcord was pulled. In the midst of the disaster and strafing we all had to laugh as we watched him run for safety with his parachute spilling out behind him. Now there were three planes blocking the end of the main runway and one on fire beside it, so the rest of the group had to land on the short runway. The strafing continued for what seemed like a long time, but it must have been just minutes, then the German fighters were gone from Seething.

**William E Ruck, radio operator, *Ice Cold Katie*, 448th BG, piloted by James J Bell.**

intruders. Harris and three of his crew survived but the six others died. Stilson and six of his crew survived. It is believed that Stilson's B-24 was brought down by "friendly" AA fire.). Two other victories were credited to Uffz Drongal and Fw. Dormsten. KG51 lost two Me 410A-1s and their crews. Oblt Klaus Kruger and Fw Michael Reichardt, his bordfunker (radio operator gunner,) in 9K+HP and Hptm Dietrich Puttfarken and his radio-operator gunner, OFw Willi Lux in 9K+MN, were lost.

Just who shot the two Me 410A-1s down is open to conjecture. One Me 410A-1 was claimed shot down by S/Sgt Raymond G Chartier, the tail gunner aboard *Peggy Jo* (before the B-24 was shot down by the *Hornisse*). S/Sgt Lewis Brumble, left waist gunner aboard *Last Card Louie* of the 458th BG, flown by Lt H W Wells, was credited with the destruction of an Me 410 at 6,000ft at 2230 hours south-east of Rackheath airfield near Norwich. This Me 410 was reported to have fell on its right wing and dived straight into the ground on fire

**Right:** The ill-fated *Cee Gee II* and 1/Lt James S Munsey, whose B-24 was named in honour of his daughter Carole Geane, and his co-pilot, Lt Robert O Crall. *Mike Bailey.*

**Below:** Victims of the intruder attack by KG51 on 22 April 1944, at Seething. B-24H 41-29240 *Tondelayo*, 41-28595 *Ice Cold Katie*, and 41-9575 *The Ruth E K Allah Hassid*, which collided at the end of the runway. *USAF.*

followed by a large explosion when he hit the ground. The nose gunner and a waist gunner aboard a 389th BG Liberator flown by Lt P T Wilkerson also claimed the destruction of a Me 410 in the same area. Local eyewitnesses say the Me 410A-1 broke away, racing seawards as Wilkerson's B-24, its engines and fuel tanks riddled, caught fire and spiralled out of formation from about 3,000ft. Six of the Liberator crew perished. The Me 410 flown by Oblt Klaus Kruger and his radio operator, Fw Michael Reichardt, crashed and exploded in a field at Ashby St Mary. Uncertainty surrounds the disappearance of Puttfarken and OFw Lux's Me 410, because no trace of it has ever been found. Quite possibly it is the one seen by eyewitnesses, and it probably crashed into the North Sea.

On 9 May 1944, 823 B-17s and B-24s were despatched to bomb marshalling yards and airfields in France, Luxembourg and Belgium escorted by 668 fighters. B-24s bombed airfields at Florennes, St Trond, Nivelles and Hody and the marshalling yards at Liege. Two B-17s and four Liberators failed to return, one each from the 389th, 448th, 453rd and 466th BGs. JG26 claimed two Liberators and two of the seven USAAF fighters lost this day. Lt Addi Glunz, CO, 6./JG26, destroyed B-24 42-52186 *Sunshine* of the 735th BS, 453rd BG, 7km east of Turnhout, and B-24 42-52584 *Worry Bird II* of the 787th BS, 466th BG, 7km south-south-west of the town in the space of six minutes. *Sunshine*, piloted by 2/Lt Edward J Perro crashed at Arendonok, Belgium, with the loss of five crew.

*Left:* II./KG51's finest hour in the bomber interceptor role was on 22 April 1944, when 15 Me 410s led by 24-year old Maj Dietrich Puttfarken's shadowed the 2nd BD returning to England and destroyed nine B-24s for the loss of two aircraft and crews, including the 5th Staffel CO, who remains missing. *Ian McLachlan.*

*Below:* B-24H *Sunshine*, photographed at München-Riem aerodrome, April 1944. B-24 H-FO 42-52106 'Sunshine' of the 719 BS, 449 BG had made a forced landing near the Italian-Swiss border on 29 March 1944 and was captured virtually intact by the Germans. *Albert Spelthahn.*

*We* were at 18,000ft. It looked a long way to the ground but I did not hesitate. I jumped and dropped several thousand feet on my back. There was a terrific jerk after pulling the rip cord. Everything seemed very quiet after the terrific noise a few minutes before. I saw the burning pieces of our aircraft falling and tremendous palls of fire and smoke coming from the target. It was a lonely feeling to see our bombers disappearing in the west when in another hour I knew they would be back at Seething.

**Maj Ronald V Kramer, 448th BG, flying in co-pilot's seat with Capt Robert T Lamberton, whose B-24 was hit by *Flak* and burst into flames just as they released their bombs on the marshalling yards at Liege, Belgium, 9 May 1944. Nine men were PoW, one KIA.**

*When* our plane was hit, the front end was nothing but a mass of flames. I had no choice but to abandon the plane. I grabbed my chest chute like a football and went out the nose wheel door. On the way down I attached it to my harness. It wasn't easy, because I had to remove my oxygen mask to see where it should be attached! Then after pulling the rip cord, the pilot chute didn't pop – it had been burned off (that is my guess). I reached in and pulled a hand full of silk out and the resultant jerk was most welcome. I judged myself to be about 3,000 ft off the ground and soon landed on top of a fence. I was taken to St Giles Hospital in Brussels for ten days, then a series of stops before arriving at Stalag Luft III, near Sagan. I was reunited with our co-pilot, H. F. Hall, in jail in Brussels. Neither of us knew the fate of all crew members until the war was over. Five of us bailed out (the bombardier, DiDomenico was never heard of). Four survived the war.

**Bob Shaw, navigator, *Worry Bird II*, 787th BS, 466th BG, piloted by Lt Allender 9 May 1944. Three chutes were seen from *Worry Bird II* before the doomed Liberator stalled and spun down. Crews said that the fighter which hit the B-24 was reported shot down. In fact, it was Glunz's wingman, Lt Peter Rober, who was brought down. Rober was able to force-land his Fw 190A-8 near Keel and suffering only slight injuries.**

*Below: Kriegie.* Maj Ronald V Kramer, 448th BG, shot down on 9 May 1944 and sent to Stalag Luft III. *Kramer.*

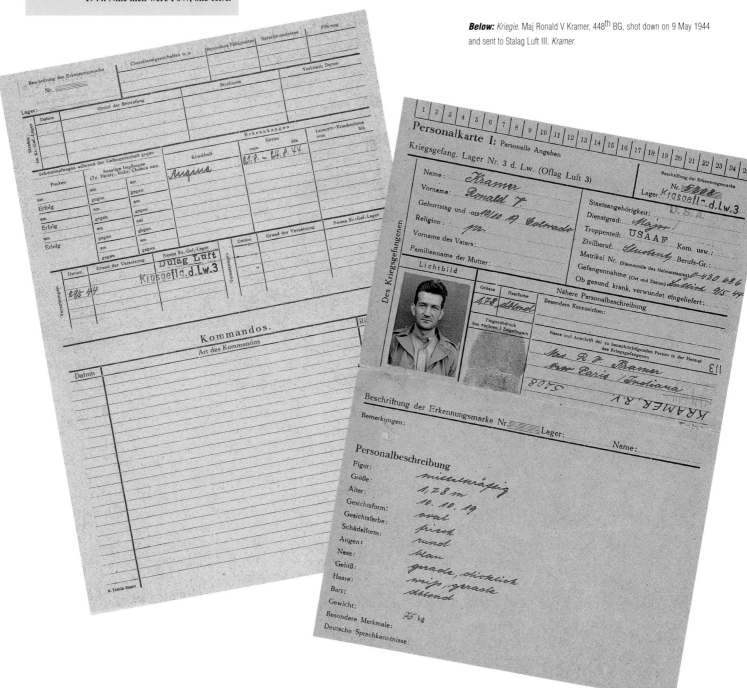

***Above:*** B-17G of the 452$^{nd}$ BG over Berlin, 29 April 1944. *USAF.*

We undertook an odyssey that should rightfully take its place in history alongside those of Ulysses, Jason and the Argonauts. For us, it was a miraculous and incredible escape from the very maw of death. By the laws of probability, we shouldn't have made it. It was our eighth mission. The target was Saarbrucken, where we would be bombing railway marshalling yards. The trip into the target was uneventful, but we knew that it was heavily defended as it was an important rail centre. We were not deceived by the good beginning. The Colonel who led the mission, a West Pointer, was a dauntless flier with an exalted reputation. The only trouble: these fearless career soldiers tended to share the opinion that combat crews were expendable; like in the "Air Corps Song" it was our destiny to live in fame and go down in flames.

We turned on the IP and opened the bomb bay doors. We were getting punishing Flak. Shrapnel cut off the navigator's oxygen supply and destroyed his radio compass, a crucial event as it turned out later. Unbelievably we were not dropping our bombs. The Colonel was not satisfied. We left the target, made a wide circle and came around again for another bomb run. This time they really had our range. It was ferocious. All of the squadrons were badly chewed up by shrapnel. Many of the Forts were trailing smoke and had feathered engines. Some of them left the formation and headed to Switzerland.

The bomb bay doors came open again and this time we dropped. Capt Long's aircraft was burning. I could clearly see the waist gunners looking at us through the waist window. These fellows were our friends and lived in our barracks. They stayed in formation until bombs away and then started down out of control. Our tail gunner saw them blow up. There were no survivors apparently. This mission would have been their final one. Ironically, their regular radio operator had overstayed his leave in London and was not with them when they went down. He went to see the families of the dead airmen upon his arrival back in the United States. By way of consoling the widow of one of the gunners, he wooed and then married her.

Flak knocked out our two outboard engines and blew off one of our bomb bay doors before we could get them closed. Smoke poured from the two disabled engines, which Chick had quickly feathered. We were strongly tempted to try for Switzerland but decided against it. We could not stay up with the formation, usually a fatal affliction. Slowly we lost altitude and forlornly watched our departing comrades in the bomber

formation. We followed them until they were out of sight.

Chick headed us in the general direction of home. When we were down to 11,000ft, we blundered over an enemy airfield. They began firing at point blank range and came within a hair of shooting us down. Chick put the ailing bomber into almost a vertical power dive to get away from the Flak. We could not move because of the G factor and thought we had "bought the farm" for sure. We could only stare at one another in mute terror. Chick and Fish pulled out just above the tree tops. They ordered us to dump overboard everything that would come loose. It all went – ammunition, machine guns, radios, clothing, anything we could find that was not fastened down. At this point we were all in the radio room, my own post. I remember that we did something that seems melodramatic at this distance, but then it made sense. We all shook hands solemnly and bade each other goodbye.

Everybody was ordered up into the nose to give us better balance (trim). I stayed back in the radio room to man the radio in case we made it out of Germany. We were now taking a scenic trip through Belgium, dodging church steeples and tree tops. People were waving at us, and terrorised farm animals were panicking and running away from our sound. After our spectacular dive, Chick had added full war-emergency power, which gave us about 140 mph airspeed. It was too much. On full power the remaining two engines became overheated, turning cherry red and threatening to explode. Chick gradually reduced manifold pressure and RPMs, which allowed the red hot engines to cool off and kept us airborne at 125mph, just slightly above stalling speed. We were right down on the deck with no room for mistakes, and it was still a long shot as far as I was concerned. Later Chick referred to this as "a piece of cake". Ha!

We had forgotten about the Channel defences and, as we neared the coast, I began to see tracers streaking at us. At first I didn't realise what they were. We must have come out somewhere between Dunkirk and Ostend. Now all of the batteries of the coastal defences started opening up on us with a vengeance. We could see the barbed wire and gun emplacements and I fancied I could see the coal scuttle helmets of the people who were firing at us. We could not shoot back. We had thrown away our guns. Shells were exploding inside the aircraft and once I leaned forward to see better through the acrid smoke. As I did, a machine gun bullet came through the floor

and creased my scalp. I yelled, "I'm hit!" I had seen a lot of war movies and I knew that was the appropriate response to the sight of my own blood.

Explosions in the nose and cockpit wounded Chick, Jasper and Ward Hudson, the tail gunner. A Flak tower was trying to depress its guns to finish us off but Chick dived lower to prevent this. Chick continued to fly the plane, although he was in great pain. There was a 3in piece of shrapnel sticking out of his thigh. We were jinking around a lot to spoil the enemy's aim. At last we saw with relief the coast pulling away from us and knew we were safe for the moment.

I tuned in the distress frequency on the liaison set. The DF station answered us immediately and started tracking us as it looked likely we were going to come down in the water. We neared the English coast, sending 'darky-darky'; the military equivalent of May Day. A fighter field either answered us, or we were directed to it by the DF station. Then an appalling realisation came to light. We had no brakes or flaps; our hydraulic system was shot out; so we knew we were going to have to crash-land. The fighter field was very small and had no runways. It was either a training field or a Spitfire base. Later we learned it was at Southend-on-Sea on the Thames Estuary.

We came in very hot and had no room to go around again. After touchdown we were quickly running out of field. The big bomber was rolling directly towards a concrete ammunition building. Quickly Chick unlocked the tailwheel, kicked the right rudder and gunned the left engine. We careened to the right and narrowly missed the ammo house. A thick barbed wire barrier surrounded the field. We cut a path through it as if it was ticker tape. The landing gear was washed out when we hit a stump or something and we started sliding on our belly. I was thrown violently around in the radio room. The bomber was completely out of control. We hit a ditch, slewed around and stopped. I jumped up and ran out of the plane.

The rest of the fellows were getting the wounded out of the nose hatch and I helped. Chick was in great distress, but Jasper was still knocked out. The meat wagon and fire trucks came roaring up and in a matter of moments we were surrounded by RAF chaps who were congratulating us on our stunning performance. They took us to the Sergeant's Mess and began plying us with whiskey. We became hilarious. We were all wound up and talking a mile a minute. The Limeys were smiling at us indulgently. What sweet relief – we had made it!

Somebody noticed my head was bleeding; so they took me to a hospital and cleaned me up. It was only a scalp wound but I spent the night in the hospital. Next morning I had a pint of tea and a hearty breakfast and considered myself a very lucky boy. I knew I would get a Purple Heart this time. I didn't! We stayed at Southend for a few days. One night we borrowed RAF uniforms from our hosts and went into town to a dance. We looked very smart and military in them. The local girls were so surprised to find that we were all bloody Yanks. I visited Chick, Ward and Jasper in the hospital before we went back to the base. We didn't see them for a good while after that. When we got back to Molesworth, everyone was surprised to see us. We were supposed to be dead. Friends had reported that we had gone down. Our stuff had already been divided among our comrades. It took us days to round up our bicycles, clothes and other property.

We did not have to fly for a while. All of us were still 'shook up' considerably. Usually a combat crew was sent to the Flak House after such an experience, but for some reason they did not send us. The Flak House was an old English manor with lovely grounds, gardens and recreation facilities, where "Flak happy" crews rested and recuperated ("Flak happy" translated is: combat fatigue).

I never flew with Chick again. He came back to the 303rd after I left, but never flew any more combat missions. When we were put back on operations, Stan Fisher became our first pilot. Fish was a survivor and at the time that was important to me. I always continued to think of him as the co-pilot even though I flew more missions with him as first pilot than I did with Chick. They were the best. Nobody could have brought Sweet Melody back to England but those two. It was an incredible piece of flying. As far as I knew, no four-engined bomber had ever before survived an 11,000ft power dive. Chick was awarded the Silver Star for his heroic performance. The Medal of Honor was what he and Fish both deserved, but these were usually reserved for heroes who were no longer there to collect them. Chick also collected a Purple Heart, as did Jasper and Ward.

**Saarbrucken, 11 May 1944**, *"Chick's Crew"* **Ben Smith Jr radio-operator,** *Sweet Melody*, **360th BS, 303rd BG. (Lt John A Long's crew in** *Bow-Ur-Neck-Stevens*, **crashed with the loss of seven crew KIA, 4 PoW).**

**Left:** Chick's Crew. Standing: Lt Anthony 'Chick' J Cecchini, pilot, (WIA 11.5.44); Lt Stan Fisher, co-pilot; Edward 'Jasper' Veigel, navigator (who, when asked by the pilot in the US on the crew's first cross-country flight, what town it was below, had replied Jasper, Texas. It was the port of Beaumont!); Theodore McDevitt, bombardier. Kneeling: Cliff 'Bachy' Bachman, flight engineer, who completed 52 combat missions; Clarence 'Alvin' Cogdell; George Kepics, ball turret gunner; Robert J 'Chunk' O'Hearn, waist gunner; Ben Smith Jr, radio operator, (WIA 11.5.44); Ward Hudson, tail gunner, (WIA 11.5.44). *Ben Smith.*

**Right:** Bullet holed B-17G 42-107147 *Sweet Melody*, 360th BS, 303rd BG, which Lt Anthony 'Chick' J Cecchini, a NY cop in peacetime, crash-landed at RAF Southend-on-Sea returning from Saarbrucken on 11 May 1944. *USAF via Robert M Foose.*

**Above:** B-17 41-21585 *Wulf Hound*, 360th BS, 303rd BG, crash-landed, 12 December 1942, at Beauvais, France, after being shot up by the 9th *Staffel*, JG26, led by Lt Otto Stammberger. *Wulf Hound* was captured virtually intact and later flown to the *Erprobungs Stelle* at Rechlin and flown on trials, whereupon it was given to the *Versuchsverband Ob d L* at Rangsdorf on 10 September 1943. *Hans-Heri Stapfer.*

On 11 May 1944, 609 B-17s and B-24s were despatched to bomb targets in Germany, Luxembourg and Belgium, while 364 Liberators of the 2nd BD were assigned a range of targets in France. Eight B-17s and eight Liberators were lost.

The 44th BG Flying 'Eightballs' were part of the bombing effort directed against the marshalling yards at Mulhouse, but the primary target was obscured by clouds, so several targets of opportunity were hit. Lt. Walsh's ship was last seen at 1411 hours.

JG26 next turned their attention to the 70 Liberators of the 486th and 487th BGs of the 92nd CW, which was on only its fourth mission. The formation had been briefed to bomb the marshalling yards at Chaumont but the leading 487th BG had flown into a *Flak* area near Chateaudun. Both the lead and deputy

*T*he time of day was very close to 1420. It's always been a habit of mine to look at watches when things occur – and I do recall that very well. We were shot down by Me 109s. Our position in the formation was Purple Heart Corner. It turned out to be just that! As an engineer, my position was the top turret, and that is where I was just before it all started. Things were rather quiet, and as we had a fighter escort, Lt Walsh suggested that I go back and transfer my fuel. It would seem to be a good time as we had used enough from our main tanks to transfer in from the outer cells. And the fuel would be out of the way in case we ran into trouble later and couldn't spare the time. So I went back to the waist section and told Sgt Lawrence Richards to cover my position while I was doing my job of transferring the fuel. I could take his position if anything happened.

Well, I had just had time to finish and was on my way back to the waist position when all hell broke loose. There was Flak banging around us as well as fighters firing at us. One Me 109 hit us in the No.2 engine, setting it on fire. Another shell exploded in front of us and blasted my headgear off just as I was scrambling to get my chest chute. Sgt Puksta helped me to snap it on and that's when I could see that he had been hit also. I opened the escape hatch and told him to jump. He looked at me and said, 'You go first!' The plane was going down and he didn't look too good, so I told him to be damned sure to follow me. Puksta bailed out, was captured and become a PoW.

My experiences are ones that I still have nightmares about. When I jumped, I counted to about 10, enough to clear the plane. We were at about 15,000ft at that time, I pulled my ripcord - and nothing happened. No chute came out! So I was falling free at 120mph and I tugged and pulled at the flaps on my chute and finally pulled out a little of the silk or nylon. As I kept pulling, the pilot chute came out and it, in turn, released the main chute. All of this took so long that when it finally blossomed out, I was about 300ft from the ground! This is one of the reasons why the Germans did not spot me coming down. When I landed, I injured my left heel and I, too, had been hit by the shrapnel from the exploding shell that had hit Puksta. I had one in my arm above the elbow and several small ones in my face and another one in my neck, which just missed my jugular vein. This all took place near Patay, a little village about 20 miles from Orleans, known for its association with Joan D'Arc. I met up with Richards a couple of weeks or so after we bailed out. To my surprise, we met on a bus, along with our Free French escorts, going to a farm camp in the Forest of Freteval, where the Germans had an ammunition dump, and these men all hid out successfully, right under the German noses. When the camp was started, there were only about eight or ten of us, but things changed rapidly and soon there were several hundred of us evadees.

**11 May 1944. Sgt Joseph O Peloquin, engineer, B-24 42-94999, 506th BS, 44th BG, flown by 2/Lt James H Walsh Jr singled out north-east of Chateaudun by Lt Addi Glunz, CO 6./JG26, who set the No.1 engine afire. The B-24 left the formation "in difficulty" but still under control. (Most of the evadees were liberated by the US Third Army on 13 August, 1944.)**

lead aircraft were shot down and a third was crippled. Among the missing was the Group CO, Col Beirne Lay Jr, who had taken command of the Group on 28 February 1944 - following a staff appointment.

Meanwhile, the 92nd BW had become badly disorganised after losing its leader and deputy leader. Lt Wilhelm Hofmann led his 8th *Staffel Schwarm* so close to the B-24s in their head-on pass that his wingman, Fhr Waldemar Busch, rammed a 487th BG Liberator, causing it to crash. Busch's propeller was knocked off, but he was able to force-land his Fw 190A-7 and suffered only slight wounds. 44km west of Chartres, Oblt Waldemar "Waldi" Radener, CO, 7./JG26, made a successful attack on a 487th BG B-24 and then accidentally rammed a second. Radener bailed out of his Fw 190A-8 with minor injuries. Both of these B-24s made it back to England, where the crew of one bailed out.

The all out RAF-USAAF air offensive on the *Reich* from early 1943 not only forced the German fighter aircraft defences to be strengthened, but also its *Flak* defences to be strengthened and reorganised. The *Flak* arm, thus far employed in single batteries for defence against single hostile incoming aircraft, was not able to cope with the newly introduced concentrated bombing attacks, both by RAF Bomber Command and by the 8th AF. Therefore, in the course of 1943, a thorough reorganisation of German *Flak* was carried out. The bulk of the *Luftwaffe*'s *Flak* was transferred from the Russian and Italian front and into Germany, for the air defence of the Reich. Thus, by the end of 1943, some 70 per cent of the total *Flak* personnel (900,000 men) were concentrated in the Western Front air defences. The single batteries, in turn, were concentrated into *Grossbatterien* ('Large Batteries'), comprising large units of two or three single batteries at all large and important targets such as the Ruhr war industries. Simultaneously, the number of guns in a single battery was increased to six and eventually to eight. By late 1944, *Flak* personnel in the *Reichsverteidigung* had expanded to 1,100,000 men and women.

From the summer of 1943, the *Grossbatterien* proved particularly effective against US daylight raids, especially when clear weather conditions allowed visual ranging. The build-up of *Flak* in the *Reichsverteidigung* went on steadily from the summer of 1943 to June

**Above:** Oblt Waldemar 'Waldi' Radener destroyed 37 American and British aircraft (including 17 *Viermots*), 1943-44 with JG26. He ended the war as *Ritterkreuzträger* and Kommandeur of II./JG300. *Walter Stumpf.*

1944; the defences in the Ruhr for example were doubled from 200 heavy batteries (8.8, 10.5, and 12.8cm guns) at the end of 1942 to 400 at the end of the next year. After the first US attacks on the *Wehrmacht*'s Achilles' heel, the synthetic oil industry, in early 1944, a formidable amount of *Flak* was rapidly concentrated around the main plants at Leuna, Pölitz, Brüx, Blechhammer, Wesseling, Gelsenkirchen, and Ludwigshaven. Up to 600 heavy guns, including a large number of 12.8cm guns, were concentrated around each of these plants. These proved very effective against the massive and compact daylight attacks, even in 10/10th cloud conditions. (On 25 November 1944, the raid against the Merseburg/Leuna oil plants, 197 1st and 3rd BD B-17s, or almost every one in four of the force despatched, returned with *Flak* damage and eight aircraft were shot down - even though the attack had been carried out through 10/10th cloud.)

The problem of manpower for the rapidly expanding *Flak* arm in the *Reichsverteidigung* was solved mainly by drawing up new sources of manpower, from the *Reichsarbeitsdienst* (Reich Labour Service), female personnel for staff duties, Russian and Croatian PoW volunteers, and – last but not least – the *Luftwaffenhelfer* ('*Luftwaffe* Auxiliaries', equivalent of the British Air Training Corps). In all, some 75,000 students from secondary schools were drafted into the *Luftwaffe Flak* arm from February 1943 onwards, manning the heavy batteries.

*If enemy aircraft enter a certain area around Friedrichshafen, preliminary alarm is given out. The code-word for this is 'Edelweiss'. The crews take up action stations. Gun crew consists of: gun chief; elevation gun-layer (K1); azimuth gun-layer (K2); loader (K3); ammunition gunner (K4); ammunition gunner (K5); fuse setter (K6); ammunition gunner (K7); ammunition gunner (K8); plus three Luftwaffe-auxiliaries as 'jamming clearers'. The FuMG (radar) is switched on. The gun crews check the lines with which the gun settings are passed from the fire control centre. An action takes place as follows:*

*'Edelweiss' shout the NCOs of the batteries 215 and 230. We run to our guns. The lines are checked. Then follow the air situation reports. 'Enemy formations, distance 80km, sector 3, heading for Friedrichshafen.' Now the battery leader shouts: 'Barrels direction 3'. Slowly the barrels swing around. The K6 turns on the centrifuge of the fuse setting machine and keeps it running. 'Aircraft sounds in direction 3.' We don steel helmets and tighten the chin straps. Cotton wool is stuffed into the ears. All is ready. The shell is in the fuse setter. The final preparations are done. I am excited about what is to come. At last the command: 'Scharfer Zielflug'. The gun-layers report: height -settings; side — settings; fuse - settings. Now the commands: 'Battery fire - battery.' Then the firing bell sounds for three seconds. The K3 removes the shell from the fuse-setter, pushes it into the breech and fires. A flame shoots out of the muzzle. The barrel recoils. The gun jumps.*

*Now a shell leaves the barrel every five seconds. 'Cartridge jamming' the K3 suddenly shouts. The K1 immediately lowers the barrel. 'Jamming clearers' are in readiness for such an event. One of them places a wooden block on the breech, the second one strikes the breech lever downward with a sledge-hammer. The third one strikes out the cartridge with a barrel wiper from the muzzle end. Firing then continues. After the action the empty cartridges are collected and counted. Fire control announces how many salvoes had been ordered and the number of empty cartridges should tally with this. With most of the guns this does not add up! The Russian 8.5cm guns, which are bored to the German calibre 8.8cm (Flak M 39) to take German ammunition, frequently jam and are therefore not very popular with us Luftwaffe-auxiliaries. Fire control: MALSI 41-43. The radar values are passed to the MALSI, which calculates the gun settings with regard to speed, direction and altitude of the aircraft. Radar is the FuMG with a range of between 30 and 300 km according to type of equipment.*

**16 year old 'Flak Boy' Luftwaffenhelfer Heinz Riediger, heavy Home Flak Battery 230/VII, Friedrichshafen, 1944.**

*B*efore the major attacks on Leipzig in December 1943, and from 12 May 1944, on Leuna and the neighbouring chemical works, there had been disruptive attacks, especially by night, in the area Halle-Merseburg since the beginning of the war. About six weeks after my call-up as Luftwaffe-auxiliary I had experienced action as gunlayer on the 8,8 cm Flak. The main sites to be protected by the Flak group Halle Leuna were the railway station of Halle/Saale, the railway carriage factory Ammendorf, the Buna works in Schkopau north of Merseburg and the Leuna Works south of Merseburg and the Lützkendorf Works (Wintershall) near Mücheln/Geiselt. During the major attacks on industrial targets and major cities in western and northern Germany by the RAF and US air forces in 1943 it had been realised that, with the range of the 8,8 cm Flak 18 and 36, only brief firing with a gun elevation of 80-85 degrees was possible. A Flying Fortress or a Halifax bomber needed about 20 seconds for the run in to the target. The bombers attacked in waves of 16-20 aircraft. The attacking heights were between 7500-8000m. In late summer or autumn of 1943 the guns were therefore replaced. Instead of six 8,8cm per battery we received four 10,5 39's and later two more, again bringing the battery strength up to six guns.

*Above:* Luftwaffenhelfer operating the *Kommandogerät 40* (command device 40) of the battery 3./406 in the *Flak Gruppe Halle-Leuna*. Albrecht Riedel.

### The air situation alarm grades for my Flak battery were:
*Air situation – approaches over the Heligoland Bight alarm readiness.*
The approaching formations cross the German North Sea coast (Weser-Elbe estuary). Duty routine continued normally. School lessons in the afternoon. At night we had to be dressed, but remained in our quarters.
*Air situation – enemy formations in the area Hannover-Brunswick – action stations.* From the area Hannover-Brunswick the formations were able to fly either eastward (eg. Magdeburg, Berlin) or southward (eg. Schweinfurt, Nurnberg). At action stations all fighting positions had to be manned. The control post (B1) with fire-control equipment, radar, computer and all six gun emplacements and the power generators. The gun captains reported the readiness of their guns to B 1.

Communication lines were tested. Gun Anton had to report the temperature of the powder. Among the ammunition at their gun was a specially marked shell without a fuse. There was a long thermometer in the opening which reached into the powder load – it would be pulled out for reading.

*Below:* During 1943, the *Kommandogerät 40* was introduced as the standard fire-control predictor in the *Luftwaffe Flak* arm. It could accept aircraft targets flying at speeds of up to 1,000 kph and flying in a steady turn. It was usually fed with data from a radar nearby and was operated by a crew of five. *Albrecht Riedel.*

*Air situation – leading bomber formations south of the Harz approaching Sangerhausen-Querfurt – air raid warning with sirens for the civilian population.* We had to take our places at the guns. There was the command: Initial position, barrel 45 degrees, direction 10. The circumference of the gun emplacement was divided in 12 sectors (12 = north, 3 = east, 6 = south, and 9 = west). Sector 10 was west-north-west. The attacks were generally expected from this direction. If aircraft entered our area and the gunlayers had covered the command pointers with their follow pointers, the gun captains reported to B1: 'Anton, Berta, etc, covered'. The decision to open or cease fire was made by the battery commander according to information from the gunnery controller. Effective fire was only possible during the run into the target because then the attacking aircraft were not able to alter direction, height or speed. This was estimated to last 20 seconds and only this time was available for the Flak. The gunlayers also had tables for barrage fire with fixed positions within the airspace surrounding the guns. In the case of equipment failure, the gun controller could then decide on firing a barrage in a given airspace.

The first major attack in preparation for the invasion in Normandy was on 12 May 1944, a beautiful spring day. In the early afternoon, about 1330 or 1400hours, we lay in the sun on the top of our gun revetment. We were at readiness, otherwise we would have had some duties or school lessons. The air situation: bomber formations in the area Hannover-Brunswick. Next report, leading formations south of the Harz approaching Sangerhausen-Querfurt (at the same time air raid alert for the civilian population). We leapt from the wall to our guns.

Next report, lead formation turns off in direction Erfurt. We thought at first that they would continue flying south. But they had only made a small detour in order to attack out of the sun. Our comrades at the fire-control equipment had difficulties. They were dazzled by the sun. Until then I had never seen so many aircraft in the sky. We, the gun-layers and the gun captains had just reported 'Abgedeckt' (Cover the formation, guns ready) when the firing bell rattled at the gun. The command to fire was given simultaneously for all the guns of the battery. In group fire all guns fire at the same time. Until now we had not fired much with the 10,5cm Flak 39 because, with the exception of one major night attack on Leipzig, we had never experienced a major attack with more than 900 Flying Fortresses.

The attack lasted for about half an hour, bombing the Leuna works in several waves. At first I thought that we had shot one of the aircraft down but it was the smoke signal of the pathfinders to commence bombing. The air was full of swishing and roaring sounds. The silhouette of the Leuna Works disappeared behind the fountains of earth thrown up by the bombs. Only because of a brief stoppage of the

gun was I able to take a quick look in the direction of the Leuna Works. As gunlayer I was stuck in my seat on the gun and had to operate the elevation control (with a wheel like the steering wheel of a car, follow the command pointer with the elevation position pointer). Our firing position was only 2000m west of the Leuna Works. One of the bombs fell beside our gun emplacement, whose surrounding revetment prevented any damage. Only the earth thrown up by the impact and perhaps a few splinters fell into our emplacement.

The unreliability of the guns was noticeable during this attack. The gun 'Emil' had fired 106 rounds during the attack. We (gun 'Anton') were in second place with 53 rounds. All the other guns were behind with 30 to 50 rounds. One gun had only fired six. Whether the fault lay with the guns or the ammunition I do not know. We were never able to find out. One of the most frequent stoppages was a stuck shell case. The cases were not ejected after firing. Firing had to cease, the barrel lowered, about half the gun crew had to leave their posts and then, using a wooden pole which lay in readiness on the revetment, eject the stuck case from the breech.

Shortly after 12 May 1944 there was an inspection of our unit by the commanding general and commander of Luftgau III/IV (Berlin/Dresden). In his short address he hinted that because of the attacks on the refineries we had to reckon with an imminent invasion in France. The next attacks came at Whitsun, 24 May, with equal ferocity, in order to interrupt the fuel supplies to the Wehrmacht. The result was a reinforcement and reorganisation of the Flak group Halle-Leuna which, when I was transferred to the 'Reichsarbeitsdienst' (Reich Labour Service) in October 1944, had not been fully completed. These measures were for us Luftwaffe-auxiliaries from the upper schools of Müchen/Geisental and Querfurt the beginning of our wanderings.

**Albrecht Riedel, born 7 April 1927, one of the German 'Flak Boys' who enlisted in the Flak arm, serving as a Luftwaffenhelfer in the batteries 3./406 and 2./540 of the Flak Group Halle/Leuna during 1943-44. These Flak batteries formed part of the 14th Flak Division, which was responsible for the anti-aircraft defences of the industrial areas in mid-Germany.**

***Above:*** Albrecht Riedel, a 16 year old *Luftwaffenhelfer* in 1943. *Albrecht Riedel.*

***Left:*** A 10.5cm *Flak* shell in the loading tray of gun *Anton* in the battery 3./406, with two of the guns crew in the background. *Albrecht Riedel.*

# *Chapter 6* – **Oil and Invasion Fever**

On 12 May 1944, 886 B-17s and B-24s were dispatched with 980 escorting fighters in the first attack on oil production centres in the *Reich* – the *Wehrmacht*'s Achilles' heel. In all, five main oil plants in central Germany were bombed. A total of 470 *Jagdwaffe* fighters were sent up to oppose the American formations and, in one of the fiercest air battles of the war, 46 bombers (all except five were in the 3rd BD) were shot down, mainly over the Rheine-Main area by JG1 (two B-24s); JG3 (10 B-17s); JG26 (one B-17), and JG27 (21 B-17s). The remaining 12 were probably shot down by *Flak*. Worst hit was the 45th CBW, comprising the 96th, 388th and 452nd BGs. The 452nd BG lost 14 B-17s, the 96th 12 (including two that collided while under attack) and a 388th. US fighters claimed 61 enemy machines shot down for the loss of seven of their own. In fact, 28 German pilots perished, 26 others being injured.

Next day, 13 May, the 8th AF dispatched 749 bombers

**Below:** Fähnrich Herwig Befeldt straps himself into the cockpit of his Bf 109G-6 at Bad Wörishofen, shortly after joining 8. /JG3, spring 1944. In 11 combat sorties in two action-packed months in the *Reichsverteidigung* and over the invasion front, Befeldt shot down a B-17 and was shot down himself or crash-landed no less than four times, finally becoming a PoW on 11 July 1944. *Herwig Befeldt.*

*It was a beautiful clear day and the usual forming of groups into wings took place over England and then proceeding over the channel to our various destinations. We picked up heavy Flak near Koblenz, but to my knowledge no planes were lost or delayed; however, for the 96th BG, this was just a harbinger of things to come. In no time at all we observed our fighter cover above us being drawn off to defend us against German fighters. Almost simultaneously, our crew was reporting attacks by enemy fighters from almost all points of the clock. With the exception of the tail gunner who wore a flat, back type parachute at all times, the remaining crew members had detachable chest type chutes. Obviously, attaching a chest chute on a buckle harness under a Flak vest was extremely awkward. However, considering the pressing attacks on our group from the German fighters, in a brief lull, I decided to loosen my Flak vest and put my chute on. Quite frankly, with all the bombers going down around us, I felt it was just a matter of time and if worse came to worse, I could, at least, make an immediate attempt to escape. It seems like a very short time thereafter, when tracking an Me109 and firing my 50 calibre machine gun as he came in from 12 o'clock high and as he passed my line of vision there was a sudden jolt and shuddering of our aircraft. It seemed to stop in mid-air and then fell off into an uncontrolled fall. As explained, with the exception of myself and my tail gunner, none of the other crew members would have had their chutes on and when our plane went down out of control, there would have been no chance whatsoever to recover any of the chutes.*

*Through a miracle I escaped through the B-17's nose hatch and the tail gunner was blown out the rear. I personally believe the German fighter was out of control and had struck our B-17 amidship as I do not recall any explosion. Incidentally, the area I went down in on that fateful day was Bad Camburg, about 28 miles north-north-west of Frankfurt, Germany.*

**Clifford D Jones, navigator, Lt Lourie's crew, 96th BG, Brüx, 12 May 1944, who with tail gunner Lewis Lanham, were the sole survivors.**

On Friday 12 May, strong formations of American bombers were reported flying into the Reich. The aircraft of our IIIrd Gruppe were scrambled in a northerly direction, among which was a Schwarm (four Bf 109s) of the 8th Staffel under OFw Ströbele. I flew as Tactical Number 2, or Wingman to the Staffel leader. Even before we had reached the point where our Gruppe should join other units, we were attacked by Lightnings and got entangled in a dogfight. A wild twisting and turning began. Aircraft Numbers 3 and 4 had soon lost contact with us, but I doggedly hung on to my Schwarm Leader, who turned in ever tighter turns (the Lightning, a twin-engined, twin-tailed fighter, had a better turning rate than the Bf 109). When OFw. Ströbele noticed that I had an "Ami" on my tail firing in my direction, he broke off the dogfight and we dived steeply towards the earth with full power. Only moments before, I had felt bullets striking my machine, but still it remained airworthy. However, my cockpit hood got increasingly smeared with oil; obviously, the oil tank which was fitted just in front of the cockpit had been hit. Soon, my view was so bad that my Schwarm leader was concealed from my sight. It was decision time: should I bail out now, or would I still be able to force-land my aircraft? I made up my mind to jettison the hood first, so I could see anything at all. Still, the oil now splashed onto my goggles – so get rid of these too. This forced me to wipe my eyes all the time, but my view was better than before.

While all this theatre was going on, I had completely lost my bearings. From a height of some 1,000m, I discovered a double rail track, which I followed. This, I hoped, would certainly lead to a city or even to an airfield. And I was lucky: after some five minutes I reached -what I later found out- Bonn-Hangelar airfield. There were no other aircraft in the circuit, so I could line up my machine undisturbed for a crash-landing. Of course, I did not lower the undercarriage, and my aircraft slid along on its belly for quite a while, before it finally came to a stop. I had successfully done my first belly landing. Completely covered in oil, I clambered out of my machine – there was no need to open the cockpit hood, as I had none left. My crate looked in a sorry state: the propeller was bent, its belly ripped open, and everything was covered over in oil.

Still, it was quite a shock when I started counting the bullet hits in my machine. If I remember correctly, there were 13 strikes, mainly in the wings. One bullet had grazed the front oil tank and the slipstream had sucked out the oil, which had so severely obstructed my view. When I had climbed out of my Bf 109, lots of people came running towards me, who, with experts' eyes began looking at the sorry mess in which my Bf 109 had been turned. Their conclusion: it bordered on a miracle that I had pulled off a neat belly landing in such a damaged condition. I rang up my unit in Bad Wörishofen, where they were very pleased to receive a sign of life from me, as they had already half written me off.

Fähnrich Herwig Befeldt, Bf 109G-6 pilot, 8./JG3, 12 May 1944. His story is perhaps typical of the replacement fighter pilots that joined the *Luftwaffe* day fighter arm late in the war. Badly trained, and hastily thrown into the battle against all odds, only a handful survived in the lethal skies over the Third Reich. His fighter pilot training completed, in mid-April 1944, 18 year old Fähnrich Befeldt was posted to 8./JG3, a *Reichsverteidigung* unit at Bad Wörishofen. His first assignments given him by his *Staffelkapitän*, (ObLt Koch) were: to become familiar with the Bf 109G-6 (he had flown only the *Emil* and *Fritz* series), R/T and the use of oxygen. This all took about a month before Herwig's name could appear on the Battle Order. On 12 May, Befeldt was one of twenty-two Bf 109s of III./JG3 which ran into a superior force of Mustangs in the Rhein-Main area. Four 109s were lost and their pilots killed. Two more crash-landed. One was Befeldt's aircraft. Maj Dahl and the 7th *Staffel* CO, Lt Horschelmann (KIA) each claimed a Fortress before the *Gruppe* ran into trouble with the P-51 escorts. Dahl barely managed to force-land his riddled Bf 109G-6 at Mannheim-Sandhofen.

**Right:** Bf 109 pilot bailing out of his doomed fighter. *USAF.*

# BOMB RUN TO BRÜX

*Now I see the planes clearly – they are Fw 190s and Me 109s; mean fighters to tangle with. They are making frontal attacks and coming in 15 at a time in a staircase formation. I pick up one in my sights and fire a five second burst. They are firing cannon shells at us. I feel them hitting our ship and I am beginning to sweat now. I pick a Fw 190 up in my sight track for one second and open fire. I follow him. He is going by off our left waist…got him. He explodes in a ball of fire. I swing my turret to 6 o' clock and I see five of our Forts going down on fire and explode, throwing flames around the sky. I see seven men bail out of a Fortress. An enemy plane circles them once and comes in firing at the chutes. They all catch fire and I can see the men falling to earth. I fire at the enemy ship for eight seconds. I see smoke trailing from his engine and sincerely hope that I got the rat. A man bails out of a ship in front of us and comes into our ship, breaking our Plexiglas nose, injuring our bombardier and navigator and throwing them into the catwalk of the ship. I look down at the ground and see many small fires and large ones burning. They are enemy fighters and our Forts. Another man bails out of a Fort in front of us. His chute hits our propeller blades. They cut the top out of his chute. I see him falling, looking back at his flapping shroud lines. I try to shoot him. He falls to the ground, still alive until he struck the earth. We limp over the target. There go our bombs. We made it….*

**S/Sgt Sam N Fain, ball turret gunner, *Lady Stardust II*, 452nd BG, flown by 2/Lt Milan "Mike" Maracek. 12 May 1944. (The crewman who hit the Plexiglas nose was Lt Fred L Myren, riding as Formation Officer in the tail turret of the lead ship flown by Lt Boris Slanin (three KIA/seven PoW). Myren bounced off into *Lady Stardust II*'s right wing.)**

*I heard a sharp snap, something like Flak. A parachute went over the right wing and also some stringy stuff was sliding back across my window. I opened the door and looked toward the cockpit. I was blinded by something - plus a terrific wind. It was blood, a lot of it. I was covered from head to foot and it went on through the ship painting it red and freezing. The bomb bays were solid red and slippery. The nose was gone, because of the fellow that bailed into it. That was what I saw on my window. The blood inside the ship came from Merle "Uncle Dudly" Orcutt, engineer. The right side of his head was gone…We were going down, but I didn't know the altitude so I took an extra oxygen bottle and started up the catwalk. There was a hard wind coming from the front. I was holding the left rope when it broke. It was weakened by an exploding shell I guess. I fell on the right rope. It was OK, but I dropped my oxygen bottle and it went tumbling down. I spent some time trying to get the bomb bay doors up with my knife. The crank and extension were gone so I gave the job up. I took some wire from the bomb pins and fixed the rope back. I went up to the engineer. He didn't look like Dud. But from the feeling inside of me I had no doubt. He was dead.*

*I went back to the waist gunners, got some first aid kits and hunted for the powder. There was none. The right waist gunner grabbed a bandage and put it on his head. The expression in his eyes reminded me of a patient taking his first look at the stub of his leg after an amputation. Red was still bleeding and as he would breathe, blood would come out the hole in his eye. I wiped the blood off his face… He returned the act, and said, "I thought you were a walking dead man."*

*The tail gunner said something about strafing, then he yelled, "Tail gunner hit". From the way he said it, I knew there was a lot of pain. I grabbed the first aid kit and ran for him. After laying him down in the waist, I began slicing my way to his wound, which was centred in his back. It was a terrible hole and I hurried to get a bandage on so he wouldn't lose too much blood. After getting the bandage on, I gave him a shot of morphine…We were alone, flying just above the ground, like a coyote sneaking among bushes in fear of yelping hounds close behind. We passed over a fighter base and could see the Germans shooting at us. We could hear the machine guns rumble above the rumble and rattle of our own plane….Then came a call over the interphone that we loved to hear. "There is the Channel ahead."*

**T/Sgt Dwight N Miller, radio operator, *Lady Stardust II*, which got as far as the Channel, where it was ditched, becoming one of the 14 B-17s the 452nd BG lost this day. 12 May 1944. Total 8th AF heavy bomber losses were 46 B-17s and B-24s and a staggering 412 bombers damaged. As a result of this raid, oil production at the Sudetendeutsche plant was 100 per cent inactive during June 1944.**

**Right:** A young Dutch family proudly posing with a 108 gallon drop-tank, which was dropped by a P-47 over Zuid-Scharwoude, northern Holland on 29 May 1944 when 187 Thunderbolts flew escort and support for the heavies attacking aircraft plants and oil installations. *Ab A Jansen.*

*In the course of the war, I was shot down three times: in flames by Flak near Stalingrad, by a Spitfire over Sicily, and again in flames in the vicinity of Frankfurt am Main. The third time - during my 'Storming' days - remains especially vivid in my memory. On 12 May 1944, we were scrambled from Salzwedel against the Viermots. In the area of Frankfurt-Limburg-Siegen-Giessen we got contact with the enemy. The bombers were well protected by Mustangs, and therefore it was of paramount importance to engage the bombers in a swift surprise attack. We succeeded by turning in to the bombers sooner than expected. I swung in some 400-500m behind a bomber and was at once met by intense defensive fire. At the same time I kept an eye on a Mustang which approached me, firing its guns. He was about 300m away and I thought he would never hit me at this turning speed. Apart from that, I was certain that he would break off his attack in order not to expose himself to the fire of his own bombers. But I was mistaken. While firing at the bomber with all my guns, I was suddenly hit from behind. At the same time there was a dull bang which shook my Fw 190A-8. In no time at all, the cockpit windows were completely covered in oil and I could see nothing. I tried to jettison the cockpit cover, but without success. It had opened only half way, which made bailing out impossible. Meanwhile flames were licking along the fuselage. I threw my machine into a steep left turn and let the aircraft slip away to the inside. The*

*flames were thus forced away from the fuselage and later on went out. I made an emergency landing in the vicinity of Dornholzhausen/Bad Homburg in the Taunus, well enough in spite of being able to see hardly anything at all. It would have turned out fatally had I not noticed a power cable immediately before landing which I was only just able to avoid by diving under it.*

*Mechanics told me later on that my aircraft had received hits from behind and in front. Hits in the oil cooler had caused the oiling up and the fire, which had then been followed by the seizing up of the engine. When I reported back to my unit, I was congratulated for my Abschuss, which I had not been able to see myself. Two of my comrades had observed and reported it.*

**Lt Walther Hagenah, IV. *Sturm*/JG3. Ofhr Nolting of IV./JG3 destroyed two Fortresses – his 6th and 7th victories. Hagenah's victim crashed near Camberg. IV./JG3 lost an Fw 190A-8, the pilot was injured. Hagenah served as fighter pilot in the *Luftwaffe* day fighter arm from spring 1942, and flew operationally almost without a break until the end of the war. When IV./JG3 was formed during spring 1943, he was posted to this unit, which was re-named IV. 'Sturm' JG3 early in 1944. He survived the hard air battles in the *Reichsverteidigung*, and was posted to another unit September/October 1944.**

**Below:** Focke-Wulf 190 captured intact by the Allies in Italy undergoing evaluation at Wright Field. *Pieter Bergman.*

*M*y short spell of very hard sorties 14 of them), were over central Germany with JG3 'Udet', which I joined on 14 April 1944. Prior to this, from the summer of 1943, I had been with the Stabs Staffel of JG51 on the Eastern Front. Over the following months, we were mainly involved in tank busting, in support of the German infantry. I completed 126 of these fighter-bomber sorties with 500kg SD, SC or Container anti-tank bombs, scoring my first three victories in the process. When my Kommodore, Oberst Karl-Gottfried Nordmann suddenly sent me to the so-called 'Reichsverteidigung' to the second Staffel of JG3 'Udet', a fighter group heavily involved in combating the American bomber offensive, based at Burg near Magdeburg, it was to "beef up" units against the 8th AF 1000 bomber a day raids. I was to fly high-altitude sorties to cover the Sturmstaffel of JG3 Udet attacking the bombers. They flew the Fw 190 with four 2cm MG151 cannons. We flew the Me 109G-6 with the methanol-injected supercharger. Often our groups were about 40 planes strong, usually assembling at 24,000ft over Magdeburg with other groups from JG3 Udet, including the Sturmgruppe. Flying the heavily armoured Fw 190, we had to protect them from above and therefore climbed up to 30,000ft.

On 12 May, we had an early rise, as soon as our radar spotted the 8th USAAF bomber formations assembling north of London. We came on one-hour combat readiness, collected all our gear and came to our Me 109Gs in the company of our mechanics for final preparations. We put on life-vest, dinghy and parachute, and then came the cockpit readiness when we climbed into our aircraft. We were now on 4-minute take off readiness. I was in Oblt Bohatsch' Staffel and had to lead the unit that day as he had reported sick. We were in seat-readiness for a long time and getting tired of it! Finally, around 11 o'clock, came the order to take off. Green flares signalled to all pilots of I./JG3 to start up the engines and Staffel by Staffel took off. We were to assemble over or near Magdeburg or Kassel at 'Hanni-8,' which meant at 8,000 metres or approximately 24,000 feet, and for us even higher at 30,000 feet to cover the Sturmgruppe Udet. We were led by 'Horizon', our ground station, who gave us the information of a 1,000 bomber raid approaching with fighter cover of P-51s, Thunderbolts and Lightnings! Well, we then knew we were in for something big!

As the Sturmgruppe and several squadrons of Me 210 and 410 rocket-carriers went into the attack, we saw the big boxes of B-17s splitting up before the target was reached. Their escort was obviously delayed and we were able to hit them fully! While we were still at 30,000ft behind our combat groups, we descended and with added speed went with them into the next bomber group north of Frankfurt am Main

and Hanau. The initial rocket attack had split the boxes apart and we could easily engage them from the front, without being bothered by the escort of P-51s. They only arrived later when the inferno was on!

The bomber box, as far as I could see, consisted of B-17s and it also split up and we could each pick out our single targets. The B-17 I picked out was flying on the outer right of the formation and grew bigger very fast in my gun sight, and when I opened up with my MK-108 and two 13mm guns, the plane soon caught fire in its outer engines and wing tanks. Parts were falling off and parachutes were coming out fast, I counted up to eight. Never, ever, have I seen so many planes falling down, ramming each other, being downed by Flak and fighters. The sky at 24,000ft was full of debris!

Then a 'pearl string' of five Mustangs came down on me from high up and from the north-east, there was only one thing to do and to head face to face with the first one, and giving a lot of deflection, about five plane lengths. My luck was to hit the P-51 first and we passed each other closely. Coming in and around to be ready for the other four, I saw my adversary explode in a large fireball! My underwear was already wet, but what came next was literally flying for my life, I was chased down from 24,000ft to ground level by four P-51s. Outclimbing them was out of the question as I was running out of fuel! When the warning light indicating the fuel running out, one is additionally nervous. Hedge-hopping to the north-east, I drew the Mustangs into 2cm quadruple Flak fire from Fritzlar airfield in Thuringia. I swiftly carried out an emergency landing, but since I had been hit several times, the landing ended in a spin around as one of my undercarriage legs broke off! Luckily, the P-51s were brushed off by a great and very alert Flak crew. I flew home to my base at Burg in another Me 109 from a Staffel buddy of mine, Fw Einenkel who had a nervous breakdown and was sent to hospital. Over base, I waggled my wings twice to indicate to our mechanics that I had two air victories. They received me with a great hello, but I definitely had enough for one day! Our losses on that day were about equal to the enemy's bomber losses.

**Fw Horst Petzschler, I./JG3 "Udet", who on 12 May 1944, shot down a B-17 at Frankfurt am Main, and a Mustang south-east of Frankfurt - his 4th and 5th victories. I./JG3 lost a Bf 109G-6 over Gieben, the pilot escaped with injuries. Two days later, Petzschler claimed a B-24 Liberator *Abschuss* N of Braunschweig.**

**Above:** OFw Alfred Müller (left) and Fw Hans-Eberhard 'Hardy' Blume of 4./JG27, in front of three of their unit's Bf 109G-6s early in 1944. Fw Blume survived the war with one confirmed victory. Müller, an ace with 15 *Abschüsse* including four *Viermots*, was KIA, 16 August 1944. *Hans-Eberhard Blume.*

**Left:** Early spring of 1944, the main undercarriage of an American bomber which was shot down over the North Sea, washed ashore on the North Sea beach of Wangerooge Island, one of the Eastern Friesian Islands. *Hans-Jurgen Jürgens.*

to targets in the Reich. Some 691 of the heavies got their bombs away and 12 B-17s and B-24s were lost. The fighters claimed 47 enemy fighters shot down for the loss of five of their own. Two days later 166 B-17s and B-24s bombed V-weapon sites in France. No bombers were lost and 128 of the heavies dropped 485 tons on the *Noball* sites. Four days later, on 19 May, 888 B-17s and B-24s were despatched, the B-17s attacking targets at Berlin and Kiel, while the 300 Liberators went to Brunswick. Fighter opposition was heavy and 28 bombers failed to return. US fighters claimed 70 enemy fighters for the loss of 19 of their own.

On 20 May, it was back to France again, when 367 B-17s and B-24s were sent to pound targets in France, while 271 B-24s and B-17s of the 3rd BD were

*After being ready for the start. I commanded with the Gruppe at 11:40 am with the order to gather over Paderborn with the I./JG1 and III./JG1 at a height of 1,000m and then proceed towards the Porta Westfalica at 7,000 to 8,000m. The unit reached the commanded destination while climbing and received the order to fly at a course of 340 degrees. After several changes of directions, the unit sighted the enemy and engaged in air battle with the battle group. The planned attack towards the battle unit was unsuccessful because the group became entangled in air battles with the fighter escorts. The unit turned away towards the east and prepared for a second unified attack. I attacked from the front and below a Liberator, which was flying as the second plane on the left in a closed Pulk. The Liberator burned immediately with a bright flare and separated from the Pulk. When it went down, I saw that the tail was separated from the plane and the Liberator exploded in the air. After this, more air battles with the enemy escort planes developed, which reached as far as the areas of Minden. After I tumbled around with several Thunderbolts in a height of up to 800m my plane lost its balance during a steep curve, when I saw under me an Fw which was pursued by two Thunderbolts. I balanced my plane again and shot from above and behind a long fire burst from a distance of up to 30m whereupon the two Thunderbolts exploded in the air.*

**Oblt Georg-Peter Eder, II./JG1, his battle report of the downing of a B-24 at 6,500m at Osnabruck-Rheine and further north at 1245 hours, 19 May 1944. Eder was flying Fw 190A-8 "Red 24". Amount of ammunition used (against B-24): MG 131, 120 rounds, and MG151/20, 80 rounds. The 2nd BD encountered 150 to 200 enemy fighters between Dummer Lake and the IP and again after leaving the target area. At Waggum airfield 30 Fw 190s and Bf 109s attacked from 12 o'clock skidding through the formation head-on. At Steinhuder Lake, more then 220 enemy fighters were encountered. A total of 12 B-24s and four P-47s were lost. Of Eder's 78 victories, 36 were four-engined bombers.**

despatched to bomb Liege and Brussels. Heavy cloud caused the 3rd BD to abandon its mission and part of the 2nd BD to be recalled. The 8th AF returned to France again the next day and on 22 May the heavies struck at Kiel and Siracourt. Five B-17s were lost.

With the good weather continuing, the heavies made visual bombing attacks on several targets in France on 23, 24 and 25 May. By 24 May, the first-line *Reichsverteidigung* fighters' strength had declined to 246 single-engined fighters and 35 twin-engined *Zerstörer*. The *Jagdwaffe* had become a mere shadow of its former self. On the 27th, the 8th switched to German targets once again. 24 bombers were lost. On 28 May, 1,341 heavies pounded oil targets in Germany. 32 bombers were lost. VIIIth FC claimed 27 enemy machines destroyed for the loss of nine of their own, while IXth FC, which dispatched 527 fighters under VIIIth FC control, claimed 38 enemy fighters for the loss of just five of their own. In fact at least 40 *Jagdwaffe* aircraft (15 per cent of the fighters that engaged the Americans on 28 May) failed to return to their bases, 18 pilots being KIA and 13 more injured. For these losses, they claimed 36 heavies and 11 fighters shot down. 26 of the Fortresses that failed to return were from the 1st and 3rd BDs. Three B-24s of the 3rd BD force that attacked Lutzkendorf/Halle and

*O*n 20 May 1944, III./JG3 received orders to move to Ansbach, a peacetime airfield to the south of the town. Here the Gruppe had a change of command. Our new commander was Hauptmann Langer whom I had known from the reserve unit at Marignane. My first operation from here was on the 27th May. The defending formation collected in the area of Karlsruhe and flew to meet the American B-17s, which were on the approach to targets in the area of Strassburg. But before we reached these we were involved in a heavy dogfight. I was unable this time to stay with my section leader OFw Ströbele. Suddenly I was alone with three or four Typhoons who were trying to get behind me. I was left with no choice, I had to dive away. During the dive I tried to shake off my pursuers but without success. I can remember the situation very well. My sole chance of getting rid of the Typhoons was in low-level flight. I had reached the Rhine valley and flew eastward. I had to fly lower than my pursuers so they would not be able to make me out against the sky. I took every risk in keeping as close as possible to the ground. Suddenly I saw a power line ahead – and flew under it. Then across the Rhine and into the Black Forest. In these narrow valleys I was safe. A look back: the Typhoons were gone. I was not very happy about this but OFw Ströbele cheered me up afterwards, he would have done the same. For we had strict orders not to get ourselves involved in a fight with enemy fighters except in an emergency. Our main task was to shoot down enemy bombers. For that purpose equipment, and especially personnel, had to be conserved.

**Fähnrich Herwig Befeldt, pilot, 8./JG3.**

**Above:** Lt Hannes Wenko (right) and his first mechanic standing on the wing of their I./ZG26 Me 410B-2/U2/R4 3U+AA at Köningsberg/Neumark aerodrome in the summer of 1944. R4 stands for a pod containing yet another extra two MG151 20mm cannon installed under the belly of the aircraft, which made this *Zerstörer* version heavily armed for the bomber-destroyer role. *Wenko via Punka.*

**Above:** Wenko and his gunner, OFw. Liebsch, have strapped themselves in for take-off on a bomber interceptor mission in Me 410 3U+AA from Köningsberg airfield, summer 1944. The six 20mm forward-firing cannon and two 7.9mm machine guns are clearly visible. *Wenko via Punka.*

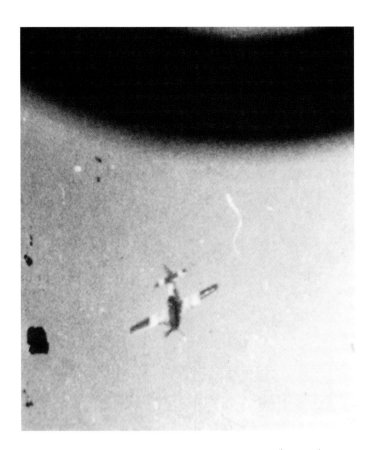

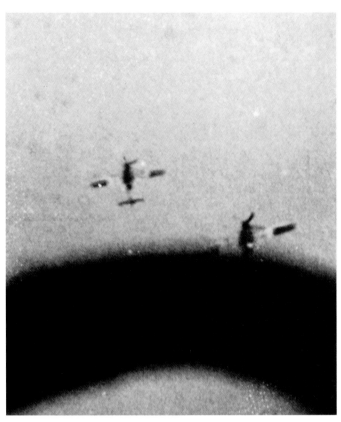

**Above:** Once locked in combat, Wenko and Liebsch were intercepted by two 328th FS, 352nd FG, Mustangs. The Me 410 had no rear-defence when Liebsch' guns proved unserviceable. He then decided to grab his camera and take this sequence of two photos of the Mustangs coming in for the kill, muttering, *These are the last minutes of my life. Liebsch via Punka.*

**Left and Above:** The crew were very fortunate when their Me 410 was shot down in flames. Wenko made a successful belly-landing. Having overcome his shock, Liebsch took these two shots of the smouldering wreck of 3U+AA, and his pilot inspecting the blazing cockpit area, which they had hastily evacuated only minutes earlier. *Liebsch via Punka.*

*Left:* B-17 42-31968 and Lt Clarence D Wainwright's crew, 381st BG, FTR, 24 May 1944 after a mid-air Collision. Near Gruental, two German women view the crashed aircraft in which seven crew were KIA. Two men survived and were made PoW. *Ulrich Lange via Ron Mackay.*

*On Sunday 28 May 1944 (Ascension Day!), I led the Staffel, as my Staffelkapitän, Oblt Walter Bohatsch was still sick and could not fly. Well, when the bomber stream came in towards Magdeburg/Kassel, to attack industries in that area, we were in position above the Fw 190 Sturmgruppe that mercilessly started attacking the B-17 boxes from head-on. Flak shot down the first B-17. They never stopped firing as we entered combat! So far, we were safe from the Flak at our height of 30,000ft, but the American escort arrived and P-51D Mustangs attacked us from higher up than 30,000ft! My wingman went down first while I still looked down on the Fw 190 attack, which I was supposed to cover. It was too late to help my wingman, but the attacking P-51D was passing me fast, I could give him a good burst of my weapons and he went down trailing white coolant and belly-landed 60km north of Magdeburg!*

*Meanwhile our whole Staffel was split up and single dogfights developed, although we were strictly forbidden to engage in it, as we had to concentrate on destroying the bombers. Well, many crazy orders had been given and these cost us dearly! Another P-51D hacked a third of my left wing off and made my machine unflyable, so I prepared to bail out. At a height of 4,800ft our balloon barrage over the Elbe ship-locks reminded me that I was low enough to jump. Not pulling the ripcord immediately, I descended low over the River Elbe to land in the middle of the wreckage of a B-17 and its crew! The Commanding Officer of a 8,8cm Flak battery, a young Leutnant, lined us all up! He had difficulties with his schoolboy-English, and asked the crew if they spoke English. The answer was given by the navigator, a 6ft plus tall American from the Chicago area: "We speak American!" Then the Leutnant noticed something different on me, my yellow armband with the text "Deutsche Luftwaffe". You should have seen the face of the Leutnant when he asked me "How did you get into this group?" I replied "By parachute!" He simply could not believe that a German pilot could get shot down too! Well, the propaganda!*

*We were all transported to my base in Burg and had a good time together until next morning, when the crew was brought to Oberursel, the interrogation camp for Allied flyers at Frankfurt am Main. I think three or four men of this B-17 crew failed to bail out and died on impact of their aircraft. Later on, we heard that this particular raid hit a dummy factory that was 20 miles away from the real Henschel Tiger Tank producing plant, which was situated between Magdeburg and Kassel. So followed one air battle after another on the eve of the invasion. We could never match the numbers, often it was 20:1. On the Eastern Front, the Russians outnumbered us by at least 10:1, but we still had many old pilots to hold the line there!*

**Fw Horst Petzschler, JG3, 28 May 1944. I./JG3 lost four Bf 109G-6s and two pilots KIA in combat with the Mustang escorts in the Magdeburg area on 28 May. Petzschler's short spell of operations in the *Reichsverteidigung* was ended as the Normandy invasion started and he was returned to his old unit, JG51, on the Eastern Front. Shot down 11 times, he survived the war and was credited with four American, and 22 Russian, aircraft destroyed in air combat.**

Wetzlar were lost. The three other Liberators lost came from the 2nd BD.

On 29 May 1944, 993 B-24s and B-17s were despatched. Some 888 of the heavies made visual attacks on aircraft plants and oil installations in Germany. For the second day running strong enemy fighter formations opposed the bombers, whose gunners claimed 62 of them shot down. Some 673 US fighters were airborne and they claimed 39 enemy fighters

destroyed for the loss of 10 of their own. Actual *Jagdwaffe* losses, on 29 May, amounted to more than fifty aircraft shot down, 44 aircrew KIA (including two leading aces), and nineteen others being injured in air combat. II./ZG1 flying the obsolete Bf 110G-2 was decimated to the south-east of Vienna, eight *Zerstörer* lost and 17 aircrew killed, seven others wounded. The *Gruppe* was unable to score any victories on this fateful day. Even so, 17 Liberators were lost and 17 B-17s also

**Below:** To counter the growing menace of Allied fighters and fighter-bombers attacking ground targets during early 1944, many *Luftwaffe* airfields built up strong, light. *Flak* defences. Many of these strongpoints were improvised, such as this battery of four heavy calibre machine guns from a damaged Fw 190 at Bourges airfield, May 1944. Hundreds of Allied aircraft fell victim to the *Luftwaffe* airfield defences during 1944-45. *Karl-Heinz Jeismann.*

29 May, Whit Monday. Our section had closed up well to the formation and we had no enemy fighters behind us. There were about 80 Boeings which the four of us attacked. During the attack (head-on) I suddenly noticed that the cannon had jammed, firing with only two machine guns, one of which also stopped firing. Bad luck! When we were through the formation I had difficulty to keep station with my leader. The most important thing was always to keep the section together. So I was unable to keep an eye on the formation. Lack of fuel then forced me to go down and I landed separated from the others at Ostschatz (near Dresden). From there I took off for Ansbach. There I was greeted with a great hello. 'Congratulations, congratulations!' etc. At first I did not know what to think of that. I had merely observed good hits in 'my' Viermot, but no kill. In Ansbach they had been listening in to our radio communication during the fight. Amongst others also my section leader's call: 'Congratulations Befeldt, that was your Abschuss!' My radio wasn't working, so I had heard nothing. It really turned out that the Boeing I had fired at had gone down, trailing white smoke, beside the one that my Oberfeldwebel had downed. Usually such a four-engined one does not go down as the result of 1 1/2 machine guns, it must have been a lucky hit. Either I had hit the pilot, the controls, or some other sensitive part. Well, that same evening I received the EK II from my commander. I spent the evening with my comrades, wearing the medal round my neck all the time as I had been ordered.- I don't know if it was the general rule to wear the EK II for 24 hours as it had been presented with the ribbon around the neck (after that only the red-white-black ribbon was worn in the top button hole).

The warm and sunny weather of early summer of the next day, 30 May 1944, held the promise of renewed strong enemy attacks. It was to be an eventful day. On the battle order again, I climbed into my machine, wearing the full panoply of my decoration of the day before, as enemy bomber formations were reported flying in the direction of central Germany. It was my 8th operational flight. The IIIrd Gruppe took off from Ansbach with orders to intercept a B-17 formation heading for Halle/Merseburg. We found it at about 10,000m altitude. It was an impressive sight: more than 100 Flying Fortresses sparkled silver in the sun. If one did not know what bomb load, what a potential of death and terror they carried, one would have rejoiced at this sight.

We, coming from the south, overtook the Boeings, who were unescorted by fighters, in a wide sweep and positioned ourselves in front of them. We had to attack the bombers principally from head-on. They were armed all over with machine guns and we had to expose ourselves to their fire-power only for the very briefest of time. The closing speed was about 1000 km/h - they flew at about 400 km/h and we at about 600 km/h. During an attack we had only a few seconds for scoring hits on the enemy bombers with our machine guns, which fired through the propeller arc and the two 20mm cannon mounted under the wings. One aims with one's aircraft, using the crosshairs of the reflector sight which is mounted in the front of the cockpit. Whether one had aimed correctly one can observe by the trail of one's tracers. The closer one is to the enemy, the greater the chance of a hit. So one doesn't press the 'button' ( in fact it is a small lever on the stick) until one is within 2,000 to 1,000m of the enemy. The success or failure of the attack is decided within only a few seconds.

As our twelve machines charged firing through the bomber formation I felt a blow. I was certain to have received a hit. My engine, too, sounded different than usual. I therefore reported to my leader by radio that I was breaking off because of engine trouble, reduced power and prepared for an emergency landing. But first I had to lose height. When I was down to about 1000 metres I spotted close to a village a field which appeared long enough for a belly landing. I continued my descent and lowered the flaps. When I was down to about 50m, smoke from the engine came into the cockpit. It is dangerous to land with a burning engine.

Instinctively, - one does not think in such a situation. I pulled up the machine, which was fairly slow by now, to perhaps 150 to 200 metres, jettisoned the roof, undid my straps and jumped out. The next moment I felt a painful blow on my right leg which almost made me lose consciousness. I had struck the rudder. In my confusion I pulled the ripcord rather late, but my 'chute opened in time to break my fall. I felt the strong jerk of the 'chute's opening and almost immediately after an enormous pain in my knee as I struck the ground. I had no doubt that my leg was broken but I was alive. I was unable to stand up. It did not take long before some men came running across the field and soon there was a stretcher there. I was carried to the nearby station building of the narrow gauge railway. My rescuers were very concerned about me. After about an hour an ambulance came along which took me to the Luftwaffe hospital at Halle-Dölau. The examination revealed that there was nothing broken, I had got away with a bruise in my right knee. I reported that to my unit at Ansbach in the evening.

I had called 30 May 1944 a day of significant consequences for my future life. I realised this only some weeks later in July when, recovered from my 'wounds', I returned to my IIIrd Gruppe in France. Amongst the pilots there were only young, strange faces. Immediately after the beginning of the invasion nearly all fighter units were withdrawn from the Reich defence and transferred to the invasion front. And of the pilots of the 'first hour' only a very few had survived, the majority were dead, missing or wounded. It had been my good fortune not to be fit for operations during this time, but I found this situation very depressing.

**Fähnrich Herwig Befeldt, 8./JG3. Befeldt rejoined his unit in early July. On 11 July, while on an escort mission for fighter-bombers and recce aircraft over the Invasion front, he became entangled in a fierce dogfight with Typhoons. He managed to withdraw from the battle and turned back at around 1435 hours. Only a few minutes later, and whilst flying over thick cloud at about 3,500ft, his Bf 109 was hit north of Caen by radar-directed AA. Befeldt bailed out and landed near a Canadian AA battery, which claimed to have shot him down, and he was taken prisoner. His unit, III./JG3, was decimated 8 to 17 July 1944. For four victory claims, the Gruppe lost 10 pilots killed or MIA, plus two PoW and 18 Bf 109s destroyed. By 5 September, when the Gruppe was withdrawn from the invasion front for rest and replenishment, III./JG3 had lost a staggering 56 pilots KIA and MIA, 23 wounded, and four PoW. Aircraft losses amounted to 210 Bf 109s written off. Only four experienced pilots, the Gruppenkommandeur and three Staffelkapitäne and four young replacement pilots, survived the three months of action over the Invasion front. Most of the young, hastily trained replacements had not survived beyond 5-10 sorties. III./JG3 claimed 54 Abschüsse 6 June to 5 September 1944.**

**Above:** B-17F 42-3524 Vonnie Gal of the 527th BS, 379th BG, pictured at Kimbolton shortly before noon on 5 June 1944, by armourer/bombsight maintenance man Joe D'Angelo, using his Brownie box camera. 1/Lt Jack Lamont, whose crew flew its second mission on this day in this aircraft, is walking almost beneath the nose. I/Lt Jack Lamont's crew flew 27 or 28 missions in this aircraft, which by July 1944 was the oldest operational Fortress in the Group. On its 50th mission, on 20 July, Vonnie Gal and 2/Lt William F Moore's crew FTR from Leipzig. Hit by Flak in the fuel lines just after bombs away, Moore put down at Payerne airfield, Switzerland. Vonnie Gal left Switzerland for Burtonwood on 25 September 1945. Joe D'Angelo via Richards.

**Right:** Strategic target. The gun crews' quarters of heavy Flak battery 3./406 were situated near the synthetic oil plants of Leuna, which are clearly visible on the skyline, late summer, 1943. By October 1944, the 14th Flak Division, responsible for the defence of the Leuna oil refinery and other industrial installations in southern Germany comprised 62,550 men and women, including 6,000 15-17 year old Luftwaffenhelfer. Albrecht Riedel.

failed to return. However, the Leuna works suffered a 50 per cent drop in production after the raids in May; the Pölitz works was even worse hit on 29 May.

Next day, 30 May, 928 heavies in six forces, escorted by 672 fighters, continued its pounding of aircraft industry targets in Germany, marshalling yards in France and Belgium, and *Noball* sites in the Pas de Calais. 12 bombers and nine fighters were lost. On 31 May, 1,029 heavies were despatched and only one bomber and three fighters were lost.

Operation *Cover* called for raids on coastal defences, mainly in the Pas de Calais, to deceive the Germans as to the area to be invaded by the Allied armies massing in Britain. On 2 June, the 8th AF mounted two strikes on V-weapons sites in the Pas de Calais. In the first raid,

633 heavies were involved. In the second raid, 293 bombers struck at the *Noball* sites. No bombers were lost. In the afternoon mission, 319 B-17s and B-24s were despatched to bomb airfields and railway targets in France. Seven bombers were shot down. For the next three days hundreds of 8th AF bombers flew two missions a day to the Pas de Calais area. On Monday 5 June, 626 bombers attacked coastal defence installations in the Cherbourg-Caen and Pas de Calais areas, together with three *Noball* sites and a railway bridge. On the

*T*he Allied invasion took place on 6 June in Normandy. The following day the orders of the day of General Eisenhower and the Supreme Commander of the Luftwaffe (Goering) were read out to us, with the usual exhortations 'to give our best'. I cannot remember exactly all that was said and ordered. We had probably not even listened properly, for we were more concerned with the summer holidays which were soon to begin, because firstly we were about to move on to the next form, secondly there were to be no lessons and thirdly we were to be granted two weeks' leave. Normally we would only get a 48 hour weekend pass.

**Albrecht Riedel, 17 year old *Luftwaffenhelfer*, or German "*Flak* Boy" and gun layer.**

night of 5 June at Rougham, near Bury St Edmunds, Abe Dolim, a navigator in the 94th BG, recorded in his diary: *There have been all sorts of rumours about an imminent invasion of the enemy coast.* That night RAF aircraft and gliders flew overhead in wave after wave. American crews knew then that they would be going in the morning and some thought *there would be hell to pay.* Many did not get much sleep that night.

On 6 June 1944, D-Day, a total of 2,362 bomber sorties, involving 1,729 B-17s and B-24s was flown, dropping 3,596 tons of bombs for the loss of only three Liberators (two of which collided over France). VIIIth FC flew 1,880 sorties and claimed 28 enemy fighters shot down. The only *Luftwaffe* presence over the invasion beaches that morning were two Fw 190s flown by "Pips" Priller and his regular *Kacmarek* (wingman), Uffz. Heinz Wodarczyk of the Stab flight at Priller's Lille-Nord command post. These were the only two fighters available to JG26. (The Ist *Gruppe* was heading for Reims while the IIIrd was en route to Nancy-Essey in south-east France. Hptm Naumann's Second *Gruppe* at Mont de Marsan and Biarritz, had taken off at 0700 hours and flew as far as Vrox, where they waited for further orders). Taking full advantage

of low cloud Priller and Wodarczyk made a full-throttle (650km/h /400mph) strafing run over *Sword* beach just after 0800 hours before returning to Lille-Nord unscathed and honour satisfied. (The Third *Gruppe* reached the JG2 airfields at Creil and Cormeilles by 0930 hours but did not begin flying sorties until noon, while the Second *Gruppe* flew from Vrox to Guyancourt near Paris and took no further part in the momentous day's events). That night in England US ground crews worked throughout the night of 6 June and all day on the 7th so that two missions could be flown. On 8 June, 1,135 bombers were despatched to communication targets in France. Bad weather prevented 400 heavies from bombing, and next day postponed any bomber strikes at all. It also severely curtailed operations on 10 June. Of the 873 bombers airborne, over 200 were forced to abort because of cloud conditions. Some 589 bombers, including 31 Pathfinders, attacked eight airfields in France and nine coastal installations in the Pas de Calais. On 11 and 12 June, bad weather ruled out targets in Germany and the 8th despatched its bombers to France again. Tactical targets in France continued to be attacked until 15 June, when 1,225 bombers attacked an oil refinery at Misburg, and the 1st BD struck mostly at airfield targets in northern France, which could be used to launch *Luftwaffe* attacks on the Normandy bridgehead. On 15 June 1944, the orders for ObstLt Josef 'Pips'

**Above:** B-24H 42-95132 of the 858th BS, 492nd BG, flown by 2/Lt David . McMurray, burning in a field near the Normandy beachhead on 15 June 1944 after it was shot down by Oberstleutnant 'Pips' Priller, his 100th victory of the war. *USAF.*

**Right:** Bf 109G-6/R3 of 6./JG300 being serviced, summer 1944. After *Wild Boar* night-fighting had been abandoned that spring, JG300, 301 and 302 were thrown into the daylight battles over the Reich. *Peter Petrick.*

**Full page:** In the build up to D-day aircraft were stockpiled at air depots throughout England. *USAF.*

**Inset:** B-24 Liberator *Fords' Folly* of the 392nd BG at Wendling, Norfolk, D-day 6 June 1944. *USAF.*

*Left:* View of the
Normandy beaches from
a 493rd BG B-24.
*Truett Woodall.*

Priller, Kommodore, *Jagdgeschwader 26 "Schlageter"*, came through very early, he was to lead II./JG26, III./JG26 and III./JG54 on an offensive sweep to an area north-west of Caen at 0625 hours. The weather forecast promised a fine day and in no time at all the three *Gruppen* had taken off and were racing over the French

countryside. Just after take off they were told to change course and fly towards five *Pulks* (big formations) of heavy bombers who were just inland of the French coast and heading east towards Paris. 'Pips' Priller was among the first to spot the Americans flying at about 16,000ft. They were B-17s. Above the bombers were the

escorting American fighters weaving to and for searching for the German fighters that would surely come. 'Pips' made the decision to attack the B-17s before the escorting fighters lost altitude and dropped down to engage his formation.

The 492nd BG was not the only B-24 outfit to lose a

*N*ever will forget when they told us we were to be the first to bomb ahead of the troops just before they landed. They read us all kind of messages from all the Air Corps generals. We were up all night getting minutely prepared. Took off two in the morning. Flak was light. Mission was very successful. There was a full moon. I have never seen as many boats of all descriptions as there were crossing the Channel. Saw the battleships firing at gun emplacements. Quite a sight. Quite a show.

**Diary entry, Lt Robert Shaffer, lead bombardier, *Naughty Nan*, 93rd BG, D-day, 6 June 1944.**

*Below:* B-17 (42-30146 *Cherokee*, 333rd BS, 94th BG, FTR, 29 July 1943) A3+CE, *Luftwaffe* serial 230146 ('2) in KG200 colours, attracting a large crowd whilst visiting Parndorf airfield to the east of Vienna in the summer of 1944. The following american 'Viermots' is also known to have been used by the Germans in *Luftwaffe* markings: B-17 42-30048 *Flak Dodger*, 544th BS, 384th BG, force-landed at Laon, France on 26 June 1943; B-17F 42-30336 *Miss Nona Lee II* flown by I/Lt Bell Glyndon, which force-landed with engine trouble near Varde, Denmark on 9 October 1943 was captured virtually intact. B-17 42-3190, 338th BS, 94th BG, force-landed at Evreux, France, after a raid on Le Bourget, 14 November 1943. It was repaired and used by *Luftwaffe*. B-17 42-38017, 349th BS, 100th BG, FTR, 3 March 1944; B-17F 42-30713 *Phyllis Marie*, 568th BS, 390th BG, made an emergency landing at Werben near Cottbus, Germany, returning from Berlin, 6 March 1944. It too was repaired and found by Allied troops in Bavaria at the end of the war. B-24D 41-23659 captured by the *Luftwaffe*, used by the Italian Air Force coded I-RAIN, (later on KG200 strength); B-24H 42-52106 *Sunshine* (captured 29 March 1944) B-24 41-28779. At least 10 B-17s and one B-24H used by the top-secret *Kampfgeschwader 200* operated on long range agent-dropping and sabotage-missions over Allied territory, some lasting up to 13 hours, mainly on the Eastern Front. B-17 41-21585 *Wulf Hound* with KG200 markings A3+BB, for example, is reputed to have been used in this role over England and Russia from late 1943 until it was shot down by American AA fire at Luvigny, France, on the night of 2/3 March 1945 whilst on its way back from an agent-dropping mission to Belgium and France. B-24 41-28779 (KO+XA) crashed on take off from Quedlinburg on 13 April 1945 and burned out. Its crew were trying to escape from approaching American ground troops. Finally, an unidentified B-17 of KG200 flown by OFw. Knappenschneider crashed on take off from Echterdingen airfield in March 1945. On board were 10 members of the Vichy-French government who were to have been dropped over the French-Spanish border. The only survivor was the tail gunner. *Dr Karl Dorscheln.*

*I made an oblique attack on the first box from the side, at the same altitude and obtained several strikes on one of the Boeings flying on the left side of the formation. After a battle at close range with the very strong escort, I attacked a formation of about 20 Liberators from the front. I fired at the Liberator flying the left outboard position in the first vee and I saw strikes in the cockpit and on the two left engines. After I dived away I saw the Liberator sheer away from the formation, bright flames coming from three engines, and dive. I could not see it hit the ground because of the continuing air battle.*

**Oberstleutnant 'Pips' Priller, combat report. In fact Priller had just achieved his 100th victory. It was B-24H 42-95132 of the 858th BS, 492nd BG, flown by 2/Lt David P McMurray, one of 26 B-24s of the 492nd BG, part of the force directed to bomb the railway bridge across the Loire River near Tours at La Frilliere. In this one head-on pass, Priller had hit the Liberator's right wing, damaging No.3 and No.4 engines.**

*I couldn't feather No.4 and it dragged along. We salvoed our bombs, but 15 minutes later No.3 supercharger went out and we had to drop out of formation. I got a heading for the beachhead and we made a run for it. When our No.2 prop governor went out I told the guys to stand by. We were at 7,000 and could see the French coast about 30 miles ahead. The navigator (2/Lt John F Ferrell) signalled we were over friendly territory (they weren't) and then bailed out. He was captured. We then lost No.1 — out of gas and in 15 seconds the whole crew bailed out. But every time I let go the ship started to top over. So I put down full flaps, put power on No.2 and No.3 and trimmed the plane for a glide. I left the seat at 1,800ft, detonated the IFF equipment and made a delayed jump. When I saw cows in a pasture, I pulled the cord.*

**2/Lt David P McMurray, pilot, B-24H 42-95132, 858th BS, 492nd BG. Ferrell landed in enemy territory and was taken prisoner. The rest of the crew landed in Allied hands and 48 hours later all nine men were back at North Pickenham. Ferrell's mistake saved his life, when on 7 July, now a PoW in Germany, the rest of the McMurray crew were killed when they were shot down over Bernberg in their B-24.**

Liberator to JG26 on 15 June. South-west of Chartres, III./JG26 caught the Liberators of the 392nd BG without escort and the Bf 109 pilots made three attacks, from the front and the rear. Maj Klaus Mietusch , the CO, claimed one of the B-24s, while his wingman, Uffz Erhard Tippe, claimed a *Herausschuss* after shooting a second B-24 from its formation. However, although very badly damaged Lt Harry A White got the Liberator back across the Channel and he crash-landed at Eye. (Mietusch was KIA on 17 September 1944 when he was

shot down by Lt William R Beyer of the 361st FG. Mietusch was a veteran of 452 combat sorties and had claimed seventy-two aerial victories.)

The 392nd BG gunners exacted some measure of revenge on III./JG26. The group claimed two victories but in actuality return fire from the B-24 gunners brought down only one Bf 109G. This was flown by the 9th *Staffelkapitän*, Oblt Victor Hilgendorff, who had an artificial right leg as a result of injuries sustained in 1942 when he was shot down. Hilgendorff jumped from

*We were attacked by fighters. John Wehunt, tail gunner, was killed. Glen Barnes, top turret gunner/flight engineer, suffered 32 wounds in his face and neck from splintered Plexiglas and Flak when his turret was hit. He never returned to the crew. Our two waist gunners, Sergeants James Braceforte and Robert Dunbar, bailed out and later became PoW after our oxygen system was hit, exploded and caught fire. We went temporarily out of control and they thought we were going down. It was our 13th mission.*

**Lt Harry A White, pilot, B-24 42-95025 of the 579th BS, 392nd BG, 15 June 1944.**

**Right:** The crew of B-17G 43-37704 *Button Nose*, 535th BS, 381st BG, at Ridgewell studying their route for the target for today. *Button Nose* and Lt Bob G Beackley's crew failed to return on 8 August 1944, when they landed on the continent. *Button Nose* was salvaged on 14 November 1944. *USAF.*

his stricken Bf 109 and landed in a French field carrying his false leg under his arm! Two P-38s of the 55th FG shot down two Bf 109Gs of JG26 and a pair of P-51 Mustangs of the 339th FG destroyed two Fw 190As.

On 25 June 1944, over 1,100 heavies were despatched to targets in France on two missions, one in the morning and one in the afternoon. In the morning, 258 Liberators of the 2nd BD, 137 B-24s of the 3rd BD, and 263 B-17s of the 1st BD, bombed airfields, power and transformer stations and an oil dump. During the afternoon, 274 B-24s of the 2nd BD attacked airfields at Bretigny and Buc, and an air depot at Villacoublay near Paris. The day's two missions cost the 8th AF 13 bombers and two fighters. Two of the B-24 losses were from the 489th BG, one of which, 42-95249 *Teaser*, flown by 2//Lt J D Coffman, was shot down by Uffz Hermann Grad of 4./JG26, who had taken off from Boissy-Le-Bois with

*It was our second trip to the oil refineries at Magdeburg. The first was on 28 May, and was our third mission. We did sustain some Flak damage, but came back unharmed. The 20th June mission was our 15th mission, and was part of the concentrated effort to destroy the German oil industry. We had no fighter escort flying with us, but we were told that there would be area escort that we could call in if needed. We flew over the North Sea, and turned in to the enemy coast, and about then our tail gunner, Tommy Rogers, started calling out fighters trailing behind us. Lt DeBrandes told him to keep an eye on them, and if they pointed their nose at us to start firing. We started our bomb run to the target through very heavy Flak, and about that time the fighters hit us. They were Fw 190 and Me 109s. We dropped our bombs, and the fighters came through their own Flak to hit us. We were the last element in the group, and were therefore prime targets. All of our gunners were firing and the ship was filled with smoke in the radio room.*

*One Fw 190 flew up along our right side, and as I swung my gun around to shoot, a burst of 20mm Flak came through the floor of the radio room, and small pieces hit my leg. I dropped the gun for a moment, and he was gone. He was so close I could see him clearly looking the damaged bomber over. By that time, our inboard engines were burning, and because of the location of the fuel tanks, that was an automatic bailout signal. I reached for my chest pack chute, which I always kept at the base of the radio transmitter, and when I picked it up, it was in shreds. The 20mm Flak must have hit it when it came through the floor. I was prepared to jump while hanging on*

to one of the others, but my ball turret gunner located a spare chute near the tail, and snapped it on to my harness. Our tail gunner had been hit, and he was helped from his position in to the waist where he bailed out with the rest of us who were in the rear of the ship.

*We all were accounted for on the ground after we jumped, except for T/Sgt. Lambrecht, our flight engineer. He was never found. When we hit the ground, the German civilians were waiting for us, and I had a few bruises and a black eye for a few days. Our bombardier was also badly beaten, but none of us except the tail gunner had to be sent to a hospital, as a result of his wounds from the enemy planes. When we bailed out, we were at about 21,000ft, and I delayed my chute opening until the ground looked close. I must have free fallen about 15,000ft. We had been told to do this to avoid Flak and fighters. I spent the rest of the war as a PoW and returned home in June 1945.*

**T/Sgt Ken Garwood, Magdeburg, 20 June 1944, when oil targets were pounded again. For the loss of 12 B-17s and 37 B-24s 17(shot down by fighters, 19 by Flak, while 19 heavies force-landed in Sweden) and 12 escorting fighters, the *Jagdwaffe* was further decimated. JG300 lost nine pilots KIA and five WIA, whereas the Me 410-equipped ZG26 and ZG76 lost 17 crew KIA and 14 injured. After the 20 June raids, German oil production was just 24,250 tons, down from 214,000 tons in March 1944.**

**Right:** B-17Gs of the 306th BG led by a PFF ship of the 36th BS, 305th BG, passing a burning enemy target. Nearest Fortress is 42-31897/S of the 423rd BS. This aircraft and 2/Lt David A McNaught's crew FTR from Junkers plant at Kothen on 20 July 1944. All nine men were made PoW. Top left is B-17G 42-38198/D of the 369th BS, then 44-6019/V of the 367th BS. On 11 May 1944 this aircraft and 2/Lt Edward J Magner's crew returned from Saarbrucken on first three, then two, and finally one engine, before putting down at Manston where the last engine caught fire! Magner's crew and 44-6019 FTR from Lille on 12 June. The Group was off course and drifted into the Antwerp *Flak* where 44-6019 was hit by three bursts of 88mm and Magner ordered the crew to bail out. Two men were KIA and a third died later in hospital in Brussels. Right is B-17G 42-97278/K *Umbriago*, also of the 367th BS. This aircraft and 1/Lt Charles C Wegener's crew were one of eight that FTR on 12 September 1944. Two crew were KIA and seven were made PoW. *Richards*.

Oblt Kemethmüller, CO, 4th *Staffel,* an ace with 89 victories and a holder of the *Ritterkreuz.* The two pilots had no trouble in catching the ailing Liberator, which had flown over their base on two engines after being damaged by *Flak* at Villacoublay. Kemethmüller presented Grad, who had yet to score a victory, with the invitation to shoot the B-24 down. He dispatched his victim at 14,000ft from 11 o'clock high, knocking out a third engine while the crew was otherwise occupied watching the wing and who failed to notice the approaching Fw 190s. Everyone aboard survived and they went into hiding with the Resistance but only two of the crew made it to the Allied lines. The pilot and the rest of the crew were betrayed to the Gestapo. On 5 August, they were captured and as they were in civilian clothing, they were transported to Buchenwalde concentration camp, on the last train out of Paris – before it was retaken by the US Army. In October 1944, a list containing the names of the Allied airmen at Buchenwald was smuggled out of the

*This was my first operational sortie in the P-51D. I flew as number two to George Preddy on "withdrawal support" for Fortress aircraft, which had been bombing marshalling yards at Belfort near the Swiss border. There was quite a large response by the enemy, however, whenever we moved towards aircraft coming within the vicinity of the bombers they rapidly departed, so the sortie was really uneventful. On the latter part of the return flight we had to give close support to a badly damaged Fortress (wing and fuselage damaged and one engine feathered) which was straggling badly, the crew of which fired on us whenever we got a little too close. We saw the Fortress to the UK coast then parted company.*

**"Ramrod 451", 17 July 1944. FLt Lt Edwin H King RAF, seconded to the 487th Fighter Squadron, 352nd FG, at Bodney, Norfolk. The 487th FS was commanded by Maj George E Preddy.**

concentration camp to a *Luftwaffe* base nearby and the OKL demanded that the airmen be turned over to the *Luftwaffe.* It was only just in time for they were due to be executed a week later. Coffman and his crew spent the rest of the war as PoWs.

On 7 August 1944, the 492nd BG, 2nd BD, was

**Right:** Casualty of the 29 June 1944 mission was B-24 42-95326, flown by 2/Lt Glenn F Jones, 712th BS, 448th BG, who force-landed in the Beemster, north-west Holland, with his port outer propeller gone and the starboard outer feathered. All 10 crew survived and were taken prisoner. *J P de Haan, Ab A Jansen.*

When I returned from leave on 17 July 1944, first we went to 2./406 (Rossbach/Schortau) for the formation of a large battery with 12 guns (2. and 3./406). From there we went to Oebles/Schlechtewitz (new position for a large battery - heavy Flak sub-group Leuna-South) the next day. We took over from a RAD-detachment in Oebles /Schlechtewitz older but well functioning guns and equipment, which were standing in the open in a wheat field that had already been harvested. There was no barrack accommodation. We slept on straw in tents for about 20 men. In the evenings we were able to bathe and swim in the nearby Saale river. On 20 and 21 July we had air attacks. The battery fired without stoppages. According to older Flak soldiers, they were 'pleasant fly-pasts from left to right' (west to east). We were somewhat south of the Leuna-Works and no longer at the centre of the attack as previously in Kötzschen.

A day or two later we (the Luftwaffe-auxiliaries) moved on to Leuna-Daspig on a lorry driven by wood-gas. At each slight incline we had to get out and push. We were now Luftwaffe-auxiliaries of 2./540 belonging to Flak sub-group Leuna-Middle (heavy inner Flak ring). The Flak sub-groups Leuna/South and Leuna/North (light Flak) were renamed Merseburg-South and Merseburg-North. The position was well built – at least as far as the gun emplacements were concerned. Gun emplacements with concrete bunkers for the ammunition and new 12.8cm Flak 40 with a much increased range, and which functioned well. With these I never experienced jammed shell cases, only the ammunition was twice the weight (50kg) of the 10.5 Flak 39. Two loaders were required who, having taken over the round from the ammunition gunners, had to place this in the loading tray of the automatic loading mechanism. Gunlaying was like with the 10.5 Flak 39 and that, apart from at the radar set, was the main occupation of the Luftwaffe auxiliaries.

But we did not remain long even here. It must have been during one of the attacks on 28 or 29 July 1944, when 168 bombs (carpet-bombing) fell into our position. We counted the craters. The entire living quarters were destroyed, but fortunately we had no losses. All our belongings except what we had on us were gone. I cannot remember whether anyone had called out 'take cover'. I only remember that suddenly there was a terrific roaring in the air and that I, together with some comrades, was squatting at the door to the ammunition bunker and that an older soldier held a rosary in his hands and prayed. The gun emplacement was covered with sand and stones. My seat on the gun was bent. It had become quiet again and we started with the clearing up. Here I had only got to know my gun emplacement and my own barrack hut. Where the barrack huts had been there were only bomb craters with bits

**Above:** The K6, on left, operating the fuse-setting mechanism of *Anton,* one of the 10.5cm guns in battery 7/142 at Berlin-Falkensee in early 1944. By the autumn of 1943, 100 centrally led and radar-guided heavy *Flak* batteries of the *1st Flak Division* could put up a formidable curtain of steel over 'Big B'. *Tony Temburg.*

of equipment and uniforms. The next day our battery commander praised us and sent us on 48 hours leave.

This position was abandoned and 2./540 was transferred to Trebnitz where I spent the last two months of my time as a Luftwaffe auxiliary. We were not involved in the transfer. For this there were special transport units. The setting up of the guns – without revetments in a cucumber field – was done by soldiers, prisoners of war and volunteers. When we returned to Trebnitz after our leave and re-equipment we only assisted in the mounting of the gun barrels. Gun carriages and barrels were transported separately. The barrel alone weighed 5 tons, as much as an entire 8.8 gun. We had to haul the barrel on to the carriage with a long rope.

Not far away was a railway Flak battery. Our quarters were at first in the dance hail of an inn, then later on in caravans parked along a road near the gun emplacements. Here I experienced major attacks on Leuna and Merseburg. During one, at the end of August or beginning of September, I witnessed two aircraft shot down from an approaching formation. The attacking Flying Fortresses came from the east. It was a clear and beautiful summer's day. We had opened fire on the leading

formation with perhaps four or five groups and searched the sky for the explosions of our shells. The first aircraft exploded at once in the air, the second went almost vertically down, then also exploded. Two crew members must have bailed out from this machine. Farmers working in the fields then brought them to our field kitchen, where they were still standing when we collected our rations after the attack. We had little time for observation, for as gunlayers we had to keep our eyes on the indicators and make the appropriate adjustments.

Daily routine at firing position, 114 (Kotzschen) up to the beginning of summer 1944: At 0600 Reveille. At 0700, battery parades beside the office. Duty NCO reports to battery sergeant Major. The duty NCO was on duty for 24 hours and was responsible for the entire daily routine (reveille, carrying out assigned duties, etc). It also had to be reported how many of the Luftwaffe auxiliaries were doing line checks and therefore not on parade. The communications to the staff and other units had of course to be maintained at all times. The report was followed by a kit inspection. The battery commander would then usually come along to greet us. The battery sergeant Major would make his report and the battery commander would say: "Good morning - battery." Our reply: "Good morning Herr Leutnant." (Or Hauptmann, depending on his rank). After 20 July, that casual "Good morning" (which we Luftwaffe auxiliaries had found rather dashing) was abolished. Then the disguised order of the supreme commander of the Luftwaffe (Reichsmarschall Hermann Göring) established the so-called 'German greeting' of 'Heil Hitler' for the entire Wehrmacht,, which until then had only been used by the Waffen-SS and the party organisations. But from this time onwards we had doubts whether the war could still be won militarily, although we hardly mentioned this amongst ourselves. We hoped for a political solution after the introduction of still-unknown wonder weapons, and wanted to make our contribution to the defence of our homeland.

0800. Daily gas drill. 0900. Individual training on equipment and guns, Flak gunnery training, cleaning of guns and ammunition or formal drill. 1000 hours, combat drill together with other units (e.g. training aircraft), during which photos were taken. The obtained results would then be used by the gunnery officer (radar unit commander, lieutenant or sergeant major) in a lecture, pointing out any mistakes that might have

been made. 1200hours. Mid-day break. 1400hours. Afternoon – school lessons (limited to 18 hours per week. English and French were dropped. Only Latin remained). 1800hours. End of duty day. Sometimes there was sweet milk soup for the Luftwaffe-auxiliaries. Then we were at leisure, which we sometimes needed for educational matters. We sometimes solved difficult questions with the help of a friendly NCO, Dr. Beutelschmidt from Vienna. His father was supposed to have been a minister of the old k. u. k. government of Austria. 2100 hours. Lights out -was put back to 2300 hours after some time as there was frequently gunnery training together with searchlights from 2200 to 2400 hours. In such cases reveille would be an hour later on the following day. These standard duty rosters could not of course be adhered to as they were interrupted by air raid warnings. Similarly where the night's rests were concerned. If we had an alert during the night, reveille would be later the next day.

*Luftwaffenhelfer* Albrecht Riedel, gunlayer,
Home Heavy *Flak* Batteries, 1943-44.

**Below:** During a break in an air battle during the first half of 1944, the gun crew of *Anton* (230/VII) at Friedrichshafen consumes a hasty meal. *Heinz Riediger.*

**Above:** B-17G 42-37889 *Pride of Chehalis*, 336th BS, 95th BG, being inspected by locals after crashing in a potato field near Vroomshoop, the Netherlands on 29 June 1944, when 1,150 B-17s and B-24s were despatched to bomb the synthetic oil plant at Böhlen, a ball bearing works and 11 aircraft assembly plants in the Leipzig area. 1/Lt J D Cook and his crew bailed out safely before the Fortress, one of 15 bombers lost, went down. Two men evaded capture. A total of 391 heavies returned with battle damage. *Coen Cornelissen.*

**Right:** The gun crew of *Anton* (230/VII) at readiness in anticipation of a raid on Friedrichshafen, spring 1944. Note the three victory rings painted on the barrel of the gun. *Heinz Riediger.*

*A* most exciting "Penetration Support" sortie. We were ahead of the bomber stream and so were in a good position to intercept a flight of 12 109s, to which we were directed by Radio from the UK. We were told that the 109's were forming up in line abreast, above a lake just to the south-west of Munich, preparatory to a head-on attack on the bombers. The enemy was at 35,000ft and we closed up on them from behind and below, climbing up from 30,000ft and aiming to be unseen as long as possible. I was again flying No.2 and managed to get in a short burst of some 362 rounds at the 109 alongside the one Major Preddy had selected as his target, this, just as they broke downwards. George, closely followed by myself, then chased his 109 to ground level, gradually closing up with it; in the descent during which we reached speeds well in excess of the permitted "red line" I got my first experience of the effect of compressibility. After a hair raising chase around trees, I managed a short burst at the 109 and saw strikes on the wing, then still following George I saw strikes from his guns on the fuselage. The pilot then zoom climbed, jettisoned his hood, and bailed out. His parachute opened successfully and his aircraft crashed nearby.

**"Ramrod 458", 21 July 1944. FLt Lt Edwin H King RAF, seconded to the 487th FS, 352nd FG. Preddy was awarded a half share in the Bf 109 kill to bring his total score to 15.5 (+ 0.333 for a Ju 88 share).**

# ATROCITIES OF WAR

**UNITED STATES v Fritz Dietrich, et al, trial date: The accused were tried at Dachau, Germany during the period 30 June-15 July 1947 before a General Military Government Court. Fritz Dietrich, Fritz Dintinger, Albert Eli, Karl Hunsicker, Johann Klein, Willy Stemmler, Richard Wandel and Otto Zeitzer did at or near Saarbrucken, Germany on or about 31 July 1944, deliberately and wrongfully encourage, aid, abet and participate in the killings of members of the United States Army…**

*We left the formation just a few minutes after dropping bombs. Rubenstein left through the nosewheel hatch, Monsulick and Sanders through the bomb bay, Carswell, myself, Woods, and Kudlo through the camera hatch in the rear. The remaining crew members I don't have any knowledge. Pulsipher was in the waist with parachute on, listening to interphone and uninjured. Berry and Good were at controls, both wore back type parachutes. Last conversation of the pilot 1/Lt Berry, was interphone conversation and order for crew to bail out, he was last seen at the controls. German interrogator told me he was dead, but gave no reason but led me to believe that it may have been civilians. 2/Lt Good was talking to the pilot on intercom when last heard, Germans told me he was dead but would not give the cause of death. But also led me to believe that it may have been the civilians. I thought that I had heard Pulsipher yell "Don't shoot" after he had landed. He was hiding in the bushes about 500 yards away…*

18 year old S/Sgt Virgil R Huddleston, right waist gunner, B-24H *Hula Wahina II*, 704th BS, 446th BG, flown by 1/Lt Emil Berry, shot down by *Flak* on the mission to Ludwigshafen, 31 July 1944. Berry, 2/Lt John B. Good, co-pilot, and S/Sgt Lewis E Pulsipher, tail gunner, were murdered by the *Volksturmer*. Police President Fritz Dietrich, Karl Hunsicker, and Wilhelm Stemmler, received death by hanging. Three others were indicted and tried. Two received sentences of life imprisonment and one received four years in jail. Huddleston was found by a dachshund and captured by a forester. Dozens of people crowded around him, some taking pictures. The SS police showed up and took him to St Wendel for holding. He and the other six crew were sent to PoW camps. The remains of the Liberator came down near Dudweiler in the district Saarbrücken. It was claimed by the Heavy *Flak* Battery 631.

**Below:** 18 year old S/Sgt Virgil R Huddleston, right waist gunner, B-24H *Hula Wahina II*, 704th BS, 446th BG, flown by 1/Lt Emil Berry, shot down by *Flak* on the mission to Ludwigshafen, 31 July 1944. *Huddleston.*

***Above:*** B-17G 43-37615 *Elizabeth's Own* of the 306th BG on fire after it cracked up on landing on 27 July 1944. *Richards.*

*T*he daylight attack of 3 August 1944 was to turn out to be even worse for the Flak than the night attack of 27 and 28 April, for 23 Flak auxiliaries in Schnetzenhausen were to lose their lives. In the morning it was drill as usual. Lie down, get up, line up, gunners' chain. Just as we are finishing the hooter sounds. We go to the guns, don our steel helmets, put cotton wool in our ears. Ready. The shell is in the fuse-setting holder. At last the order 'scharfer Zielflug!' The first round thunders from the barrel. Command follows command: 'Group fire-group!' We have a new auxiliary from the Black Forest. His face shows a mixture of fear and laughter. Suddenly the bombs scream down. It thundered, and everything, the protective wall, the gun, shook. Instinctively everyone looked for what cover he could find. Clumps of earth strike my back. I felt, now you die the hero's death, and an indescribable fear. I hope it's soon over, I thought. Then it was all over. At first it was like night all around. Dust hid everything. As it got lighter I climbed onto a bench within the gun revetment.

What I saw outside was terrible. At 'Berta' the gun lay outside its revetment, the carriage up in the air. No one survived there, I thought. Smoke rose up at 'Cäsar', a bomb had torn open the revetment. A couple of powder-blackened and dirt-smeared figures, their clothes torn, were just rising up from the confusion. At 'Dora' a demolished barrel stood sadly. Nothing moved. I was the first out from our revetment and hurried to 'Cäsar' to give assistance. Groaning figures lay between the guns. An almost unbearable smell of powder and blood was everywhere. The Obergefreite M stared at us from maddened eyes, he kept moaning "Oh shit" and "oh God, I am ill, I want to die". He was in a bad way, the poor fellow. Some had been flung out and lay there with amazingly contorted limbs. One man lay on the gun with a dusty and sunken face.

**16 year old 'Flak Boy'** *Luftwaffenhelfer* **Heinz Riediger, heavy Home** *Flak* **Battery 230/VII, Friedrichshafen, 3 August 1944.**

**Inset:** Gun crew of *Dora*, in the Heavy Heimat Flak Battery 230/VII at Friedrichshafen. All these 16 year old boys perished, 3 August 1944. *Heinz Riediger.*

**Above:** 16 year old *Luftwaffenhelfer* Heinz Riediger, a *Flak* gunner in battery *Anton*, an 85mm gun in the *Schwere Heimat Flak Batterie* (Heavy Home *Flak* Battery) 230/VII at Friedrichshafen during 1944. *Heinz Riediger.*

**Right:** On 3 August 1944, a 15th AF raid hit the *Flak* defences of Friedrichshafen. Of the six 85mm guns (captured from the Russians) in Schw H *Flak* Batterie 230/VII, four were destroyed and one more damaged. Of the 16 year old *Hitlerjugend Flak* crews, 23 were killed and 34 wounded. *Heinz Riediger.*

**Left:** The battered remains of *Dora* after a direct hit killed its 11-man gun crew, 3 August 1944. *Heinz Riediger.*

We were to escort the bombers to the target area (Magdeburg) joining up with them as they coasted in at Den Helder which meant getting to height over the UK. One could hear the bombers climbing whilst we were still at briefing and since the weather was poor we had to climb in sections through cloud from 600 to 18,000ft, joining up as a squadron and then a group on top. Over the continent the cloud began to break up and there was considerable opposition almost all the way in. I was again Number 2 to Major Preddy and watched him get two Me 109s. I only got a squirt at one. After the target we were relieved and returned direct to UK with no further action, just the usual Flak.

"Ramrod 483", 5 August 1944, FLt Lt Edwin H King RAF, seconded to the 487th FS, 352nd FG. Preddy was awarded confirmation of one Bf 109 destroyed and one probable. Next day he shot down six confirmed Bf 109s before going on leave until October 1944. He returned as CO, 328th FS. On 25 December 1944, Preddy scored his two final victories to take his score to 26.8333. Preddy was killed by friendly fire the same day.

This was a most eventful close escort sortie. I was leading a section initially of four reduced to three when one of my members aborted shortly after leaving the UK coast line and after the spares had returned to base. We were flying just north of the bomber force, at around 30,000 ft, with considerable enemy activity to the south,

looking like swarms of bees. We were instructed to protect the northern area when regretfully, we allowed ourselves to be jumped by Fw 190s the first knowledge of which was enemy fire as they came down past us. We broke to port into the attack - I was still feeding from the drop tanks - and in executing a maximum rate turn with combat flap to avoid enemy fire the aircraft flicked and went into a spin. By the time I had got rid of the drop tanks, recovered from the spin, and regained full control I had lost much height and was now at around 10,000ft and on my own, my number two not having managed to stay with me. When I had climbed back to a sensible height I found myself still alone, well north of the Ruhr. Initially I set course northwards then north-west, aiming to cross out to sea in the area of the Walcheren Islands. Since no one seemed to take any interest and as visibility was poor I called up for radio assistance from the homing facilities, receiving steers for the UK. I eventually arrived back not having been troubled other than by AA fire from Walcheren Island area. It transpired that my colleagues were more fortunate having dropped their tanks and so were in a better position, but were far too occupied looking after themselves than to follow me and assumed that I had been shot down. Much alcohol was consumed that evening.

"Ramrod 522", 18 August 1944, FLt Lt Edwin H King RAF, seconded to the 487th FS, 352nd FG. In all, King flew 15 combat sorties with the 352nd FG.

**Above:** 44<sup>th</sup> BG Liberators dropping supplies over Best, Holland, during Operation *Market-Garden,* 18 September 1944. *Steve Adams.*

withdrawn from combat having lost 54 aircraft in May to July 1944. This was the heaviest loss for any B-24 group for a three month period. The 491<sup>st</sup> BG moved from the 45<sup>th</sup> Combat Wing to take the place of the 492<sup>nd</sup> in the 14<sup>th</sup> Combat Wing. In late August to early September the Liberators transported supplies to the Allied ground forces in France and to the Allied airborne divisions involved in Operation 'Market Garden'.

**Left:** During the 7 July 1944 raids against oil targets in Germany, 28 Liberators and 9 Fortresses were lost, the Majority to the heavily armoured *Sturmjäger* FW 190 A-8s of IV (*Sturm*)./JG3 and II./JG300. Two of the nine B-17Gs that failed to return, however, were lost in a tragic accident on the way in, when 42-97983 FC-Z, 571<sup>st</sup> BS, flown by 2/Lt. Larue F Cribbs, and 42-10707 *North Star* of the 579<sup>th</sup>, flown by Lt. Lawrence J Gregor, both of the 390<sup>th</sup> BG, collided over Hoorn, the Netherlands. The smashed tail of *North Star* (shown here) plunged between the garage and the house occupied by the Sleutel family at the Westersingel. Thirteen of the 20 crew members from the two Fortresses, and one of the inhabitants of Hoorn, perished in the tragedy. *Jan de Groot via Ab A. Jansen.*

*F*rom 23 July till 17 October 1944, I was with the 2nd Staffel of JG76. Staffelkapitän was Hptm Schianowski. I flew some 10 or 12 sorties, all with enemy contact, and claimed two Mustangs shot down around Recklinghausen. Dogfights with Mustangs and Thunderbolts were for us flying the Me 109 a question of altitude, we were about even up to 6,000 to 8000m, at higher altitudes only with extra fuel injection which one could not use for very long. The 109 was hard on the controls, but after being used to flying the Me 110 and 410, not too much so.

After a sortie in the area of Arnheim on 16 September 1944 – during which I fired at the landed gliders – I led the so-called Holzaugenschwarm (literally 'wooden-eye', or 'remain vigilant' section). Hauptmann Schianowski led the Gruppe and was on the return flight to Störmede airfield near Geseke. Suddenly, I saw a flight of Mustangs coming in for an attack. As I had received a hit in my radio set, I was unable to warn the Gruppe of the impending danger. During the ensuing fight I also lost sight of my section comrades. I was able to shoot down two Mustangs after a tough fight, but had suffered much damage myself too, I received splinters in my forehead and the engine of my Me 109 was on fire. With a great deal of luck I was able to make a belly landing at a colliery near Recklinghausen. The works firebrigade was close by and so were able to rescue me and I was taken to hospital.

On this day the Gruppe was fired on by our own Flak, several Me 109s were shot down. Amongst them our Lt Reich, he was severely injured and lost one foot. Other comrades were dead. When I returned after four weeks in hospital and a short leave, the Gruppe had been transferred. Our new airfield was Schafhof near Amberg, I flew several sorties from here, frequently together with Eugen Meier, then Gefreiter, later Unteroffizier. He was a good chum, tough and full of energy. During a sortie around Creilsheim we got into contact with Mustangs. We had a tough dogfight, Eugen shot down one Mustang and I two. Then I was again hanging on my parachute. I got a good reception by an army unit who confirmed our successes.

When I returned to the airfield two days later I had a special reception by my Hauptfeldwebel Hermann. I believe we were now off to Reinsdorf. Jüterborg was near there with another Gruppe and the Geschwader staff, Kommodore was Obstlt Dahl. A fantastic man who did not spare himself. There, after one particular sortie, I got to know Oblt Klaus Bretschneider, the most successful pilot in the Geschwader, who was later killed during a ramming attempt [Oblt Bretschneider distinguished himself as a *Wild Boar* night fighting pilot in 5./JG300, claiming 14 RAF Bomber Command aircraft in just 20 sorties at night during late 1943-early 1944. When JG300 was re-employed in day-fighting during spring 1944, he went on to claim 17 American *Viermots*, becoming *Staffelkapitän* of 5./JG300 in August 1944 and receiving the award of the *Ritterkreuz* on 18 November 1944. Bretschneider was KIA on Christmas Eve 1944 when he was shot down in his Fw 190 A-8 *Sturmbock* by Mustangs].

**Uffz Walter Ibold, Bf 109 pilot, 2./JG26, who in late autumn 1944 was posted to 14./JG300, still flying the Bf 109G.**

*Flying alone, we became sitting ducks for German fighter planes. An easy target, this crippled B-24. Indeed, a fighter plane did pick us up, but thank God, it was American and not German. He was flying a P-47 and came within eyeball range. He called over the radio, 'Hello Big Friend, this is your Little Friend. How much fuel do you have?' Just then a Flak battery had our range again and began firing, hoping to finish us off. Our 'Little Friend' dove earthward, heading directly toward our enemy. His courage and skill put a stop to the German firing. We were saved. At this point, we could have headed for Sweden and internment for the rest of the war, but with the P-47 at our side as escort, I was determined to get our old B-24 safely back to Old Buck. The aircraft had stabilised by now; it was losing altitude steadily, due to the loss of the No.3 and No.4 engines, but once we reached 10,000ft, it levelled off and maintained level flight. We were confident now, that 'Big Friend' would return us even though the two right engines were inoperative. In the distance, I could see a sight that never looked better to those weary eyes: the White Cliffs of Dover. We were home! We landed without any problems, but our faithful B-24 was full of holes. It had no brakes or flaps and was damaged beyond repair. She never flew again.*

**Eino V Alve, pilot, B-24, 453rd BG, 25 August 1944. V-2 fuel dump, Belgium.**

**Above:** Liberators of the 492nd BG attacking the Schulau oil refinery near Hamburg, 6 August 1944. *USAF.*

**Left:** B-24 Liberators of the 453rd BG in formation. *USAF.*     **Above:** B-17G 42-97976 *A Bit O' Lace* of the 709th BS, 447th BG. *Charles E Brown.*

As I recall, 24 August 1944 was the first day that the 8th Air Force was hit by jet fighters. It was our sixth mission I believe, and prior to that day our ball turret gunner had remained in his turret from takeoff until the return landing. However he had been talking to his buddies, other gunners, and they had told them that once they arrived at the "IP" they got out of the turret until after the bomb run because enemy fighters "NEVER" flew through their own Flak. Therefore on this day he was not in position. We were on our bomb run when the tail gunner announced "SOMETHING'S COMING IN ON OUR TAIL". Almost immediately after his announcement the turret gunner got into his turret. A few seconds later we sustained a direct hit in the bomb bay. We still had not arrived at the target so we still had full bomb load, 500lb bombs, and the hit was partly under the floor of my radio room. The Flak had knocked out some of the bombs but some were still in the bay and fusing. Several of us managed to release the rest. There was a fire in the cockpit and in the radio room, which we extinguished. Fortunately, we had dropped from about 35,000 to approximately 12,000ft. I say fortunately, because our oxygen system had been punctured so we had no oxygen. Also one of the wing tanks had been hit and so it was another miracle that we did not have any problem there.

Of course there was a radio check immediately after we were hit and the only crew member not to respond was our turret gunner. A fragment had gone through his gunsight and critically injured him directly in his head. We had taken him out of the turret but even when the emergency oxygen mask was placed on him he did not revive.

Later the Flight Surgeon told us that there was nothing more we could have done because of his injuries.

All of the radios and navigation equipment was destroyed with the exception of the "Gibson Girl". I fortunately was able to run out the trailing wire antenna and attach it to the "Gibson Girl". I must have cranked on it for nearly 30 minutes and it was a welcome sight to see a P-51 just above us in, again I estimate about 30 minutes from the time I first began transmitting our SOS on the emergency radio equipment. Another miracle was the fact we never encountered another enemy fighter from the time we were hit. The P-51 guided us to a crash landing field on the coast, I believe was Woodbridge. I have not mentioned yet that many of our plane's controls were so damaged that it took both Capt Bosko and our co-pilot Curt Kohnert to maintain as level flight as possible. Consequently when we arrived over Woodbridge it was impossible for the pilot and co-pilot to bail out. Because of the damage to controls and possible brake damage the pilot ordered the rest of the crew to bail out. It turned out that he had neither flaps nor brakes but due to the field length they had no problem. We all were picked up at various points by the RAF and taken to their hospital where the injured were treated. A miracle for me personally, was the fact I did not sustain even a scratch on this mission, even though my radio room was a shambles.

**Bishop E Ingraham, Merseburg, 24 August 1944. Some 25 B-17s and B-24s were lost during raids on oil and industrial targets on 24 August 1944.**

# *Chapter 7 –* **Bloody Battles**

On 27 September, the Liberators of the 2nd BD got back to the bombing war with tragic results. While the B-17s headed for oil targets and engineering centres at Cologne, Ludwigshaven and Mainz, 315 B-24s went to the Henschel engine and vehicle assembly plants at Kassel in central Germany. For the 445th BG it was a mission which would live forever as one of the most tragic and probably the most disastrous raid for a single group in the history of American air warfare. The 445th BG flew into an area a few miles from Eisenach where three assault *Gruppen*, or *Sturmgruppen* (II./JG4, IV./JG3 'Udet' , and II./JG300), each with a strength of around 30 Fw 190s, were forming for an attack. (The Fw 190A8/R2 fighters, also called *Rammbock*

(Rammer) or *Sturmbock* (Battering Ram) were specially equipped with two heavy MG 131 13mm machine guns and four MG 151/20 2cm cannon and heavy armour plate which could deflect the American .50 calibre shells with ease.) In addition, three 'cover' *Gruppen*, I. and III./JG4 and I./JG300, were equipped with Bf 109s and were to pick off any badly damaged stragglers left by the Fw 190s. The fighters were directed by radio by the 1st Fighter Division at Doeberitz but much to the chagrin of the ground commander, the *Luftwaffe* pilots at first failed to see any bombers. Then they did. The *Sturmgruppen* attacked at about 1003hours in three waves, each wave with fighters in line abreast from the rear and with cannon and machine guns blazing. In less

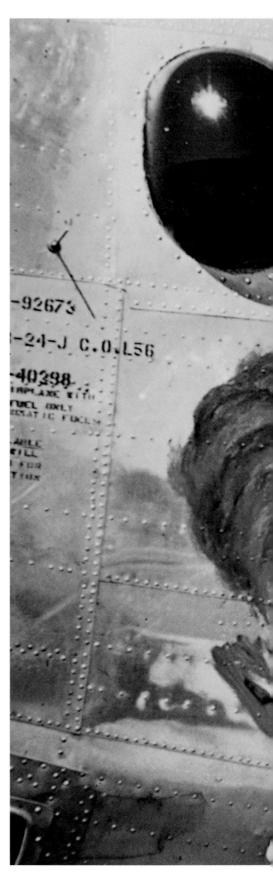

*Above:* B-17G 43-37993 *Mah Ideel* was assigned to the 91st BG on 23 July 1944 and completed 72 missions with only one recorded abort. Pilot Jack Green (back row, right) and co-pilot Bert Stiles (back row, centre) led the first crew assigned to this B-17. Stiles wrote "Serenade To The Big Bird" during his 35 mission tour on B-17s. He was killed in a P-51 in November 1944 while gaining his only victory as a fighter pilot. *Mah Ideel* was finally broken up for scrap at Kingman, AZ, December 1945. *Tom Fitton.*

**Below:** B-24J 44-40298 *The Shack*, which transferred from the 493rd BG to the 458th BG in the summer of 1944, when the 3rd BD converted fully to the B-17. *USAF.*

**Above:** Uffz Ottomar Kruse, replacement fighter pilot with 8./JG26 during summer 1944. In his short spell of operations over the invasion front (eight combat missions in four weeks), Ottomar shot down a Mustang (16 August) and a Lightning (25 August), before he was shot down by 56th FG Thunderbolts and became a PoW on 16 September 1944. The attrition rate among the *Tagjagd* pilots, and especially the green and hastily trained replacement pilots, was horrendous – none of Kruse's 8th *Staffel* comrades survived the war. *Ottomar Kruse.*

*W*hen we approached the bombers in a closed formation, suddenly some of these large aircraft started to catch on fire, some even blew up. This led us to believe that other German fighter formations had attacked the Americans before us. But then it was very quickly our turn. My Staffel Kapitän and I had had a test gyro-sight installed in our aircraft. With the aid of this sighting mechanism I was able to down two B-24s within seconds. The [first] aircraft turned on its side and plunged. Also, the neighbouring machine was already smoking from a previous attack. Both left engines were burning. I only needed to change aim to shoot again. Then this one stood in bright flames. The new aiming device was functioning astonishingly. I was so surprised and fascinated that I flew alongside my victim and stared at the metro-high flames which were pouring out of this Liberator all the way back beyond the elevator. Then this great machine clumsily laid itself over on its back and went down...

**Above:** Gefr Ernst Schroeder, pilot, *II.Sturm/JG300*. Schroeder.

After passing each other, we both turned our aircraft around and headed at each other with blazing guns. During the first approach I received two hits in the tail unit. During the second approach, my guns failed. Evidently, I had used up all my ammunition when firing at the two bombers, or my guns were jamming – I do no longer know exactly what happened. We made about four or five more frontal passes at each other, but all that was left for me to do, in order not to get hit again, was to take evasive action. After the last frontal approach of the American I finally 'hugged' the ground and was lucky enough to escape – most likely because of the camouflage paint job of my aircraft, 'Red 19'' Kolle-alaaf!' [Cologne-aloft - Schroeder was born in Cologne].

**Left:** B-17G 42-31726 *Duration-Plus*, 368th BS, 306th BG, which FTR from Merseburg with 1/Lt Clayton A Nattier's on 13 September 1944. The aircraft was shot out of formation by *Flak* at the target and crashed at 1132 hours at Ammendorf, near Halle. Nattier and five others survived to be taken prisoner. Three of the officers died in the crash when two of them were still trying to get the third out of the B-17. *Richards.*

**Gefr Ernst Schroeder, pilot, II.*Sturm*/JG300 27 September 1944,** who duelled with a P-51 of the 361st FG, which was escorting the 1st BD, 100 miles away, until it got the call to help the B-24s. However, six precious minutes elapsed before they could reach the beleaguered 445th BG and two other P-51 groups arrived after the enemy had departed. One 361st FG pilot, 2/Lt Leo H Lamb, died when he collided with an Fw 190. Altogether, 29 enemy fighters were shot down by the American fighters and bombers and 18 German pilots were killed.

*O*ur ship had been hit several times, two engines were on fire and the interior of the plane was in a shambles. The gunners kept firing but finally they were all wounded or dead. At this time I knew we were in serious trouble with no hope of flying any longer. I finally gave the bail out order because at this moment only one engine was running and not too well at that. I asked my co-pilot to unbuckle my seat belts before he bailed out. Just as he stood up to do so a 20mm cannon shell cut him in half. I really knew it was the end of our flight. The right wing was rammed by a German fighter, tearing it off. Next, the left wing blew up and only the fuselage remained. We were then at 19,000ft. It must have just exploded because the next thing I knew I was clear of the plane and hurting very, very much.'

**William Bruce, pilot, *Bonnie Vee*, 27 September 1944 (only one other member of his crew survived) broke his neck and his right pelvis and badly damaged his right shoulder. After capture, German officers fractured his jaw with a pistol butt. Almost totally paralysed and black and blue all over, Bruce spent three days on a train which took captured airmen to Frankfurt interrogation centre and then another week on a train before his severe injuries were at last treated by a German doctor. Bruce was finally sent to Stalag Luft I.**

*T*he leading Liberator, on fire from nose to tail, came swinging toward us like a severely wounded animal, then peeled away as if to pick a spot away from us to die. The next bomber moved up in its place...One Liberator with two engines on fire on the left wing came up from below us to explode when it had reached our level. A human form fell out of the orange coloured ball of fire. As he fell through space without parachute or harness, he reached up as if to grasp at something.

A 20mm shell tore through the bomb bay, ripping off the doors and severing fuel lines. Two fires started simultaneously in the bay. What strange mystery of fate kept us from exploding, I'll never be able to fathom. The engineer, T/Sgt Robert Ratchford, threw off his parachute, grabbed a fire extinguisher and put both fires out before the 100 octane gas had been ignited. Then we attended to the gas leaks from which fuel was pouring out like water from a fire hydrant. Gasoline had saturated the three of us in the ship's waist and we all had a difficult time moving about. The two waist gunners were slipping and sliding as they sighted their guns. A large puddle of gasoline accumulated on the camera hatch, blown in by the slipstream outside.

A bullet from a Focke-Wulf probably saved my life. My oxygen mask had become disconnected and before I realised it I was losing consciousness. A 20mm shell came through the waist above the head of waist gunner S/Sgt Joseph K Selser, and caused S/Sgt Robert J Cannon, to look around from his position at the right waist gun, notice my trouble and connect the oxygen line again. I gained consciousness to find the battle continuing...

One wave of enemy fighters followed another, until after six minutes the attacks ceased as suddenly as they had started...In spite of the loss of one engine, our ship managed to keep in contact with the others for a while. When the navigator, 2/Lt Robert M Kaems, informed us that we had reached friendly lines, the sickening feeling relaxed its hold in the pit of my stomach, but a dry muddy taste remained in my mouth. It proved impossible to stay with the other bombers for long and an escort of P-51 Mustangs picked us up in answer to a call from the radio operator, T/Sgt Jake S Monzingo. We were approaching a landing field in northern France [near Lille] when the second engine on our left wing cut out and a third engine spit and sputtered. Those of us in the waist rushed to crash-landing positions in the nick of time. Hunter cleared a clump of trees by inches, clipped a set of high-tension wires and brought the ship down on a potato patch, skillfully jumping several ditches, only to have one wheel catch in a hole, buckle and dig the right wing into the ground. We all took a severe bouncing but our only casualty was a cut hand for the bombardier, 2/Lt George E Smith.

**Sgt Tom G. Spera, photo-observer, *Terrible Terry's Terror* piloted by 1/Lt. William F Hunter. Hunter's crew, which came down at Willems, near Lille, on 27 September 1944, returned to England and the majority of them were killed on a raid on 9 March 1945.**

*Below:* B-17Gs of the 96th BG taxi out at Snetterton Heath. On the runway, left, is 42-97775/L of the 413th BS, which crash landed on 14 January 1945. Right, foreground, is 43-37794/T of the 337th BS, which was lost on 19 September 1944 with Lt Raymond W Bauman's crew (all PoW). Behind is 43-37687/Y of the 338th BS, which FTR when it landed on the continent on 15 February 1945. *USAF.*

*I noticed an unusual red glow in the sky around us. As I turned my head to the right, through my co-pilot's window, I saw a parachute floating down. Then the plane in front of us burst into flames. Other parachutes appeared on all sides. Suddenly, an Fw 190 swooped in front of us from underneath and behind. At the same time my arm was being pounded by my co-pilot, Newell Brainard. One engine was on fire and while working to feather the prop, other German fighters came into view. All around us was on fire...black smoke...planes going down...more parachutes...machine guns firing...the shudder of 20mm...shells hitting...another engine gone...intercom out...plane out of control...a gripping fear – near panic...then, fire! The bomb bay was a roaring inferno. Our escape route was blocked. On the flight deck behind me the radio operator stood petrified, fascinated, staring into the flames. Brainard quickly got out of his seat. I never saw either again.*

**Ralph Carrow, pilot.** *Patches,* **700th BS, 445th BG, 27 September 1944. It is possible that Brainard was one of at least nine airmen landing in or near the village of Nentershausen who was murdered or executed by German civilians, and in one case, by a German soldier home on leave. Carrow bailed out and landed in a field near a group of buildings surrounded by a high fence. A German soldier who approached him, pointed a rifle at the American and asked,** *Jude?* **Carrow had landed near a slave labour camp!**

*A wolf pack of Fw 190s...came out of the high clouds behind us and hit us so fast that our tail gunner never got to call them. He and the two waist gunners must have been hit almost immediately. The top gunner, Eppley, got in a few shots as he watched the 20mms hitting the top of the fuselage and crawling toward him. I was in the front turret and wondered what those small Flak bursts directly in front of us were. I soon found out, as there was an explosion directly under the turret, which blew out all the controls for the turret and the guns. I was helpless as the Fw 190 streaked past. He couldn't have cleared us by more than 6ft. We were in the High Right Squadron and I could see the fighters attacking the lead squadron like a swarm of bees...At this time I heard the bail-out bell ringing, so I got out of the turret and found Corman Bean, the navigator, putting on his 'chute. The whole nose compartment looked like a sieve. Those exploding 20mms had blown up right between us but neither of us were hit. By this time we were nosing down and the whole left wing was on fire. We opened the nosewheel door and bailed out.*

*In the meantime, Sgt Eppley was still firing from the Martin turret and failed to hear the bail-out bell. He happened to look down and saw the pilot coming out of the cockpit and starting across the flight deck, so he decided it was time to leave. He followed the pilot down into the bomb bay. Imagine his surprise when he found the bomb bay doors closed.*

*Schaen was going up the tunnel toward the nose following the radioman and the co-pilot. Eppley automatically reached for the bomb door handle and to his surprise, the doors opened, so he went out there. He was no sooner out than the ship blew up. We learned later that the radioman, Sgt Collins, and the co-pilot, Bobby McGough, got out, but were wounded. Unfortunately, Jim Schaen never made it. He left a wife and baby. We never found out why the men didn't go out of the bomb bay as they were supposed to do. Perhaps the first one down pulled the handle the wrong way and thought the doors were stuck.*

**2/Lt George M Collar, bombardier, describing the sad demise of Lt James W Schaen's ship, 27 September 1944, which went down 800m south of Forstgut Berlitzgrube. Collar was among five of the crew captured.**

**Below:** Pilots of 7./JG26 at five minute readiness, Stevede-Coesfeld airfield, autumn 1944.
L-R: Uffz Stumpf; Lt.Siegfried Sy; Lt Peter "Pit" Andel; Uffz Heinz Meiss (KIA 13 Mar 45) ;
Lt. Ahrens. *Walter Stumpf.*

*Above:* Fw Gzik of 2./JG300 at cockpit readiness in his Bf 109G-4 'Red 2', Borkheide aerodrome, autumn 1944. Note the name 'Rita' painted aft of his cockpit. *Kees Mol via Roba/Lorant.*

*A* mist of gasoline was floating forward onto the flight deck. The first thing that entered my mind was to try to stop the gas flow. If those shells ever entered the ship, the ship would explode. So I climbed down into the bomb bay to look at the holes in the gasoline tanks, hoping they would seal themselves. The holes were too large to seal up, so I decided to open the bomb bay doors to let the slipstream blow it out of the ship...During that time I got soaked from head to foot with gas. The slipstream started to clear up the inside. I turned around to get on the flight deck (all of this took less than a minute) to tell the pilot we had been hit bad and were losing gas fast. Before I could move one or more 20mm shells went off under my feet, wounding me in the right foot and both legs. The blow lifted me up and hurt my back and I fell on my back on the catwalk. Then I saw a blinding flash and I was on fire from head to foot. I felt. my face burning and that was all I remembered as I thought I was dying.

**Theodore J Myers, top turret gunner, *Hot Rock*, piloted by Lt William J Mowat, 27 September 1944. Myers regained consciousness to find himself hanging in his parachute. He and Frank T Plesa, tail gunner, who was also badly wounded, burned and blown out of the B-24, were reunited in a German hospital.**

than five minutes the *Luftwaffe* fighters decimated the 445th BG, shooting down no fewer than twenty-two Liberators in the space of just three minutes and three more in the following three minutes. Three of the bombers were shot down in one single attack by *Staffelkapitän* Oskar Romm of *Sturm 15./JG3 'Udet'*. The very next day, Romm claimed two more B-17 kills, which took his tally to eighty-five.

The 445th lost 25 bombers shot down and five more crashed in France and England. Only five made it back to England. It proved the highest group loss in 8th AF history. There were 236 empty seats in the mess-halls at Tibenham that evening. Altogether, the 445th lost 117 men killed and 45 officers and 36 enlisted men had been made PoW. Some of them were ordered by the Germans to collect the burnt and charred remains of their colleagues from the crashed aircraft. Even though JG3, 4 and 300 reported 39 *Viermot Abschüsse* on 27 September, and another 23 were claimed destroyed by the *Tagjagd* on the 28th, the *Jagdwaffe* again suffered serious losses. Within 48 hours, 63 pilots were posted killed or missing, 26 others being injured in air combat over mid- and western Germany. In England meanwhile, all new American replacement crews coming into the 2nd BD would be diverted to the 445th. 10 crews were

*Above:* Oblt Karl-Heinz Bendert, *Ritterkreuzträger* with 55 victories in JG27 and JG104. Bendert claimed 40 British fighters, a Blenheim, and a French Morane fighter between May 1940 and December 1942, when he was awarded the *Ritterkreuz*. After a spell of instructing, he joined the *Reichsverteidigung*, taking over 5./JG27 in December 1943, and command of 2./JG104 in April 1944. Bendert claimed a further 13 kills in the *Reichsverteidigung*, including 10 American *Viermots*, ending the war with 55 confirmed victories. In this photo, taken in 1944, the strain of continuous combat is clearly visible in his face. *Hilde Bendert.*

# CANNON FODDER

**Uffz Fritz Wiener, born on 24 July 1925, was one of the young replacement fighter pilots joining the Reichsverteidigung during the final stages of the war. His story vividly illustrates the situation of the Tagjagd at the end of 1944, when, as Fritz puts it, the young pilots, who had only limited chances to survive in air combat, were misused as 'cannon fodder.'**

*Above:* Flieger Fritz Wiener, photographed on the occasion of the award of his Wings in December 1943. *Fritz Wiener.*

*I*n 1944 the German fighter pilot generation consisted of combat experienced pilots, about three to four years older than myself (about 50 per cent), the remainder being replacement pilots. The majority of the latter category had only a minimum of flying experience with the Messerschmitt Me 109, and no combat experience at all to compensate the heavy losses from which the German Air Force then severely suffered. When I joined JG11, in the beginning of October 1944, I had never flown the Me 109 with the additional 300 litre belly tank; I had never practised take offs and landings in formation; and I had never fired the Mk108 cannon and MG151 machine guns with which my Me 109G-14 was equipped. Combat tactics, combat formation flying and combat manoeuvring in formation were entirely new tasks to be learned. All of this occurred during a period of about two months with severe restrictions on flying time, because the gasoline supply was already very limited even at combat units.

During this period I had my first serious accident. While flying at high altitude as a wingman in a flight of four, the oil pipe of my engine broke and within seconds an oil film covered my entire canopy. The oil pressure went to zero and smoke developed in the cockpit. I could barely see the ground through the side windows. Nevertheless, I decided to make a belly landing. I forgot, however, to drop the additional belly tank, which was still well filled. I managed to find a plain area for a belly landing. Fortunately, shortly before touching down, the belly tank got caught in a barbed wire fence and was torn off. As I had no forward visibility at all I was unaware that a line of trees was right ahead crossing my landing area, and both wings were torn off by the trees though which I slithered. The aircraft was completely destroyed, but I escaped without any injuries.

Three or four days later I was ordered to travel by train from Wunstorf near Hannover to the airfield at Eger [now Cheb, in the Czech Republic] and to pick up a replacement aircraft for my wrecked Me 109G-14. A brand new latest type Me 109 K-4, serial nr. 330 366, was handed over to me. On my return flight to Wunstorf airfield the Me 109K-4 with a more powerful engine (DB605 D) of almost 2000hp, an additional 300hp in comparison to the G-14, performed very well. However, after about 40 minutes of flying time, the oil pressure suddenly decreased rapidly and, again, a thin oil film covered the canopy of my aircraft. Fortunately, I saw an airfield and made a successful 'gear down' emergency landing there. It turned out to be Quedlinburg airfield in the Harz mountains. During a technical inspection it was found that the motor block had a small hole, through which the motor oil had leaked. Three days later, after an engine change, I returned to Wunstorf airfield and continued the combat flying training with this aircraft. It was from then on permanently assigned to me and received the marking 'Yellow 5' of the 7th Staffel. I am deliberately describing some of the technical deficiencies of the Me 109 aircraft, because we had to cope with these quite frequently during the end of 1944. Rumours said that the production of these aircraft in Poland and

Czechoslovakia was sabotaged. Among other minor technical deficiencies I experienced problems with the fuel supply system and the braking system.

My 'Yellow 5' was also equipped with one of the first Secondary Surveillance Radar (SSR) systems used by the Luftwaffe from 1944 onwards in the Reichsverteidigung. Only two aircraft of II./JG11 were equipped with this new system. It enabled identification of one single friendly aircraft in a formation by German radar stations on the ground (the 'Jägerleitdienste') and subsequently allowed the manoeuvring of these German fighter units into favourable tactical positions for attacks against enemy formations. The other SSR-equipped aircraft belonged to the Stabsschwarm (Gruppe Command Flight). It was the principal aircraft to be used for SSR identification when missions were flown under the command of our Gruppen Kommandeur. I was only allowed to switch on the SSR-equipment in my 'Yellow 5' when receiving the specific order "Light you star" from my Staffel leader over the R/T.

*B*ohlen was my 29th mission. That morning the 94th was split. Part of the group was designated to complement the 385th, which had suffered such tremendous losses (11planes) over Berlin the previous day, that it was unable to put a full group in the air. Their destination was Merseburg. The 331st Squadron was assigned to the 95th Bomb Group, with Bohlen its destination. Both targets were in the Leipzig area; however, Merseburg was the most dreaded target the 94th visited during my combat tour. Damage and losses sustained there were enormous. The Flak was terrifying. The Flak at Bohlen, on the other hand, was meagre; and though we had experienced Luftwaffe opposition on previous trips, it seemed a "milk run" by comparison. So we of the 331st considered ourselves fortunate.

Several of the crews on this mission were in the early stages of their tours. As we neared the initial point, Raymond "Speed" Spediacci, our tail gunner, made an observation about the looseness of our formation and commented that we'd surely be hit. The words were hardly out of his mouth when I heard machine gun fire and shouts of, "Bandits", and "We're being attacked" over the intercom. I left my radio and rushed back to my gun, the right waist, just as the Me 109s and Fw 190s were passing through our formation. They were attacking us from the rear and coming in six or seven abreast. The total number was later estimated at 60 or 70. The entire encounter didn't last 5 minutes. Then at 2 o'clock level I saw a Fortress with its left side afire from wing to rudder. And just to show how strangely- most certainly a defence mechanism – the mind works sometimes, all I could think of at that moment was the beauty and the brightness of the orange flame. I almost felt like a spectator. Lt. Jay "Mac" McIntosh identified the plane as Major Lambert's. Then a helpless feeling came over me as I watched the pilot at the wheel trying to hold the craft on a straight course. I wished I had arms long enough to reach out and snatch these boys from their "vehicle to eternity". Then slowly it peeled away from us... back... back... back.. .and at 5 o'clock low it exploded. Mac's voice then came over the intercom asking how the formation was holding up. "Speed" responded in a strained voice that no planes were behind us and he thought all were lost. I looked out the right waist and saw nothing. It was the same with Miltie Storm at the left waist. Then we just stared at one another. Obviously we were the only ones left. My eyes focused on the damage to our right wing. A large blackened hole was on top. It had apparently started to burn. Some of the boys thought we took a 20mm burst there. A huge section of the bottom of the wing was ripped loose and flapping in the air. Gasoline was pouring out in a stream like a contrail. But we were still aloft.

Mac tagged on to another squadron and we continued to the target. Reaching the I P, I breathed more easily. A feeling of security actually came over me knowing we were over the target. Why, no German fighter would dare go through his own Flak. Then Kenneth "Boots" Allmond, our co-pilot, ended our moment of respite by calling our attention to the "squirt jobs" manoeuvring around 2 and 3 o'clock. One of them mustered enough courage to make a pass. It was an Me 163 rocket propelled plane.

To me it looked like something out of "Buck Rogers". It was at 1 o'clock and still out of range when I fired a short burst for the assurance that my gun was working. Boots said to save my ammunition and wait until it was within range. I didn't think it necessary to explain. I waited... I watched the plane as it drifted toward 3 o'clock. I felt my eyes were deceiving me; it was actually in a "pursuit curve". I saw the flashes in his wings and the bursts of the exploding 20mm shells nearing our plane. My initial reaction? I started to drop down behind the armour plate below my gun. Then just as suddenly came the realisation that I, my eight crewmates, our plane – armour plate and all – were facing destruction. I started shooting. I continued firing until he was at about 4 o'clock. From my recollection, I sent 200, possibly 300, rounds in his direction. He stood there suspended for a moment. Then it seems the plane quivered, rolled over, and started down. There was no fire, no parachute, no explosion. The last I saw of him, he was in a slow spiral heading earthward; and I could hear the boys yelling over the intercom, "You got him, Chuck. You got him!"

When we reached base, we learned that Lt Brown and his crew had returned from the mission. Probably assuming that the entire squadron was lost, they turned around after the first fighter attack. A third plane, piloted by Lt Schumacher, I believe, aborted about midway during the mission because of a mechanical malfunction.

**T/Sgt Guy "Chuck" Chookoorian, radio-operator-gunner, 331st BS, 94th BG, Bohlen (Leipzig) 7 October 1944.** By this time the *Tagjagd* had only 360 fighters and pilots available for combat duty in I./Jagdkorps, 90 of which were in action against the USAAF, 7 October. Some 42 *Viermots* were destroyed for the loss of 20 pilots KIA and four injured. Between 8 October and 2 November 1944, the *Tagjagd*, in an effort to give the battered arm a breather, and to conserve forces for Galland's proposed *Grosse Schlag*, did not rise in force against the bomber formations. Only on 2 November, defensive fighter forces were again hurled en masse against the 8th AF attacking oil plants in central Germany, notably Leuna. However, of the 490 fighters in action that day, 120 were shot down, 78 pilots surviving. 40 *Viermots* FTR, thirty of which were destroyed by Fw 190s of *Sturm Gruppen* IV./JG3 and II./JG4. They lost 30 of the 61 aircraft dispatched – almost a 50 per cent loss rate.

**Below:** Me 163B Komets of 13. or 14./JG400. The *Kraftei* or 'Power Egg', rocket-fighter had a maximum speed of 955kph and was introduced into JG400 early in 1944, but it never developed into an effective bomber-interceptor. Before the end of the war only 370 Komets had entered service. Many, including their pilots, were written off in landing accidents when the residual rocket propellants exploded. The top-scoring Komet pilot was Fw Siegfried Schubert of I./JG400, with three *Viermot* kills (including two B-17s on 24 August 1944) whilst operating from Brandis airfield. He was killed in a take-off accident on 7 October. *Kees Mol.*

**Above:** B-17Gs of the 413<sup>th</sup> BS, 96<sup>th</sup> BG taxi out at Snetterton Heath. 43-37792/N was MIA with Lt. Henry Chrismon's crew on the mission to Osnabruck on 21 November 1944. *USAF.*

*I crank the nose turret to the "0" position, push the bar handle holding the two tiny doors closed down to full open, slip my hands under the second navigator's armpits and pull on him. His head falls back against my right shoulder. I look at Miller and vomit into my oxygen mask and nearly drown from it. I have never seen a human head hit by a shell. I pull him out and lay him on the strewn floor of the navigator's compartment....With a note of the macabre, I make an entry into my navigation log explaining the absence of fixes. I write it in the blood lying on my table. All this time the aircraft is making a slow, wide turn to the right because its controls are shot away and the number three engine is knocked out. We are slowly losing altitude. The noise of the wind blowing in through the holes in the front of the airplane creates an awesome, ghostly sound. The stun of the incident is blown away by the sound of the three rings on the bail out bell.*

**2/Lt Robert L Ferrell, 20 year old lead navigator, B-24 *Jolly Roger*, 755<sup>th</sup> BS, 458<sup>th</sup> BG, piloted by 2/LtWilliam Klusmeyer Jr, Cologne, 14 October 1944. All 10 crew were made PoW.**

*Over the target the sky looked like some surrealistic painting by Hieronymous Bosch. There was a pall of smoke as thick as a forest fire. With all the firing that was going on, it looked like the lights on the Los Angeles Freeway. Trailing long plumes of smoke, planes were falling, bombers and fighters alike. Parachutes dotted the weird landscape like random wildflowers. The Flak was unbelievable, barrage Flak from one end of the sky to the other... Dogfights were going on between our escort and their fighters among the bomber formations... To make it an authentic Wagnerian apocalypse, the lurid sky-scape was lit up ever so often by spectacular rocket explosions...Suddenly, as I gazed out on this, a feeling of exaltation swept over me. It was magnificent. I had the sudden revelation: This would not be happening if men didn't love it.*

**Ben Smith Jr, radio-operator, *Chick's Crew*, 303rd BG, Leipzig 1944.**

scraped together for the mission the following day, ironically to Kassel again. *Patty Girl*, flown by another crew, was the only Liberator from the 27 September mission to fly. All 10 crews returned safely to Tibenham on this occasion.

Late in the morning of Sunday 26 November, over 1,000 Fortresses and Liberators, escorted by 15 fighter groups, headed for the hydrogenation synthetic oil plant at Misburg near Hanover - a target partially destroyed three weeks before. Timing began to go awry and the 1st BD formation was spread over 40 miles instead of 20 as briefed and the three escorting groups could not hope to protect all the B-17s. *Jagdkorps* I prepared to launch some 550 fighters, although in the event, just over 400 would make contact with the enemy formations. As the heavies passed Oldenburg in the north and headed south-east towards the Elbe, Fw 190A-8/-9s of I and II./JG1, and Bf 109G-14s of III./JG6, were sent off from Mecklenburg, and JG301 was brought to a state of readiness on its airfields at Stendal, Sachau, Solpke and Salzwedel. 50 Fw 190s of III./JG1 attacked the tightly packed boxes of bombers on a wide front between Uelzen and Perleberg. Three escorting groups of P-51s battled with the enemy for about 20 minutes. II./JG1, alone lost five fighters to the P-51s in as many minutes. JG6 lost three pilots near Salzwedel, and the 9<sup>th</sup> *Staffel* lost four fighters.

At this point the Liberators, now over Wittenberge, changed direction and headed south. Then they flew west past Stendal to cross the high ground at

**Above:** B-17G 43-37877, 836th BS, 487th BG, on fire after a direct hit over Merseburg, Germany, 30 November 1944. The aircraft crashed at Halle. Seven of Lt Lloyd W Kerten's crew were killed. Two were made PoW. *USAF.*

Gardelegen and headed for the target from the east. All three *Gruppen* of JG301 had taken off from their bases at Salzwedel, Sachau, Stendal and Solpke, and they converged on the bombers just as the leading elements were approaching Hanover. Some 150 enemy fighters broke through and carried out mass wave tail attacks on the Liberators out of the sun in waves of three and five. Mustang pilots and the B-24 gunners replied to the onslaught with heavy machine gun fire. Three Fw 190s were shot down and their pilots killed, while over Rethen, Oblt Vollert, 5./JG301 CO, was intercepted by two Mustangs while hard on the tail of a Liberator and

was downed after a tense dogfight.

Without fighter escort the 491st BG, which was the last over the target, was extremely vulnerable. The anti-aircraft guns ceased firing and over a 100 fighters bore in for the kill. Lt Col Charles C Parmele, CO of the 854th BS, flying as Air Commander in *Ragged But Right* (piloted by Capt. Joseph R. Metcalf), decided to miss the *Flak* ridden target area and ordered a sudden left turn to the south and then to the west to reach the original Rally Point with the rest of the bombers in formation. This may have been a mistake, as the fighter attacks from the south and east appeared to be on the

increase. Parmele's decision effectively split the group and placed the 854th BS about 1,500 yards behind the leading 855th BS and off to the left by itself. At 1240 hours, two minutes after bombs away, the 491st was attacked over the Teutoburger Wald and the Ems, by about 75 single-engined fighters of III. and IV./JG27 from Rheine, Hopsten, Achmer and Hesepe, and

The 491st Bomb Group was flying tail end Charlie for the air force that day, and as such, we would be a prime target for fighters. We didn't have fighter support the last 30 minutes of our flight to Misburg because they didn't have the range to go all the way. Enemy fighters attacked us as we turned on our IP toward the target. On the initial attack we lost three to four of our planes. We were determined to drop our bombs, which we did, and immediately turned away from the target because of heavy Flak. After leaving the target area we were under constant attack for the next 20 minutes or so until we got over the Minden Canal, where we received fighter support from P 51s. To the best of my recollection we started out with a flight of 36 planes and arrived back at our base with from 16 to 18 planes. We were very fortunate in our plane since we did not sustain any injuries nor was our plane damaged to the point that we could not get home. We did have several bullet and Flak holes in our plane. I recall the plane flying on our right wing flipping over to the right. Our crew members reported seeing parachutes opening. As you can imagine, the flight back from the target to where our fighters were was a hairy one. My gunners claimed one plane shot down and a possibility of another one.

**Capt Joseph R Metcalf, pilot, *Ragged But Right*, 491st BG, Misburg, 26 November 1944.**

I was a 20 year old kid who had 29 missions with one more to go…I cannot say why the 491st was hit so hard by fighters that day. I can say why the ship I was in was hit. The pilot was never able to get into his spot in formation. When we were hit we flying far behind the rest of the formations. There was a definite lack of training and combat experience. We were hit by two Me 109s who came in from the left side and to the front, sweeping the ship with their cannon fire from front to rear. There was no communication of the attack over the intercom and the first I knew of the attack was the sound of their shells ripping through our ship. The first 109 finished his run at us and I was able to get a short burst off at him but it was an impossible shot. As far as I could determine afterward, it was the only return fire by our ship. By then the second 109 made his run and our ship went into a shallow dive to the right and the inside filled with smoke. I climbed out of my turret and snapped on my parachute and then is when I made a near fatal mistake. In my haste I forgot to plug in my walk-around oxygen bottle. There was a plywood door between the tail position and the escape hatch, it was jammed shut and I had to force it open, as I approached the escape hatch, I saw one of the crew members bail out and then the hatch cover fell shut. Inside the ship at this time it was almost impossible to see due to the intense smoke, but I seemed to be aware of one other crew member near the hatch cover and that is when the lack of oxygen caught up with me and I passed out. I came to, falling through the air and I can remember telling myself that I had better pull the ripcord. When my chute opened I looked for other parachutes and they were all tiny specks above me.

On the way down to the ground, one of the 109s flew past me at about 50 yards, with the pilot taking a good look at what he had shot down. To this day I don't know how I got out of the ship. It is possible that there was another crew member near the escape hatch and that he threw me out or I may have been blown out if the ship had exploded. I was taken prisoner by citizen militia members and ended up in a German Army hospital along with the other four survivors in the crew. They were the co-pilot, engineer, radio operator, and one of the waist position gunners. None of them could shed any light on how I got out of the ship. We were in the hospital until 23 December 1944 when we were shipped out to the German interrogation centre in Frankfurt, we spent one day there and were then shipped out to our first PoW Camp at Wetzlar.

**Carl W Groshell, tail gunner, l/Lt. John S. Warczak's crew, 854th BS, 491st BG, Misburg, 26 November 1944.**

**Below:** Uffz Walter Stumpf of 7./JG26 getting strapped into his seat of a Fw 190A-8 in preparation for a mission from Coesfeld airfield, autumn 1944. *Walter Stumpf.*

IV./JG54 from Vorden. The enemy fighters dived through the 854th, flying low-left, breaking up the squadron formation and attacking again, alone, or in pairs. They singled out stragglers and made their attack from 5 to 7 o'clock – a little high.

Wave after wave of fighters tore through the Low Squadron. Coming directly out of the sun, at 10 o'clock high, the *Luftwaffe* attacked in waves of up to eight abreast, breaking away below the bombers. About 10 waves attacked, followed by simultaneous attacks from 3 and 9 o'clock, by German fighters four abreast or in echelon. When the attacks finally subsided, no less than 16 Liberators had been blasted out of the sky, in the space of just 15 minutes. Further bomber losses were prevented by the timely arrival over the Minden Canal of eight P-51 Weather Scouts led by Bob Whitlow, which held the Fw 190s at bay until reinforcements could arrive to save the dozen remaining B-24s. The Weather Scouts claimed five enemy fighters shot down and one damaged. Escorting Mustangs accounted for seven fighters of III. and IV./JG27. Oblt Heinrich Sterr, 16th *Staffel* CO, IV./JG54 was shot down by a P-51 over Vorden whilst coming into land. Sterr had 130 victories, 127 of them on the Eastern Front. Hptm. Haase, CO I./JG3 "Udet" was killed in a crash on take off after he collided with his wingman.

**Above:** Fighter pilots of 7./JG26 hide in the forest near Coesfeld aerodrome in autumn 1944 while a formation of *Dicke Autos* passes overhead. L-R: Lt Peter "Pit" Andel; Lt Siegfried Sy; Uffz Walter Stumpf; Uffz Leopold Speer (KIA 1 Jan 45). *Walter Stumpf.*

**Left:** 1/Lt (later Maj) Urban L Drew, 375th FS, 361st FG. On 7 October 1944 flying P-51 *Detroit Miss*, Drew shot down two Me 262s of *Kommando Nowotny* over Achmer airfield, the first Allied fighter pilot to down two of the jets in one sortie. Upon his return the American ace was recommended for the award of the DSC, but was turned down because of insufficient information. Drew's camera-gun had jammed and his wingman, Lt Robert K McCandliss, had broken away during the attack to avoid *Flak* and had not witnessed the actual shoot downs (McCandliss was shot down over Rheine airfield and became a PoW). In 1967 Drew received confirmation of the two victories from none other than Maj Georg-Peter Eder, who witnessed everything from the ground after aborting his take-off with engine failure! In May 1983 Ben Drew was presented with the award of the Air Force Cross (modern equivalent of the DSC, and ranked second only to the MoH). He and Eder, two former adversaries, became firm friends. *Steve Gotts.*

**Above:** A brand-new FW 190D-9 has just been flown in from the Focke-Wulf works to II./JG26 at Reinsehler airfield, south of Hamburg in September 1944. Ogefr Werner Molge, is seen here checking out the controls of the aircraft. Note the tactical number 'White 9' from the ferrying unit on the tail. *Werner Molge.*

**Above:** A brand-new FW 190D-9 has just been flown in from the Focke-Wulf works to II./JG26 at Reinsehler airfield, south of Hamburg in September 1944. Ogefr Werner Molge, is seen here checking out the controls of the aircraft. Note the tactical number 'White 9' from the ferrying unit on the tail. *Werner Molge.*

*W*e were well into Germany and at bombing altitude (27,500ft) when a tube in the turbo-supercharging system of No.1 blew. The engineer, Matt Gravanic, looked at the equipment and said there was nothing he could do without a spare. At this altitude, without a supercharger, the engine had about as much power (or drag) as if it were feathered. Since we would be coming down later we left it running. We were about at the IP when No.3 ran away from having too much applied power. Obviously we couldn't keep in formation so started to descend. No point in aborting at this time as we were so close to the target, and we wouldn't have received credit for the mission. As a result, we went over Hamburg at 20,000'. Since we weren't flying formation I got a good look at the city and remember an impression of red roofs. We didn't have a bomb sight but our navigator, Larry Moore, had been a bombardier before checking out on the "G-Box", so at least we dropped bombs, à la RAF, on the city.

At the time we were the only plane over Hamburg so the AA gunners used us for target practice. Each gun seemed to be aimed individually instead of sending up a box barrage. Larry stood up in the "astrodome" looking back and telling me which direction to turn depending on the last bursts of Flak. We cost the Germans a lot of Reichsmarks that day. One burst was close enough to come through the right side behind the co-pilot, Walt Woodrow, knocking out his oxygen system and tearing a hole in Matt Cravanic's pants. The rest of the bomber stream had turned South to make a Cook's Tour of Germany (avoiding Flak zones). I put the nose down to pick up speed and turned north-west to get to the North Sea as quickly as possible. We went over Cuxhaven at 15,000ft and spent some more of Hitler's money. About this time I had the auto-pilot on, oxygen mask off, enjoying a cigarette, feet up on the rudder bars, when Walt picked up the mike and announced over the intercom, "Don't shoot unless they shoot first." I jumped up and said "What?' He pointed off our right wing and there were four Fw 190s almost flying formation with us. I got on the "horn" and called our Group Leader (Foxhole) to get Fighter Control to send some '51s. Larry Moore, in his excitement, gave me the co-ordinates as being somewhere over Denmark (I heard about that later). He quickly changed them and I relayed the information to Foxhole. The 190s pulled ahead and made a pursuit curve approach from l2 o'clock, went under us - so close you could almost reach out and touch them. To this day I have no idea why they didn't shoot. We were way off the main Bomber Stream, at a relatively low altitude with all four "fans" going (we hadn't feathered No.3 either, because even with it being pulled way back (the throttle) we were getting a little power from it), so perhaps they thought we were a German "decoy". Or perhaps they were on a training mission without ammo. Who knows?

Somewhat later a couple of flights of '51s did show up. We were out over the North Sea by this time headed for home at 10,000'. We had power again from No.1. By coincidence we reformed on our Group as we reached the coast of England. Because of our experiences I had the "honour" of landing first that day.

**1/ Lt Cy Broman, pilot *Hubert*, 92nd BG, Hamburg, 26 November 1944.**

*Y*es I went to Misburg. Yes I came back unscathed. I led the slot element. According to the best of my memories, the 491st. was a decoy group. More than one Group could have been involved in the decoy "thing". We had lots of fighter cover that was supposed to take care of us. Well, the main body of the bomber train was hit by lots of German fighters and our cover was called in to help. We were left to end for ourselves. The high right was hit first from the rear. They were picked off one by one until they all were gone. All this was out of my field of vision. The low left was next. They were picked off with the exception of about three or four. The remainder joined with us the 855th Sq. We really closed ranks and returned blistering fire from about 70 50's. I saw only a couple of Fw 190s, which passed about 30 yards to my left, peeling to left. O L Hicks, my engineer-top turret gunner bounced tracer or "fireball" ammo off the belly of one. My crew was credited with one kill. The left waist gunner, a bombardier from another crew, on his last mission, got the credit. I'll never forget his elation when we returned and he hit the ground, kissing it.

**Lloyd Murff, pilot, *Big Un*, 855th Bomb Squadron, 491st BG, Misburg, 26 November 1944.**

Total B-24 losses this day were 21, while 53 returned battle damaged and with 15 crew aboard KIA. The B-24 gunners claimed 12 fighters shot down while the escort fighters claimed 42 kills, of which the 361st FG claimed 23 enemy aircraft shot down. The *Luftwaffe* had suffered very heavily: losing 122 fighters, with 57 pilots killed and 30 wounded. JG301 alone lost 39 fighters and 26 pilots KIA or MIA, and 13 wounded. JG1 lost 11 pilots killed or missing. P-51s of the 364th FG, one of the groups protecting the 1st BD,

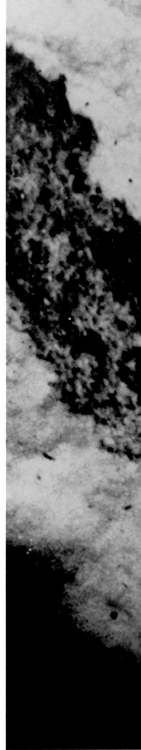

**Above:** *Blue Streak*, 834th BS, 486th BG, hurtles down in flames at Merseberg, 2 November 1944. All the crew perished. *USAF.*

*Oil targets were the absolute roughest. When the routes to targets would be uncovered at the early morning briefings and those red ribbons extended to Leipzig, Merseberg and Lutzkendorf an immediate feeling of dread was evident throughout the room. Those were always the targets with the most defensive guns and the most probability of German fighters. I know that those who ended their combat days while attacking marshalling yards, missile sites, airfields and aircraft manufacturing plants, and whatever other type targets might offer opinions somewhat different but in my mind the oil targets were those where there was no doubt of intense opposition. This one was certainly one of my roughest missions. The Flak was horrendous and its effect on the bomber force was devastating. Its been a long time since that day but the memory of airplanes falling, exploding in mid-air, spinning down out of control some of their crews escaping by parachute will probably remain always. On the bomb run itself, with the formations holding altitude, position and direction was the time of the great losses being inflicted. One could look in any direction and see the big planes going down.*

*While on the bomb run our own aircraft took a hit, which became most obvious as we left the target. The engine instruments for numbers 1 and 2 engines were indicating loss of oil pressure, erratic temperatures and manifold pressures with smoke trailing from the left engines. We were obviously losing power but it was impossible to identify the specific problem due to the instrument indications and we were a long way from home to think about making it on two engines. I elected to monitor the engines more by visual means of the engines and smoke rather than the instruments. I did shortly feather number 1 as the smoke increased but came to suspect that we had taken a hit somewhere in the instrument panel as well as the port engines which proved the case after we made it back to base. It was the battle damaged aircraft which caused us to be among the aircraft landing out of normal landing sequence and which allowed us to witness the disaster of two B-17s colliding on final approach.*

**1/Lt Bob Voss, pilot *The Dorothy V*, 94th BG, 30 November 1944, Lutzkendorf. The main oil production plants at Bohlen, Leuna, Lützkendorf and Zeitz, were severely damaged in a raid by over 1,200 8th AF heavies. Some 33 B-17s and B-24s were lost, the majority shot down by *Flak*.**

shot down two Bf 109G-14s of JG26. Lt Erich Ahrens of 3./JG26 shot down Lt Jack Gaston of the 364th FG. (Nine P-47s and P-51s and 13 B-17s were lost this day). Next day, 27 November, the ranks of the *Tagjagd* arm were further depleted with another 51 fighters and 31 pilots KIA, to Mustangs. By December 1944, *I. Jagdkorps* had only just over 1,000 fighter pilots left alive, two-thirds of them hastily trained and very green replacements.

Command acted quickly to replace the 491st BG losses. The control Tower log entries for 26 November

# THE REVOLUTIONARY ME 262 SCHWALBE

**Left:** Me 262 dispersed in the woods near Frankfurt, April/May 1945. *Kees Mol.*

*U*nbelievable. Rumours of new miraculous aircraft had long made the rounds of the Geschwader. 'Jet fighters', 'turbine fighters', 'rocket fighters', 'power eggs' and 'Hitler farts' had been the expressions since 1943, if a pilot wanted to show that he was up to date. In spite of that, no one knew whether this implied a number of secret weapons, or just some invention of the Ministry for Propaganda. 'The new fighter climbs vertically to 12,000m in 20 seconds, flies at 1000km/h and carries several 3cm cannon in the nose!' Such claims appeared wonderfully desirable amongst us of course, and perhaps we believed it for a while, because it would have been such a good thing. Later, the reality came fairly close to these figures. Which warrior does not wish for a better weapon when his present one is inferior to that of the enemy. And we German fighter pilots had for a long time now been the 'hunted' ones. Now things were going to change ‐ It was unbelievable...

One day – it was autumn 1944 – I heard and saw the Me 262 at Rechlin and Lärz. When watching, I had to use 'deflection' as the kite was always further than its noise suggested. This noise, which today leaves even babies unaffected, was then most unusual and made one hold one's breath. It was incomparable to the Me 109, for what I saw was no progress by usual standards, this machine was truly one of the hoped-for miracles. A testbed nearby, on which one of the jet engines was running, was shaking under the developed power, the air was vibrating and stones and earth were flung far by the pressure of the thrust. Up in the sky, Me 262s and Ar 234s drew their courses in wide and elegant turns and I stood amazed. Later, at Lechfeld, I was allowed to admire the Me 262 close by, and in the end was given theoretical and practical instruction on the aircraft.

There were many novelties such as rudder trim, electrical elevator trim, compensated airspeed indicator which showed true airspeed at all altitudes. And then the engines! There were no accurate horsepower values in the usual sense. Jet engines are rated at thrust in kilograms and this varies with altitude, speed and other factors. I heard for the first time new conceptions such as axial compressor, combustion chamber, jet pipe diameter reduction etc. Most importantly it was impressed on us to increase power only slowly both on the ground and in the air. Otherwise the engine would overheat and the turbine blades would exit the jet pipe as a glowing mass with all kinds of entertaining consequences. I remembered that only too well. First, take-offs. Having practised taxiing using engines and brakes, at which the nosewheel had shown itself as having a mind of its own, came the first take-off. A mechanic assisted in starting the engines. It was not so simple. Frequently there were fires and extinguishers always had to be at the ready. As a consolation we heard that a device was under development which would automatically keep the throttle within permissible limits. A battery cart was connected to the electrical circuit of the aircraft

to supply power to the auxiliary motor, which got the engine turning. In emergency – and if sufficiently charged – the aircraft's own battery would do this as well, or one used a starting rope, as with an outboard engine. Only when the engine had reached 2000rpm could the fuel supply, 'J 2' (diesel oil), be turned on. Before that, petrol had to be used briefly.

At the first take-off I was too cautious. I was still opening the throttle as the end of the runway approached uncomfortably close. I only just managed to drag the aircraft into the air. During the following take-offs I stood on the brakes while giving power.

In flight I then noticed the weight on the controls. At 850km/h, on average the maximum speed of the Me 262 in level flight, the control column was rigid like a tree and only the smallest movements were necessary and possible. The later introduced gearing, which was activated at high speeds and allowed much more sensitive flying, was of great advantage especially during attack and firing, where quick and accurate corrections were required.

As a previously unknown problem the question now cropped up, how one was to get rid of the so easily achieved speed. In a shallow dive near ground level, the Me 262 quickly speeded up to 950km/h (beyond that it became so nose-heavy that it could barely be held), and it was difficult for the beginner to get it back to 350km/h - the maximum speed for extending the undercarriage. No wonder that in the initial stages, a minimum cloud base of 1000m had been imposed for flying activities.

As the engines were liable to flame-out at low throttle settings and no one relished having to do a relight on his first flight, there were sometimes circuits which would have counted as minor cross-countries at initial training. These beginners' circuits often extended to beyond sight of the field and it happened frequently that two such 'world travellers' approached the field at the same time. Then occurred one of the critical moments: the overshoot! There were many unnecessary losses through an insensitive opening of the throttles. It was not necessarily a case of turbine blade failure or the 'Onion', the jet pipe, parting company; no, it was enough for the engines to accelerate unequally to cause a machine flown by a beginner to flip over and crash. In single-engined flight the Me 262 reached about 550km/h, but could not be held with the undercarriage extended and descended at about 2m/s. I had unpleasant moments when, during one of my first circuits, the port engine failed on the downwind leg. I was unable to retract the already extended undercarriage, as the undercarriage pump was driven by the port engine. Against all the rules I turned against the dead engine with the live one running at full power and just managed to make the field. This proved to me what could be done with this kite.

The crushing Allied air supremacy forced us to place the aircraft dispersals in woods wherever possible. NSU tracked motorcycles towed the aircraft sometimes for *kilometres to the runway. As the jet's endurance was only about one hour, the engines were not started until just before take-off. For quick scrambles the serviceable jet aircraft were lined up wingtip to wingtip on both sides of the runway and also serviced there. Engines could be changed relatively quickly.*

*Radio communication was ideal compared with other aircraft as there were no sparking plugs to cause interference. A new approach aid was often useful as at these high speeds even some of the old hands could get disoriented at the beginning. The Me 262 only carried armour plating at the front: steel plates, about one cm thick, in front of the ammunition boxes and a thick bulletproof windscreen at an angle of about 30° in front of the pilot. I know of no case where this armour had been pierced. There was no armour behind the pilot and was not really needed. Who was likely to bother us from behind? Regrettably that changed when the fellows from the other side realised their impotence in the air and began to greet us heartily from behind during take-offs and landings, when high-speed aircraft were extremely clumsy. The armament satisfied all fighter pilots' dreams. Four MK 108, with 360 3cm shells of all kinds, mounted in the nose, brought down any 4-mot even with only a few hits. When, in the final weeks of the war, 12 R4M rockets (5cm) were mounted under each wing, which could be fired successively or as a salvo, we felt like being captains of a battleship. There was no enemy aircraft able to survive even a single R4M hit.*

*I flew my first operational sorties alone, later in a section, against reconnaissance aircraft (Lightnings) with or without escort (Lightnings or Mustangs) and Mosquitoes over southern Germany. We were guided by our own ground control station called 'Sturmvogel', or 'Storm Bird', up to visual contact. If one got into attacking position from behind without being spotted, an Abschuss was assured. But fighters and reconnaissance aircraft are no 'barn doors' (as we called the huge four-engined Allied bombers) and the time available for firing was extremely short. Also, one had to pull up sooner than with piston-engined machines, otherwise the victim would disappear up the air intake. So, at the beginning, frequently we missed. And if the approach was spotted soon enough by the enemy, their agile aircraft were able to twist or dive away forcing the jet fighter with its wide turning radius to save his ammunition for another day. To score a hit in such an alerted formation was all but impossible. If the enemy fighter was particularly clever and twisted tightly, he could even throw something at the Messerschmitt. Sometimes a few Lightnings hung around over Lechfeld at 8000m, waiting for us. They had noted our weaknesses, but not yet our strengths. That came later. Too late!*

*Our strength lay in our superior speed and armament. One should visualise what power is behind a heavy jet fighter. A pull-up started at low level with 950km/h would end on one's back between 2500 and 3000m and 300km/h! The jet fighter pilot must reckon in different dimensions. Especially in those days, when the enemy had nothing comparable and the difference in speed amounted to 200 to 400km/h. The opponent had to be, if at all possible, recognised earlier, the attack begun sooner and more accurately and the firing carried out with the utmost precision. A few seconds - and with the high rate of fire the ammunition was quickly exhausted.*

*At reduced speed the Me 262 was, like the Me 109, easy to manoeuvre, with leading-edge slats extended and the nicest of condensation trails at the wingtips. At relatively high humidity and high speed straight and level flight there were even fog banks across the entire wing which, when at low level, could even be seen from the ground. In the tightest of turns, the Me 262 would begin a pitching movement prior to flipping over, enabling the pilot to ease off on the controls before it was too late. Even though one was pressed into one's seat with several G in tight turns, one had to remember that the propeller-driven fighters were capable without exception of even tighter turns.*

*At the beginning it had been assumed that the 'flying soldering torch', as our fast kite was called, would be too vulnerable with its unprotected engines and 2,500 litres of fuel and attacks against four engined formations with their dense curtains of fire were prohibited. After trials against reconnaissance aircraft and fighters this ban was lifted. Although there continued to be scrambles against the latter and successes scored, the main targets now became the Boeings and the Liberators. Now our new weapon would show what it could do.*

*Some hotheads who attacked the 4-mot formations alone had successes, but also had to pay the price for their dash. Old hands knew that bomber formations had to be attacked in at least sections of flight strength in order to spread the defensive fire. We too therefore assembled small units before attacking the bombers. Operating these fighting formations sometimes led to problems. We tried a formation in echelon with only 50-80 metres between each aircraft. Although protection to the rear was partially lost, this was not so important thanks to our superior speed, and the closing up for the attack was quicker. Only during the climb, and especially when R4M rockets were mounted (which meant a loss of about 50 km/h), had attention to be given to enemy fighters who, coming from above, were then able to match our climbing speed of 650km/h.*

**Lt Fritz R G Müller, Me 262 day fighter pilot, credited with six victories in III./JG7 and the *Erprobungs Kommando* 262, November 1944 to April 1945. He was known in III./JG7 as 'Kondens Müller or 'vapour-trail Müller' because one of his specialities was to use the electrical elevator trim and a great deal of manual effort, to make tight turns close to the ground causing vapour trails to appear at the wingtips of his jet. Müller previously flew the Bf 109G in III./JG53, 1943-44.**

**Below:** Me 262, possibly of III./EJG2. *Müller via Heilmut Detjens.*

**Above:** Lt Fritz R G Müller, one of the most successful Me 262 jet fighter pilots (six *Abschüsse* in III./JG7 and the *Erprobungs Kommando 262*, November 1944 to April 1945) playing with the *Staffel* dog whilst serving with III./JG53 in Italy at the end of 1943. *Müller via Heilmut Detjens.*

*Above:* B-17G 42-32099 *Fightin' Carbarn Hammer Slaw*, named after a comic strip character, 367th BS, 306th BG, March 1944. This B-17 and 2/Lt Charles F Manning's crew FTR from Berlin on 5 December 1944 when the plane ditched in the North Sea. All nine crew perished. *Richards*.

*A*fter a dog fight with bomber-escort fighters over Hamburg I had to make a forced landing in a field near Zever after receiving damage to my cooler, which I succeeded in doing without significant damage (apart from the oil tank and propeller). After another dogfight in the area of Rheine on 14 December 1944, in which Heinz Richter was killed, a further emergency landing went awry. I made a rough landing in a meadow and ended in a wood where my Bf 109 suffered total damage. I was taken from the wreckage with concussion. But intensive oxygen treatment soon restored my fitness to fly. The first take-off after my concussion, it must have been on 27 December 1944, was a test flight. I had been asked by a comrade who had gone down with flu to test his aircraft which had been fitted with a new engine. When I was about to return to Rheine after this test flight I found that the airfield was blanketed with thick fog and I was therefore not able to land. As I was about to set course for the nearest available airfield I was attacked by four Spitfires and shot down. The aircraft crashed next to the village of Kattenvenne. I was able to bail out and returned with my parachute

**Fähnrich Otto Theisen, who joined 2nd *Staffel* of I./JG27 December 1944.**

said, '*Sixteen replacement B-24s arrived from Stansted, Shades of Dawn Patrol.*'

On 16 December 1944, using appalling weather conditions to his advantage, Field Marshal Karl von Rundstedt and his panzer formations attacked American positions in the forests of the Ardennes on the French-Belgian border. They opened up a salient or "bulge" in the Allied lines supported by an estimated 1,400 fighters in 12 *Geschwader*. In England the Allied air forces were grounded by fog and it was not until 23 December that the heavies could offer bomber support in the "Battle of the Bulge".

On Christmas Eve, a record 2,034 8th AF bombers and 500 RAF and 9th AF bombers, took part in the largest single strike flown by the Allied Air Forces in WW2, against German airfields and lines of communication leading to the "Bulge". The 1st BD made a direct tactical assault on airfields in the Frankfurt area and on lines of communication immediately behind the German "bulge". Crews were told that their route was planned on purpose to go over the ground troops' positions for morale purposes. Brig-Gen Fred Castle, commander of the 4th BW, led the 3rd BD on his 30th mission in *Treble Four*, a 487th BG Fortress, with Lt Robert W Harriman's crew. All went well until 23, 000 ft over Belgium, about 35 miles from Liege, his right outboard engine burst into

On 17 December 1944, the Second Gruppe was ordered to transfer from Wunstorf to the airfield at Zellhausen, near Seligenstadt/Aschaffenburg on the Main river, from which we then operated within the frame of Reichsverteidigung West. In spite of very bad weather all of the more than 60 fighter aircraft, led by Ju 88s, arrived safely there. The Ju 88 aircraft also remained at Zellhausen airfield. Already in the afternoon of 17 December we flew our first combat mission in conjunction with our ground offensive in the Ardennes, the mission objective being to render support to the advancing German ground forces. The first combat experience, which we young pilots gained, was the effectiveness of the anti-aircraft fire capacity of the American ground forces, and our inability to take effective avoiding action to escape from their accurate fire. Consequently, we suffered our first losses. During the following days, until 31 December, we were only able to fly missions on seven days due to the prevailing extremely bad weather conditions. And whenever the weather was favourable we had encounters with the American fighter forces, mainly P-47s, and incurred severe losses. Very often we had encounters in which we were outnumbered five to one. Accordingly, during this short time span, a total of 41 aircraft of my Second Gruppe JG11, were either completely destroyed or damaged, with nine pilots killed (predominantly the young replacement ones) and five wounded.

Encounters with the American fighter forces were less vulnerable for us when we flew in larger formations. I remember quite vividly one day between 20 and 24 December, when flying in group formation, i.e. four Staffels and the Staff Flight, we met a large formation of US fighters in the vicinity of Bad Kreuznach. We were flying at an altitude of about 8000m in a suitable position to attack and we engaged the enemy fighters. I was the wingman of the flight leader and my primary task was to stick to his tail. Rapid manoeuvring started and my flight leader vehemently pulled his aircraft up in order to gain additional altitude. In order to be able to follow him I had to use my emergency power, i.e. a methanol injection for a duration of about two minutes. My whole attention was concentrated on following the manoeuvres of my flight leader. Suddenly I saw P-47s ahead of us and I started firing with my MK108 cannon and the machine guns. I think I scored some hits but I had to break off because my flight leader executed evasive manoeuvres. When trying to reduce the engine power, in order to stop the methanol injection, I experienced a malfunction of the gas throttle and I kept going at full power. After scanning over the instrument panel in order to establish my situation, I could move the throttle back and forth but it had no effect on the running of the engine. During this short period I had lost my flight leader and I went into a steep dive to get away from the area where the fighting was going on. Somehow I managed to operate the engine power by regulating the gasoline flow with the 'Schnell-Stop' lever and finally landed safely at my home airfield.

The subsequent technical inspection revealed that the 'Gasgestänge' had broken. Had this very seldom technical failure perhaps again been caused by sabotage during the production of the aircraft in Czechoslovakia?

**Uffz Fritz Wiener, II./JG11.**

**Below:** B-24J 44-40271 *House of Rumor*, 854th BS, 491st BG, which was lost with Lt George A Meuse's crew at Misburg, 26 November 1944. Three gunners ignored the bail out bell and went down with the ship, firing their guns to the end. *USAF.*

24 December 1944 - Christmas Eve. My brother had just arrived on a visit. Towards 1400 hours, I and a section comrade, were scrambled, with orders to chase away or destroy a few lone-flying aircraft, probably reconnaissance machines. We spotted the enemy near Kassel and had to climb to around 10,000m. Suddenly my cockpit iced up and the visibility became practically zero. With my experience of flying on instruments, I tried a slow descent. Suddenly I felt hard strikes on my tail, obviously from enemy fire. My 109 stood on its nose and down we plunged. I tried to jettison the roof and bail out, but had to push against it for a long time with my shoulders before it came off. I finally got out at fairly low altitude, so pulled the ripcord at once, one panel tore, and the impact on the ground was very hard, I suffered contusions to my legs and lower body. I had come down on the railway line Kassel-Bebra, near a train which stopped, people got out, amongst them were some acquaintances from my home town. We wished each other a 'Merry Christmas'.

**Uffz Walter Ibold, Bf 109G pilot, JG76.**

**Above:** The wreckage of *Treble Four* piloted by Gen Fred Castle on Christmas Eve 1944. *Rougham Tower Assn.*

**Above:** FW 190A-8s of 7./JG26 returning safely from a mission, late 1944. *Walter Stumpf.*

**Above:** Face of a lost generation. Othr Alfred Scharf, 7./JG26, KIA in his Fw 190A-8, 16 September 1944 either by a P-47 or a P-38, two months after turning 20. He claimed one victory, a P-47 of the 356th FG, on 18 August, during his few short weeks in the lethal skies over Germany. *Walter Stumpf.*

flame and the propeller had to be feathered. The deputy lead ship took over and Castle dropped down to 20,000ft. But at this height the aircraft began vibrating badly and he was forced to take it down another 3,000ft before levelling out. The Fortress was now down to 180mph indicated air speed and being pursued by seven Bf 109s of IV./JG3. They attacked and wounded the tail gunner and left the radar navigator nursing bad wounds in his neck and shoulders. Castle could not carry out any evasive manoeuvres with the full bomb load still aboard and he could not salvo them for fear of hitting Allied troops on the ground. Successive attacks by the fighters put another two engines out of action and the B-17 lost altitude. To reduce airspeed the wheels of the Fortress were lowered and the crew ordered to bail out with the terse intercom message, *This is it boys.* Castle managed to level out, long enough for six of the crew to bail out, but at 12,000ft the bomber was hit in the right wing fuel tank, which exploded, sending the B-17 into a plunging final spiral to the ground. Brig-Gen Castle was posthumously awarded the Medal of Honor; the highest ranking officer in the 8th AF to receive the award. Harriman and Castle were buried in the American cemetery at Henri-Chattel.

For four B-17s destroyed, IV./JG3 lost two pilots MIA, and five PoW, on 24 December. The *Reichsverteidigung*

suffered the loss of 85 pilots KIA/MIA, plus another 21 wounded or taken prisoner.

Overall, the Christmas Eve raids were effective and severely hampered von Rundstedt's lines of communication. The cost in aircraft though, was high. Many crashed during their return over England as drizzle and overcast played havoc with landing patterns. Tired crews put down where they could. Only 150 aircraft were available for another strike on 26 December. Next day the wintry conditions were responsible for a succession of crashes during early morning take-offs. On 30 December, the 8th again attacked lines of communication. On the final day of the year, the 1st BD kept up the attacks while 3rd BD crews returned to oil production centres. This time they were assigned Hamburg. It was the scene of another disaster for the 100th BG, which lost 12 Fortresses to JG300 and to *Flak* over the target; half the total lost by the 3rd BD. *Reichsverteidigung* units lost 37 pilots KIA/MIA,

**Below:** A 12./JG77 pilot looks on as his engine fitter inspects the Daimler-Benz engine of his Bf 109K-4 at Neuruppin airfield, at the end of 1944. From October 1944, JG77 was employed in the *Reichsverteidigung*, first in the defence of Berlin. On 1 January 1945, three *Gruppen* of JG77 were involved in Operation *Bodenplatte*, attacking Antwerp-Deurne airfield. *Kees Mol via Nitsch/Roba.*

***Above:*** B-17G 44-8355, a PFF ship in the 710<sup>th</sup> BS, 447<sup>th</sup> BG, flown by 2/Lt Miles S King, takes a direct *Flak* hit on the bomb run on 24 December 1944. Eight crew were KIA and two made PoW. *Derek Smith.*

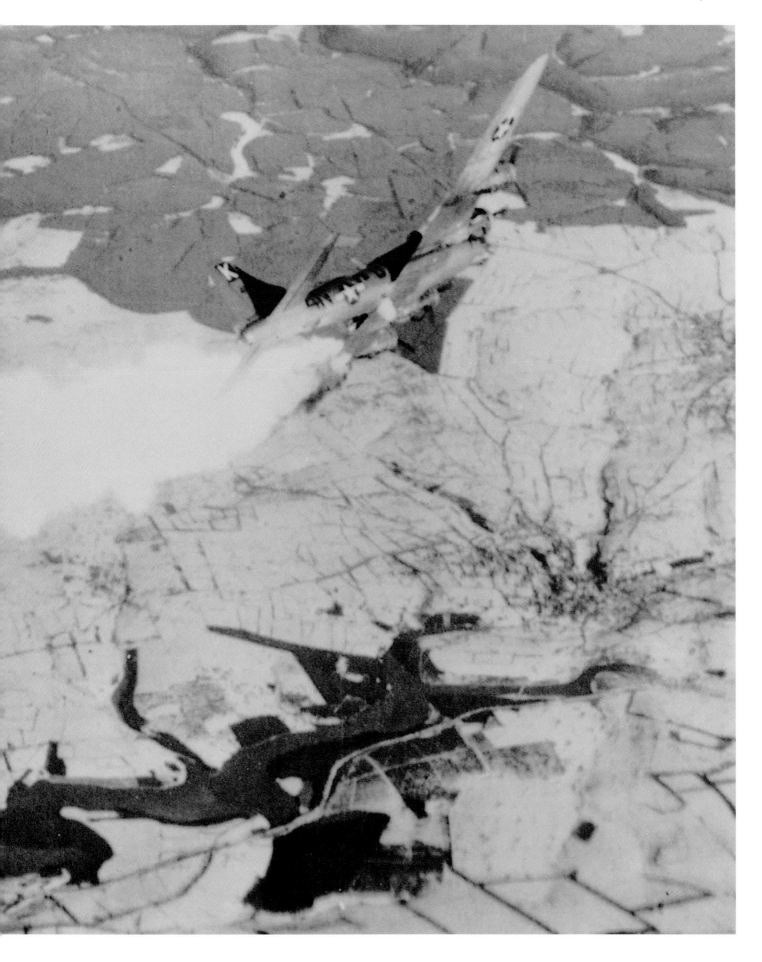

# STURMJÄGER OR 'STORM FIGHTERS'

*T*he tactical idea to combat the American bomber boxes by specially armoured Fw 190s attacking from behind in tight and massed formations was born in the late summer of 1943. Maj Hans-Gunther von Kornatzki is acknowledged to be the father of this concept, which he practised in the Reichsverteidigung in Sturmstaffel 1 or 'Storm Squadron 1' which he formed and led October 1943 to April 1944. Equipped with the Fw 190A-6 (from February 1944, the A-7, and from April the A-8) Sturmjäger or 'Storm Fighters', Sturmstaffel 1 became operational at Dortmund in January 1944. Although during the ensuing months the unit managed to notch up a fair amount of Viermot victories whilst operating from Dortmund and Salzwedel aerodromes, losses from defensive fire and American escort fighters were also very heavy, at least 14 of the volunteer pilots having perished by April 1944. Incorporating the remains of Sturmstaffel 1 as its 11th Staffel at Salzwedel airfield in April 1944, IV./JG3 became the Sturm Gruppe IV./(Sturm) JG3, practising the same 'Storm' tactics in the Reichsverteidigung. One of the all-volunteer fighter pilots serving with IV./JG3 was Uffz Karl Kapteina;

I arrived at IV./JG3 'Udet' at the end of September/beginning of October 1944. I had volunteered for 'Storm' duties at the holding unit at Liegnitz after the then commander, OLt Volkmann, had asked the men for volunteers to come forward. IV./JG3 was then stationed at Schafstädt. I was posted from the Gruppen staff to the 4th Staffel at Langeneichstädt. There I was told by the Sergeant Major, in the presence of OLt Gerth, to sign a declaration. This was to confirm my obligation to the Sturmgruppe. If I remember correctly there were eight parts, but I can only recall three precisely. 1.After alarm start to fly in tight formation. 2.To attack the enemy formation from behind. 3.If the enemy cannot be downed with gunfire, he is to be rammed.

After signing the declaration, OLt Gerth explained each point. First he played down the commitment to ramming. He said that our guns were so good that the enemy was bound to be destroyed – unless one had a stoppage. In actual ramming, one had to arrange it so that one could still bail out and save oneself by parachute. When attacking from behind one had to expect the concentrated firepower of the Viermots. We had however, other than the usual fighters, special armour plating. These were the so-called blinkers, bulletproof glass screens on either side of the cockpit cover, and 8mm armour on both fuselage sides. Our close formation flying made us very vulnerable to enemy fighters, but we had fighter cover from the other three Gruppen of the Geschwader. On subsequent sorties, however, I saw little of this fighter cover.

Fourteen days later, having done some training on the Sturm machine, I was transferred to the 15th Staffel at Nehmsdorf, which was commanded by Lt Romm. I remained with this Staffel until I was shot down over Belgium on Christmas Eve 1944. I don't want to talk about the numerous sorties where we never caught sight of the enemy. But I have several other tales to tell. At the end of November1944, the Gruppe was transferred to the west to Stormede. At this time the High Command was preparing for the Rundstedt or Ardennes offensive. On our first sortie over the western front we had no contact with the enemy, but Hanne Kleinchen was shot down – by our own Flak near Bonn. By this time we were no longer flying in tight formation, but well apart, as was usual for fighters. On one of these sorties our Staffel was at the rear, while comrades from another Staffel ahead had a dogfight with enemy fighters. I was flying as wingman to our Staffel commander, Lt Hecker, when he became ever slower, then jettisoned his cockpit cover and bailed out. Once he was hanging on his 'chute I circled about 200m above him. And it was very well that I did so; shortly afterwards a Lightning came along and fired tracers at him. I went for him at once and fired a burst of tracer across his bows. He turned in and we had a dogfight. I did such a violent turn to port that the machine started to shake. That was the sign that it was about to stall over the starboard wing. I had to ease off the elevator a bit. That widened my turning radius. Then the pilot of the Lightning made a grave error. He dived away and flew westward at low level. I was able to shoot him down with ease. He must have been a beginner. Lt Hecker returned the next day by train, he told me that he had bailed out because his engine had failed.

On one of the first days of December, the Gruppe was flying at 2000m east of Cologne in a southerly direction under the command of Hptm Weydenhammer. We could see the bombing of Cologne. There was a thick layer of cloud above us. In spite of that Hptm Weydenhammer tried to get through the clouds with the formation. Four of us came out of the tops, Hptm Weydenhammer, Fw Hopfensitz, Fw Martin and myself. Hptm Weydenhammer was an old hand and had all the blind flying qualifications. The remaining three of us had been instructors and had the instrument ratings 1 and 3. 3 was the fighter instrument rating. Probably none of the others had this.

There was nothing left to see of the Viermots. We flew westwards and after some time the clouds disappeared. At that moment we were fired on by German Flak. Hptm Weydenhammer continued to fly with us westwards. Why, I do not know. We crossed the front line and American Flak took over from the German, with an intensity I had never experienced before. The Christmas trees of the light and medium Flak flew past our machines in masses. In between, the bursts of the heavy shells made our machines bounce about. Then the 190 of Hopfensitz caught one. He dived away, I, as his wingman, went after him. He was able to level off near the ground and we flew eastwards. We landed in Werl. The machine of Hopfensitz had three hits, mine had none.

I personally only participated in two 'Sturm' attacks. On the first one, on 23 December 1944, we were flying with the Gruppe to the south of Bonn. Uffz Hoffmann was leading our Staffel. I was his wingman. Fw. Hopfensitz flew on my left. We sighted a formation of Marauders [322nd BG formation going in too attack rail bridges at Euskirchen. Two were lost to IV./JG3] and attacked from behind. I fired at an enemy machine and scored hits but as these showed no particular effect I proceeded to fire with all my guns. The machine exploded in a huge ball of fire. Afterwards Hopfensitz remarked that it had been the most beautiful Abschuss. He had also shot down a Marauder. I had dived away and as I saw some of the remaining Marauders slinking off to the west I climbed up again and tried to fire at one of the machines. But I had no ammunition left! As my fuel was getting low I went off alone in the direction of Gütersloh. I was flying low down when a fighter approached me in the opposite direction. As we passed the pilot waved at me. I waved back. It was a Mustang. He was probably also low on fuel.

Invariably the pilots would peel off downwards after delivering their attack to seek out the nearest airfield, then after refuelling returned to our own base. The fighters were frequently obliged to do so as they had been in the air for a long time and had jettisoned the drop tanks, at latest just prior to the attack.

It might be of importance that, shortly before the successful attacks in which I participated, the commanders had received new directives on tactics. Previously the formation leader had received the courses to fly towards the enemy force from the ground. For example, fly 270, then perhaps 303°. Now the formation leader was given the enemy's position and decided himself the courses to fly. That appeared to be better. I had previously been on a number of flights where we never found the enemy as we had been wrongly directed from the ground. Whether that had been due to incompetence of the controllers or, as rumour had it, 'sabotage'? In the Reich Defence we flew in two vic's astern and the Staffeln would alternate their positions. I have never experienced an assembly after an attack and have never heard about such a thing.

One day after my first successful Sturm attack, the Sturmgruppe took off at 1115 hours from its base Gütersloh against American four-engined bombers. It had been reported that the Americans, having formed up over southern England, had made their way towards Germany on an easterly course.

I flew in the 1st section of our Staffel as pair leader. Fw. Hopfensitz was section leader, his Kaczmarek (wingman) Fhr Ott My Kaczmarek was OFw Schulze. In addition, one other pair flew with our Staffel. Altogether there was about 35 aircraft in our group. We first flew to the Möhne dam, where we were to meet other groups. As however there was nothing to be seen of these, our commander, Hptm Weidenhammer, flew in the direction of the western front line, climbing to 7000m. We were receiving a running commentary about the position of the enemy over the radio so that we were able to fly directly towards them. In the area of Liege-

Bastogne we started to circle in order to await them there. Suddenly a call over the radio:

*'Questionmark ahead, probably Indiaper (Red Indians, or enemy fighters)!'* I switched on my reflector sight, the guns had been readied shortly after take-off.

The next moment the supposed *Indianer* flew past us – they were Me 109s! These had, as I discovered later, already attacked the *Viermots* over Belgium. We continued to fly our port turns, when suddenly my engine started to splutter. I noticed that the temperature showed under 500. I cursed and begged my engine to hold out until the Americans turned up. It must have understood me, for it did so.

After a while some small specks appeared in the west which came rapidly nearer and revealed themselves as the 'Fat Cars' (enemy bombers). Some restlessness became noticeable in our formation. The comrades closed up more tightly and Hptm Weidenhammer led in a wide turn to port, during which we climbed another 300m, to the attacking position behind the *Viermots*. We were now about 200 metres above and 800m behind the enemy.

Our commander now said to ground control: 'We are attacking!', then we gave full throttle and lowered our noses. We had selected the formation on the extreme left. Ott, flying next to me to starboard, now became restless and I had to take great care that he should not ram me. Then I took aim at my first opponent. After the first burst I had destroyed his tail turret. Then I fired with all I had at the wings. By now I had got so close that bits of his tail section were flying past my ears. The kite was on fire all over. The undercarriage dropped out, then the machine went down over its port wing. Whether the crew had been able to save itself I could not tell. On breaking off I saw my comrade Hopfensitz go down, trailing white smoke.

After a dive of 500m I took a look at the formation we had attacked. All that was left was a burning bunch of disintegrating machines, from which two intact ones sheered off to port. These too must be downed! I got excited and started to climb again, which was easy after my speed in the dive. During the climb I saw that an Fw 190 from the 16th *Staffel* also climbed and positioned itself behind a *Viermot*. Three of the crew bailed out before the 190 had fired a single shot. The rest followed, after it had been raked by the Fw. Meanwhile I was some 500m behind my new opponent when three Americans also jumped. The *Viermot* now took wild evasive action. At 200m I gave a short burst with my 2cm guns. Having observed hits, I fired with the 3cm guns as well, covering the wings. This had a catastrophic effect. The entire machine burned, then the port outer wing broke off and the machine went down. At the same moment my rudder received a hit and I could not move the pedals any more. I did not know whether the elevator had also been hit and did not dare to break off to the side. I flew past the crashing aircraft, then there was banging in my engine and the cockpit filled with smoke. Two small flames came out of the right footrest.

I wanted to release my harness but it would not come open! When I failed to do so after another two attempts, I jettisoned the cockpit roof. Then hell was let loose! The resulting draught beat the flames into my face. I again tried to release the straps, then I gave up. I put my hands, which had already suffered burns and were now painful in the flames (I had taken off my gloves before firing), on the cockpit sides. Meanwhile the machine must have presented a gruesome sight as it went down like a blazing torch from 7000m. Slowly my senses left me, I could see nothing but red. The worst was breathing in the flames, which streamed past my head. My sole hope was the crash, then the pains would be over. Suddenly there was a bang and a terrible pain went through my limbs. Then I felt nothing. I floated through space. Was I dead? I slowly returned to my senses. The earth was alternately below and above me. Then I was out again. Then conscious once more. I thought: you are saved, just now you were in a burning aircraft. As it became dim again about me I subconsciously pulled a red button which was hanging on my right side. The same moment there was a bang and I was hanging on my parachute!

Now I was fully conscious and I felt the terrible pain of my burns. I looked down at myself and tenderly felt my head and face, as far as this was possible with my burnt hands. It was all a charred and bloody mass. The rest of my body was unharmed, saved by my leather flying suit, which was singed all over. I was hanging on my parachute and it seemed as though it wasn't going downwards at all. Suddenly there was a swishing noise and my left boot, which I had missed already, flew past me and downwards. It became ever smaller until I lost sight of it.

**Above:** Uffz Karl Kapteina (here while a Gefreiter (AC1) preparing for a training flight early in the war) served as a *Sturmjäger* in 14. and 15./JG3, October to December 1944. He claimed a Lightning shot down at the end of November and a Marauder on 23 December. After destroying two B-17s on 24 December 1944, his Fw 190 was hit by return fire. Kapteina, who bailed out with severe burns, was taken prisoner. *Karl Kapteina.*

Only the slight draught from below showed me that I was going down. In the final 300 to 400m the 'chute began to swing about and I discovered that I would land in a wood. That could have fatal consequences for me! But I was lucky to land in a clearing. I had to roll over to break my fall. After all, one's descent is at the rate of 5 to 6 m/s.

As to my escape there are several possible versions. 1. As I no longer used the controls, the machine started to go down. After perhaps some 1000m it exploded and I was flung out of the burning wreck. 2. The front fuel tank exploded after some time and flew off past me. That dragged me out of the machine as the straps had possibly been burnt. 3. The straps had been burnt and the draught had dragged me out of the machine. Whichever way it had been, I now lay in a miserable heap in a forest clearing somewhere in Belgium. After some time I was discovered by American soldiers, who took me in a Jeep to Banneux (near Liege) where my wounds were treated. I was then taken to a hospital in Liege. Whilst I was recovering in hospital, Liege was bombarded by V-1s. One of these exploded about 150m from the hospital. All the window panes, together with their frames, were flung into the rooms.

At the beginning of 1945 I was taken via Carentan, France, in a hospital ship to England and there to the General Hospital in Reading. It was interesting to watch the *Viermots* assembling over England. The Americans started in the early mornings, before it had got really light and it took a very long time before they had formed up and gone on an easterly course. The British started in the late afternoon while it was still light. They did not form up but went on course in a stream.

**Left:** One of the most successful *Sturm* pilots and formation leaders in IV./JG3 during the first half of 1944 was Lt Hans Weik, who destroyed 22 *Viermots*, 21 of them in 9./JG3, before being severely wounded in combat after shooting down a B-17 for his 36th kill near Kempten on 18 July 1944. Nine days later, Lt Weik was awarded the *Ritterkreuz*. Hans Weik.

including one *Gruppen Kommandeur*, three *Staffel Kapitäne* and a further 12 Jagdflieger injured.

German production of fighter aircraft actually increased through 1944 into 1945. It had peaked in September 1944, when an astonishing 1,874 Bf 109s and 1,002 Fw 190s were completed. (Though that same month, an average of three German fighters – and two pilots KIA - were lost for every B-17 or B-24 shot down.) The dispersed manufacturing plants were beyond the power of the 8th AF to seriously damage. Therefore, some postwar surveys concluded that the 8th AF bombing offensive was a failure. But the bombing was just good enough that the *Luftwaffe* fighters had to keep rising to attack, and then

they were mostly destroyed by the P-51s and P-47s. The USSTAF was clearly winning the battle of attrition in the conflict with the *Jagdwaffe* as trained fighter pilots at this stage of the war were impossible to replace. January 1945 marked the Eighth's third year of operations and it seemed as if the end of the war was in sight. On 1 January the First Air Division (this day the prefix "Bomb" was officially changed to "Air") encountered enemy fighters in some strength during raids on the tank factory at Kassel, an oil refinery at Magdeburg and marshalling yards at Dillenburg. The Magdeburg force came under heavy fighter attack while the Kassel force was badly hit by *Flak*.

Though the final great offensive of the *Wehrmacht* under von Rundstedt had ground to a halt in the Ardennes, and Germany had no reserves left, there were signs that the *Luftwaffe* at least, was far from defeated. The overwhelming air superiority of the Allies led to German plans to try to simultaneously destroy the RAF and American aircraft on the ground in Holland, Belgium and Northern France in a single, decisive, blow. *Unternehmen Bodenplatte* began at about 0900 hours on New Years Day 1945, using 875 single-engined fighter aircraft, primarily in support of von Rundstedt's Ardennes offensive. Total Allied aircraft losses during *Bodenplatte* amounted to 424 destroyed or heavily damaged but German losses however were catastrophic. 300 aircraft were lost, 235 pilots were killed, and 65 pilots were taken prisoner. The big gamble had turned into a disastrous defeat.

*Above:* 7./JG26 pilots are briefed at Stevede-Coesfeld airfield, October 1944. L-R: Lt Gottfried Dietze; Ahrens; Uffz Heinz Meiss; Hoffmann; Uffz Hans-Joachim Zutz; Mischkel; Lt. Peter "Pit" Andel; Ogfr Otto Puschenjack; Lt Gerhard "Bubi" Schulwitz; Lt Siegfried Sy; Uffz Walter Stumpf; Fritsch. *Walter Stumpf.*

*Right:* A member of 416 Repair & Salvage Unit posing with locals in front of the crashed Mustang OC-R 415268(?). 1944-45. *George Reedman.*

**Above:** *Bodenplatte* struck hard at Eindhoven airfield. Black clouds of burning aircraft rising behind Spitfires of the Recce Wing on 1 January 1945. *Baird via Putz.*

**Right:** Fw Haralds Makars (left) and Lt Arnolds Mencis, two Latvian volunteer pilots who flew on the Eastern Front in ground attack aircraft and in 3./JG54, 1943-44, and JG1 in the *Reichsverteidigung*, November 1944. Mencis shot down two Spitfires during *Bodenplatte*, 1 January 1945, before he was forced to crash-land his Fw 190 10km east of Hengelo airfield with his fuel tank holed. *Arnolds Mencis.*

**Right:** B-24 42-51707 *Dorothy*, 453rd BG, in the snow at Old Buckenham, which finished her days in warmer climbs, at Kingman, AZ after further service in the 445th and 389th BGs. *USAF.*

On the evening of 31 December 1944, all pilots of II./JG11 were ordered to assemble in the village gymnasium near our airfield. Here, we were informed about 'Bodenplatte' and received a thorough briefing on our tasks and objectives. We now learned why the Ju 88 aircraft had remained attached to our Gruppe. Their task was to act as pathfinders and lead us to our designated target, which was Asch airfield near Maastricht. Contrary to most other missions, which were normally outlined in general terms during 'ad hoc' briefings, the mission 'Bodenplatte' was explained and pre-planned in great detail. Of course, all aspects of this operation were discussed at length between the pilots and there remained little time to find some sleep in the provisional bedding arrangements. I do not recall any abnormal emotional reactions being apparent among the pilots when we were briefed for Bodenplatte.

At dawn on 1 January 1945, II./JG11's four Staffels and the Staff Flight had lined up on opposite sides of the airfield and were ready for take-off. Departing first in formation were the Staff Flight and the 5th Staffel, followed by the 6th Staffel, which took off in the opposite direction. The remaining two Staffels followed likewise and within two minutes the whole Gruppe was airborne. I flew as a wingman in one of the four flights of the 7th Staffel. The group assembled and proceeded at low level in the direction of Frankfurt am Main. There we joined up with the other Gruppen of JG11, which had departed from Grossostheim and Biblis aerodromes. The Ju 88s then took the lead and navigated JG11 to our target, Asch airfield. The idea behind this mission 'Bodenplatte' was to carry out surprise attacks very early in the morning with as many German fighter forces as could be assembled, on airfields in France, Belgium and the Netherlands, and from which the Allied Air Forces operated against the German offensive in the Ardennes. It was hoped that the Allied aircraft would all be on the ground, nicely lined up and presenting good targets for strafing attacks and that the alcohol consumption during the New Years' eve celebrations would have affected their defensive capabilities

Unfortunately for us this turned out to be wishful thinking. As our Fighter Wing arrived over Asch airfield, P-47s and P-51s were already airborne and immediately engaged the Me 109s and Fw 190s of JG11 in air combat. Also, heavy anti-aircraft fire was hurled at us from the ground. Our intention to carry out organised ground attacks was further hampered by numerous patches of fog in the vicinity of the airfield, which forced us to abandon maintaining close formations and many individual flights were now largely on their own. Consequently, our losses were heavy.

In my capacity as wingman of the flight leader I had to stay in formation with him and await his orders. We flew in loose formation, about 50m apart, in the combat area of Asch airfield, and because of the unfavourable weather conditions, I had difficulties to remain in visual contact with my flight leader. During the attack manoeuvres over Asch, with rapid course changes, I lost contact with my flight and

was on my own. Considering that about 200 aircraft were operating over Asch airfield and in poor weather, it was impossible for me to get a picture of what was going on. The anti-aircraft fire from the ground added to the confusion. Since the supplementary belly tanks had been dropped and the remaining gasoline in our main tanks allowed for a total of only 50 minutes flying time (intended for the attacks on Asch airfield and for the return flight), we had to leave the combat area after about 10 minutes of engagement there and I decided to return on a direct course to Zellhausen airfield. To top it all off, when crossing the front line on our return to our home bases, German anti-aircraft batteries started firing at our own aircraft in the belief that they were the enemy, and shot down many of them! The losses of my Gruppe, II. /JG11 were, six pilots killed, two taken prisoner and 11 aircraft destroyed or damaged.

During the first half of January 1945, our missions were flown mostly in Staffel strength (consisting of four Flights) or in single Flights of four aircraft. Our main objective was to hinder, to the maximum possible extent, Allied aircraft carrying out ground attacks on German military installations and supply columns. Because of the overwhelming air superiority of the Allied Airforces, our efforts were of negligible harm to them. The negative psychological effects caused by this situation were further deepened by an order from Hermann Göring, the Supreme Commander of the Luftwaffe, that any combat mission aborted by a pilot for alleged technical reasons was rated as cowardice, which, by the law of war, could be punished with the death penalty. Only after an immediate technical inspection had proved that the malfunction reported by the pilot was actually existing, was he freed from the accusation. This situation constituted a heavy blow for the morale of all pilots, and particularly for the younger ones like me who were still highly motivated, even though our losses were the most numerous among the fighter pilots because of our limited combat experience.

**Uffz Fritz Wiener, pilot, 7./JG11. JG11 lost a catastrophic 24 aircraft, or 40 per cent of its front-line strength, as well as nineteen pilots killed or MIA on 1 January 1945. JG11 was withdrawn from the western front on 17 January 1945, and re-deployed to the east of Berlin on ground attacking missions against the advancing Russian armed forces. During one of these risky low level strafing runs, on a large convoy on 29 January, Fritz Wiener was hit in his back by an explosive round. Although large pieces of shrapnel had penetrated one of his lungs and some 30 others had peppered his back, he managed to remain conscious for about 10 more minutes and make an emergency landing on a snow-covered field near Vietz, some 20km from the front. He remained in hospital and was taken prisoner by US forces in early May, after which he was operated and had the shrapnel removed from one of his lungs. Wiener was not released from captivity until October 1945.**

*It was at about 0830 hours when the first strike took us by surprise. Fw 190s jumped our fighter base at St Trond, Belgium. I was on my way to our supply trailer when I heard AA fire and swoosh down they came. I stumbled into the nearest foxhole I could find and looked out to watch the action. Two 190s had already made their pass and two more were coming in. Damn, they were moving fast. Surprisingly, little damage was done. Two P-47s were shot up in their revetments and a machine shop trailer was damaged. The raid only lasted about 15 minutes or so but it seemed a hell of a lot longer. There was one casualty however. One of our cooks had gone into St.Trond walking down a cobble stone street when an unexploded AA shell fell beside him and then blew up. Those AA crews were something else. They were firing at anything that moved. They crippled one 190 and the pilot bailed out. He landed in a field nearby and two of the AA crew gunners raced over to him and almost beat him to death. Two weeks later the two were courtmartialled and transferred to combat infantry. Two P-47s returning from an early morning mission intercepted the last two 190s, shot one up so bad he dropped his wheels down and they let him land. The MPs took over and we were the proud new owner of one of Herman's fighter planes. Shortly afterwards one of the P-47s tried to come in and the AA opened up on him. That "Jug" pilot left in a hurry. He must have been low on fuel because he came back again waggling his wings and finally got down.*

**S/Sgt Ray A Rhodes, supply, 379th Air Service Squadron, attached to 404th P-47 FG, 9th AF, New Year's Day 1945. In fact, Fw 190A-8, serial no. 681497 of 5./JG4, was one of five attackers shot down during the attack on St. Trond. Gefr. Walter Wagner belly landed his virtually intact "White 11" just to the north of the airfield. It was repaired by 404 FG mechanics and painted bright red. A new serial no. "1-1-45", was applied to the tail. Though fully airworthy, higher authority decreed that the aircraft was forbidden to be flown, even by Lt Col Moon, CO, 404th FG!**

*On New Year's Eve, we were stationed at Rheine. 2nd Staffel of I./JG27 had all of five pilots available for operations (many pilots had been killed, missing, dead) our Staffel commander, Lt Heinrich Wiese, (who after some time had taken over from Lt Wunsch who had failed to return from a sortie on 21.11.44); Heinrich Braun, Ewald Lang and myself. Lt Joachim von Stechow, who had been trained as a fighter pilot but had not yet been in action, had joined us in the last few days. With the exception of our new comrade, we all had combat experience. Lt Wiese, had shortly before brought down a B-17 by ramming; unintentionally, as he later told me (he had nosed down too late) and had to bail out. Braun and Lang had several aerial combats.*

*The orders for 1 January 1945 were issued in two parts: On New Year's Eve we were advised of the imminent large-scale effort and ordered to readiness early on New Year's Day. At dawn on New Year's Day itself we were briefed on our particular task which concerned the airfield of Brussels-Melsbroek. Some 180 Marauder bombers were stationed there. Other bombers and fighters had also been sighted there by the jet-powered Ar234 reconnaissance aircraft. Our task was to destroy aircraft and hangars there. We took off shortly after 8 o'clock. We assembled in a formation which was led by a Ju 188. We flew at low level over the Rhine and through Holland as far as Utrecht. From there we headed in a left turn for Brussels. Our second Staffel, which was represented only at flight strength, occupied the port outer position. The flight was led by our Staffel commander, Heinz Wiese. His wingman was Lt Joachim von Stechow who flew on the extreme left. I flew to the right of Wiese and Lang was on my right.*

*As we crossed the arms of the Rhine to the south, we were at a height of about 300m. Here the port wing of our formation was met by heavy Flak. The machine of Wiese received a direct hit. I saw a ball of fire on my left and knew that our Staffel commander had been killed. His inexperienced wingman now attempted to escape the Flak by evasive action. I called out to him to dive down close to the ground to escape the fire. I myself dived down at once and Lang followed me. When I looked around for von Stechow's machine I found that it had been hit. The Bf 109 broke apart and crashed to the ground. Von Stechow was unable to get out.*

*Soon we had reached Brussels. We circled the airfield, which was easy to make out, first in the direction of the city. Over the city we pulled up and let ourselves fall, one after another, upon the airfield of Melsbroek. The machines, which still stood as they had been shown on the photos, were attacked with cannon and machine guns. After the second and third attack the place and the hangars were in flames.*

*After several attacks we turned for home. We had orders to make our way individually. Near Eindhoven I ran into Flak in spite of being at low level. From this moment onward I remember nothing. As I was later told in hospital, I had been shot down by the Flak, crashed with my machine and was found – still strapped into my seat, which had evidently broken loose in the crash – many metres away from the wreckage. According to this report my aircraft had then burned out. I awoke again on the 10th January 1945 in a Canadian field hospital near Turnhout where I was looked after well in every respect. The English surgeon, Mr Cowell from Newcastle-on-Tyne, looked after me particularly lovingly. I had suffered a heavy concussion (on the limits of a brain contusion), severe facial injuries, a dislocation of the left shoulder and a fracture of both right forearm bones.*

**Fähnrich Otto Theisen, fighter pilot, 2./JG27. I./JG27 lost six pilots killed or MIA. Theisen was the only one of his Gruppe to be taken prisoner.**

**Right:** Fighter pilots of 7./JG26 discuss tactics before setting off on a mission against the Americans from Stevede-Coesfeld airfield in October 1944. L-R: Uffz Walter Stumpf, one kill, 366th FG P-47, 9.3.45; survived the war; Lt Peter Ahrens,11 victories, killed in accident on 4 March 1945; Uffz Meihs. *Walter Stumpf.*

# *Chapter 8 – Gotterdämmerung*

On 2 January 1945, the B-17s once again pounded lines of communication and raids of this nature continued for several days until the position in the Ardennes gradually swung in the Allies' favour. The severe wintry weather on 5 January over England, was responsible for several fatal accidents during take-off for a mission to Frankfurt. A period of fine weather, beginning on 6 January, enabled the heavies to fly missions in support of the ground troops once more. These were mostly against lines of communication, airfields and marshalling yards. Finally, the German advance in the Ardennes came to a halt and ultimately petered out. Hitler's last chance now lay in his so-called "wonder weapons"; the V1 and V2. Missions were flown to tactical targets throughout the remaining days of January but when the weather intervened the 8th mounted shallow penetration raids on *Noball* targets in France. The 8th also attempted several tactical missions but the weather was so bad morale sagged as mission after mission was scrubbed, often just after take-off.

*Whilst serving with 14./JG 300, I was promoted to Feldwebel on 1 January 1945 by Kommodore Dahl, for particular valour in the face of the enemy. I cannot remember my first operational flight with 14./JG300. We were frequently sent off but failed to approach the enemy. Eugen Meier and a Feldwebel Deutscher frequently flew with my section from Reinsdorf. I think my next sortie was on 14 or 15 January 1945 with about 25 Me 109s of our Gruppe under the command of ObLt Müller from another Staffel. After a short while he broke off saying: "My horse is lame", and ordered me to continue in charge of the formation. We received enemy contact in the area of Stendal. There had been some fights already and with a number of Fw 190s about. A mad dogfight was going on. We were able to carry out one attack against a formation of Boeings. Some were certainly downed, but there was no time to make observations, as the Red Indians (enemy fighters) scattered us. There was a mad dogfight, ratio about 10 to 1. I was able to shoot down one Mustang, but then once again it was my turn. I came down by parachute at Sandau near Havelberg. I found out that people from my home town of Moere had been evacuated to this place, so we had a good celebration that evening. Hardly anyone from my unit had made it back, the Gruppe had high losses that day. When I returned to Reinsdorf a couple of days later the commander, Ofterdinger, asked: 'Ibold, where is my Gruppe?' My wingman, Fw Deutscher, was also killed on this day. I can still see his twisted face in my mind's eye.*

**Uffz Walter Ibold, Bf 109G pilot, JG76.**

**Above:** The pock-marked landscape at Pölitz oil refineries 3 March 1945. *USAF.*

By 3 February 1945, Marshal Zhukov's Red Army was only 35 miles from Berlin and the capital was jammed with refugees fleeing from the advancing Russians. Accompanied by 900 fighters, 1,200 B-17s and B-24s dropped 2,267 tons of bombs on the centre of Berlin, killing an estimated 25,000 inhabitants and destroying 360 industrial firms, heavily damaging another 170. Photo-reconnaissance revealed that an area one and a half miles square, stretching across the southern half of the 'Stadtmitte' or city centre, had been devastated. The 8th lost 21 bombers shot down and another six crash-landed inside the Russian lines. Of the bombers that returned, 93 had suffered varying

forms of major *Flak* damage. Further German disruption in the face of the Russian advance occurred on 6 February, when 1,300 heavies, escorted by 15 groups of P-51 Mustangs bombed Chemnitz and Magdeburg, and the 8th resumed its oil offensive with raids on synthetic oil refineries at Lutzkendorf and Merseburg. Bad weather forced all except one 1st AD Fortress to return to England while over the North Sea. Altogether, 22 bombers were lost in crash-landings in England.

On 9 February, the heavies returned to the oil

**Left:** On 6 July 1944 HM King George VI and the royal party visited Thurleigh, where HRH Princess Elizabeth christened B-17G 42-102547, a lead ship in the 367th BS, 306th BG, *Rose Of York.* The aircraft was lost over the North Sea on 3 February 1945 returning from Berlin. All the crew perished. *Richards.*

**Below:** A P-38 Lightning of the 9th AF framed by the wrecked buildings of a former *Luftwaffe* airbase in Belgium, December 1944. *Pieter Bergman.*

*I* was born in 1925 and did not get to the Eastern Front as a day-fighter in the 2nd Staffel of the famous JG52 until towards the end of the war in December 1944, straight from fighter training on Me 109Gs. I was a beginner as far as flying hours were concerned and somewhat fearful at the thought, what I should do once the dogfight was over when, not knowing where I was, I would have to find my way back and how many minutes fuel I would have left. The training for the German fighter pilots was simply too short with too few flying hours and in particular far too few overland flights to practice navigation. As a young fellow one had the necessary fighting spirit, for me today unimaginable physical condition, quick reactions and a carefree nature. Today I can only sadly shake my head about all that. During our aptitude tests we had looked upon the older Luftwaffe doctors (all of some 30 years old) with quiet amusement. Our Gruppe commander was about 32 years old, Major Adolf Borchers, a very level-headed man whom we called 'Papa Borchers'. These were the circumstances under which a young fellow came to the front. I had not wanted to be a fighter pilot but would have much preferred to have become a long-range reconnaissance or bomber pilot as this would have involved a far better training. As such I could then have become a Lufthansa pilot later on. Or so I thought. Eight days after arriving at the night and cross-country instrument flying school at Sprottau/Sielsia we ensigns were told that the entire training was to cease due to lack of fuel. We could go either to the Reich Defence, the fighters over Germany, or to the Regiment Hermann Göring as infantry. We obviously opted for fighter training. Fortunately I was posted to the East to JG52 in Krakow in Poland and therefore did not become part of the well-known statistics which said '5 sorties against the allies, then the name would be removed as shot down and dead or in hospital.'

**Günther Wiedenbruck, who served as a pilot with II./JG52 between December 1944 until the end of the war on the Eastern Front, commenting on the lack of sufficient training of the *Luftwaffe*'s replacement fighter pilots in the latter stages of the war.**

In January 1945, I was promoted to Leutnant and was posted to the 3rd Staffel of JG105, flying the Fw 190 and based at Zeltweg (on the southern edge of the Alps north of Graz). There was deep snow here and three Fw 190s crashed on landing. For that reason the Staffel was transferred to Absdorf-Bierbaum on the Danube (some 40km west of Vienna). It was a grass field with no hangars or fuel installations and with only a small hut for flying control (by one NCO), a crash unit (one lance-corporal with about 20 girls and a fire cart without tractor) and parachute section. The airfield was north of the Danube. On the other, southern side of the Danube was the synthetic oil plant Moosbierbaum (post-war the atomic power station Zwentendorf). This power station was attacked several times by the 15th AF during January to March 1945 and was finally put out of action during the middle of March. The bomber formations of 600-800 machines flew from Italy towards Vienna, passed Vienna to the East and then turned north of Vienna onto a South-westerly course. That took them right over our airfield, which was struck by quite a few bombs. On one occasion a farmer and his horse, who was delivering the mid-day meal to working parties around the airfield, became a victim of the bombs.

We continued to receive reinforcements so that in the end we had 25-30 aircraft instead of 10 to 12 as originally. The fuel however was lacking. At the end of February we received a single delivery of 20.000 litres (one railway tank wagon). An Fw 190 had a fuel capacity of 500 litres. As we had no storage tanks, we had to leave the bulk in the wagon and store the rest in petrol barrels placed in pits around the airfield. The petrol had been stretched by the addition of some 15 to 20 per cent alcohol. As some people kept experimenting as amateur chemists in order to get at the alcohol for private use, we had to keep a check on their accommodation to prevent accidents.

As a protection against bomb splinters and gun fire the aircraft were placed in bays with walls of heaped earth around them. We had problems with ground water and dragging out the machines. Some of the machines were dispersed around the sides of the field under groups of trees.

Due to the shortage of fuel the aircraft were not to be moved under their own power but were dragged by teams of oxen. We had some 20 to 25 of these which the local farmer had had to supply. A particularly hefty one, whom we called Hannibal, pulled the starter trolley (which was about the size of an air compressor as used in the building industry). It was amazing to see the stoicism of this powerful beast as the 1,700hp engines burst into life beside him. We also had a tracked motor cycle as a tractor. A Norwegian NCO was in charge of the oxen. Two Letts were in charge of the refuelling, whose teeth fell out as a result of the lead in the petrol, although they got a litre of milk per day.

We had to surrender part of our technical personnel to ground troops. In exchange we got about 15 girls (hairdressers, dancers, secretaries) who had been given a crash course as mechanics. As they could not be used for work in the open at sometimes – 10° we employed them in the parachute store, office or kitchen. We had removed the 2cm cannon from damaged aircraft, mounted them in twos and thre's on homemade turntables, equipped them with sights and batteries and placed them around the field and we had some 40 guns all connected by telephone to a central fire-control.

The bomber formations arrived regularly between 11 and 12 o'clock, but about an hour before that the fighter escort of 60 to 100 Mustangs turned up and patrolled the area around our airfield and kept an eye on us. Several times we considered taking off against them, but in view of their superiority in numbers it would have been pointless.

**Lt Karl-Heinz Jeismann, pilot , 3./JG105.**

**Right:** Due to the severe shortage of fuel, by early 1945 teams of oxen were used to tow tank wagons and other roiling *Luftwaffe* stock on operational airfields. Here, a Fw 190 of JG105 is being serviced. *Karl-Heinz Jeismann.*

**Above:** On 8 February 1945, a 77th FS, 20th FG attack on Esperstedt airfield broke all 8th AF records when Maj. Jackie Gilbertson led his Mustangs in a surprise strafing attack on Esperstedt airfield, destroying 31 Fw 190s, a Bf 109, four Me 410s, and an unidentified biplane. Two more Fw 190s, two Bf 110s, and one Me 410 were damaged. This photo was taken just before the 20 minutes' destruction was unleashed, from the cockpit of Mustang 44-11324, and shows smoke screen pots around the airfield. *Pieter Bergman.*

Myself and another pilot, were ordered to a special assignment from Jüterborg, probably because I was the last member of ZG76 still alive with blind-flying experience. We were to simulate German fighter units by transmitting radio traffic on courses between 270 and 360°. We talked, gave orders and received instructions from the ground. This sortie coincided with strong enemy bomber formations flying in an easterly direction, to Leipzig, Chemnitz and Dresden. The escorting fighters were to be tempted away towards us, two fake Geschwaders! Soon we could see vapour trails coming towards us from all directions. With a great deal of luck and under considerable difficulties we were able to land in one piece at Neustadt-Gleve. The Me 109s went into the bays and down we went into the slit trenches. Some Me 262s, having got to the unescorted bombers, were said to have shot down 16 of them.

**Uffz Walter Ibold, Bf 109G pilot, JG76.**

refineries in the ever diminishing Reich, now seriously threatened by the Russian armies converging from the east. At the Yalta Conference early in February 1945, Josef Stalin, the Russian leader, and his army chiefs asked that the RAF and 8th AF paralyse Berlin and Leipzig and prevent troops moving from the west to the eastern front. British Prime Minister, Winston Churchill and American President, Franklin D Roosevelt, agreed on a policy of massive air attacks on the German capital and other cities such as Dresden and Chemnitz. These cities were not only administrative centres controlling military and civilian movements but were also the main communication centres through which the bulk of the enemy's war traffic flowed.

Spaatz had set the wheels in motion with a raid on Berlin on 3 February. Magdeburg and Chemnitz were

bombed three days later but the most devastating raids of all fell upon the old city of Dresden in eastern Germany, starting with an 800 bomber raid by the RAF on the night of 13 February. Two waves of heavy bombers produced firestorms and horrendous casualties among the civilian population. Next day 400 bombers attempted to stoke up the fires created by RAF Bomber Command while 900 more bombers attacked Chemnitz, Magdeburg and other targets. On the 15th over 1,000 heavies bombed the Magdeburg synthetic oil plant and next day almost 1,000 B-17s and B-24s hit oil targets at Dortmund, Salzbergen and Gelsenkirchen. 8th AF crews were to return to the pottery city of Dresden again in March and April 1945 on similar raids but the Allied air forces' top priority remained the oil producing centres. On 16 February, the heavies hit the Hoesch coking plant

*Above:* B-17G 44-6814 *Choo-Z-Suzy* of the 368th BS, 306th BG at Thurleigh. This aircraft FTR from the mission to Fulda on 6 February 1945 when it landed on the continent. It was later flown back to the UK and in May 1945 was transferred to the 381st BG at Ridgewell. *Richards.*

at Dortmund, estimated to be producing 1,000 tons of benzol a month. Bombing was completed visually and the *Luftwaffe* was noticeable by its virtual absence but bomber losses continued to occur, mainly as a result of the bad weather which often affected forming up operations over England, and to *Flak.*

On 22 February, *Clarion,* the systematic destruction of the German communications network, was launched. More than 6,000 Allied aircraft from seven different commands were airborne this day and they struck at

*The remaining serviceable aircraft in Reinsdorf were moved to Erfurt-Stotternheim. Here we were accommodated in private houses with pleasant hosts. We did a handful of sorties, but without much success. For some days we had visits from a section of two Mustangs who hung about high above the airfield. They destroyed several aircraft during take-off and landing. Frequently a section took off in order to catch the American fighters. One day I took off with a section of four Me 109s, we flew around at some distance to the airfield, were then directed to the field by radio, placed ourselves up-sun and bounced the Mustangs. Both were heavily hit and went down. The entire section took part in this attack.*

**Uffz Walter Ibold, Bf 109G pilot, JG76.**

transportation targets throughout western Germany and northern Holland. All targets were selected with the object of preventing troops being transported to the Russian front, now only a few miles from Berlin. Despite the low altitudes flown, only 7 bombers were lost, including two B-17s to an Me 262 jet fighter of III./JG7 flown by Gefr Notter. Next day only four bombers were lost from the 1,274 despatched and on 26 February three bombers only were shot down over Berlin. On 4 March the 466th and 392nd BGs bombed Swiss territory by mistake. The US Ambassador had only recently attended a memorial service and visited reconstruction projects of the previous bombing on 18 September 1944. Gen Marshall urged Gen Spaatz to visit Switzerland secretly and reparations, involving many millions of dollars, were made to the Swiss Government.

By March 1945, the systematic destruction of German oil production plants, airfields and communications centres, had virtually driven the *Luftwaffe* from German skies. Despite fuel and pilot shortages Me 262 jet

**Right:** B-24 42-50390, 577th BS, 392nd BG, one of eight B-24s at Wendling damaged in three strafing attacks lasting 20 minutes, carried out by *Luftwaffe* twin-engined intruder aircraft around 2115 hours on 21 March 1945. Timed delay frag bombs were dropped in and around parked B-24s, along with 20mm cannon fire of 200 to 300 rounds. The 577th was hardest hit, with seven B-24s damaged. One man was slightly injured and 14 bomb bay fuel tanks were destroyed. *Ed Shapley via Ben Jones.*

**Below:** 5th ERS ASR OA-10A Catalinas, in co-operation with RAF high speed launches and Warwicks, rescued hundreds of downed airmen in the North Sea during the latter part of WW2. On 23 March 1945 three OA-10As were on ASR patrols and they rescued six RAF airmen, including P/O Strafford, navigator with 612 Squadron, being lifted from Catalina 44-33915 at Halesworth after being rescued from off the Dutch coast. *Charles J. Johnson.*

fighters could still be expected to put in rare attacks and during March almost all enemy fighter interceptions of American heavy bombers were made by the Me 262 equipped JG7, Galland's *Jagdverband 44,* EJG2, led by OLt Bär, and I.KG(F)54. On 3 March the largest formation of German jets ever seen made attacks on the bomber formations heading for Dresden and four separate oil targets. III./JG7 despatched 29 Me 262s, whose pilots claimed six of the nine bombers which failed to return in the area of Hannover-Braunschweig. *Ritterkreuzträger* Hptm Gutmann of 9./JG7 was killed during this action.

On 15 March, 1,353 bombers escorted by 833 fighters hit the German Army HQ at Zossen near Berlin and a marshalling yard at Orienburg. Two days later 1,328 B-17s and B-24s, escorted by 820 fighters, bombed targets in west and north-central Germany. On 18 March a record 1,329 bombers bombed Berlin again. 12 B-17s and a B-24 were shot down. 37 Me 262s of the *Geschwaderstab* and III./JG7 claimed twelve B-17s shot down and six *Herauschüsse* (HSS) as well as one fighter. The jet menace became such a problem, that beginning on 21 March the 8th flew a series of raids on

airfields used by the 262s. The raids also coincided with the build up for the impending crossing of the Rhine by Allied troops. For four days the heavies bombed jet airfields and military installations.

On 22 March 1,301 B-17s and B-24s bombed targets

**Right:** B-17G 43-37516 *Tondalayo,* 406th Night Leaflet Squadron, at Cheddington. On 4 March 1945, while returning from a NLS mission over Holland, *Tondalayo,* piloted by Lt Col Earle Aber, the Squadron CO, was set on fire off Clacton by British shore batteries which had opened up on a German intruder. *Tondalayo's* crew bailed out as Aber and his co-pilot, 2/Lt Maurice Harper, remained at the controls in a desperate bid to reach the emergency field at Woodbridge. Both pilots were killed when *Tondalayo* crashed into the sea in flames. *Mike Bailey.*

**Below:** B-17G 44-6604, 367th BS, 306th BG, put down in emergency on the continent on 18 March 1945. 44-6604 joined the 381st BG in May 1945. *Richards.*

*I took off with a section against a major attack in the area of Leipzig-Dresden. Our radio communications suffered particularly heavy interference on this day. At 7,500m I came upon a Boeing flying on an easterly course south of Dresden, separated by about 10 kilometres from the rest of the formation at the same height and escorted by four Mustangs flying above and behind. I assumed that this aircraft had some special duty and decided to attack it. The radio interference was now so heavy that no communication was possible. I passed close below the Mustangs and although they followed my section trailing black smoke (full throttle), my airspeed indicator showed that I no longer had to bother myself about them. The Boeing was now ahead of me in a gentle turn to port and I was approaching it at an angle of about 10 degrees from port and about 5° from above. At a range of about 1,000m the rear gunner opened continuous fire. What now happened took only seconds. At about 300m I and my wingman gave a short burst with a little deflection. We observed about a dozen hits in the fuselage and between the engines of the Boeing and then we had passed above it. Flying a wide turn (with the Mustangs behind us, trailing black smoke and getting ever smaller) we observed the end of the bomber. It spun for some 2000m, several large parts broke away from the fuselage and wings and then it literally burst asunder. All of a sudden the radio interference had ceased. We had received no hits, set course for home and the Mustangs eased the strain on their engines as they realised the pointlessness of any further chase.*

*The effects of damage to the outer skinning at high speed was enormous. A dislodged, hand-sized piece of plywood from the undercarriage cover lost at 300m*

*height and at a speed of some 900km/h made the Me 262 suddenly so nose heavy that I was only, and using all my strength, able to pull out just before striking the ground. A strong rushing and rumbling noise made the background music. A harmless hit near the wingtip made a small hole in the slat and a flower-like hole at the exit. The effect: instant turning of the machine around the lateral and longitudinal axis and it seemed that the fuselage would break apart. Again hard work on the control column and rudder pedals. Only after a considerable reduction of speed and trimming out did the machine again become reasonably controllable.*

**Lt Fritz R G Müller, III./JG7, 21 March 1945, who claimed the lone B-17 (despatched to Oberusel to drop two tons as Micro H Mk II test) at 0950 hours at 7,500m, south of Dresden. However, this B-17 does not appear in any loss listings. Müller was credited with 16 *Abschüsse* whilst serving with III./JG53 1943-44, and six (one RAF Mosquito and five US aircraft) flying the Me 262. On 25 March 1945, he shot down a Liberator in flames at 1025hours at 7,000m south of Luneburg. No parachutes were observed. (The left turbine of Müller's 262 was hit by return fire, and he force-landed at Stendal, where he rammed into a Ju 88 parked in Hangar No. 5. He managed to douse the fire before it got out of control.) On 4 April 1945, he shot down a Liberator at 0945 hours at 7,000m in the Bremen area. On 9 April 1945, Müller destroyed a Thunderbolt at 8,000m west of Berlin. 17 April 1945, he shot down a B-17 at 7,000m in the Elbschleife, north of Prague.**

east of Frankfurt and 10 military encampments in the Ruhr in preparation for the Allied amphibious crossing of the lower Rhine on 23 and 24 March. The 8th bombed the Bottrop military barracks and hutted areas directly behind the German lines while 136 B-17s of the 15th AF attacked Ruhrland again and caused extensive damage to the plant. 27 Me 262s attacked the bomber formations and claimed 13 B-17s shot down but only one Fortress was actually lost, while P-51s claimed two of the jets (OFw Lübking with thirty-eight *Abschüsse*, and Fw Eichner, both KIA) destroyed. Next day 1,244 heavies bombed rail targets as part of the rail interdiction programme to isolate the Ruhr and cut off coal shipping. Since the loss of the Saar basin the Ruhr was the only remaining source of supply for the German war machine. On 23 and 24 March, under a 66 mile long smokescreen and aided by 1,749 bombers of the 8th AF, Field Marshal Bernard Montgomery's 21st Army Group crossed the Rhine in the north while further south simultaneous crossings were made by Gen Patton's Third Army. Groups flew two missions on 24 March, hitting jet aircraft bases in Holland and Germany, while 240 B-24s, loaded with 600 tons of medical supplies, food and weapons, dropped vital supplies to the armies in the field. Flying as low as 50ft, the Liberators droned over the dropping zone at Wesel at 145mph, using 10-15° of flap to aid accuracy in the drop. Spasmodic and highly accurate small arms fire and 20 mm cannon fire brought down 14 Liberators and 103 B-24s returned with battle damage.

**Left:** P-51 44-14923 *See Me Later,* 335th FS, 4th FG, flown by 2/Lt Kenneth Green, one of eight Mustangs lost from a force of 743 dispatched on 3 March 1945. *See Me Later* was hit by *Flak* and crashed near Rotterdam. Green was taken prisoner. *Ab A. Jansen.*

**Above and left:** Two B-17s - 42-102555, 366th BS, 305th BG, piloted by Lt D G Shoemaker, and 42-102501 *The Challenger,* 546th BS, 384th BG, flown by 2/Lt Robert C Long, were forced to ditch in the North Sea on 3 February 1945. Two men survived from Shoemaker's crew and six from Long's. These men were rescued after three Warwicks of 280 Squadron from Beccles, on ASR escort patrol, spotted two dinghies, some six miles apart, west of Texel. HSR launch 2631 was directed to the position; and the survivors were hauled on board. *Bert Waller.*

**Above:** B-24J 44-40439 *Shady Lady,* 566th BS, 389th BG, was lost with 2/Lt. George S Crock's crew on 31 March 1945. *USAF.*

Bomber crews were now hard pressed to find worthwhile targets and the planners switched attacks from inland targets to coastal areas. Beginning on 5 April, the weather over the continent improved dramatically and the B-17s were despatched to U-boat pens on the Baltic coast. Everywhere the Allies were victorious but while the Germans kept on fighting, missions continued almost daily. Such was the 8th AF's superiority that the B-17s assembled over France on 5 April, before flying in formation for an attack on the

*We were suddenly transferred from Stotternheim to Bremen-Neulanderfeld. From here we were to fly low-level attacks on the British troops who had crossed the Rhine at Wesel. Nothing much came of that. When we returned from the first sortie, with little fuel left, the airfield had been bombed. Some Me 109s got in and parked on undamaged areas, some put down in meadows, some tried it on the airfield. Like a few others, I was turned on my back in a bomb crater and that was the end of my machine. I was lucky again to get away virtually unscathed, as two comrades were killed. We returned almost without any aircraft to Erfurt-Stotternheim. The Gruppe was reinforced to no more than half its normal establishment and off we went to Plattling. There we experienced a bombing attack, we thought it was against our airfield, but the large marshalling yard was being attacked. It was full with trains carrying refugees. We rushed to their aid, what had happened there was terrible.*

**Uffz Walter Ibold, Bf 109G pilot, JG76.**

*When one of our sections was returning from a high-level sortie on 26 March 1945, it was immediately attacked by the Mustangs. One Fw 190 was shot down but the pilot was able to make a belly landing in spite of having been hit in the neck. After some difficulties with the Mustangs and under the cover of our Flak the remaining three machines managed to land safely. The Mustang which had succeeded with the first one came down so low in a renewed attack that it struck a tree and crashed. The dead pilot had been a Pole. I visited our pilot the next day in a Bulgarian hospital. I did not fly again at Absdorf because of the shortage of fuel. At the beginning of April 1945 the Geschwader was disbanded. Some of the more or less trained pilots went to another Geschwader, the rest – myself included – to ground forces. I cannot tell of great deeds, only of the dawning of the end. While I was annoyed, like most of my comrades, not to get into action, I now of course see these things in a different light.*

**Lt Karl-Heinz Jeismann, pilot, 3./JG105.**

**Above:** Despite the high attrition rate and the prospect of crushing defeat, there was always an opportunity to relax and have fun. Lt Peter Ahrens, an ace with 11 victories in 3.& 7./JG26, rides the auxiliary tank for a Fw 190 early in 1945. He was killed in an accident on 4 March 1945. *Walter Stumpf.*

*M*y time at Molesworth was from February 1945 to June 1945. We arrived at the base but had several weeks of waiting to be called into action. Our crew or gunners were assigned a barracks near the big hangar. We were assigned to the 427th Squadron, which was located just behind the bunker next to the main runway. On our first day at the barracks about 12 of us from two crews walked through the door. Someone's first remark was, 'When did the men in this empty barracks go home: A voice called out, "They didn't go home; they're visiting Germany as guests of the German PoW camp, or else they're dead. You rookies look around and pick out a bed." It was a very quiet time after that remark was made to us. None of us "new men" ever knew if 'the "old timers" were pulling our leg, and we didn't ask.

Six of our crew finished 53 missions in 57 days, starting on 27 February and ending on 25 April 1945. This was as short a time for fifty-three missions as I have ever heard of. Our waist gunner was the first to be voted off the crew. He fell asleep on us on missions 2 and 3. Our co-pilot was hit by Flak over Berlin and lost his foot from Flak damage. He was a great pilot. We were members of Lt Denison's and co-pilot Chuck Haynes' crew. Our plane was named El Screamo. Three trips to Berlin were plenty for all of us. We always had lots of "black" Flak. The third man to drop from our crew got drunk and tried to break into the Red Cross barracks. Of course, he was not welcomed with open arms. Our 26th mission was the most frightening of all. It was to Oranienburg, Germany, almost within sight of Berlin, 40 miles to the south, on 13 April 1945. Our group was hit by six to eight Me 262 jet fighters that day. One B-17G in the 555th Squadron, belonging to Lt Murray, was shot down in this air battle. Eight men were killed and the flight engineer got out of the aircraft. During this time, an Me 262 dove past me so fast I couldn't turn my two .50 machine guns on him. This 262 dropped down about 5,000 to 6,000ft in a wide turn and then came up directly behind our B-17. We were flying "tail end Charlie" so I had this aircraft all to myself. I made the very most of this situation; I started firing at him from a long distance and never let up but kept hitting his right engine. I continued to score hits on the engine until he was about 120 feet from me. At that time the engine and wingtip blew off. The 262's momentum carried it to within 55 to 45ft from me; we were both looking at each other. Just as suddenly he began his fall from about 25,000 feet, approximately 43 to 63 miles from Oranienburg, Germany. The 303rd Bomb Group interrogation officer really had no interest in a buck Sgt's report on a 262, which may have been the last Me 262 shot down by an enlisted man in World War II. Lt Denison put me in for a DFC but it was not even considered. The Flak was what really startled a B-17 tail gunner to get jumpy. They called us "Flak happy," and that we were.

**Walter "Don" O' Hearn, tail gunner, 303rd BG.**

marshalling yards at Nürnburg.

In Germany, the now desperate situation called for desperate measures to be taken against the all-powerful bomber streams and last ditch attempts were made by the *Luftwaffe* to try to stem the tide. One plan, in the autumn of 1944, had been Adolf Galland's "*Grosser Schlag*" ("Big Strike"). The *General der Jagdflieger* had worked out detailed plans to launch a mass-attack by 3,700 fighters in 18 *Geschwaders* against a large-scale

Allied daylight bombing raid in order to deliver a knockout blow. His assembled force however, bled to death during the Ardennes offensive and *Bodenplatte*, and during raids like 26 and 27 November 1944. Another plan also conceived late in 1944 that now reached fruition, in the spring of 1945, however, was the deliberate ramming of American bombers by converted Bf 109 fighters, called *Rammjäger*, flown by pilots of *Sonderkommando Elbe*. On 7 April 1945 the *Luftwaffe*

employed the *Rammjäger* fighters against American bomber streams attacking underground oil refineries in central Germany. The *Rammjäger* dived into the bomberformations from a height of 33,000 ft and destroyed 17 aircraft.

*Below:* A little Belgian boy's dream come true, playing in crashed Fw 190 *Sturmbock* somewhere in Belgium, 1945. *Kees Mol.*

# RAMMJÄGER

*I*n March 1945, I was stationed at Morlitz. Here the edict of Hermann Göring was read out to us. Although we realised that there would be no returning from this operation, the entire group volunteered. What kind of operations these were to be we did not find out at this time. My motivation was, that I would be able to lessen somewhat the high losses of the civilian population resulting from the Allied bombing. There was also a powerful spirit of comradeship amongst us pilots. We did not want to leave each other in the lurch. About 8 to 10 days after our volunteering the first of the comrades were ordered away. Fenten, Wischhofer, Hertel and I received orders for Stendal. I remember clearly that we were screened off at Stendal. We were confined to the camp and guarded by SS. We were given lectures about ramming tactics and political matters (about these I remember nothing). After some time the four of us were taken to Gardelegen to take over our operational aircraft. My machine, an Me 109, was brand new. When we took off for operations on 7 April we were given a specific area to operate in. Our aircraft were equipped for radio reception only. We were unable to transmit. We were to ram a bomber formation from above; the formation was reported by radio. Also, we were totally unarmed.

But the four of us got our cockpit covers heavily iced up. The cockpits were totally covered by ice on the inside and we had virtually no visibility. I jettisoned my cockpit cover and found that the other three had done likewise. As we were unable to communicate by radio, I used hand signals that I intended to go down. We only had light helmets and got unbearable headaches at the height of about 10,000m. I noticed that my hand signals had been understood and all four of us abandoned our task.

Then we lost one another. I found the airfield of Gottingen. But I soon discovered that I was being fired at on my approach to land. I assumed that the Americans had got there first. I also noticed that the airfield had been made unusable by ditches. I was able to overshoot at the last minute and landed at Goslar. I had hardly landed, when a soldier in a foxhole indicated that the place was under attack. The airfield was being attacked by Thunderbolts. After the attack I saw that my aircraft had remained undamaged. The groundcrew collected petrol for me from damaged aircraft so I could take off again. I flew back to Gardelegen. The operations officer told me that a number of my comrades had had cockpit icing and that excused my own actions. Now we returned to Stendal. Our own belongings had meanwhile been lost. The part of the barracks, where they had been stored, had been bombed. As there was suspicion of an unexploded bomb, we were unable to get back our baggage. Incidentally, it is today still beneath the rubble.

The following figures trickled through: approximately 120 fighters had taken off from various places for the ramming mission. Two-thirds of the aircraft were lost, through cockpit icing, crashes and being shot down. The *Wehrmachtsbericht* (armed forces Report) stated that about 60 Flying Fortresses had been hit. This could not be confirmed later on. We were sent to Klagenfurt for further operations (i.e. Kommando Bienenstock). Fortunately it never came to this. Soon I became a prisoner of war of the Americans. My thoughts today about this operation are that it had been utterly senseless to sacrifice such young and enthusiastic men against such overwhelming odds.

**25 year old OFw Ernst Rummel, who was an experienced flying instructor when he had joined I./JG300 as a *Wild Boar* night fighter pilot in the autumn of 1943. His unit had switched to day fighting in the *Reichsverteidigung* in March 1944, and he survived being twice shot down during the next month.**

*Right:* OFw Ernst Rummel did not get to ram a *Viermot* on 7 April 1945 when the cockpit canopy of his Bf 109 became heavily iced up and he had to break off the ramming mission. *Werner Zell.*

*Above:* Bf 109G-10 of JG300 at Prag-Gbell aerodrome, May 1945. It has been fitted with a DB605 A5 engine, probably taken from another aircraft. *JaPo.*

*Left:* At the end of hostilities in May 1945, hundreds of aircraft wrecks still littered the countryside on the continent. This Fortress, 42-97781 BN-O *Eight Ball III*, 359th BS, 303rd BG, came down on the edge of the Apeldoorn-Diemen Canal at Eerbeek, Holland, on 2 November 1944. Nine of Lt Jack T Davis' crew were taken prisoner and one man was KIA. During the next year, souvenir hunters continued to strip the aircraft of parts. *Brouwer via Ab A Jansen.*

*Although we hit the target visually, there was no Flak. However, we did draw fighters this time. Three Me 109s attacked, then a single Me 109 came straight at the formation from the rear. Lanny in the tail and Charles Stewart, the tail gunner on Burich's plane, which was filling in the low diamond, opened up on him. We speculate that one of them must have killed the pilot since the 109 kept straight on and rammed Burich. Whatever else the Germans were, they weren't suicidal. Both the B-17 and the 109 went down.*

2/Lt William W Varnedoe Jr, navigator, 385th BG, 7 April 1945.

**Fw Walter Otto was trained as a fighter pilot during 1943-44, and after graduating on both the Ju 88 and Me 109, in the summer of 1944 he received further specialist training.**

*On completion of my training as a pilot, I was posted to a Special Command at Hirsching near Linz where I was instructed on the four-engined Flying Fortress. We were told that we were to be flown to Italy in a Ju 52, with the aim of capturing the Allied heavy bombers whilst their engines were being warmed up at the break of dawn and ferry them to Germany. Fortunately, nothing came of the whole thing. In the autumn of 1944, several combat units were disbanded due to lack of aircraft fuel. I was given the choice of either being sent to the infantry on the Eastern Front, or to become a ramming fighter. I chose the latter and received further instruction on the Me 109. On 7 April 1945, I finally became operational for the ramming mission, operating from Prague Gbel airfield. Our Me 109s were fitted with an additional belly fuel tank and with an armoured frontal windshield, but without any guns or camouflage. With the bellytank, we had about three and a half hours flying endurance. If I remember correctly, we were informed that 200 aircraft were to take part in the ramming mission, but I don't know if all the machines did in fact start on the mission. At 0900 hrs, we were scrambled in the direction of Brocken, and climbed to a height of some 10,000m. During the flight, I heard the Deutschland Song and the Horst-Wessel Song in my headphones, and we were also told to 'save your Fatherland, think of your women and children'.*

*At last, at 11 o'clock, we were ordered to go ahead with the ramming mission. The four-engined Fortresses came in from Belgium and were on a heading probably for a bombing attack on Stendal. I successfully rammed one bomber and was fortunate to bail out, coming down back to earth by parachute at Stadthagen, near the Steinhuder Lake. From there I travelled by train through Celle, Leipzig, Chemnitz to my home town, where I stayed for two days between 9 and 11 April before going back to Prague. On arrival, I found out that there were only few of my comrades left there. From Prague we transferred to Pocking and from there we were posted to a small satellite airfield at Klagenfurt, which was situated near the railway yards for goods trains. A handful of Bü 181s were stationed on this field, and I received orders to take off and try and blow up the bridge over the Danube at Pressburg. I took off on 5 May at 2100 hrs in my Bü 181 and headed for Pressburg. It was my luck to receive hits from ground fire forcing me to crash-land on the Feld mountain, which precluded me from having to blow up the bridge. Early on the next morning, I travelled back to Bruck on the Mur by train, where I was taken prisoner. I was taken to a PoW camp at Ulm, from which I was released 14 days later.*

**Above:** Fw Walter Otto was trained to fly a captured B-17 during the latter half of 1944, for a 'kidnapping' mission of Italy-based Fortresses. Several surprise commando type raids, involving KG200 B-17s, were planned during the final phase of the war. The intention of one of these was to land several KG200 B-17s with commandos on Algerian airfields, wreaking havoc with flame-throwers among the American bombers based there and then try and take off again in the KG200 aircraft. None of these missions went ahead and Fw Otto volunteered for ramming duties instead. He was one of the few pilots to survive a successful ramming attempt during the *Rammkommando Elbe* operation of 7 April 1945. *Walter Otto.*

**Above:** B-17G 43-38775, 602nd BS, 398th BG, dropping bombs early in 1945. This aircraft crash-landed on 21 April 1945, was repaired,and saw out the rest of the war. *Frederick L Carr.*

*O*ur P-51 escort was cruising up and down the bomber stream when the alert, 'Red Bandits in the area!' was given. Our whole crew really perked up. I looked out. In the distance was a plane that resembled a P-51. Something was hanging below the wings, like a belly tank. Our fighters had already dropped their belly tanks on the bandit alert! And this 'plane was flying alone, something our fighters never did. I called the waist gunners to alert them and they had already seen the same thing. This Me 109 turned toward us on a pursuit curve and our right waist gunner opened up. The German flew past our tail where Pete began firing, and he came on around to our left side where Nick got him. In a short time they got another Me 109 I never saw but which was confirmed. We began to relax a bit when suddenly the engineer's guns behind me started shooting. I looked out my cockpit window to see an Fw 190 shooting at us and the lead plane, just to our right. He appeared to be trying to ram the lead plane if he wasn't successful in shooting him down. His wheels fell down and he began to wobble from side to side. Had he wobbled to his right he would have rammed the lead plane and we would have gone too in the explosion but he passed in front of us, wobbling to his left. I could see his head slumped down. I'm sure he must have been dead.

**Lt Robert L Miller, B-17 pilot, *Sonof A Blitz*, 863rd Squadron, 493rd BG, 7 April 1945.**

***Right:*** *Sonof A Blitz*, 863rd BS, 493rd BG, 7 April 1945.
Truett Woodall.

211

At the beginning of July 1944, our group at the FF5 B 5 at Neubrandenburg had completed the instrument training on Do 17/Do 217, but there appeared to be no requirement on appropriate units. Not until December did a number of pilots receive a posting to Altenburg for night fighting, which was changed to 3./EKGr (J) at short notice. I was sent together with some comrades to Pilsen, and from there to Ansbach for conversion to the Me 109. We first got about a dozen take-offs on Fw 44, Bü 181 and Ar 96, to help us make the transition from heavy aircraft to light ones, and we practised aerobatics, formation flight and dogfights. Then followed six circuits on Me 109 two-seaters with an instructor and the next flight would be solo. The flying itself was no problem, but take-off and landing on an Me 109 was quite different to that on a Do 217! I managed well with the undercarriage and the tendency to break out at take-off. Most of the 26 solo flights were circuits, only the last four were formation practices. After my last flight on 23 March 1945 my flying licence was endorsed: Ready for operations on Ar 96 and Me 109. But – fighting tactics, firing, baling out in emergency – had been only taught in theory! What this short training was to be for only became clear to us later on.

After this conversion training we returned to our unit in Pilsen. During a parade a letter from Reichsmarschall Göring was read out. Volunteer pilots were required for participation in special duties. We were given little time to think about this. Certainly, such a decision ought really have been considered with some care. My friend Günter Wittenberg, with whom I had been together in a unit in Neubrandenburg, and I, together with some others, put our names down in the office. Our reasoning was that we would be able to continue flying, while the others were faced with the prospect of ground fighting. The dice had fallen, now we had to go through with it!

I was sent to Klecan, to the west of Prague, together with some 30 others. Our quarters were in a school building, messing was a few hundred metres away in a small mansion with a small former private airfield beside it. During the day there were lectures about the situation at the front, tactics and experiences on ramming operations. That finally clarified the purpose of it all. But it appeared that there would be a few days of respite yet and as a result we did not think about it more than was absolutely necessary. A stroll to the nearby Moldau after supper and an hour's pedal boating were a pleasant diversion.

On 6 April, rumour had it that operations would begin the next day. Most of us packed their kit that evening. How I slept that night I can no longer remember. On 7 April, following briefing, preparations were made for take-off. Orders: Fly along the Elbe as far as Magdeburg, height 10,000m, further instructions from control – on contacting enemy, destruction by ramming. The aircraft had been specially prepared for this operation: the radio transmitter had been removed, armament only one 13mm machine gun with 50(!) rounds of ammunition.

Who was to fly with whom was left to the pilots. It was mostly friends or men who knew each other well who clubbed together. As already at briefing it had become clear that difficulties due to cloud cover were to be expected and, that after having passed the layer of cloud, there would be no sight of the ground for some while. We four of our section took another look at the chart and agreed that we would fly a course of 330°. Further communication during the flight would not be possible. Having been assigned our aircraft, we went to the machines which were dispersed around the airfield. I had been given 'Black 2', the third aircraft of our section. So that's the one, I thought to myself. Two mechanics were standing beside it. I went up to them and introduced myself. For a long time I was unable to forget the look in the older one's eyes. Did he see in me the man who was to wreck his machine?

On the order for cockpit readiness the two men assisted me into the machine. And now we waited. The weather conditions for the operation, which was to be flown with sight of the ground, was still very unfavourable - low, unbroken cloud cover. I can no longer remember how long we sat there in our straps, certainly long enough for my bladder to stir itself. I undid my straps, got out and went over to the tailwheel. Our fourth man grinned down to me from his cockpit window.

Then came to order to be off! I was still standing by the wing when the first engines burst into life. Now it was a matter of seconds. Into the cockpit, parachute, straps, oxygen mask. The engine started straight away. Cockpit cover closed and off. My assistants waved me off and I was following the man in front to the take-off point, a few hundred metres away. Aircraft of the preceding sections were standing along the edge of the field, probably having problems. Pilots and ground crews were having

discussions. There was not much time for looking, for we were taxiing close one behind the other. The take-off point was at the far end of the place. It was a grass field and it was just long enough.

Two or three sections were already in the air but not complete, then it was our turn. One after the other, at short intervals, the aircraft left the ground. After a wide turn we passed over the airfield in echelon to starboard on a course of 330° and immediately afterwards entered the cloud. The first disappeared, then the second, and then I too was in cloud. That was my first instrument flight in an Me 109! I carefully watched the instruments. No deviation from course, steady climb, watch the artificial horizon. The steady drone of the engine was reassuring. If the forecast was right and it was only a thin layer, then I must soon get out of the murk at this rate of climb, so I thought. But still the layers were passing the window, from top left to bottom right. If one were not to have an artificial horizon to rely upon!

I knew that I had two aircraft ahead of me. Suddenly I had a terrible vision before my eyes and at once altered my course 2° to starboard. Doing that, I believe to have chosen the lesser of two evils. That time in Ansbach, two Me 109s had been approaching the landing mark so close together that they had been ordered to overshoot by firing off reds. The two pilots had not seen each other. While the one held its height, the lower one pulled up and its propeller cut open the fuselage of the other behind the pilot's seat. Both crashed while still over the airfield. One of the pilots died of severe burns after a few days. That was what had suddenly come into my mind, for we too had been close to each other when we had entered into the clouds. I felt beads of sweat on my forehead. And still no visibility.

The altimeter showed a little over 2500m when it began to get lighter -and then I was flying in beautiful sunshine above a slightly irregular sheet of cloud. But all alone. Then I spotted two aircraft far off to port. I increased power and approached them at an acute angle. They were in fact the two comrades who had taken off before me. We showed our pleasure at meeting up again with gestures. A motion with his hand from Günter, who was in the lead, indicated that we should climb, for we could no longer wait for our fourth man. We slowly increased our height. It was a strange feeling to be without communication with our comrades only a few metres away, and with ground control. Absolute radio silence was the essence of this operation, in order to be able to utilise the element of surprise. But it was of great handicap in our situation, as we were badly in need of a wind report!

A clumsy movement caused the map covering our flight route to slip from my knee. As I was fumbling for it with my left hand, I suddenly had the tube of my oxygen mask in my fingers. In the haste of the departure we had forgotten to connect it to the oxygen supply. And now? The breathing tube was dangling behind me to my left. With much effort I succeeded to push it under my thigh. And all with only my left hand, for I could not let go of the control column. Another difficulty was to plug it into its socket. Günter, who was flying beside me, said after we had landed that he had been worried by my erratic flying and my business in the cockpit.

The altimeter showed 7000m. We had been under way for 45 minutes, without sight of the ground. Then the clouds were gone as if they had been cut off. Far below us an unknown countryside. Of the Elbe, which would have been easily recognisable even from this height, there was no trace. So our course had not worked out. I assumed that a northerly wind might have driven us off to the south. Judging by the countryside that appeared more likely than being north of the Elbe.

It was a peculiar situation to be in! A section of Me 109s was crawling through the air, the three pilots tried to recognise prominent roads and railway lines on a map, gesticulated like deaf-mutes to each other, but no-one knew where they were until a motorway junction appeared. At this time there were only two of these in the area, at Schkeuditz and Hermsdorf. It could only be Hermsdorf, for in the vicinity of Schkeuditz one should have been able to see Leipzig. We had been blown quite some distance to the south! So, alter course. I suggested a course of 350° by showing three fingers, five fingers and thumb and index finger forming a zero. My comrades had understood at once and confirmed it by nodding their heads. No communication problems, even without radio! As we were now on our way to the operational area of Magdeburg-Hannover, we climbed to the intended height of 10,000m. Below us the Harz. There was still some snow in a number of valleys. Never before had I looked down on the ground from such a great height. If only we were not engaged on this serious task with an uncertain outcome!

*Suddenly Günter was close beside me, made a gesture as if he wanted to drink, pointed downwards – and was gone. I tried to discover something in the direction he had pointed. Nothing! I banked the aircraft a little for a better view below, but without success. Günter had simply disappeared! Not knowing that this searching around was shortly to be fateful for me, I tried to close up with my leader. He had not noticed this incident. Three or four minutes had passed since Günter's disappearance when I got a strong headache and then lost consciousness. I came round again some 2000m lower down. Vertically below me the earth – an indescribable racket in the cockpit. The entire machine vibrated as the engine was running at top speed! So, power off, pull out. What was that? No pressure on the controls! Airflow gone! I had heard about that during theoretical training. I was still high enough for that to be corrected. The altimeter showed 7000m.*

*Then, a little lower and on the port bow, a P-38 Lightning appeared, coming directly towards me. In my helpless situation all I could do was to drop my head between my shoulders and wait for the bullets. Without moving, I risked a glance out of the corners of my eyes. Meanwhile, our machines were level with each other. For a moment I saw the pilot. Then he went past me in a steep turn. As I again looked in the direction from which he had come I saw a formation of bombers heading towards the land. So the fighter was part of the escort. Why had he not fired? Had he realised that this was no attack but a dive out of control? My aircraft was still hurtling vertically earthward and without pressure on the controls. I was already able to make out details down there. There was a single farm house there - The nose of my aircraft pointed to a ploughed field about 200m beside it, that's where it would hit the ground!*

*I looked at the altimeter: 4000m. Baling out seemed to be the only solution. I undid the straps. My eyes were already wandering to the lever for jettisoning the cockpit roof. I still hesitated. Would I get out of the cockpit in this attitude, and get clear of the tail, without getting injured? Seconds passed. The earth got closer! Then I felt a slight resistance on the control column. Hope appeared! But the direction of the dive did not change, still dominated by the heavy engine.*

*Although it was getting critical, I now staked all on one card. The pointer on the altimeter was still continuing to unwind while the pressure on the controls increased. Then suddenly the farm house disappeared below my wings. At 700m I had the machine back on an even keel. If only there had not been this splitting headache! I had to get down. I flew towards a town I could see, in the direction from which we had come. I had almost reached it when I spotted an open space which turned out to be a grass airfield without a concrete runway, landing tee, or wind sock! I chose the longer side for my approach. Flaps down, wheels down. Down! Soon it became clear that I was too high and I went round again. After a short circuit I came close over the fence and touched down immediately behind it, somewhat hard, for the surface was uneven. During the landing run the starboard wing dipped lower and lower until it touched the ground, the machine did a 360 and stopped with a jerk. I had to brace myself against the instrument panel with all my strength in order not to bang my head against the windscreen. I was no longer strapped in!*

*A car was coming towards me from the edge of the field. I had opened the cockpit roof and wondered what had happened. Men came along and said I should hurry up and get out for there were enemy aircraft around. We drove to a bunker and there I discovered that I was in Halberstadt. An air raid alert was on. Therefore no landing tee.*

*One of the soldiers who had picked me up told me that shortly before an Me 109 had landed, which had quickly been pushed into a hangar. I at once thought of Günter. And it had been him! After the all-clear I found him in operations talking to the duty officer. What had been suggested to him now applied to me as well: We should first go and get something to eat and return in about two hours. By that time the engineer in charge would know whether and when the aircraft would be serviceable again.*

*On our way to the mess, Günter told me that the engine had suddenly started to run rough due to lack of fuel. He had been left with no choice but to land. He landed with an empty tank, but with a full auxiliary one and taxied to the edge of the field. Some mechanics pushed the aircraft at once into a hangar, for shortly afterwards a bomber formation had passed in the immediate vicinity. The one I had seen during my dive! Günter of course wanted to know why I had been forced down. When I described to him with what difficulty I had managed to connect up the oxygen supply, his curiosity about my erratic flying had been satisfied. Did he want to console me when he said that fortunately I had fallen forward at my "black-out"? Had I pulled the stick back my*

*aircraft would in all probability have gone into a spin. I had not thought of that! In any case, for us both the operation had ended unexpectedly and involuntarily. But, the target had not been reached, nor the task completed! At the time this depressed us of course, but it cannot be supposed that the war had been lost because of that! When we returned to operations after two hours we got the result of the checks: Günter's Me 109 was serviceable again. The fuel transfer pumps had been repaired, the main tank filled, largely from my own machine which could not be repaired for lack of spares. The crash damage: 4 per cent. I was handed the receipt for my machine. Günter was to take off the following morning. I would be able to accompany him if I would squeeze myself into the small space behind the pilot's seat. But that I declined. I had heard about this possibility, but with the air superiority of the other side? I was so relieved to have survived the past dangers. Besides, I had an unrestricted railway ticket in my pocket. No one took my decision amiss.*

*The next day was a Sunday - Günter went to the airfield and I to the railway station. There I discovered that the tracks had been destroyed by an air raid and that the trains would start and end at Wegeleben. A small group of people had assembled and some locals knew of a relatively short path across the fields of some 6 to 7km. We had covered about half of this distance when increasing engine noises filled the air. And then one could see the bomber formations in the clear blue sky. They passed by as if on a parade, and even without fighter cover. They appeared to expect no defence. Then an unearthly rustling and whistling, and seconds later it thundered and crashed. Clouds of smoke and dust rose up and left the buildings of Halberstadt disappearing in the haze. These were the minutes during which the town was almost entirely destroyed. It was infernal!*

*All stood there, rooted to the ground with horror in their faces. At this moment we would have been a certain prey for low-level attackers for there was no shelter, not even a ditch near the road. Then some ran back to the town. What would they have found there? Most families had had their midday meals prepared when the raid took place. For many it had been for nought! With these gloomy thoughts in my mind and a great anger I looked for a while towards that place of horror, until I noticed that most of the people had left in the direction of Wegeleben. Only a few had remained standing near me. We followed the others in silence.*

*We had a long wait for the train. And then, again distressing scenes, for most of the arrivals were bound for Halberstadt and now got news of the attack on the town. The train went straight back to Aschersleben. There, the station master only knew that in a couple of hours a train would be arriving from Dessau and then returning there. I went out to the front of the station and stood in the shade of some trees, my parachute over my shoulder and helmet and oxygen mask hanging over my chest. A woman in mourning came up to me. "Well, young man, been lucky?" she asked. I nodded. Then she told me that her only son had also been a pilot and had been killed in action three weeks before. I expressed my commiserations and she said that I should take care to survive this war. In spite of her sorrow, such compassion for a stranger!*

*Towards evening the train went to Dessau, its terminus. Further travel would not be possible until the next day. I had already found accommodation in a barrack hut when there was an air raid alert. There was an air raid shelter not far away. In! A bomber attack followed on the town. The shelter wall shook from the explosions close by. We left the bunker at dawn and discovered that the railway station had been destroyed. We had to go through the town to the southern station; in many places fires were still burning and the streets were covered with rubble.*

*Again only a shuttle service as far as Leipzig. Then to Wurzen for the night. The following day as far as Dresden. Waiting for the train to Bad Schandau. There I had time for a visit to my relatives before I was able to continue in the direction of Prague. Overnight in the waiting room. When I arrived the next day in Klecan there was an air of expectancy for departure. I had the impression that they had not thought to see me again. I was to write a report but in the end it was so hectic that I never handed in the report or the receipt for my aircraft, but kept both in my pocket until I reached home. I then went with the Sonderkommando Bienenstock, the 'Special Unit Beehive' to Pocking and Klagenfurt, where I saw the end of the war*

**21 year old Ogefr Gerhard Richter, who had been trained as a bomber pilot during 1943-44, but converted to the Bf 109 early in 1945.**

*T*he officers were called to the mess of our Danish airfield for the opening of a secret letter from the Reichsmarschall. The special order of the Reichsmarschall was read out to us in a secluded room:

'Special operations of the Luftwaffe! With this operation the fortunes of war will change. Jet fighters! At long last the long promised change! In order to prove to the German people and the world that the German Luftwaffe is not asleep, special operations will be flown: Ramming sorties. Only volunteers will be accepted. 99% will barely survive. No guns on board!'

All our Staffel officers volunteered and the strictest secrecy is ordered. Some time passes before we receive our orders to proceed to Stendal. I went to Stendal with four other officers. There I was to report to Oberst Herrmann who was keen to get the Brillanten (diamonds to the Ritterkreuz) and had been placed in command for this operation by Göring. Whom do I meet, much to my surprise? My former commander, Köhnke! The pleasure is great and we celebrate. The mess was placed at our disposal and we now knew what the game was. We were totally segregated from the outside world, we were not allowed out, nor to listen to the radio, got the best of food, the finest drinks, everything we could wish for. There were daily film shows, but of the happenings at the front we knew nothing. That went on for 14 days, then we were told: 'You will stand little chance to get away with your lives, we suggest you write farewell letters home.' I also write a letter of eight pages to my wife. Then I was ordered to Leipzig with my Staffel. During the night we were taken to the airfield in a lorry. We were in Leipzig for three days with food and drink like in peacetime.

Then came 7 April 1945. We received orders at 8 o'clock in the morning. Then readiness until just before 12. Damn, the engine of my Me 109 Nr. 21 would not start and I was to lead the Staffel! 5 minutes before take-off my machines becomes serviceable, and I climbed aboard. 'Death candidates!' The airfield was crammed with airwomen and soldiers. The commanding officer stands by the Reich War Flag and salutes each machine as it takes off. At precisely 11.30 I commence my take-off run with my Staffel. We are in radio contact with the ground. Orders: climb to

11,000m. The British and Americans generally flew at 10,000m and, as we carried no guns, we were to be well above them. I keep my men closed up within sight of each other, we do not speak. It takes three quarters of an hour before we are at 11,000m. We jettison our drop tanks over the Harz mountains. A female voice kept repeating over the radio: "Comrades, think of your wives and children lying under the ruins, think of them and try to do them justice through your efforts!" Exhortations to the last. Once in the air our anxiety evaporates. Before Hannover we get a report: "Fat Cars have crossed the Rhine. Get ready!"

I flew as far as Hamburg and approached the bomber stream from the north. It was a wonderful sight. Suddenly I spot vapour trails coming from the north. I think - our own people! I do nothing about it, but is it possible? I see red noses: 'Mustangs'. So, treachery again! For it seems impossible for me to assume that these could be enemy fighters as these had never flown at 11.000 metres before. At that moment I saw two of my men being shot down. Eyes closed. I think, this is it. Behind me I see the enemy machines turning to chase me. Ice on the machine, it is freezing cold. Below me I suddenly see an entire bomber stream, about 24 heavies. I shout: "At them!" Stand the kite on its nose, full power, aim and have about 900kph on my 109. The bombers get ever closer. I see them firing, no matter, get at them. There, a bomber below me, I aim at him, oh, the gunner is a Negro, at the last moment he raises his hands, is horrified. Finished! A terrific noise, then silence. I can see the bomber disintegrating and going down. I am still alive! But out now, out of the machine. I am at 8000 metres, try to release the cockpit roof, but it jams. What now? They are but moments, diving. How to get out?

Suddenly a bang, the cockpit roof flies off, perhaps my saving! The cover is ripped off by the slipstream, I want to release the straps, get out, but my foot is jammed and I feel a pain in the leg, but I manage it, my foot is free, raise myself up and am sucked out of the aircraft. The tail of my machine strikes my shin. I feel nothing any more. A reach for my parachute, I release it and - float. Wonderful! I look at the earth from above and float gently towards it. At the last moment a power line, I pull at the lines,

the parachute drifts away, I strike the ground. "There's one coming down!" I hear people call. I am lying on a meadow, call for help. Two Frenchmen come along, place me on a stretcher and take me to the nearest house. First good news: Eight Viermots had been rammed! The sequel of events: Take-off at 11.30, rammed at 13.10. Down at 13.30.

The doctor came at 4 o'clock, meanwhile they had cut open my flying boots. I had got off lightly with a thigh wound and a broken shin. The doctor makes an emergency dressing and orders my immediate transfer to the Gau hospital at Hannover. I get to Schwarmstadt at 6 o'clock. "What, another one?" asks the head surgeon. Five of my comrades were already there. We are put together in a room. And all five from my Staffel! Some had rammed, some had been shot down by the fighters. One was blinded but recovered his sight later on.

Then we get the incredible news, having been out of touch with events for 14 days, that the British are only 6km away. We have lost all desire for further fighting, we are depressed. And how lucky I am! I ask one of the nurses to phone Stendal and talk with my commander, Major Köhnke, give him our names and ask him not to send off our letters home. Three days later the rattle of tanks, the British are coming! At 11 o'clock in the night we are taken to the hospital town of Celle in American ambulances. We had been without food the whole day. A Red Cross nurse begs some bread for us. I sit on a bench with my leg in plaster and a sergeant sits down beside me. He remains silent for almost two hours, then gets more friendly! After Munsterlager I was taken to a prisoner-of-war camp and was released to Bonn in charge of a working party.

**Hptm Roman Pesch, one of only few *Rammkommando Elbe* pilots who succeeded in bringing down a *Viermot* by ramming on 7 April 1945.**

**Left:** Hptm Roman Pesch of *Rammkommando Elbe*, who survived ramming a *Viermot* on 7 April 1945. *Werner Zell.*

By April 1945, Lt Joachim-Wolfgang Böhm was a 21-year old pilot who served with IV./JG102 at Frederikshaven/Denmark, flying the Bf 109. When the call for volunteers for the 'Training Course *Elbe*' came, he was one of the 2,000 pilots to step forward and was transferred to Stendal.

*If my memory serves me, the call for volunteers was made known by a Oberstleutnant in an informal talk with the pilots of the over-manned Staffel at Frederikshavn. He emphasised that it would be an operation to the death and that we should consider our preparedness for it thoroughly. It was all so secret that there was nothing in writing about it and that he too had only been informed verbally. The Oberstleutnant again emphasised that this operation was strictly on a volunteer basis and that pilots not volunteering would suffer no adverse consequences. We were all dismissed and only those considering to volunteer turned back and put their names down on a sheet of paper with no or a meaningless heading. As we were not to discuss the matter, we did not even mention it further amongst ourselves. It had been a true volunteering matter.*

*I had grown up in a strongly patriotic family with a Prussian-German sense of history. Amongst other Prussian virtues were a sense of duty and such as Schiller's maxim: "And if you do not stake your life, never will you win your life" were for me obvious and sacrosanct aims. My German A-level essay had been headed by Goethe's words: "What is your duty? The needs of the day." These I looked upon – like thousands before me – in staking my life for the saving of my fatherland and the protection of my homeland of Silesia. With this attitude of mind I could not otherwise have looked myself in the face, neither after a possibly relatively lenient end of the war and certainly not after a total defeat. The war aims of the enemy having become known made my readiness to stake my life absolute, especially as I had spent my 24 months of war service doing mainly guard duties, military academy and flying training, while many of my school friends and comrades had already been killed. Even if it should be incomprehensible for most people today: I had a great love for my fatherland and homeland and was ready, conscientiously and knowingly, to give all – a true patriot.*

*I was deeply impressed by the men and personalities who were collected there. The getting together and the enthusiasm, not least by the showing of films such as 'The Great King', 'Kolberg' and 'Bismarck', and the great effort, the aim of which appeared obvious, had dispersed any doubts and fears for the future. I found the impending visit of Goebbels unnecessary; but when it was cancelled I was annoyed because it gave me the impression that our mission was not after all seen as that which we had been told.*

*The basic situation was the absolute air superiority of our enemies which made every major troop movements impossible by day. I remember the statement that there was an intact army in Czechoslovakia whose break-through to Kurland would only be possible if enemy air attacks could be stopped for a while. An according encirclement of the Russians would, amongst other things, save streams of refugees from the Russians. The idea was to shake the enemy command and bomber crews (especially the pathfinders) to such a degree in their resolve by the use of three in large numbers undertaken ramming missions, that they would break off their massive operations over Germany until they had discovered what the Germans' intentions really were. The resulting quiet of x days over Germany would then be sufficient for the deployment of the Bohemian army in the direction of Kurland into the Russian flank. I cannot remember who had explained to us this plan which, not knowing the true situation at the beginning of April, had at the time appeared reasonable to me.*

*Our initial operating height would have to be about 11,000m in order to gain sufficient speed for the attack. As the Me 109 at its normal weight was unable to reach this height, we would have to make do without guns and ammunition and also radio, not least in order to maintain absolute radio silence. Ramming targets were to be, as far as possible, the leaders of the bomber formations. Experienced pilots recommended and discussed how one should ram in order to make one's own chances of survival as good as possible. We were to take off in sections. It was left up to us who was to fly with whom, but each section was to include at least one pilot with combat experience.*

*I am fairly certain that I was in the 8th section to taxi out for take-off at Gardelegen and that we were not the last ones to do so. There must therefore have been 48 Me*

**Above:** Lt Joachim-Wolfgang Böhm was severely injured when his *Rammkommando Elbe* Bf 109K-2 crashed between Wehningen and Tripkau on 7 April 1945. *Werner Zell via J-W Böhm.*

*109s intended for the operation. Of the total number involved at the airfield I have no idea, but fewer actually took off. In my own section were Leutnant Thiel, myself to his right, than a Feldwebel with combat experience and a Gefreiter. The last did not even get airborne and the Feldwebel gave me a sign with his hand soon after take-off that he would have to land again. As far as I am able to remember, I estimate that something like 30 or 35 Me 109s went into action.*

*I do not know for certain, but I suspected technical problems; the day before we had pleaded to do at least a circuit with the Me 109s which had been parked for some considerable time, but this could not take place due to lack of fuel. I had been assigned a brand new Me 109K2. In any case, only Me 109s took off from Gardelegen. How many of these were G or K I cannot even estimate.*

*I did not get as far as ramming. Before reaching operational height, oil squirted across the windscreen and ran over the Galland-cockpit canopy; whether due to enemy action or an engine or oil tank defect could not be ascertained. In any case, I was sitting in the dark. In order not to arouse a suspicion of 'cowardice before the enemy' by bailing out, I decided to go down in a spin. I wanted to simulate a crash to any possible enemy. In my ignorance I turned on the windscreen washer too soon which was soon exhausted of its five litres and I again sat in the dark at 200m. So, shortly after levelling out without being able to see, I went into a row of poplars and was rescued from the wreckage, seriously injured, by some civilians. The site of my crash was between Wehningen and Tripkau, 100m off the road (to the north) from Domitz/Elbe to Bolzenburg/Elbe.*

**Left:** B-17G 42-37840
*Combined Operations*, 367th BS,
306th BG. On 15 April 1945 Lt
Robert A Vielle flew into a hill on
the Isle of Man while en route to
Langford Lodge, Northern
Ireland. All 11 people aboard,
including Miss Emily Rea,
American Red Cross,
Capt George E Cubberly,
squadron executive officer and
Capt W Bradley Butterfield,
squadron operations officer,
were killed. *Richards.*

**Above:** Lt Gottfried Dietze, St Kpt, 7./JG26, February-May 1945, with five confirmed victories. *Walter Stumpf.*

On 8 April, the 8th put up 23 groups of B-17s and ten groups of Mustangs to bomb targets in Germany and Czechoslovakia. In excess of 1,150 B-17s and B-24s escorted by 14 groups of Mustangs, bombed targets in the Leipzig, Nuremberg and Chemnitz areas. On 9 and 10 April the German jet airfields were again bombed. As a result, about all Me 262 units were forced to withdraw to the Prague area. On 14 April an estimated force of about 122,000 Germans holding out and manning 22 gun batteries along the Gironde estuary in the Royan area, which was denying the Allies the use of the port of Bordeaux, were bombed by 1,161 heavies. The 467th successfully dropped all their 2,000lb bombs within 1,000ft of the MPI; half the bombs falling within 500ft. This was a bombing pattern unsurpassed in 8th AF

history. The 389th BG lost two Liberators when 3rd AD B-17s, making a second run over the target, released their fragmentation bombs through their formation. Two more crash-landed in France and a fifth limped back to England.

On 15 April, nearly 850 heavies of the 2nd and 3rd Air Divisions carrying *Napalm* for the first time, dropped 460,000 gallons in 75 to 85 gallon liquid-fire tanks on the stubborn defenders of Royan. The 1st AD added 1,000 and 2,000lb GP bombs while three fighter groups put down fire on gun emplacements. No *Flak* was encountered and French forces later captured the port. On 16 April Orders of the Day No.2 from Gen Spaatz ended the Strategic mission of the 8th AF and only some tactical missions remained.

*I was commander of II./JG11 during the fierce battles and consequent heavy losses in the Reich Defence, April-December 1943, when I shot down 12 Viermots. I was pulled out by Göring and given the task of setting up the new department 'General Recruiting Luftwaffe' in the Reich Air Ministry. At the same time I was appointed in agreement with Reich Youth Leader (A Axmann) honorary Reich Inspector of Hitler Youth Airmen. So I was saddled with the running of two departments at the same time. The Hitler Youth Airmen had 250,000 members who received pre-military training in Hitler Youth camps, followed by flight instruction (in a selective process for suitability) by the NSFK (the Party Flying Corps, Generaloberst Keller) in their gliding camps. About March 1944 I was ordered to report to Göring on the Obersalzberg, together with Prof W Messerschmitt, in order to express my opinion on the Volksjäger (peoples' fighter) project and the possibilities of using selected Hitler Youth pilots. About June 1944 there was a meeting at the Reich Air Ministry under the chairmanship of Keller with Milch, Sauer, Knemeyer, myself and others to discuss the Volksjäger project. Here things began to take shape with a reference to a development by*

Heinkel. *It so transpired that, when I was once again with Göring at Karinhall to make my report, the idea of a Jagdgeschwader 'Hitler Youth' with the name 'Oesau' was to be realised. It was also decided that this Geschwader was to be equipped with Volksjäger (which were still in the development stage). In September 1944 I took part in the so-called Volksjäger conference at Rastenburg. Galland and Messerschmitt were in favour of giving priority to the Me 262. But Sauer, Galland having meanwhile fallen out of favour with Göring, succeeded with his idea of mass production of the Volksjäger. In the middle of December 1944 I was ordered to Vienna to attend the first display of the He 162, which ended tragically. Back in Berlin a few days later I had a serious clash with Generaloberst Keller about the possible use of the He 162 for "my Hitler Youth airmen". He did not share my doubts about the Volksjäger and advised for its mass production at another meeting with Göring a few days later, in the presence of Gollob. I did not suspect at the time how heavily I would be involved with the He 162 later.*

*In January 1945 I was ordered to Rechlin in order to fly and test the He 162. I was given initial instructions on it by Bär (Obstlt Heinz Bär), with whom I had been in Tunisia. After the first circuit it had become obvious to me that, unless decisive changes were made to the machine, this aircraft would be out of the question for Hitler Youths coming straight from gliders without intermediate training on other and proven fighters. I informed Göring about my impressions in a priority report! I also informed Keller who meanwhile had flown the He 162. At the beginning of March I was ordered to Goslar to form a yet unnamed fighter Geschwader where I, under Gollob, first assembled ground personnel made up of various former fighter Geschwaders to a 'new mob'.*

*In the middle of March the first 32 He 162s arrived, from Travemünde, I believe, and*

*we began immediately with the training of the pilots (not Hitler Youth) who had meanwhile arrived from various fighter training schools. It turned out that the conversion training brought no problems, only the lack of fuel caused us difficulties! Enemy formations daily passed overhead without us being able, nor permitted to interfere. On 15 April 1945 I was able to take off for a sortie with the first section, but as we had been sent to the wrong place by fighter control, we failed to make contact with the enemy. We did not operate again until the 21st of the month because of bad weather, when I was able to score the first Abschuss, a P-47, with the He 162. On landing the weak undercarriage collapsed under me and I ended up on my belly. On 22 April Lt Bartz also shot down a P-47 and that was the end of this nameless Geschwader which was to have been named 'Hitler Youth'. As the Americans were meanwhile getting uncomfortably close to the Harz, the remaining He 162s were flown from Goslar to Travemünde and the entire Geschwader was sent to the Harz for ground fighting as infantry. I received orders, again from Loerzer, to take over the Bücker project at Friedersdorf, where I, together with Hptm. Purps, on 1 May 1945 did a night sortie against approaching tank units of the Red Army between Küstrin and Landsberg, but without success as the defensive fire of the Russians was so heavy that, riddled with hits from infantry arms, we had to give up further attempts. I spent the remaining days with Loerzer in the personnel department of the Reich Air Ministry.*

**Oberst Adolf Dickfeld, *Ritterkreuz* with Oak Leaves who finished the war with 132 *Abschüsse* on the Eastern and Western fronts, recounting his involvement in the development of the He 162 *Volksjäger* 1944/early 1945, and his experiences flying the jet in April 1945.**

**Full page:** On 4 April 1945 when Me 262s of III./JG7 attacked the American formations, Lt Fritz Müller shot down *Trouble N Mind* of the 448th BG, flown by Capt John M Ray and Lt Rudolf Rademacher shot down 44-50838 of the 448th BG, piloted by Robert Mains, pictured. Only one man survived aboard Mains' ship and six parachuted to safety from Ray's. The deadly R4M folding-fin air-to-air missiles were mounted on wooden racks beneath the outer wing of the Me 262. They could be fired in salvoes, or ripple-fired in waves. One hit was normally enough to destroy a four-engined bomber. Rademacher is reported to have destroyed 24 aircraft flying Me 262s and had a grand total of 126 victories.

At 3.30 the ringing of the alarm clock woke us up. My friend Gerd and I hurried to catch the bus which took us to the airfield. It was still dark with a clear, star-spangled sky above. The bus arrived on time and we had breakfast in the mess. Here we were told to hurry as we were to go straight to our dispersals, and after about ten minutes we were off. We could hear the engines running from far away. We were in a proper fighting mood. In our Storm Gruppe we knew none other, for we were all volunteers. By the time we arrived at the dispersals it was already 5 o'clock and the day was beginning to break.

We went into our rest room and awaited further orders. Then our chief came in, Hptm Wolf. OFw Walter reported 12 pilots of 5th Staffel ready for briefing. We were allocated our sections and briefed for the sortie. As always, I flew with our chief as pair-leader. Our section consisted of our chief as leader with Rudi Rank as his wingman, then myself with my wingman Heinz Richter. Rudi and Heinz were old comrades with whom I had been flying for a long time. We were the most senior pilots in our Staffel and had had considerable successes on fighter-bombers. After briefing everyone went to his aircraft to check it over. As always I had my white 15. It was the third aircraft I had had in a year. Each time it had been destroyed by enemy action. Twice I had made a belly landing and the third time it had been destroyed on the ground after a sortie.

When I got to my machine it was being readied. The 250kg bomb was installed, the parachute lay ready, the headset and oxygen tube of the helmet were plugged in. Meanwhile it was 7.30, the sun was well up and there was not a cloud in the sky. After a bare half hour the loudspeaker at dispersal summoned all pilots to the operations room and 10 minutes later all the pilots were there.

Major Mortise, who wore his Ritterkreuz, told us: "Comrades, I don't have to tell you that the situation is serious. But I have some good news too. With immediate effect we shall no longer be operating as fighter-bombers but as fighters. The bomb racks will be removed at once and that will give us a better performance, allowing us to achieve quite a lot. I now expect you to be quite clear about this during your future operations and to achieve victories. Until now this had hardly been possible, but now we have all the more chance to shoot enemy fighters from the sky. You know that all the hopes are on the Sturmgruppe and we shall do honour to our name, just as we had done when we were fighting the Viermots. There will be continuous operations from now onward. Now go back to your machines and make certain that everything is in good order. That is all I have to say to you. The pilots are dismissed to go to their dispersals."

The sun was already high in the sky and it was an unusually hot day. We were at 30 minutes readiness at the dispersals. Meanwhile, the bombs and bomb racks were removed by the mechanics. The clock showed 11.30 and the mess van was in sight. During the meal the following words came over the loudspeaker: "Attention all! Attention all! Alarm, Scramble! Enemy formation from the east approaching Straussberg, bombing of town and airfield must be prevented, then independent chase."

We dropped everything and hurried to our aircraft. Here my chief mechanic stood ready to assist me with the straps. After a brief warming up of the engines our chief taxied out for take-off, followed by Rudi Rank, myself and then Heinz Richter. We lined up quickly and did a formation take-off. Under the prevailing conditions at the airfield this was not always easy, but with 100% concentration and mutual trust we had often managed it. We formed up immediately after take-off and departed on a course of 0450, climbing up to 3,500m. The sunlight was intense and it was unusually hot in the cockpit. After 20 minutes our top cover, flying about 300m above us, reported Mustangs behind us. Everyone looked behind him but we were unable to see anything yet. But as I looked to my left, I noticed a Mustang flying straight towards Rudi, as usual at number 2, diving and firing with all his guns. I snatched my machine around and fired at the enemy aircraft which broke off at once. But my comrade's machine was on fire and he was already hanging on his parachute.

Now followed a violent dogfight, during which I succeeded in bringing the Mustang down. Having observed him going down trailing intense smoke, I pulled up steeply to

**Above:** Broken Eagle (I). Fw 190A-8 'Yellow 9', probably of *Stab*/JG6, rests with its back broken at Reichenberg airfield, May 1945. *JaPo.*

the left. And now my own fate caught up with me. A bullet went through the side window, through my foot and ended up in the fuel tank. After the first shock I noticed fire on the right side. The cockpit quickly filled with smoke and I could get no air. At this moment I thought that all was finished. But then I jettisoned the cockpit roof, undid my straps, kicked with my left foot against the stick and jumped out. By then I had suffered 2nd and 3rd grade burns in the face and hands. I pulled the ripcord of my parachute right away which opened at once. I was hanging there at 3000m, below me a huge forested area and not far from that a large lake. My position was about 30km south-east of Konigswusterhausen. The aircraft which had shot me down circled a couple of times and then disappeared.

The time during which I hung on the parachute seemed to take no end, but it took only ten minutes until I was down. In spite of all my pain I hoped that I would land well, for it was the first time that I had bailed out. I made every effort to guide the 'chute away from the lake, but in spite of all my misfortune I was lucky with my landing, dropping into a small clearing in the woods. The 'chute was caught in the trees and I was dragged only a little way along the ground. I released the straps and saw a road about 20m in front of me. I dragged myself to it, then lay down, for I was completely exhausted.

A short time later a whole crowd had gathered around and I found by their speech that they were not Germans. Later on I discovered that they were Poles. One of them, who spoke a little German, came along and asked whether I was German or English. At first I did not know what to reply, but then I said that I was German. Then I was really pleased and amazed, for they placed me in the shade, gave me something to drink and did everything I asked for. Then they got a car to take me to the nearest doctor. The Poles had behaved exceedingly well. Then I lost consciousness and did not wake up again until I was in hospital, where I found my comrade Rudi Rank. We were taken westward in stages until I ended up a few weeks later in a Hamburg hospital. After three years and 45 operations in various hospitals I was finally discharged.

**Oblt Hans Zepuntke, fighter/fighter-bomber pilot, *Sturm Gruppe JG4* describing his last sortie of the war, 16 April 1945. The core of second *Sturm' Gruppe* in *JG4* had been formed in October 1944 from the *Sturmstaffel* led by Maj von Kornatski, and was equipped with specially armoured Fw 190s. The unit was decimated during the ensuing months over central Germany, and during both the Ardennes Offensive and Operation *Bodenplatte*. In mid-January 1945, JG4 was transferred to the Eastern Front where it became involved in the heavy fighting over the Oder bridge-heads. By early April 1945, the remnants of JG4 returned to Schleswig-Holstein and against the overwhelming might of the RAF and US air forces. Against all the odds, Oblt Hans Zepuntke survived his spell of operations, 1944-45.**

**Right:** Maj James McPartlin, 401st BS, 91st BG, is dunked in a trailer filled with water following his last mission of his combat tour. He was responsible for the naming of B-17G 42-97061 *General Ike*, which flew its first operational mission on 13 April 1944, two days after it was christened by Gen Dwight D Eisenhower. On 29 May 1944 *General Ike* led the 91st BG to Poznan, Poland, on the longest daylight raid of the war up to that time. *Ike* completed 75 combat missions, returned to the USA in June 1945 and was broken up for scrap. *USAF via Thomas J Fitton.*

*In mid-April, the 15, 16 or 17, I was leading a section which included Eugen Meier and two other comrades. We were to reconnoitre in the area of Nuremberg. Suddenly we spotted a large assembly of tanks and lorries near Hof, where the tanks were being refuelled at a service station. This discovery surprised me, but obviously the Americans were also startled by our appearance. We attacked the assembly twice and fired at some lorries on the roads, scoring some solid hits and then getting home safely. What we had achieved we could not make out. Another attack would have been suicide for the tanks fired like mad with their machine guns. After coming back from this ground-attacking sortie, we suffered an attack on our airfield. There were not only Mustangs, but Lightnings as well. They destroyed nearly all our machines. I lay behind a wall on the south-west side of the airfield beside a transformer station. Behind it stood our NCO armourer with an MG 15 machine-gun, firing at the attackers. He hit a Lightning and it went down behind the field.*

**Uffz Walter Ibold, Bf 109G pilot, JG76.**

On 17 April, Dresden was bombed by almost a thousand bombers. Eight B-17s and 17 fighters were shot down, including six B-17s by Me 262s of JG7.

The end of the Reich was nigh. During the week 18 to 25 April, missions were briefed and scrubbed almost simultaneously as the ground forces overran objective after objective. The German corridor was shrinking rapidly and the American and Russian bomb lines now crossed at several points on briefing maps. Gen Patton's advance was so rapid that on one occasion at least crews were lining up for take-off when a message was received to say that Gen. Patton's forces had captured the target the B-17s were to bomb! The end came on 25 April 1945 when 306 B-17s of the 1st AD bombed the Skoda armaments factory at Pilsen in Czechoslovakia, while 282 B-24s, escorted by four fighter groups, bombed four rail complexes surrounding Hitler's mountain retreat at Berchtesgarden. Ten Me 262s of I./JG7, fighting to the last, claimed seven B-17s shot down.

During the first week of May the German armies surrendered one by one to Montgomery at Lüneberg Heath, to Devers at Munich and to Alexander at

**Right:** B-17G 42-107180 *The Eagles Wrath/Lucky Rebel*, 410th BS, 94th BG, on display beneath the Eiffel Tower in Paris at the end of the war. *USAF.*

An exercise which was to test the co-operation with ground control again showed the lead which German aircraft development had achieved. A supposed enemy formation in the area of Brandis was to be attacked simultaneously by propeller, jet and rocket fighters. I took off with a section from Brandenburg-Briest and represented the jet fighters. Height and course were ordered and monitored from the ground. The weather was varied with clouds at different heights and haze layers. Visibility of the ground was virtually zero. In the target area I saw four Me 109s, the representatives of the piston-engined fighters, in battle formation. According to fighter pilot usage I approached the section from behind. But they were not asleep. Suddenly all four stood on their noses and disappeared through a cloud layer some 1,000m below us. While in a wide turn to observe them, a condensation trail shot almost vertically out of the cloud layer below me. At the head of this rapidly growing trail there was a tiny something which, as it approached, turned out to be a Me 163. This 'power egg' was showing us its strength. It flashed upwards only a few hundred metres beside us,

ignoring or perhaps not even seeing us and continued to rush higher until it disappeared into a layer of cloud. For quite some minutes the two layers of cloud were connected with a vertical white line. The object of the exercise had been successful. Had we been able to do this a year sooner, the air war over Germany would have turned out differently. On 8 May 1945, coming from Czechoslovakia, I landed for the last time at Lechfeld, after having given a small show for the Americans celebrating there. As I later heard, my proud kite was taken to America by sea and air.

**Lt Fritz R G Müller, III./JG7, who on 8 May 1945 flew Me 262A-la 500491 to Lechlade airfield, where he surrendered to US troops. His aircraft is now on display at the National Air and Space Museum, Washington DC.**

*Below:* Broken Eagle II. Bf 109G at Wunsdorf airfield. *Mike Henry.*

*I was one of the pilots then transferring from Ottingen to Salzburg. We were there for some days, but with only a few aircraft. A number of Me 262s of the 'Galland Gruppe' were also there. There was talk of a transfer to Steinach in Ennstal. Then orders came in for us to carry out relief attacks in the Prague area. I was to take part, as was also Eugen Meier. Still, my 109 could not be made serviceable in time, and so I remained in Salzburg. As I walked from my 109 to the barracks some of our officers drove away in cars. We never saw them again. The rest of our Gruppe with pilots, mechanics, clerks and Blitzmädchen ('Lightning Girls', equivalent to the WAAF) drove to the Alps in lorries. Just short of the airfield at Steinach, at a small village, we set up camp. It was 8 May 1945. Whilst on our way we were frequently fired at by partisans. As we had our office with us, our service books were there too. We tried a trick to get home, if possible, as civilians, by changing the discharge date to 4 May 1945. I then travelled north in a workshop truck filled with all kinds of things and people. On our way we arrived at an American checkpoint, they were nice people, even giving us some diesel to continue our journey. But in Burghausen we were directed to a sports ground. That was the beginning of captivity. I gave my service book to a Blitzmädel who later sent it back to me, and stuck my flying licence into one of my boots. Soon we were taken to a PoW camp in Salzburg, then to Ulm on the Danube. Many thousands of soldiers were held there in meadows and open fields. It was a bad time, but luckily, through fortunate circumstances I was amongst those men who were preferentially released and was home at the end of July 1945.*

**Uffz Walter Ibold, Bf 109G pilot, JG76. At war end he had 25 confirmed victories (including six American *Viermots*) in 60 to 70 *Reichsverteidigung* sorties, and was decorated with the German Cross in Gold.**

Casserta and finally to Eisenhower at Rheims in the early hours of 7 May. Starting on 1 May, before the Germans surrendered, Fortress crews flew mercy missions, called *Chowhound*, to starving Dutch civilians in Holland (together with RAF *Manna* operations, which had begun on 29 April) until the end of hostilities, carrying food. VE (Victory in Europe) Day took place on 8 May. Then the B-17s airlifted troops from the United Kingdom to Casablanca where they continued on to the China-Burma-India Theatre and also acted as "moving vans" for fighter groups going to Germany as part of the occupation forces there. The bomb groups returned allied PoWs to England and France and airlifted displaced persons from all over Europe. Then *Trolley* or *Revival* missions in bombers crammed with ground personnel were flown at heights ranging from 1,000 to 3,000ft over bombed out cities to show them the outcome of Allied bombing over the past four years. On 13 May 1945 the B-17s and B-24s, led by the 467th BG, flew the Victory Flypast over the 8th AF Headquarters at High Wycombe.

*Right:* Remains of a Fw 190 and other German aircraft discovered by advancing US forces. *Jack Rude.*

*I*nstead of us, fully trained and eager pilots, the powers that be placed former and highly decorated bomber pilots in our fighter aircraft. These men missed the company of their crews, and were little at ease in the small cockpits of the Fw 190. One day in Prague, whilst we watched the proceedings from the ground, 11 out of 12 of these ex-bomber pilots were shot out of the sky within the span of just two minutes.

**Martin Hoffmann, flieger and former *Hitler Jungen* (Hitler Youth), who had been posted to JG105 at Schonering near Linz/Austria in October 1944. Due to the acute shortage of fuel, he did not see action, but in February 1945, he received theoretical ground instruction on flying the Me 262. In April 1945 he was posted to *Kommando XIII* (in III./JG105) at Prague-Gbell airfield, where he was trained on the He 162 jet, or *Volksjäger*. However, Lack of aircraft and fuel kept him and his fellow novice pilots on the ground.**

*Right:* Nazi flag which fluttered over the Kugelfischer ball bearing plant, the largest of the four plants at Schweinfurt, was presented to the 305th BG at Chelveston by an Air Force journalist after the US 42nd "Rainbow" Armoured Division captured it on 11 April 1945. The 305th BG lost 13 crew on the second raid on the plants on 14 October 1943. *Bill Donald.*

**Above:** Germany lies in ruins as a B-17 on a *Trolley* mission flies overhead. *Thorpe Abbotts Memorial Museum.*

# German Ranks and their Abbreviations

| German Ranks | US equivalent |
|---|---|
| Reischmarschall | no equivalent |
| Generalfeldmarschall | General (5-Star) |
| Generaloberst | General (4-Star) |
| General der Flieger | Lieutenant General |
| Generalleutnant | Major General |
| Generalmajor | Brigadier General |
| Oberst | Colonel |
| Oberstleutnant (Obstlt) | Lieutenant Colonel |
| Major | Major |
| Hauptmann (Hptm) | Captain |
| Oberleutnant (Oblt) | 1$^{st}$ Lieutenant |
| Leutnant (Lt) | 2$^{nd}$ Lieutenant |
| Stabsfeldwebel (StFw) | Flight Officer |
| Oberfähnrich (Ofhr) | no equivalent |
| Oberfeldwebel (Ofw) | Master Sergeant |
| Fähnrich (Fhr) | Officer candidate |
| Feldwebel (Fw) | Sergeant |
| Unteroffizier (Uffz) | Staff Sergeant |
| Obergefreiter (Ogfr) | Corporal |
| Gefreiter (Gefr) | Private First Class |
| Flieger (Flg) | Private Second Class |

# Glossary

| | |
|---|---|
| **Abschuss** | Confirmed victory in air combat |
| **Abschussteiligung** | Contribution to a confirmed air-combat victory |
| **Alarmstart** | Scramble |
| **Bordfunker or Funker** | Radar/radio operator |
| **Deutsche Kreuz im Gold (DKG)** | German Cross in gold |
| **Dicke Autos** | 'Fat Cars' (B-17s and B-24s) |
| **Eichenlaub (El)** | Knight's Cross with Oak Leaves |
| **Eisernes Kreuz I, II (EK I, EK II)** | Iron Cross (1$^{st}$ and 2$^{nd}$ Class) |
| **Einsatz** | Operational flight |
| **Ergänzungsgruppe (EGr)** | Replacement or complement wing |
| **Express-Express** | R/T code for 'hurry up' |
| **Flak (Flieger Abwehr Kanonen)** | Anti-Aircraft Artillery |
| **Feindberührung** | Contact with an enemy aircraft |
| **Führer** | Leader |
| **Geschwader** | Roughly equivalent to three RAF wings. Comprises three or four *Gruppen* |
| **Gruppe** | Group containing three or four *Staffeln,* designated by Roman figures, eg: IV./JG26 |
| **Gruppenkommandeur** | Commander or Captain, a Gruppe command position rather than a rank |
| **Herausschuss** | Claim for a bomber shot out of formation |
| **Horrido!** | Tallyho! |
| **Jäger** | Fighter |
| **Jagdbomber (Jabo)** | Fighter-bomber |
| **Jagdgeschwader (JO)** | Fighter wing, includes three or four *Gruppen* |
| **Jagdwaffe** | Fighter Arm or Fighter Force |
| **Kampfgeschwader (KG)** | Bomber Wing |
| **Kommandeur** | Commanding officer of a *Gruppe* |
| **Kommodore** | Commodore or Captain, a *Geschwader* command position rather than a rank |
| **Kurier** | R/T code for 'Allied heavy bomber' |
| **Luftwaffe (LW)** | Air Force |
| **Maschinen Gewehr (MG)** | Machine gun |
| **Maschinen Kanone (MK)** | Machine cannon |
| **Nachtjäger** | Nightfighter |
| **Pauke-Pauke** | R/T code for 'going into attack' |
| **Reflex Visier (Revi)** | Gunsight |
| **Reichsluftfahrtministerium (RLM)** | German Air Ministry |
| **Reichsverteidigung** | Air Defence of Germany |
| **RitterKreuz (träger) (RK/RKT)** | Knight's Cross (holder) |
| **Rotte** | Tactical element of two aircraft |
| **Rottenflieger** | Wingman, the second man in the *Rotte* |
| **Schlachtgeschwader (SG)** | Ground attack wing |
| **Schwarm** | Flight of four aircraft |
| **Schwarmführer** | Flight leader |
| **Schwerten (S)** | Knight's Cross with Oak Leaves and Swords |
| **Stab** | Staff flight |
| **Staffel** | Roughly equivalent to a squadron, designated sequentially within the *Geschwader* by Arabic figures, eg: 4./JG1 |
| **Staffelkapitän (Stk)** | Captain, a *Staffel* command position rather than a rank |
| **Transportgeschwader (TO)** | Transport wing |
| **Viktor** | R/T code for 'have received and understood message' |
| **Viermot** | Four-engined bomber |
| **Wilde Sau** | 'Wild Boar', freelance night fighting tactic over bomber command's targets under attack |
| **Zerstörer** | 'Destroyer', Bf110 fighter aircraft |
| **Zerstörergeschwader (ZG)** | Heavy fighter wing (Bf 110 or Me 410 twin-engined fighter) |
| **Zweimot** | Twin-engined bomber |

# Index

# Index

# Bibliography

- **Gebhard Aders & Werner Held,**
  Jagdgeschwader 51 'Molders' (Stuttgart 1985).
- **Air Ministry,**
  The Rise and Fall of the German Air Force 1933-1945 (London 1948).
- **Paul M Andrews and William H Adams**
  Heavy Bombers of the Mighty Eighth 1995.
- **Cajus Bekker,**
  The Luftwaffe War Diaries (London 1967).
- **Allan G. Blue,**
  The B-24 Liberator. A Pictorial History (London 1979).
  The Fortunes of War; The History of the 491st Bomb Group
- **Manfred Boehme,**
  Jagdgeschwader 7. Die Chronik eines Me 262-Geschwaders 1944/45 (Stuttgart 1983).
- **Martin W. Bowman and Theo Boiten,**
  Raiders of the Reich. Air Battle Western Europe: 1942-1945 (Airlife 1996).
- **Martin W Bowman**
  Great American Air Battles of WW2 (Airlife, 1994).
  Home By Christmas? The Story of US 8th/15th AF Airmen At War (PSL, 1987).
  Four Miles High (PSL, 1992).
  Castles In The Air (PSL.1984).
  Fields of Little America (Wensum, 1977).
- **Various issues of Bulletin Airwar 1939-1945**, magazine of the Studiegroep Luchtoorlog 1939-1945 (Airwar) (Leiden).
- **Donald J. Caldwell,**
  JG26. Top Guns of the Luftwaffe (New York 1991).
  The JG26 War Diary (Grub Street, 1998).
- **Ed Castens**
  The 446th BG (H) Revisited.
- **Wolfgang Dierich,**
  Die Verbände der Luftwaffe 1935-1945 (Stuttgart 1976).
- **Fred Dittmann,**
  Der Einsatzflughafen Esperstedt der deutschen Luftwaffe 1935 bis 1945. Eine Dokumentation (Kelbra 1995).
- **John Foreman and S E Harvey**
  The Messerschmitt 262 Combat Diary (ARP 1990)
- **Roger A. Freeman,**
  Mighty Eighth War Diary (London 1981).
  The Mighty Eighth
- **Adolf Galland,**
  Die Ersten und die Letzten. Jagdflieger im zweiten Weltkrieg (Munchen 1970).
- **G . W. Gellerman,**
  Moskau ruft Heeresgruppe Mitte (Koblenz 1988).
- **Werner Girbig,**
  ... im Anflug auf die Reichshauptstadt (Stuttgart 1970).
- **Werner Girbig,**
  Die Nicht Zurückkehrten (Stuttgart 1970).
- **Steve Gotts,**
  Little Friends: A Pictorial History of the 361st FG in WW2 (Taylor Publishing 1993).
- **Jim Hamilton,**
  The Writing 69th (Privately Published 1999).
- **Maj-General Haywood S Hansell Jr.,**
  The Air Plan That Defeated Hitler (1972).
- **Ian Hawkins,**
  B-17s Over Berlin - Personal Stories from the 95th Bomb Group (H) (Brasseys, 1990).
- **Werner Held,**
  Fighter! Luftwaffe Fighter Planes and Pilots (New York 1979).
- **Werner Held,**
  Reichsverteidigung. Die deutsche Tagjagd 1943-1945 (Friedberg 1988).
- **Janet Howard**
  Boots From Heaven (Cross Cultural Publications Inc).
- **Ales Janda & Ing. Tomas Poruba,**
  Messerschmitt Bf 109K (Prague 1997).
- **Russell Ives**
  The 491st BG (privately published).
- **Jägerblatt**, offizielles Organ der Gemeinschaft der Jagdflieger e.V., various issues
- **Ab A. Jansen,**
  Wespennest Leeuwarden, Deel II 1942-1943 (Baarn 1979).
- **Ab A. Jansen,**
  Sporen aan de Hemel. Kroniek van een Luchtoorlog 1943-1945, three vols (Baarn 1979-81).
- **Ab A. Jansen,**
  Fliegerhorst Schiphol. Onze nationale luchthaven in bezettingstijd. Volume 2: Zet en tegenzet (Amsterdam 1998).
- **Harold E Jansen,**
  The History of the 446th Bomb Group (H) 1943-1945
- **Werner Kock,**
  Das Kriegstagebuch des Nachtjagdgeschwaders 6 (Wittmund 1996).
- **Beirne Lay Jr.,**
  I Saw Regensburg Destroyed
- **Richard H Lewis/as told to William R Larson,**
  Hell Above And Hell Below (Delapeake, 1985).
- **Will Lundy**
  The 44th Bomb Group History
- **Erwin Van Loo,**
  Vliegveld Woensdrecht in het Vizier (Historical Graduate Thesis, University of Amsterdam 1996).
- **Samuel W. Mitcham,**
  Eagles of the Third Reich. Hitler's Luftwaffe (Shrewsbury 1989).
- **Eric Mombeek,**
  Defending The Reich; The History of JG1 "Oesau" (JAC Publications, 1992).
  Luftwaffe A Pictorial History (Crowood, 1997)
- **Lt. Fritz R.G. Müller,**
  Flying Log Books 1940-1945, and diary 1943-1945.
- **Walter A. Musciano,**
  Messerschmitt Aces (New York 1982).
- **Hans-Dietrich Nicolaisen,**
  Gruppenfeuer und Salventakt. Schuler und Lehrlinge bei der Flak 1943-1945 (Volume II, Busum 1993).

# Bibliography

- **Ernst Obermaier,**
  Die Ritterkreuzträger der Luftwaffe 1939-1945.
  Band I Jagdflieger (Mainz 1989).
- **Office of Air Force History. Strategic Air Warfare.** An
  Interview with Generals Curtis E LeMay, Leon W Johnson,
  David A Burchinal and Jack J Catton (1988).
- **Simon W Parry,**
  Intruders Over Britain, the Luftwaffe night fighter
  Offensive (ARP 1987).
- **Dr. Alfred Price,**
  Luftwaffe Handbook 1939-1945 (London 1986).
- **Jochen Prien, Peter Rodeike, and Gerhard Stemmer,**
  Messerschmitt Bf 109 im Einsatz bei der III. und
  IV./Jagdgeschwader 27 1938-1945 (Eutin 1995).
- **Josef Priller,**
  JG26. Geschichte eines Jagdgeschwaders.
  Das JG26 (Schlageter) 1937-1945 (Stuttgart 1980).
- **George Punka,**
  Messerschmitt Me 210/410 in Action
  (Squadron Signal Publications, Carrollton, Texas 1994).
- **Ron Putz,**
  Duel In de Wolken. De Luchtoorlog in de gevaren-driehoek
  Roermond-Luik-Aken (Amsterdam, 1994).
- **Heinz Riediger,**
  Jungen von der Flak (unpublished manuscript,
  Albstadt 1 (Ebingen) 1991).
- **Karl Ries,**
  Luftwaffe Photo-Report 1919-1945 (Stuttgart 1984).

- **Hans Ring & Werner Girbig,**
  Jagdgeschwader 27. Die Dokumentation über den Einsatz
  an allen Fronten 1939-1945 (Stuttgart 1994).
- **Harry E Slater,**
  Lingering Contrails of the Big Square A; A History of the
  94th Bomb Group (H) 1942-1945 (1980).
- **Mike Spick,**
  Luftwaffe Fighter Aces (Ivy Books 1996).
- **Carroll "Cal" Stewart,**
  Ted's Travelling Circus.
  Sun/World Communications Inc (1996).
- **Russell A Strong,**
  First Over Germany;
  A History of the 306th Bombardment Group (1982).
- **Christiaan Vanhee & Peter Celis,**
  Vinnige Valken, Vlammende Blirsems. De Vliegbasis Van
  Sint-Truiden 1941-1945 (Luxembourg, 2000).
- **Tony Wood & Bill Gunston,**
  Hitler's Luftwaffe (London 1979).
- **Gerrit J. Zwanenburg,**
  En Nooit Was Het Stil Kroniek van een luchtoorlog,
  Luchtaanvallen op doelen in en om Nederland (Den Haag 1993).

**445th BG Group History**
**453rd BG History**
**93rd BG History**
**305th BG History**
**392nd BG History**

# Acknowledgements

Eino V Alve; Frau Lisette Arend-Willius; Frau Anneliese Autenrieth; Mike Bailey; Eric Bakker; Herwig Befeldt; Hilde Bendert; Pieter Bergman; Günther Bielicke; Karl Bleckmann; Hans-Eberhard Blume; Joachim-Wolfgang Böhm; Don Bradford; the late Dave Brett; Cy Broman; Eberhard Burath; Frederick L Carr; Guy "Chuck" Chookoorian; Pete Clark, Rougham Tower Assoc.; Ralph S Cohen; George M Collar; Helmut Conradi; Henry Cordery; Coen Cornelissen; Arthur T Cullen; Hellmut Detjens; *Deutscher Luftwaffenring e.V.*; Adolf Dickfeld; Fred Dittmann; Abe Dolim; Bill Donald; Dr. Karl Dörscheln; Albrecht Dress; Douwe S. Drijver (Friesche Luchtvaart Documentatie 1939-1945); Georg-Peter Eder; Hans Fahrenberger; Sam N Fain; Otto H. Fries; Robert M Foose; "Hap" Galfunt; Ken Garrett; Artur Gärtner; Ken Garwood; Larry Goldstein; Wayne T Gotke; Steve Gotts; Walter Hagenah; Willi Hahn; Heimkehrer magazine. Stimme der Kriegsgeneration; Jim Hamilton; Ian Hawkins; Dr. Jan Heitmann; Mike Henry; Jan A. Hey; Derek Hills and the staff of the 2nd Air Division Library, Norwich; Martin Hoffmann; Hans Höhler; Douglas E J Hunt DSC*; Bishop E Ingraham; Ab A Jansen; Ben Jones; Clifford D Jones; Hans-Jürgen Jürgens; Karl Kapteina; Myron H Keilman; Ted King; Fritz Koal; Frau Irene Kohl; Ottomar Kruse; Hartmut Küper; Richard E Lewis; Christian Loop; Will Lundy; Ron Mackay; Ian McLachlan; Dr. Fritz Marktscheffel; Carlo Marlow; Jim Marsteller; Arnolds Mencis; Gus Mencow; Dwight N Miller; Robert L Miller; Kees Mol; Werner Molge; Eric Mombeek; Bryce S Moore; Jan Mulder; Aad Neeven; James O'Brien; Walter Don O'Hearn; Werner Oeltjebruns; Walter Otto; Peter Petrick; Horst Petzschler; Heinrich Freiherr von Podewils; Tomas Poruba; the late Gen Maurice Preston; George Punka; Ron Pütz; George Reedman; Ray A Rhodes; Connie and Gordon Richards; Gerhard Richter; Albrecht Riedel; Heinz Riediger; Bill Rose; William E Ruck; Jack Rude; Ernst Rummel; Mrs. Dorothy Saunders; Bob Scalley; Dr. Heinz Schlechter; Karl-Heinz Schramme; Ernst Schroeder; Ellis B Scripture; Robert J Seelos; Robert Shaffer; Ben Smith Jr.; Derek Smith; Albert Spelthahn; Peter Spoden; Otto P. Stammberger; Hans-Heri Stapfer; Frau Elis Stumpf; Lou Szabo; Toni Temburg; Terschellinger Museum 't Behouden Huys; Paul W Tibbets; Friedrich Ungar; Edo van der Laan; William W Varnedoe Jr.; Rob de Visser; Bob Voss; Todor Walkow; Fred O Walsh; Hans Weik, Gunther Wiedenbrück; Fritz Wiener; Hans Wijers; Peter Wood, Rougham Tower Assoc.; Truett Woodall; Werner Zell.